D1598214

William J. Walsh
Archbishop of Dublin
1886

THE

ROMAN CATHOLIC

CHURCH

and the

PLAN OF CAMPAIGN IN IRELAND
1886 - 1888

EMMET LARKIN
Professor of British and Irish History
University of Chicago

Cork University Press
University College Cork

Copyright © 1978 by Cork University Press

ISBN 0 902561 12 X

282.415
L326
87052029

TO
MINA CARNEY

CONTENTS

ILLUSTRATIONS

Preface

In a previous volume I have explained how and why I have embarked on writing a history of the Roman Catholic Church in Ireland in the nineteenth century. I will not, therefore, burden the reader with what I have already said on that score, but since the technique previously adopted as regards style and scholarly apparatus has been used again, and inasmuch as it is not quite orthodox in either case, I think it would be helpful to repeat to some extent what I have already said as to technique. The richness in the quality and quantity of both the general archival materials and the personal papers of the principal characters in this study was indeed once again very great. In presenting this evidence, therefore, I have again consciously adopted a technique that I have called "mosaic." The many varied and colored bits and pieces of evidence have been selected and arranged to create a portrait of the Church between 1886 and 1888. There are, I believe, a number of advantages in using the "mosaic" technique when the materials are appropriate. Since the writing of history can never result in more than a representation of what was "true," an historical portrait in "mosaic" is perhaps more "realistic" than might at first be supposed. The technique of "mosaic" allows for the inclusion of a great deal more of the evidence in its original form and contributes, therefore, not only to the immediacy of the actual experience but to the authority of the representation, thereby enhancing the reality of the historical portrait. As in all representations, and perhaps even more so in a mosaic, the appreciation has a great deal to do with properly relating it to the mind's eye — in a word, in achieving perspective. If I have been successful, then, in constructing my mosaic, the numerous details should integrate and the various parts should harmonize when this volume is read whole.

Since the system of footnoting in this volume is also

somewhat unorthodox, I think an explanation to the reader is again in order. Most of the ecclesiastical as well as the lay correspondences quoted from have not been catalogued in any more systematic way than by date. These correspondences, therefore, have been simply footnoted in the text as K (Kirby), W (Walsh), C (Croke), Sy (Salisbury), R (Ross) and so forth, and the dates and correspondents have been acknowledged in the text. The problem of indicating a break or omission in any particular letter quoted from has again been resolved by using the word "then" in parenthetical interpolation. For example, "The situation here now," Archbishop Walsh informed Kirby from Dublin on May 19, "is not only critical but dangerous"(K). "Moreover," he *then* added, "Rome must take care not to offend the people by any untoward pronouncement," indicates that between the last quote and the previous one there has been a break in the text. Sometimes the letter quoted from was a copy rather than the original, and this is resolved in the designation. For example, if Walsh wrote Kirby and the designation is W rather than K, the letter quoted from is obviously a copy. If there has been any variation from this, it has been noted in a footnote. The various abbreviations used in this volume for the respective correspondences quoted from are listed on page xii.

In turning once again to the many obligations that I have incurred in the researching and writing of this volume, there is still no one that I am more indebted to than the Most Rev. Dr. Donal Herlihy, Bishop of Ferns and formerly Rector of the Irish College in Rome. I must also sincerely thank the Most Rev. Dr. Dominic Conway, Bishop of Elphin, and formerly Spiritual Director and then Rector of the Irish College in Rome for all his help and kindness. I am also under considerable obligation to the present and late Archbishops of Dublin, the Most Rev. Drs. Dermot Ryan and John Charles McQuaid, respectively, for granting me permission to research in the archdiocesan archives. I must also thank once again the Most Rev. Dr. Thomas Morris, Archbishop of Cashel, for his permission to read the Croke correspondence on microfilm in the National Library of Ireland. I am also under obligation to the late Bishop of Elphin, the Most Rev. Dr. Vincent J. Hanly, for his permission to read the Gillooly correspondence on microfilm. I must also thank both Dom Mark Tierney, O.S.B., who has arranged and catalogued the Croke papers in the Cashel archives, and Father Kevin Kennedy, archivist of the archdiocese of Dublin, for their very considerable help. Finally, I must once again acknowledge my gratitude to the staff of the National Library of Ireland and particularly to its Director, Mr. Ailfred MacLochlainn, for their incredible patience, kindness, and generosity. As I have also explained before, however, no words can convey my obligations to the late Mina Carney, who perhaps more than anyone else has contributed the most to the making of this volume, and that is why I have dedicated it to her.

In conclusion, I must also take this opportunity, inadequate as it is, to thank all those who have had hand or part in the making of this book, and especially the Marquess of Salisbury, the Earl St. Aldwyn, the Trustees of the British Museum, and the Deputy Keeper of Records of the Public Record Office, Northern Ireland, for their respective permissions to quote from the Salisbury, St. Aldwyn, Balfour, and Ross papers. Finally, and once again, I must explain that no one but myself is responsible for the errors that may yet be found in this volume.

Emmet Larkin

The University of Chicago
1977

ROMAN CATHOLIC ARCHBISHOPS
AND BISHOPS IN IRELAND, 1886 - 1888

Archbishops of Ireland

Armagh:
Daniel McGettigan, 1870-1887
Michael Logue (Coadjutor), 1887-1924
Dublin:
William J. Walsh, 1885-1921
Cashel:
Thomas William Croke, 1875-1902
Tuam:
John MacEvilly, 1881-1902

Bishops of the Province of Armagh

Ardagh and Clonmacnoise:
Bartholomew Woodlock, 1879-1894
Clogher:
James Donnelly, 1865-1893
Derry:
Francis Kelly, 1864-1889
Down and Connor:
Patrick McAlister, 1886-1895
Dromore:
John Pius Leahy, O.P., 1860-1890
Thomas McGivern (Coadjutor), 1887-1900
Kilmore:
Bernard Finegan, 1886-1887
Edward MacGennis, 1888-1906
Meath:
Thomas Nulty, 1866-1898
Raphoe:
Michael Logue, 1879-1887
Patrick O'Donnell, 1888-1922
Bishops of the Province of Dublin
Ferns:
James Browne, 1884-1917
Kildare and Leighlin:
James Walshe, 1856-1888
James Lynch, C.M. (Coadjutor), 1869-1896
Michael Comerford (Coadjutor), 1888-1896

Ossory:
   Abraham Brownrigg, 1884-1928

Bishops of the Province of Cashel

Cork:
   T. A. O'Callaghan, 1886-1916
Cloyne:
   James MacCarthy, 1874-1893
Kerry:
   Andrew Higgins, 1881-1889
Killaloe:
   Michael Flannery, 1858-1891
   James Ryan (Coadjutor), 1872-1889
Limerick:
   Edward Thomas O'Dwyer, 1886-1917
Ross:
   William Fitzgerald, 1877-1897
Waterford:
   Pierce Power, 1886-1889

Bishops of the Province of Tuam

Achonry:
   Francis MacCormack, 1875-1887
   John Lyster, 1888-1911
Clonfert:
   Patrick Duggan, 1872-1896
   John Healy (Coadjutor), 1884-1903
Elphin:
   Laurence Gillooly, C.M., 1858-1895
Galway:
   Thomas Carr, 1883-1886
   Francis MacCormack, 1887-1908
Killala:
   Hugh Conway, 1873-1893

ABBREVIATIONS

W	—Walsh Papers
K	—Kirby Papers
H-B	—Hicks Beach Papers
C	—Croke Papers
M	—Manning Papers
S	—Smith Papers
Sy	—Salisbury Papers
B	—Balfour Papers
F.O.	—Foreign Office Papers
R	—Ross Papers
G	—Gillooly Papers

Prologue

This is the story of the part played by the Roman Catholic Church in the first phase of the consolidation of the modern Irish State. That State had been made real by Charles Stewart Parnell and his Irish Parliamentary Party between 1878 and 1886. When, in the latter year, William Gladstone finally introduced his first Home Rule Bill, he gave notice as prime minister that he and his Liberal Party were now committed to making Parnell's *de facto* Irish State as legal as it was real. Fundamental, then, to this ratification of the *de facto* Irish State by the British Parliament was the alliance between the Irish and Liberal Parties signalized in Gladstone's conversion to Home Rule. Though the Liberal-Nationalist alliance was indeed fundamental to any eventual ratification of the *de facto* Irish State by the British Parliament, that alliance was itself largely the consequence of a more fundamental alliance. In making the Irish State real between 1878 and 1886, Parnell had architected a concordat between the Irish Church and the Irish Party. This Clerical-Nationalist alliance had been consummated in October, 1884, when the Irish Bishops, as the custodians of the interests of the Church, swore allegiance, in effect, to the new Irish State. Without this accommodation of the Church, Parnell certainly could not have made his *de facto* State as strong as it was real, and without that strength, Gladstone and his Liberal Party probably could not have been persuaded to attempt to make that State as legal as it was real. The essence of the Clerical-Nationalist alliance was that Parnell and his Party agreed that the initiative and control of the Education Question at all levels was to remain with the Bishops, while the Bishops as a body signified that the Party was now *bona fide* as far as their own and their clergy's participation in politics was concerned. The actual terms of the alliance were worked out pragmatically between 1884 and 1886, when the limits of clerical participation in politics, as well as the meaning of Home Rule and what constituted a satisfactory solution to the Land Question were evolved.

Since the Clerical-Nationalist alliance was as basic to the strength of the *de facto* Irish State as the Liberal-Nationalist alliance was necessary to the making of that State *de jure,* the Conservative government that succeeded, under Lord Salisbury, in the summer of 1886 on the failure of Gladstone's third ministry to pass the first Home Rule Bill, did everything in its power to break up those alliances. The occasion for the Conservative government's assault on these alliances was the launching of the famous Plan of Campaign in Ireland in the autumn of 1886. Two successive bad harvests and a continued precipitous decline in agricultural prices had resulted in many Irish tenant farmers being unable to meet their rents, without facing either a considerable reduction in their income and standard of living, or perhaps even eviction and emigration. The Plan was devised to force the Irish landlords to reduce their rents and enable the Irish farmers to keep their homesteads. The Plan certainly paid scant respect to such favorite Victorian concepts as the sanctity of contracts and the rights of property, and was denounced, therefore, as being subversive of both government and society. By emphasizing the revolutionary nature of the Plan the Conservative government hoped to persuade those Liberals who were still personally attached to Gladstone, but were lukewarm on Home Rule, to forsake their recently made alliance with the Nationalists. Lord Salisbury, moreover, attempted to persuade the Pope, Leo XIII, in the light of the doubtful moral implications of the Plan, and the Boycotting that was attendant on it, to condemn the land agitation and forbid the Irish Bishops and their clergy from giving it either their approbation or support. The Irish Bishops were greatly embarrassed by this attempt on the part of the English government to drive a wedge in the Clerical-Nationalist alliance at Rome, for it resulted in the very formidable agrarian wing of the Irish Party becoming more aggressive and eventually encroaching on the terms of the alliance worked out between 1884 and 1886. When Rome did finally condemn the Plan and Boycotting in May, 1888, the Irish Bishops, in order to preserve their own power and influence, in the face of an outraged national conscience, refused to enforce the Roman condemnation, and coolly opted instead for the maintenance of the Clerical-Nationalist alliance.

At the same time that it was attempting to undermine the Clerical and Liberal-Nationalist alliances at home and at Rome, the Conservative government was also attempting through coercion to break up the *de facto* control of Parnell and his Party in Ireland. A very stringent Crimes Act was finally passed for Ireland in July, 1887, which provided, among other things, for courts of summary jurisdiction, special juries, removal of trials, and the outlawing of dangerous associations by the proclamation of the Lord Lieutenant. These extreme legal measures were, in fact, only another testimony to the grip of Parnell and his Party on the country. Indeed, the further efforts of Arthur Balfour, Lord Salisbury's nephew, and chief secretary for Ireland, to shake Parnellite power in the country, only resulted in the further consolidation of that power. By the summer of 1888, after more than a year of coercion, for example, the Party's political machine on the local level, the Irish National League, was still entrenched, and the Plan of Campaign was still in operation on those estates where the landlords had not capitulated. The Plan had, in fact, sounded the death-knell for Landlordism in Ireland, for by the summer of 1888 the vast majority of them had given way to their tenants' demands for reductions in rents. The success of the Plan, which was in effect essentially Irish-made law, enforced by Boycotting, demonstrated, moreover, that the alliance between the Bishops and the Party had more to do with maintaining Irish respect for law and order than did Her Majesty's chief secretary and Dublin Castle with all their legal machinery backed up by their police and military. In a word, then, in both sustaining and working the Plan of Campaign between 1886 and 1888, the Clerical-Nationalist alliance contributed mightily to the consolidation of the *de facto* Irish State.

Part I

THE PLAN OF
CAMPAIGN

I. The Plan of Campaign

October, 1886 - March, 1887

When the first Home Rule Bill was defeated in early June, 1886, William Gladstone immediately asked the queen to dissolve Parliament. In the ensuing general election in July, Gladstone and his Liberal Party were decimated at the polls. In a House of 670, only 191 Liberals supported by 85 Irish Nationalists were returned, while the Conservatives increased their numbers to 316, and could count on the support of 78 Liberal-Unionists for a majority of 118 against Home Rule. Shortly after forming his second Conservative ministry in August, Lord Salisbury was confronted with a deteriorating situation in Ireland. The harvest was not only threatening to be a failure, but there was a further decline in agricultural prices, and a depression in trade. At the opening of Parliament, Parnell, in moving an amendment to the Queen's Speech, warned that if something were not done immediately to relieve the Irish tenant, the result would be a serious increase in social disorder in Ireland during the coming winter. After his amendment was rejected, Parnell introduced his own Tenants' Relief Bill, which provided that any tenant who would pay fifty per cent of his rent and arrears should not be evicted pending the investigation of his case by the Land Court.

When this measure was defeated in the House of Commons by a vote of 297 to 202 in late September, the leaders of the constitutional movement in Ireland found themselves in a very awkward situation. Since the tenants were scheduled to pay their half-yearly rents in November, they must either produce an effective agrarian policy or allow the more desperate among the tenants, as indeed they were already doing in Kerry and Clare, to take the law into their own hands by not paying their rents and in resisting evictions. In a word, if the leadership did not take up the cause of the tenants, it was certain that the tenants would, as they had in 1881 when Parnell and his Land League colleagues were arrested and jailed, revert to the leadership of "Captain Moonlight." If, on the other hand, they did encourage the tenants to combine in not paying their rents and resisting the law as far as evictions were concerned, there was a very good chance that they would further alienate English public opinion and endanger the Liberal-Nationalist alliance, with was essential to achieving Home Rule in their generation.

With the approach of the November "gale," or rent, however, the time, which allowed for the making of such nice distinctions, was rapidly running out. In the third week of October, therefore, the die was finally cast when the nationalist weekly, *United Ireland,* published an unsigned article entitled, "A Plan of Campaign." Though the article was actually written by T. M. Harrington, the secretary of the National League, it had the wholehearted approval of both William O'Brien and John Dillon, two of the most prominent members of the Irish Party. Harrington proposed in bold and measured terms that the tenants on each estate should combine and offer their landlord what they thought was a fair rent. If the landlord refused to come to terms, the tenants were to place the proffered rent in the hands of trustees chosen by themselves, and if the landlord proceeded to evict for non-payment of rent, the money in trust would be then used to fight the evictions and support those who might be eventually evicted. Harrington further guaranteed that if the tenants' "campaign fund" were not sufficient, the resources of the National League would be used to support the tenants until the landlord came to terms. Finally, Harrington declared that anyone who should dare to take the farm of an evicted tenant should be boycotted.[1]

The Plan was naturally denounced in the Conservative and Tory press as a criminal conspiracy, involving no less a principle than the destruction of the sanctity of contracts. At first the archbishop of Dublin, William J. Walsh, and leader among the Irish bishops, was very chary about whether the Plan was morally justifiable, and privately told Harrington about his doubts.[2] After careful consideration, however, the

---

[1] F. S. L. Lyons, *John Dillon* (Chicago, 1968). p. 84.

[2] Patrick J. Walsh, *William J. Walsh, Archbishop of Dublin* (Dublin, 1928), p. 237. Cited [hereafter *in footnotes*] as *Walsh.*

archbishop, who was a canon lawyer by training, declared that, given Irish circumstances, the Plan was morally within the Pale. Some six weeks after the Plan had been launched, Archbishop Walsh decided to make his views public in one of those set newspaper "interviews," which allowed him to perform at his dialectical best. The "interview" appeared on December 2, in the widely read Liberal daily, the *Pall Mall Gazette.* "What have you to say," asked W. T. Stead, the celebrated editor of the *Pall Mall,* "about the famous Plan of Campaign?"[3] "Does not such a scandalous outrage," he added indignantly, if not spontaneously, "on the principles of common honesty scandalise you, the official chief of the Christian Church in Ireland?" "Well, I confess," Walsh responded candidly, "that at first I was a little startled at it." "I was not only startled," he added, "but grieved. I had never yet cause to express my dissent from the programme of the present national movement."

"The great difficulty," he then noted pointedly, "indeed I may say the only one, was that the Plan of Campaign leaves it practically to the judgement of the tenants — that is to say, to the judgement of one of the parties to the contract of tenancy — to fix the terms on which that contract is to continue in force." "That, no doubt, in the abstract," Walsh confessed, "seems at first sight a formidable difficulty; but, we must look at the other side of the question." "If the tenant," Walsh posed, "is to be viewed merely as one of the two parties to the rent contract, in what other light are we to view the landlord?" "He, too," Walsh added, making the crucial distinction, "is only one of the contracting parties, and he has had the fixing of terms of the contract long enough." "Is it quite clear that the tenants," Walsh asked, "are to be blamed if they claim to have their turn now?" "But does not that argument," Stead asked, in turn, "ignore the fact that the tenants are setting aside contracts already in existence?" "In the view of the case I am now contemplating," Walsh replied, "practically no. The old contracts, even those that have taken the form of 'statutory' tenancies under the Land Act of 1881, with judicial rents, are not at present 'in possession' to use a technical phrase." " 'In possession,' I should explain," Walsh continued, at his canonist best, "is a term familiar to churchmen and, possibly, also to lawyers, which implies that the agreement or contract being

---

[3] *Pall Mall Gazette* (London), December 2, 1886; quoted in *Walsh,* pp. 237-38.

valid and 'in possession' has nine points of the law on its side; and that therefore the *onus probandi* is thrown on the other side."

"Do you maintain," Stead asked Walsh somewhat incredulously, "that there are practically no contracts of tenancy now valid and binding in Ireland?" "I would not," Walsh replied, "put it exactly that way." "It is admitted on all hands," he then explained, "that practically all over Ireland, reductions, and large reductions are to be made in the rents, even in the judicial rents. The question is as to the amounts of these reductions." "Whatever inconvenience there may be," Walsh pointed out, "in having that great question decided by the tenants, I must maintain that there is just the same inconvenience — indeed I see in one way a much greater inconvenience — in having it decided by the landlords." "The landlord, like the tenant," Walsh emphasized, "is now merely 'one of the contracting parties' — neither more nor less." "This is, of course," Walsh lamented, "a bad, a deplorable state of things." "It is a disgrace," he added, "to the legislature of the country that things should be left in this state of disorganisation, but surely we are not to blame for it."

> Within the past six or seven months two proposals had been made by the friends of the Irish tenants, the adoption of either of which by Parliament would have saved us, or rather I should say, would have saved the Government of the country from the responsibility of the present deplorable state of affairs. I refer to Mr. Gladstone's Land Purchase Bill and to Mr. Parnell's proposal for the relief of the tenants. Both of these proposed to take this whole question of the present fair value of the land out of the hands of the landlords on the one side, and of the tenants on the other, putting it altogether into the hands of the constituted judicial tribunal of the country.[4]

"But ought not a tenant," Stead then asked Walsh, "who wished for a change in the existing condition of the rent contract, to begin by giving up the holding which he has hitherto held on those terms which he now repudiates as unfair and impossible?" "That," the archbishop replied, "for a time, was one of my chief difficulties, but recent land legislation has

---

[4] *Ibid.*

cut the ground from under every objection of the sort." "For now," Walsh explained, after referring to the land acts of 1870 and 1881, "beyond all question, the system of land tenure in Ireland is a system of *dual ownership.*" "It is no longer a system of landlord ownership exclusively," he insisted, "the tenant now is recognized by law as having his ownership as well." "This fact," Walsh emphasized, "is recognised even by the present Tory Government, who have proclaimed their intention of getting rid of dual ownership — of buying out the landlords." "That is to say," Walsh added for good measure, "the Government has adopted Michael Davitt's policy of 'abolition of landlordism in Ireland.' "

The day after his considered endorsement of the Plan of Campaign appeared, the *Freeman's Journal,* which had been cautiously playing the waiting game, became noticeably more enthusiastic. "The Plan of Campaign," the *Freeman* noted significantly on December 3, 'advances rapidly. A few days ago it was a little driplet. Today it is a great stream."[5] The most telling analysis of the implications of Walsh's remarks, however, appeared only two days after the "interview" in the English Catholic weekly, the *Tablet.* "His Grace," the *Tablet* noted on December 4, "has answered the questions put to him by the representative of the *Pall Mall Gazette* with the utmost frankness and directness, and we make little doubt but that this 'interview' will long be famous in the history of journalism."[6] "The Archbishop's bold and unequivocal defence," the *Tablet* maintained, "of the action of the tenants in the present crisis is well calculated to cause a sensation in this country; but for all that, if any man can see his way to accept his Grace's facts, he must not hesitate at the conclusion."

> What we have got to do first is to rid our minds of all notions of the tenures of England. The State has recognised a dual property in the soil of Ireland. Recent legislation has made the word "owner" in relation to Irish land a word of equivocal meaning. The fields of Ireland belong neither to the landlord nor the tenant, but to both. The tenant is lord of the land he tills, subject to the payment of a certain money tribute known as "fair rent." Judicial tribunals have been busy for years all over the land fixing these money tributes. It is asserted that since

[5] *Freeman's Journal* (Dublin), December 3, 1886; quoted in Conor Cruise O'Brien, *Parnell and His Party, 1880-1890* (Oxford, 1958), p. 205.
[6] *Tablet* (London), December 5, 1886.

these legal rents were settled there has been a heavy unforeseen, and permanent fall of prices all over Ireland, so that the sum which two years ago represented a fair rent represents a rent unjust and impossible today.[7]

"Is, then," the *Tablet* asked, "the landlord taking advantage of the seasons to make profit out of his neighbour's extremity, and to be free, not only to do what he can to exact an unjust and extortionate tribute, but also to go further and by resorting to eviction, to invade the property of another, and possess himself also of the tenant's lawful share of the ownership of the farm?" "Upon the question of principle," the *Tablet* then argued, "there is no room for dispute. For it is obviously idle to urge, as many are doing, that the judicial rents were fixed for a term of years." "The question is not one of contract at all," the *Tablet* emphasized, as indeed had Walsh, "but of *status*."

The judicial rents were not contract rents arrived at by the haggling of the market and agreed to be paid. They were fixed by an outside power, and as representing not what the tenant thought he could afford to pay, but what it was equitable that he, with his part ownership, should pay. The rents were fixed as fair rents — have they ceased to be fair? That is the question.[8]

"If the fall of prices in Ireland has been so heavy and so unforeseen," the *Tablet* argued, returning to the issue of fact, "and at the same time so permanent in its character as to make the recently fixed judicial rents no longer equitable, the tenants are entitled to a readjustment." "The legislature," the *Tablet* finally came to its point, "by declining to intervene, has practically decided against the tenants' claim and in favour of the landlords." "To advise the tenants, therefore," the *Tablet* concluded ominously, "to disregard the decision of the legislature and treat it as ill-informed, and to act on their own judgement and knowledge, is the tremendous responsibility which the leaders of the National League have accepted."

The following week, the *Tablet* was even more to the point as it finally drew its alarming conclusions from its ominous premises of the week before. "Let the leaders of the League," it declared, "be ever so convinced of the truth of their statements

[7] *Ibid.*
[8] *Ibid.*

and the equity of their claim, and the question will remain — are they justified in counseling the tenants of Ireland to take the law into their own hands?"[9] "We have certainly no wish to resort," the *Tablet* continued, after describing the technique of the Plan for its readers, "to the feeble device of damning a cause with an epithet, but we have no choice but to say that such doctrines amount to anarchy and revolution." "We are quite prepared," it added, in the great English political tradition, "that such words are not final, for there are times when the sacred duty of obedience may have to give way to the still more sacred duty of rebellion." "It is for the advisers of the League," the *Tablet* maintained, placing the responsibility squarely on Archbishop Walsh, "to say whether such a time has come now."

> What we want our readers to feel is that the teaching of the League, whether they realise it or not, is revolution, and what we want the leaders of the League to do is to tell us whether they have any better grounds for the propagation of this most demoralising doctrine that the people are free to defy the legislature, to judge their own cause, and to be a law unto themselves, than the fall in the agricultural prices in a single year. We take it then that the policy of the League, whether moral or immoral, is a policy of anarchy.[10]

"On the other hand," the *Tablet* then concluded, returning once again, though obliquely, to Archbishop Walsh, "we fully recognise that there may be a necessity overriding all law of the kind to justify the preaching of this bloodless rebellion — but the burden of the proof lies heavy with the defenders of the League."

The *Tablet* had indeed raised a fundamental question by asking whether Parliament was really to be sovereign in Ireland. While Walsh might argue that the new concept of dual ownership of land in Ireland had transformed the landlord-tenant relationship to one of status, as the *Tablet* admitted, rather than contract, the fact still remained that since it was Parliament who had created that status, it must be Parliament who not only ultimately decided the terms of that status, but even more particularly whether that status should be modified to suit the changed economic conditions of the times. As far as

[9] *Ibid,* December 12, 1886.
[10] *Ibid.*

the niceties of representative government, and the maintaining of law and order were concerned, therefore, the *Tablet,* certainly, had the best of the argument. The Irish leadership and their advisers, however, who had now, in effect, actually become responsible for maintaining law and order in Ireland, still had to meet the larger and more fundamental problem of how to contain agrarian crime and to maintain control of the National movement in the face of an outraged tenantry who were being reduced by economic circumstances to thinking in terms of survival rather than in terms of law and order.

After the appearance of Walsh's "interview" in the *Pall Mall* on December 2, the tempo of events with regard to the Plan began to accelerate. Five days later, Parnell, who had obviously become very concerned, asked John Morley, late chief secretary for Ireland in Gladstone's last ministry, what effect he thought the Plan was having on public opinion. "In England," Morley replied, "the effect is wholly bad; it offends almost more than even outrages."[11] After explaining to Morley that he had been out of political action because of illness, and had not, therefore, approved of the Plan, Parnell promised that he would try to curb at least the violence of the language being used. Parnell then summoned O'Brien to London, and complained about the language of the "Campaigners," and especially Dillon's, as well as the spread of the agitation. His remonstrances with O'Brien seem to have had little effect, however, as the Plan gathered strength in the country as well as adherents in the Party. Less than a week after O'Brien's interview with Parnell in London, in fact, both he and Dillon were arrested in connection with their being Trustees for a Plan which had just been inaugurated in Loughrea, County Galway.

Walsh, who had only just had an interview with Sir Michael Hicks Beach, the chief secretary for Ireland, on the question of higher education, was obviously very upset by the arrests, for he immediately wrote the archbishop of Cashel, Thomas W. Croke, and second only to himself in influence among the Irish Bishops, who replied on December 17, posthaste. "The arrest of Dillon and O'Brien is serious"; Croke agreed, "but it brings matters to a head, which, I think is not undesirable."[12] In his

---

[11] John Morley, *Life of William Ewart Gladstone* (London, 1906), II, 610.
[12] Walsh Papers (W), Archives of the Archdiocese of Dublin, December 17, 1886.

letter to Croke, Walsh had also sought some encouragement on his recent endorsement of the Plan of Campaign as being both legal and moral, for Croke replied at great length with his customary vigor. "There certainly is, as you say," Croke began, "no law compelling a tenant to 'surrender' his tenancy; but there is it seems to me, *a law* (?) that obliges him not to hand over the Landlord's money (it must be his, or else it would not be offered to him) to a third party who has no claim to it, who may never give it to the rightful owner, and who declares, moreover, that he will not only strive to induce all his other tenants to do likewise, but will actually expend all or a portion of, said landlords [*sic*] money in a campaign against him." "I do not see how you can justify this 'plan of campaign,' " Croke then confessed, "if you admit that there is a lawful government here, and that that lawful government has declared the above conduct illegal and immoral."

"Now, the Government — i.e., the Legislature —" Croke added, taking what was essentially the *Tablet*'s line of the previous Saturday, "has actually declared it to be so; for when asked to oblige the Landlords to accept — say the £8 out of £10 — they not only refused to intervene, but distinctly stated that there was no good ground for doing so, and that they would, therefore, assist the Landlords as usual, in squeezing the full £10 out of their tenants." "For me," Croke declared, "the answer to this is easy. The so called *law* as expounded by Irish Judges and enforced by British bayonets is simply no law at all, inasmuch as it is for the benefit of the few to the grave and obvious detriment of the many, and inasmuch, moreover, as it is upheld *as law* by an alien Legislature for the purposes other than, and antagonistic to, the peace, prosperity, and social progress of the whole Irish Nation." "Them's my sentiments," Croke further declared, " — they have always been so." "I do not mean, of course," he added, and Walsh must have breathed a sigh of relief, "to make them public." "But," Croke concluded pugnaciously, "if forced to it, I should not hesitate to do so."

The day after he received Croke's reply, Walsh wrote Tobias Kirby, rector of the Irish College and official representative of the Irish Bishops in Rome, to ensure that the situation and issues in Ireland were well understood in the Eternal City. "The *Moniteur de Rome,*" Walsh informed Kirby on December 19, "is standing to us splendidly."[13] "I take care," he pointed out,

---

[13] Kirby Papers (K), Archives of the Irish College, Rome, December 19, 1886.

"to have the articles translated — sometimes I translate them myself! — for the Freeman's Journal. We also get Canon Daniel to write articles calling attention to them." "Now that the famous 'Plan of Campaign,'" he further explained to Kirby, "has been pronounced illegal, and a conspiracy, &c &c there are some points that should be clearly understood in Rome." "It would be well," Walsh advised, laying out his points about the condemnation of the Plan of Campaign one by one, "if they were conveyed to the Moniteur."

> I.   It is notorious that the mere application to that Court of Queen's Bench for such a decision was quite sufficient to ensure the decision being given.
>
> II.   The *very same decision* was *given by the same Court* on *O'Connell* and his Association, although of course we now hear nothing but praise of O'Connell, and of *his* way of working, from those who are opposed to the present movement.
>
> III.   The decision of the mere *judges* is all that has yet been given. Dillon is determined to have it tried before a jury. This will be the real test, and I have no doubt it will result in his favour.
>
> IV.   Yesterday, the Government admitted they had made a bad mistake in their arrest of Dillon and others in Loughrea. The proceedings based on that arrest (which was *clearly illegal*) are already abandoned! Law proceedings will now at once be taken against them, and no doubt heavy damages will be recovered!(K).

The Plan, meanwhile, continued to gain ground rapidly, and the vast majority of the Irish landlords, in order to avoid trouble, generally gave way before their tenants' explicit or implicit demands. Even on the 116 estates in which the Plan was eventually put into operation, only some two dozen of the landlords refused to come to terms. The result was that the expected difficulties regarding agrarian outrage and crime, with the exception of Kerry and Clare, where the landlords were notorious as both rackrenters and absentees, did not materialize. "The state of things in poor Ireland," the bishop of Ross, William Fitzgerald, lamented to Kirby on October 28, from Skibbereen in County Cork, "is not at present, in some parts, at all events, quite satisfactory"(K). "The people however," he then reassured Kirby, "are extremely quiet, & with the exception of some of those most wicked nocturnal raids in a neighbouring County [the country] is quite peaceable." Two days later Archbishop Croke also wrote Kirby reassuring him as to the reasonable and religious disposition of his people. "The October devotions," Croke reported on October 30, referring to the fact that October had been designated the "Month of Mary" by the pope, "everywhere, I think, in Ireland, have been a great success"(K). "I can answer for this diocese," he declared confidently, "and safely say, that they were a most striking success." "We had missions pretty generally. Here, two Dominican fathers preached to enormous congregations, three times a day — the first sermon daily, having been given at 6-1/2 o'clock a.m. Our cathedral was crowded and, on last Sunday, fully 1700 people received Holy Communion, of which number 1496 were males — Deo Gratias." "It will be impossible," he then warned Kirby, "for many of our farming folk to pay *full* rents this year." "But," he added reassuringly, making the crucial distinction between the grain and potato crops, "there cannot be real distress in the country at large, as the potato crop is very plentiful."

A little over a week later, the new coadjutor to the bishop of Waterford, Pierce Power, also wrote Kirby confirming all that his episcopal colleagues from the South had reported. "The depression," he explained to Kirby on November 8, "in all departments of trade & commerce from which we have been suffering for the past few years, has I am sorry to say, been intensified by the bad weather of the last few months, which has ruined the harvest prospects"(K). "Still," he added firmly, "there is no great suffering and the cause of religion[,] of law and order is all that we deserved or hoped for. With the exception of a few isolated spots on the Western coast, the country was never more peaceful. That is what I hear from Bishops." "We have not had an outrage," he then concluded confidently, "in this County during the 5 yrs. of agitation."

In forwarding some £500 in Peter's Pence to Rome two days before Christmas, the archbishop of Tuam, John MacEvilly, writing from St. Jarlath's College, summed up the political situation in the west of Ireland for Kirby. "The outlook as regards public affairs," MacEvilly began, "is, I am sorry to say, not very promising. The present Goverm[t], are a lot of blunderers. I hope they do not mean to drive our people to extremes, tho' it looks like an idea of coercion"(K). "While suppressing *legal* associations," MacEvilly argued, "they will drive our people into secret societies at which I shudder." "I am myself," he boldly announced, "in favor of legal, well ordered Associations and agitation within the limits of law and justice, as the best means of giving vent to the feelings of the people, and of informing our rulers of the proper way, of the wants of the people." "In truth," he confessed, "in a *country like ours,* agitation within the lines indicated is the Constitutional way of securing beneficent Legislation."

"There can be no doubt," MacEvilly further maintained, turning obliquely to the burning question of the Plan of Campaign, "but our poor Landholders — all good Catholics — have been robbed for years by the enforcement of excessive rents on the part of Orange Landlords. This is now admitted by the Government representatives — the Land Commissioners — who have given sweeping reductions, and who can blame our people to agitate, within proper bounds, however, to set themselves right?" "The hopes of the people," he shrewdly noted, "have been raised so high, that nothing short of Home Legislation will satisfy them. They will never be content with less." "May God," he added, in pious invocation, "who does all for the best, inspire our rulers to listen to the just demands of our people. We are all very quiet here, but I tremble at the idea of coercion as opening the way to secret societies." "The Govmt," he concluded somberly, "seem to be proceeding in the lines they went on when they provoked the horrors of 1798."

The recent arrests of Dillon and O'Brien in his province had obviously upset the archbishop of Tuam as much as it had his colleagues in Dublin and Cashel. MacEvilly was, in fact, both right and wrong about the intentions of the government. Needless to say, while the Conservative ministry was not acting the part of *agent provocateur* in Ireland, there was a growing tendency in London and at Westminster among the ultra Tories for a stronger line in Ireland. On the other hand, Sir Michael Hicks Beach, the chief secretary, who was responsible for the Irish executive in Dublin, was anxious to keep the "rod in pickle" for as long as was possible.[14] Sir Michael, and even more, his recently appointed undersecretary, General Sir Redvers Buller, were both sympathetic to the tenants and had only an unmitigated contempt for the Irish landlords as a class. "For 120 years," Buller had written Beach on November 15, "British bayonets have backed up landlords in extracting

[14] L. P. Curtis, *Coercion and Conciliation in Ireland (Princeton, 1963), p. 147.*

excessive rents, and have supported them in grossly neglecting their tenantry."[15] "What is the result of these 120 years," Buller asked, " — the tenants have combined against the injustice and persecutions; and where are the landlords?" "Nowhere," Buller answered, "Bankrupt in money, in political, and in moral power." "Is there not," he asked Beach pointedly in conclusion, "a lesson in this?"

There was, in fact, a lesson in it. By the time MacEvilly had written Kirby shortly before Christmas, Beach and Buller had already, for several months, been applying executive pressure on the most difficult landlords in an effort to persuade them to come to reasonable terms with their tenants. By going so far as delaying or even refusing to supply the evicting landlords with the necessary police protection, the Irish executive was, of course, "coercing" those landlords who refused to grant abatements in rent. The advocates of the Plan, naturally, were quick to point out that they were now being prosecuted for openly doing what the Irish government had been covertly sanctioning for months, and what apparently was sauce for the goose was not sauce for the gander. Dillon and O'Brien, after their arrest on December 15, were returned for trial in Dublin early in January. They secured a series of adjournments which postponed the prosecutions until the middle of February, and after the new Parliamentary session had begun.

The Plan, meanwhile continued to gain ground in Ireland, and the cabinet, which began its meetings in London in the middle of January, considerably weakened by Lord Randolph Churchill's resignation as chancellor of the exchequer and leader of the House of Commons shortly before Christmas in a huff over the budget, became very alarmed over Beach's reports that the ordinary law was no longer sufficient to maintain order in Ireland. The government announced, therefore, in the queen's speech on January 28, that a crimes bill would be introduced for Ireland as the first order of business, and the Irish members proceeded to obstruct the debate on the address for the next seventeen nights running. "I am coming to the conclusion," Buller encouraged Beach on February 2, from Dublin, "that Ireland was never in a worse state."[16] "There is not so much outrage," he noted, explaining the paradox, as well as who was

[15] St. Aldwyn Papers (H-B), Williamstrip Park, Coln; St. Aldwyn, Gloucester, Buller to Beach, November 15, 1886; quoted also in Curtis, *op. cit.*, p. 155.

[16] *Ibid.*, February 2, 1887; quoted also in Curtis, *op. cit.*, pp. 167-68.

really running the country, "because the League is so firmly
established, but the people are rapidly losing any regard for the
law, and unless you can get the full act you are proposing
passed soon, the whole country will join in the Plan of
Campaign against the payment of the March Rents." "If
Paddy," Buller then warned, "once gets regularly to no rent you
will require to kill a good many before you get him back
again."

Dillon, O'Brien and their fellow "traversers," were finally
brought to trial in Dublin and the prosecutor, Serjeant Peter
O'Brien, had once again attempted to live up to his sobriquet,
"Peter the Packer," in empanelling the jury. The *Freeman's
Journal* opened a fund for the defendants and Archbishop
Walsh headed the list of subscribers. "I should gladly
cooperate," Walsh wrote in making his contribution on
February 16, "in any way in my power in an effort to secure, if
it were possible, a fair trial for the traversers."[17] "But in the
present instance," Walsh maintained, "a fair trial is
impossible. The first essential element of fairness — a fairly
empanelled jury — is wanting. The jury before which John
Dillon and his fellow-traversers are arraigned in Green Street
has not been fairly empanelled. It has been most unfairly
packed." "And," he concluded most emphatically, "as this
most recent instance of jury-packing has been effected by the
wholesale exclusion of Catholic jurors of the County Dublin, I
send this subscription to the fund, not merely as a mark of
sympathy with the traversers, but as a protest, which, as
Archbishop of Dublin, I feel it my duty to make against the
gross insult that has thus been inflicted on many upright,
conscientious members of my flock."

The next day Archbishop Croke also contributed his mite.
The letter which accompanied his subscription, however,
almost defies comment, and must be quoted in full in order to
be appreciated.

I enclose £10 towards the Defence Fund. But when is this style
of business going to cease? I opposed the "No Rent Manifesto"
six years ago, because, apart from other reasons, I thought it
was inopportune and not likely to be generally acted on. Had a
manifesto against paying taxes been issued at the time I should
certainly have supported it *on principle.* I am precisely in the
same frame of mind just now.

---

[17] *Freeman's Journal,* February 17, 1887; quoted in *Walsh,* p. 269.

T. W. Croke. Archbishop of Cashel —

Our line of action, as a people, appears to me to be in this respect both suicidal and inconsistent. We pay taxes to a Government that uses them, not for the public good and in accordance with the declared wishes of the taxpayers, but in direct and deliberate opposition to them. We thus supply a stick to beat ourselves. We put a whip into the hands of men who use it to lash and lacerate us. This is suicidal.

In the presence of the actual state of things in Ireland just now, it is inconsistent besides. We run the "Plan of Campaign" against bad landlords, and stop what we call their rent; and we make no move whatever against the Government that pays "horse, foot, and dragoons" for protecting them and enforcing their outrageous exactions. Our money goes to feed a gang of needy and voracious lawyers; to purchase bludgeons for policemen, to be used in smashing the skulls of our people; and generally for the support of a foreign garrison, or native slaves, who hate and despise everything Irish and every genuine Irishman.

The policeman is pampered and paid, the patriot is persecuted. Our enforced taxes go to sustain the one — we must further freely tax ourselves to defend the other. How long, I ask, is this to be tolerated?[18]

What indeed was there to be said for this incredibly imprudent, though characteristic, manifesto, bristling with revolutionary implications?

Croke's letter not only proved to be a real provocation to his enemies, but a most serious embarrassment to his friends both at home and at Rome. Still, none among the Irish bishops, no matter how imprudent they thought the letter was, dared to call on the redoubtable archbishop of Cashel for an explanation. Several days after the letter had appeared, however, his old friend, Henry Cardinal Manning, archbishop of Westminster, wrote Croke gently asking him for some further explanation of his words. "I have read your letter in the Papers," Manning wrote Croke from London on February 21, "and see how inexorable is the logic."[19] "But," he added significantly, "the matter is larger than syllogisms, & I have a hard time of it among my friends who do not forgive my love of Ireland." "What," asked Manning, "shall I say to them?" "They will

---

[18] Ibid., February 17, 1887; quoted in Walsh, pp. 269-70.
[19] K, February 21, 1886. Croke forwarded this letter of Manning's to Kirby.

not," he explained, "admit my 'benique interpretatis.' And it does not soothe them to say that if I had been at Cashel instead of Westminster, I should have been less patient and guarded in my words." "Let me have a few words from you," the cardinal concluded, deftly introducing the Roman dimension, "which I may use here and elsewhere." "I am in receipt," Croke replied the next day to what in effect was the cardinal's polite invitation to retract, "of your Eminence's kind favour of yesterday."[20] "As regards my letter to the Freeman," Croke unrepentantly came straight to the point, "I have no explanation whatever to offer, beyond what appears on the very 'face of the record.'" "I recommend nothing in it," he proceeded to explain, "I do not tell the people not to pay taxes; but I distinctly state, I own, and firmly believe, that, were they to refuse to do so, except under compulsion, in every instance they would be fully justified in that course."

"I believe, moreover," he continued, "that it would be simpler, a straighter, more effective, and more logical course than the one that has been adopted here whether in accordance with the 'Plan of Campaign,' or otherwise." "The landlords *naturally* look for their rackrents," Croke maintained, "without Government aid they could never secure them. Warring, therefore, as we are, against rackrents, would it not be more natural to try and punish the Government for collecting them, than to punish the landlords for desiring to get them?" "I think it would," he declared bravely, "and I say so. That is 'the head and front of my offending.'" "I am sincerely sorry," Croke added, softening a little, "that your Eminence has been worried about anything, said, or done, by me. But surely anyone reflecting on the distressing scenes that are being enacted at this moment in various parts of Ireland and of which the Irish papers give detailed accounts — hundreds of people fleeing out daily on the roadsides to pine or perish — must be formed of strange clay indeed, if he can measure his words while writing about them, or believe that there is a Government here entitled either to the respect or obedience of Irishmen." "As for me," Croke concluded disconsolately, "I wish I were out of the country altogether, or that I had never returned to it from the Colonies."

---

[20] Croke Papers (C), Archives of the Archdiocese of Cashel, Thurles. There is a microfilm copy of the Croke Papers on deposit in the National Library of Ireland, Dublin.

On the very day that Manning was writing to him from London, Croke wrote Walsh expressing his surprise that the Dillon defense fund was getting on so slowly. "I thought," he naively explained to Walsh on February 21, and obviously still oblivious as to the consequences of his letter, "it would be *five times* as much as it is by this time"(W). Croke then noted that several of the more advanced Nationalist bishops such as Kilmore, Dromore, Down and Connor, and Meath had not yet subscribed. Two days later, and the day after he received Manning's letter, a more aware, but still unrepentant Croke wrote Walsh again. In his letter to Walsh, however, he did not mention his correspondence with the cardinal. "I am getting," he complained on February 23, "a dreadful mauling about in the English papers." "And, of course," he then added, half-humorously, "in due time my Roman friends will interrogate, and put me possibly to the torture." "'Tis hard to know what to do," he conjectured, discreetly inviting Walsh's advice, "Perhaps the best thing to do is to do nothing — but wait upon events." "The Bishops," he complained again to Walsh, "are slow in coming out."

Why the bishops were reluctant to commit themselves should have been, and probably was, obvious to Croke. A subscription to the Dillon defense fund, especially after his letter, would imply that they agreed with his views on the question of not paying taxes. Indeed, even the most forward among them might be forgiven for being unwilling to go that far, at least in print, while the more timid must have certainly realized, as did Croke, that the matter would undoubtedly be referred to Rome. The pressure of the mounting criticism and the disappointment in his colleagues' reluctance to support him in the crisis soon began to tell on him. "I am suffering dreadfully," he reported to Walsh on February 27, four days after his previous letter, "and have been for some time, from headaches and sleeplessness"(W). "In fact," Croke added, even more significantly, "I am quite beaten up: and the uncertainties of the moment are not calculated to soothe or strengthen one." Even Walsh, it seems, who had replied in the interim, had not taken advantage of Croke's discreet invitation to offer advice as to what he should do. "I hope more of our Brethren in the Episcopacy," he concluded forlornly, "will be out tomorrow. I give them up."

The expected word from Rome was not long in coming, for

on March 2, it appears, Kirby wrote both Croke and Walsh. While Kirby's letter to Croke does not appear to have survived, except in terms of Croke's reply, his letter to Walsh which has been preserved may be taken as a true token of the mind of Rome in this crisis. "The authorities," Kirby began dolorously, "are intensely grieved and displeased at the letter recently written by Dr. Croke recommending or suggesting the non-payment of taxes."[21] "The impression produced by it here is exceedingly bitter," Kirby explained, "as such things, they seem to fear, coming from an archbishop, embarrass and compromise in some way the Catholic Hierarchy and the Holy See itself." "I think it would be most useful," Kirby suggested, "if your Grace wrote a good letter to Cardinal Simeoni giving him an account of the state of things in Ireland and stating what you think may be proper and opportune regarding the letter of Dr. Croke, as I fear our good English friends may be tempted to press forward their own views on the subject." "The present moment," he significantly pointed out, "seems critical both in Ireland and here with regard to our Irish affairs. But we must not despond." "By prayer and patience," he added piously, "and the prudent use of the legitimate means in our power, we may hope for better times." "I sincerely trust and pray," he concluded characteristically, "that our Divine Lord and His Blessed Mother will firmly sustain your Grace, so as always to do the right thing and say the right thing — the *verbum sanum et irreprehensibile, ut ü qui ex adverso sunt nihil habeant malum dicere de nobis.*"

In his letter to Croke, Kirby not only brought the question of his alleged recommending the non-payment of taxes under his notice, but unfortunately also made it the occasion for mentioning several other complaints that were currently being made about the archbishop of Cashel in Rome. Croke, who was already obviously in very bad humor, wrote a stinger of a reply. "I have just received your kind letter," Croke began on March 5, "in which you inform me that the authorities in Rome are 'grieved and displeased because of a letter of mine openly recommending the nonpayment of taxes' "(K). "I never wrote such a letter," he declared emphatically, "I never openly, or otherwise, recommended the nonpayment of taxes." "The Pall Mall Gazette, March 1st," Croke noted, "one of the most influential of the London papers, distinctly states that I

21 *Walsh*, p. 271.

recommended nothing." "I enclose extract," he pointed out, and then added, "I also enclose a letter from Cardinal Manning on the subject, which I pray you to return to me."

> Second, you say, "that, some time ago, I recommended in public that in the pious association of the League of the Cross, the latter the sign of man's redemption, should be set aside and *the HARP* substituted in its stead.
>
> That is a deliberate and outrageous *lie*. I recommended that the title, "The League of the Cross" should be changed, *FOR IRELAND* to "*St. PATRICK'S League* of The Cross" — a recommendation which was unanimously adopted at a meeting held in Cork, on 21st of last October, which was presided over by Monsignor Sheehan P.P. and represented over 40,000 teetotalers. I send you a report of meeting transmitted to me for presentation to the *Irish Bishops*.
>
> Three, an appeal was made to Mr. Gray of the Freeman on behalf of Stephens [the Fenian leader of the 1860's] and his wife who are living in comparative poverty in Belgium, in order to get some little annuity for them. I subscribed 5 pounds — on the grounds, "That *though DELUDED*" he loves his country and had suffered for it. It was an act of charity — and nothing more. 1500 pounds were got for him(K).

Croke then asked Kirby to show Manning's letter to Cardinal Simeoni, the prefect of Propaganda, and assure him, "that I never recommended the people not to pay taxes, and that I simply said, our taxes were misapplied, and that a 'no tax manifesto' would be more reasonable than a 'no rent manifesto,' that I oppose the one, but would not oppose the other — if started by anybody." "And now," Croke added for good measure, "the fact and truth of the case is, that it would be better for me to resign this See altogether, than be perpetually worried and misrepresented as I am and have been, by the enemies of Ireland because I am true to the country, and a fearless and outspoken advocate of its rights." "Who could quietly submit," he demanded further, "to the treatment which the Tory government are giving to the Catholics of Ireland, declaring them *unfit* to serve on juries. Cardinal Manning has, over and over again, declared to me, that if he was an Irish Bishop, he would have been, *long since hung as a rebel*."

Croke, in fact, as soon as he finished this letter to Kirby, wrote to alert Cardinal Manning. After explaining that he had just received a letter from Kirby and its nature, Croke then reported the substance of what he had answered in reply. "I suppose," Croke finally came to his point, "as the Government have 'reported me to the Vatican' that I will be severely handled by the powers that be; and I ask your Eminence to use your kindly offices in this matter as you have done on similar occasions in the past"(C). "The most foolish thing," Croke added, and admitting what he had refused to admit some ten days before, "anyone, I believe, could do would be to recommend a strike here against taxes; for the sufficient reason that it could not be successful, though, of course, it would be annoying to the Government." "Still," he noted somewhat lamely, "everyone sees that our taxes are misapplied, as Mr. Dillon proved in the House of Commons, on Thursday night last." "Your Eminence will, I know," Croke concluded tamely, "excuse me for this trouble."

Once Croke, it seems, had retracted privately in his letter to Manning of Saturday, March 5, he found it that much easier to make the necessary public *amende.* Before he had even received Manning's encouraging letter by return of post on Tuesday, March 8, he had already written, the day before, a second letter for the *Freeman's Journal,* considerably modifying his earlier one. "I thank you from my heart," Croke replied to Manning on March 8, "for your very kind letter"(C). "I have had to reply," he explained, referring to a prominent Dublin weekly, "to a leader in the 'Nation,' and turn the fact to account by writing a few lines to the 'Freeman,' which I send your Eminence herewith." "This *second* letter of mine," Croke assured the cardinal, "clears the air considerably, and really confirms my views." "Perhaps your Eminence," he suggested, "would think it well to forward it, with 'Freeman's' comments and your own, to Cardinal Simeoni." "I do not care," Croke confessed in conclusion, "for '*a fall*' with the Government, but am unwilling to quarrel with the Romans."

By deciding to take action, it appears, Croke had recovered his emotional balance. Not only does his letter to Manning breathe renewed confidence, but his reply the following day to a letter from Walsh, who had only just returned from London, reads more like his buoyant self. "Welcome home," he greeted Walsh on March 9, "I intended leaving for London today, but now find I cannot do so"(W). "I have a Pastor dead"; Croke explained, "I have a priest on the run in connection with the 'plan of campaign'; and I have Rome preparing anathemas against me." "As for me," Croke then confided, "I do not intend to take any course, until I hear *directly* from the Roman authorities. In fact, I have nothing to add to what I wrote in yesterday's Freeman. I had no more notion of sending forth a 'no tax manifesto,' than I had of shooting myself; nor do I believe my words capable of any such interpretation — except, indeed, indirectly, and by implication." "I have said as much," he reported, "to Cardinal Manning who has been extremely kind and sympathetic over the whole affair." "I cannot agree with his Eminence," Croke noted interestingly for Walsh, "that I should write directly to H— H— Indeed, I have nothing to say to him, beyond what I have already said. If I were to add anything it would be to the effect, that I wished to resign the See of Cashel, and retire for the balance of my days into private life." "I am tired," he confessed, "of battling with Rome. I do not dread an encounter with the Government, and should be always prepared to try a fall with it; but for various reasons, which I mentioned frequently to poor Dr. Butler, it does not suit me to be brought into collision with the Romans." "I strive to have respect for them," Croke pointed out, " — especially for the *Head* — but it sometimes puts me to the pin of my collar to be in thought as reverent, and in act as obedient as I ought, I suppose to be." "Meanwhile," he finally asked Walsh in conclusion, "what is to be done? Write."

Walsh, meanwhile, had already decided what was to be done as soon as he read Croke's letter in the *Freeman*. "On landing at Kingstown yesterday evening," he explained to Manning on March 9, "I at once sent your Eminence a copy of yesterday's Freeman's Journal containing an important letter from Cashel"(M). "Would it be well for your Eminence," Walsh suggested, unknowingly echoing Croke's suggestion of the previous day, "to follow up your former letter to the Holy Father by another now stating that the Archbishop finding that such a construction was put on his words had written in the most explicit way disavowing the project of suggesting a strike against taxes, and unequivocally declaring himself in favour of constitutional means of action and of constitutional means only?" That same day, Walsh also wrote Kirby sending him a copy of Croke's letter appropriately marked and underlined. "Nothing could be more explicit," Walsh loyally explained to Kirby about Croke's letter, "than his indignant repudiation of the gross calumny that he advised the people not to pay taxes, or than his unequivocal declaration that he is for constitutional means and for constitutional means only" (K).

"The fact is," Walsh cautioned Kirby, "that, do what we can, it will be impossible for us much longer to keep the people within these lines." "It would be very easy," he argued, "for Dr. Croke, for myself, and for the body of the Bishops who wish to save our people, to stand aside, as two or three have done, and leave the people in the hands of the secret organisations that are so ready to spring up if they only get the chance." "The Government," Walsh maintained, "are determined practically to suspend the Constitution in Ireland. They would have done so before this, but for their dread of the episcopal influence." "It is plain that if they do it now," he asserted interestingly, "we should be only laughed at if we persisted in advising the people, as we have hitherto done so successfully, to confine themselves within the lines of the Constitution." "The Government think," Walsh further argued, "they can succeed in crushing our people by coercion. They will simply succeed if they try it in throwing our unfortunate country into a storm of revolution."

"But in the meantime," Walsh prophesied accurately, "they will try to clear the stage for themselves by putting pressure once more on the Holy Father to exert his influence so as to leave our poor people at their mercy." "It would be far easier for us to stand by," Walsh reiterated, "and give them their way. But it is our duty not to do so without a struggle." "I should not think," he added, referring to Kirby's suggestion that he write Cardinal Simeoni directly, "of writing such a letter as Y.G. suggests. Unless officially requested to do so, I could not interfere in an affair which lies outside my diocese and province." "But what has appeared in the newspapers," Walsh noted, explaining his present interference, "is public property." "Kindly read it," he requested Kirby, referring to Croke's letter, "or so much of it as is to the point for H.E., and for H.H." "You may say to both, from me," Walsh further charged Kirby, "that *they should not believe one word that is said to them on Irish subjects,* until they have given me, or some of us, an opportunity of showing whether it is true or false."

Manning also wrote Kirby, on receiving Walsh's note, enclosing Croke's most recent letter to the *Freeman.* "In your charity, & in your love of Ireland," Manning advised Kirby on March 10, "go to the Holy Father, & show him the inclosed, which we ought to take as a true disclaimer of ill intent"(K). "It is blowing over here," Manning explained, "but I am afraid of Whisperers in Rome." Some days after receiving both Walsh and Manning's letters, Kirby had his customary audience on March 17, with the pope, in connection with the celebration of the Feast of St. Patrick. "He spoke to me about the affairs of Ireland," Kirby reported to Walsh on March 18, "I gave him my poor views, which I confirmed by reading in Italian what your Grace wrote to me on the subject."[22] "His Holiness is much grieved that he cannot read English," Kirby explained, "at the end of the audience he told me to see Cardinal Simeoni, and to explain to him what I had mentioned to himself." "I had gone to the audience," Kirby confessed, "with much anxiety, knowing of the bitter and galling impression which the letter of our friend of Cashel of the month of February had produced on the minds of the authorities here — an impression which the second letter of March 7, helped to assuage, but by no means could wholly efface." "I explained to Cardinal Simeoni," Kirby assured Walsh, "the state of our case at some length, I hope with some favourable or at least some less unfavourable impression being left on his mind." "I do trust and humbly pray that God may preserve your Grace," he piously but discreetly warned Walsh, "in your difficult and delicate position, from the danger of giving any pretext to our enemies to implicate you in the meshes of law proceedings." "Write now and again to Cardinal Simeoni," Kirby again advised, "and give him an account of current matters." "*Viva la fede*," Kirby then concluded this very important letter with an hurrah in Italian, "dell Irelanda, di Pietro, e, di Patrizio!"

The implications of the Plan of Campaign were certainly revolutionary. What the proponents of the Plan were saying was simply that the British Parliament was no longer the effective sovereign power in Ireland. In promoting the Plan, they were, in effect, not only making law in Ireland, but enforcing it as well. The Bishops, moreover, as the moral component of the Clerical-Nationalist alliance, were sanctioning that law and its enforcement as both right and just. Through the alliance's local political apparatus, the National League, furthermore, the Party and the Bishops were not only making themselves responsible for enforcing the law, but also for

---

[22] *Ibid.*, pp. 275-76.

maintaining order. When Archbishop Croke, therefore, wrote his famous letter, he was simply suggesting that taxation should be added to what was already effective Irish control over justice and the police power. In a word, the Plan of Campaign was the most formidable engine yet devised for consolidating the power of the *de facto* Irish State.[23]

If the revolutionary implications of the Plan of Campaign were not lost on the editor of the *Tablet,* it is certain they were not lost on either the British government or the Roman authorities. The government, however, was having great difficulties in sustaining itself in the House of Commons. There was little it could do, therefore, to give purpose and direction to making its will effective in Ireland. Of those traditional mainstays of British power in Ireland, the landlords, Dublin Castle, and the army, moreover, only the latter could still be relied on. The Castle had indeed given up on the landlords as a class, whom it regarded with unmitigated contempt by refusing to enforce the law on their behalf; while the Castle itself apparently lacked both the will and the means to attempt to break up the *de facto* power being consolidated under the Clerical-Nationalist alliance. Indeed, the Castle preferred at this stage to conciliate rather than to coerce the Irish, for early in November, 1886, the chief secretary for Ireland, Sir Michael Hicks Beach, opened negotiations with Archbishop Walsh for a settlement of the question of higher education for Roman Catholics in Ireland.

---

[23] The implications of the Plan, for example, were certainly not lost on that class of Irish Whig politicians and landlords represented by Lord Emly and his friends. On the very day that Archbishop Walsh's considered endorsement of the Plan appeared in the *Pall Mall Gazette,* Aubrey de Vere was explaining to Emly that as far as their interests were concerned, he thought it was now or never. In writing Emly on December 2, De Vere reported that he had recently spoken with the bishop of Limerick, Edward Thomas O'Dwyer, and his lordship was of the opinion that "the National League was losing strength, & that the Clergy who had joined it would at least *moderate* its proceedings." "If they have any such intention," De Vere argued, "*now* is their time; & they should at once set themselves against the new plan of campaign which is so outrageous as to have no plausibility, allowing the Tenants to settle all rents irrespectively alike of Contract & of Governmental & legal Arbitration. Should this scheme succeed the whole Rental of Ireland would be handed over to the National League. Either therefore it must be put down *at once,* or Home Rule must be granted immediately afterwards. I do not suppose that England has gone mad. But it is absolutely necessary that the *first* attempts at the new warfare should be put down at once & at any cost, or the example will spread; & a great civil war, or absolute surrender ensue. Pray write strongly as you can both to Statesmen on the subject & to such Cath. Bishops as you know." Monsell Papers, 3818(14), National Library of Ireland.

This is why the Roman authorities, though increasingly disturbed by the implications of the Plan of Campaign, continued to be passive about Irish affairs. They understood very well that Walsh was dealing from a position of great strength with regard to the Education Question, and they did not wish to compromise his negotiations with the government.

In entering into these negotiations with a Conservative government, however, Walsh had placed himself in an extremely delicate situation with regard to the terms of the Clerical-Nationalist alliance. While the Bishops, under the terms of the alliance, retained both initiative and control in educational matters, they also had to subscribe to the priorities implicit in that alliance. This meant that the Education Question had to take a subordinate place to the settlement of the Home Rule and Land Questions. Indeed, before he had even entered into negotiations with the government, Walsh had taken occasion at the distribution of prizes at the Christian Brothers' Schools in Dublin to acknowledge publicly the precedence of Home Rule over the Education Question.[24] "I make it plain," Walsh emphasized to Kirby in referring to this speech, on November 8, "that we insist on a settlement of the Education Question, so far as an English parliament can settle it, but at the same time we make no 'bargain' of any kind on the question of Home Rule"(K). What Walsh neglected to tell Kirby, however, was that the recently appointed bishop of Limerick, Edward Thomas O'Dwyer, had taken issue with him both privately and in the public press on the wisdom of subordinating the Education Question to Home Rule.[25] In exalting the Education Question, O'Dwyer was, in effect, questioning the very basis of the Clerical-Nationalist alliance.

---

[24] See *Freeman's Journal,* October 18, 1886, for report of speech by Walsh on October 17, 1886.

[25] W, O'Dwyer to Walsh, October 18, 1886. "I am very much obliged indeed, to you by affectionate and kindly references to myself in your beautiful speech. I just read it before going to the Jesuits today and I took the liberty of qualifying the passage in which you deprecated any attempt at a political bargain with the party in power./I think it would be a most deplorable thing to postpone this question much longer. Do you know that there is a strong — very strong body of Queen's College men amongst the professions in Ireland and that they form a very influential secularist opinion; and in your Irish Parliament when it comes, you may not find as much consideration for ecclesiastical authority as we might expect. If you and Mr. Parnell agreed on a University bill it would be passed, and Home Rule need not be touched one way or another." For O'Dwyer's speech see *Freeman's Journal,* October 19, 1886.

What was perhaps even more serious from Walsh's point of view, however, was that O'Dwyer was not only questioning his authority to speak for the Bishops as a body on the Education Question, but that he was also questioning the authority of the Bishops as a body to speak authoritatively for him on that Question.

In any case, when the opportunity for opening negotiations with the government presented itself in early November, Walsh eagerly seized it.[26] "I am a good deal engaged," Walsh alerted Kirby on November 8, "in the Education Question — trying a little diplomacy!"[27] "I have every confidence," he explained, "that the present Government will do a good deal for us in this most important matter." "Perhaps indeed," Walsh added most interestingly, "on this account, as on some others already mentioned by your Grace, it is no harm that the establishment of our Home Rule system was a little delayed." Some three weeks later in early December, when the chief secretary, Sir Michael Hicks Beach, returned to Ireland after the parliamentary recess in London, Walsh had an interview with him at Dublin Castle. Walsh explained what he thought would satisfy the educational requirements of Irish Roman Catholics, but that he spoke only for himself, since only the standing committee of the episcopal body could authorize him to speak for the Bishops as a body. Shortly after this interview, Walsh informed Beach on December 9, that his colleagues on the standing committee had given him the necessary authority(H-B). "This in the circumstance," Walsh went on to explain, "means that I am now in a position to say to you in a fully representative capacity all that I said [to] you last week when I

---

[26] A group of English and Irish Roman Catholics, including an Irish bishop, John Healy, the coadjutor to the bishop of Clonfert, had met privately on October 30, 1886, with Lord Salisbury in London to promote both diplomatic relations between Great Britain and the Vatican and higher education for Irish Roman Catholics. (See supra, pp. 48-50.) Healy, who was a good friend and ecclesiastical confidant of O'Dwyer obviously wrote him explaining the government was amenable to a solution of the Education Question, for O'Dwyer wrote Walsh (W) on November 2, 1886, "I have the very best reason to know that Lord Salisbury is quite prepared to deal with the Education Question, and I am convinced that he would do [something] if it were taken up and urged in earnest by our Parliamentary Party."

[27] K, That same day Walsh also wrote Cardinal Manning giving him a strong hint as to his negotiations. "I am very hard worked just now at our Irish Education question. We must try to get all we can out of the Conservatives. I think that in this matter, they will do something substantial for us." Manning Papers (M), Archives of St. Mary of the Angels, Bayswater, London, November 8, 1886.

saw you at the Castle — supplemented, but in no way modified, by some further points, which, I feel confident, you will not regard as unreasonable." "I think it important," Walsh pressed, "I should see you as soon as possible." "It is a matter for consideration," he hinted delicately, "whether your Lodge would not be a more convenient place for the purpose than the Castle. My carriage is well known. I see that it must have been recognised in the Castle Yard and that its presence there led to all sorts of ridiculous comments being made both in English and in Irish newspapers."

Immediately after their second interview at the chief secretary's Lodge in Phoenix Park on December 15, Beach and Walsh exchanged letters in an obvious and polite effort to commit their conversations to paper. "Of course I understand," Walsh noted on December 16, "that you would make any official use you thought right, of anything I had said to you"(H-B). "As for the University," Walsh then explained, turning to the heart of the matter, "I can only say what I have said from the beginning."

> So long as Trinity College is allowed to stand, as it does, the most prominent public building perhaps in Dublin, representing the highest favour of the State on the matter of University Education exclusively reserved for the central stronghold of the non-Catholic education of this mainly Catholic country, so long we must continue to protest against the policy which withholds from us all that we ask for — equality.
>
> It is a question of one University or of three — unless indeed some scheme can be devised in which our Catholic College can be placed on a footing of perfect equality with Trinity, within the University of Dublin. But then there would remain the difficulty of the Queen's Colleges. This possibly could be got over. The result then would be to have our Dublin Catholic University College (equal to Trinity College) a College of Dublin University, leaving the Royal University outside, as an examining body for all the *provincial* Colleges of Ireland: changes should of course be made for the more effective distribution of the endowments of these making it say, depend upon the results of their work, in some such way as I have suggested for the Intermediate Colleges and Schools(H-B).

"You are probably aware," Walsh politely reminded Beach in a postscript, "that Isaac Butt elaborated a scheme for giving us a

Catholic College in the University of Dublin." "If you wish it," Walsh added, "I can send you a tract that he published on the subject."

Three days later, on December 19, Walsh forwarded Beach a copy of Butt's tract, considerately marking the appropriate passages. Walsh again reminded the chief secretary that Butt's proposal for a National University or an enlargement of Trinity College, Dublin, so as to include two colleges, one of them Roman Catholic, had only been put forward when the proposal for a government endowment of a Catholic University appeared impossible. "I can answer for all the Bishops of Ireland," Walsh further assured Beach, "that we look for nothing but equality. We are not especially anxious for any special way of bringing this about." "It may be by one University, or by two, or by three." "As I have more than once said to you," he again reminded Beach, "I regard any settlement of it impracticable for your Government that would interfere in any way with T.C.D." "I regard the project of a third University then," Walsh finally came to his point, "as the only one feasible in the circumstances. At all events, I do not see how we can be placed on a footing of absolute equality in any other way." "And absolute equality," he repeated once again, "is the one essential requisite."

That same day, December 19, in writing Kirby explaining that Dillon and O'Brien had been arrested and that the Plan of Campaign had been declared illegal by the Court of Queen's Bench, Walsh noted that it "will gratify H. H. to learn that amid all this turmoil I am in close and frequent relations with Sir Michael Hicks Beach, the new Chief Secretary"(K). "We are working out a full settlement," he assured Kirby, "of the Education question, to make it 'denominational,' and to give us full equality of endowments &c. for our Catholic Schools and Colleges, in all three departments, primary, intermediate, and University." "Get your good community," Walsh asked, "to pray hard for the success of my little effort at diplomacy." "But you understand of course," he warned, "you cannot give a hint of it as yet. It is *MOST STRICTLY CONFIDENTIAL*." "Of course," he corrected himself, "you will tell H. H. You may say that I feel every confidence that we shall *very soon* receive the first, and a very substantial installment of justice so long deferred in this important question." "Sir Michael understands *distinctly,*" Walsh emphasized in conclusion, "that I am above *bribery* on the Home Rule Question!"

After the Christmas holidays, and early in the New Year, Walsh and Beach resumed their negotiations in another private conversation at the chief secretary's Lodge in Dublin. The interview, which took place on January 6, mainly involved, as Beach's "Memo" indicates, the question of University Education(H-B).

> (1) College, with Trin. Coll:, in Univ of Dublin. Equal endowment: examining Board for Cath. (2) Separate, equally endowed, Catholic University. £38,000 a year Trin Coll. (3) Would not support, but protests again, merely making Catholic endowed Coll: one of Royal Univ. Colleges.
>
> If (2) were adopted, would accept it as a final settlement, squashing [?] Northern Catholics who might come to Dublin; and would allow us to capitaliz. revenues of Belfast Coll & give them to trustees as a separate Coll of Royal Univ. Would not trouble about other Queen's Colleges: except that they ought not to confer College scholarships on those who could not get a certain position in University. Would like to see more pass and less class, in University Examinations. This is a matter for the Senate(H-B).

Walsh was indeed obviously very pleased with his interview as he indicated briefly to Manning the next day at the end of a long letter. "P.S. (Confidential)," he reported to the cardinal on January 7, "Our Education question is now, thanks to Sir M. H. Beach, on the high road to settlement"(M).

Meanwhile, for nearly two months, and amidst his negotiations with Beach, Walsh was struggling with another very serious situation. Finally, almost in exasperation, Walsh decided to ask Kirby to alert Cardinal Simeoni, and, if necessary, the pope, to the developing crisis precipitated by the bishop of Limerick. In a long letter to Kirby on January 22, marked both *"CONFIDENTIAL,"* and *"KINDLY DESTROY THIS WHEN READ,"* Walsh laid out the whole story(K). "I think it well to let your Grace know," Walsh reported, "that in the opinion of several of our leading Bishops we are at least in some danger of a reopening of the old dissensions within the episcopal ranks." "The Royal University," he explained, "an institution which many of us have from the very start regarded with serious misgiving, is the present source of trouble." "At its opening, the Bishops were asked," Walsh continued, and

referring to his predecessor in the see of Dublin, Edward
Cardinal McCabe, "through the late Cardinal, to approve of
two members of their body to be nominated (by the Lord
Lieutenant) to the Senate — it being understood that the
selection of the Bishops so to be nominated should be left
practically to the body."

> Even with this proviso, it was only by a bare majority that the
> Bishops consented to be represented at all. When it *was* decided
> by the majority, then the Cardinal & Dr. Woodlock were
> named for the posts. The Lord Lieutenant, as a matter of
> course, nominated them.
>
> While both were alive, Dr. Healy, then Professor in
> Maynooth, was appointed to the Senate by the Lord
> Lieutenant. He was known at the time to be *practically* a
> Bishop. Still *technically* he was not one, and in the formal
> representation of the episcopal body continued in its *two*
> representatives, matters were allowed to proceed(K).

"When the Cardinal died," Walsh then pointed out to Kirby,
"no Bishop was appointed in his place." "But a month or two
ago, to the surprise of the whole country," he added, "it was
announced that the Lord Lieutenant had appointed Dr.
O'Dwyer of Limerick — the junior member of our body!"

"Great annoyance was, of course, felt at this," Walsh noted,
"— the more so as the young prelate had shown on several
occasions in public a strongly marked disposition to break off
from his brethren and to act for himself." "At a recent meeting
of our Episcopal Standing Committee," Walsh continued, "a
strong expression of opinion was made to him, and he at once
promised to resign the seat on the ground that faith had not
been kept with the body, in their making an appointment of a
Bishop to the Senate without any reference to them." "That
promise, however," he apprised Kirby, "he has not even as yet
kept. *There is reason to fear he will not do so.*" "Now we feel,"
Walsh argued, "that if the Government can thus pick and
choose for such positions on Education Boards individual
members of our body who may be altogether out of harmony
with the body generally, the influence of the Bishops in the
matter of Education is at an end." "It will in fact," he warned,
"be necessary to refer this case to the Holy See." "But
meanwhile," he suggested to Kirby, "it would be well for Y.G.
to mention the matter in a general way to Card. Simeoni, or

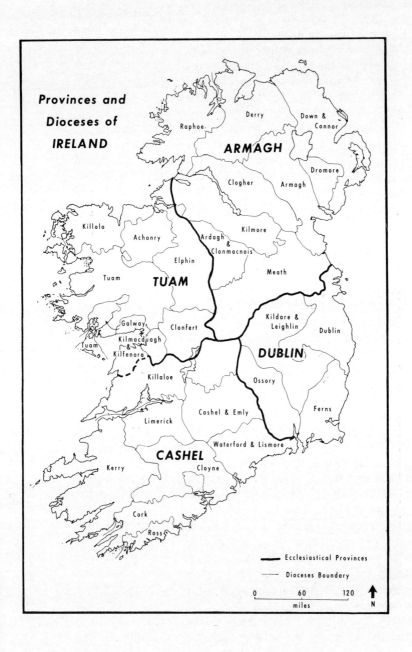

Provinces and
Dioceses of
IRELAND

Raphoe

Derry

Down &
Connor

ARMAGH

Dromore

Clogher

Armagh

Killala

Achonry

Kilmore

Elphin

Ardagh
&
Clonmacnois

Tuam

TUAM

Meath

Galway,
Kilmacduagh
&
Kilfenora

Clonfert

Kildare &
Leighlin

Dublin

Tuam

DUBLIN

Killaloe

Ossory

Ferns

Limerick

Cashel & Emly

Waterford & Lismore

CASHEL

Kerry

Cloyne

Cork

Ross

Ecclesiastical Provinces

Dioceses Boundary

0   60   120

miles

N

even to the Holy Father himself, saying that I have some fear that the seeds of dissension may have been skillfully sown amongst us. Thus the authorities will be on their guard."

For well over a month before he had taken the drastic step of writing Kirby on January 22, about the conduct of the bishop of Limerick, Walsh had been in close correspondence with Croke about the affair. After the meeting of the standing committee of the Bishops in early December, which had authorized Walsh to treat with Beach, and which had called O'Dwyer to order for accepting a seat on the Senate of the Royal University, and he had replied that he would indeed resign, Walsh forwarded his letter to Croke. Croke, who liked to poke fun at the bishop of Limerick's fondness for signing all his communications " + Edward Thomas," replied on December 13, "I return + E.T. There is plainly only one course open to him — that which you have suggested. Having undertaken to decline the honour, he cannot possibly accept it"(W). When Walsh informed Croke a week later that O'Dwyer had still not resigned, Croke noted on December 23 that — "+ E.T. is a nice fellow. He is 'cutting up' curiously. But people who know him best prophecised [sic] all this, and plenty more to come"(W). "You, probably," Croke noted, referring to an address presented by the corporation of the city of Limerick to O'Dwyer, "have not seen the full text of his reply to the Corporators. Nothing could be saucier or more assuming, or in worse taste." "He must be tamed," Croke then declared, "and will, please God, in due course." "We are surrounded by water here completely"; Croke then explained why he must close his letter, "and my right hand, owing to chilblains, is advancing fast towards the condition of a boiled turnip."

Immediately after his critical and encouraging interview with Beach on January 6, Walsh wrote Croke reporting on the negotiations. "The education question," Croke congratulated Walsh in reply on January 11, in his best telegraphic style, "appears to be progressing favourably. Training College question practically settled, and the great bulk of our N.[ational] schools denominationalised, would be a great step in advance"(W). "There is a great prejudice against Molloy," Croke warned Walsh, referring to the rector of the Catholic University and Walsh's candidate to succeed O'Dwyer as Senator, if and when the bishop of Limerick should resign, "throughout the Country. He is invariably regarded as an

unmitigated Whig, and a Jump-Jim-Crow man in politics."
"The sooner the Royal University," he then declared
emphatically, "is done up the better: so I have no interest in its
Senators." "I knew well," Croke wrote Walsh again the next
day, returning to the theme of O'Dwyer, "ever since the display
at his Consecration dinner that + E.T. would give trouble."[28]
"He must be put down": Croke then declared emphatically,
"and will not, I apprehend, except by the interposition of
Propaganda." "At our meeting," he reminded Walsh, referring
to the standing committee, "we went distinctly on the grounds
that we had ruled to have only two Bishops on the Senate, and
that no Bishop should be on it except as a nominee of the
Coetus — as Dr. Woodlock is fond of calling our aggregate
body." "He promised," Croke added, referring to O'Dwyer,
"unmistakably to resign forthwith." "How practically," Croke
then asked, "had we better approach + E.T.?" " 'Frappez et
frappez vite,' " he suggested, "should be the word." "I have got
rid of my man William, and my Cook," Croke then turned to
his own domestic problems in a postscript, "So, *eviction* is the
order of the day." "William got as drunk as a Lord," Croke
explained, "on Christmas night, broke everything before him,
and pummelled his fellow domestics after that — so, he has gone
adrift."

In what was rapidly becoming a daily news letter, Croke
wrote Walsh again the following day. "I have just had a letter
from Gray," Croke reported on January 13, referring to the
owner and publisher of the *Freeman's Journal*, "in which he
tells me that he got a fearful rating from + E.T., *through his
Secretary,* because of the 'Freeman' paragraph about his
resignation"(W). "I do not think we can do anything," Croke
then advised about O'Dwyer, "until we meet in Dublin." "The
'plan,' " Croke then reassured Walsh in conclusion, "is going

---

[28] W, January 12, 1887. Walsh had obviously enclosed his latest and what would
be his last letter from O'Dwyer on the subject. O'Dwyer had written (W), on January
8, 1887, "I am not sure that I understand the purport of your letter which I have
just received. You say that 'arrangements were considered for filling up the vacancy.'
Does this mean a vacancy to be created by my resignation or one already in
existence? If the first I should think the negotiations have progressed too rapidly;
and the assumption that it was essential that no bishop should be put on, the
ostensible grounds on which I have been asked to resign being that faith was broken
by not having a bishop selected in a particular way put on, seems to me inadvisable.
But to prevent any further misconception, I wish to say explicitly that,
notwithstanding the announcement in the Freeman, I have not resigned, and as
things have gone, it is less likely than ever that I shall."

ahead pretty briskly in the South. Here, we have no trouble whatever; as the Landlords, without exception, have caved in, and given a substantial abatement." "I leave home tomorrow," Croke again reported to Walsh the next day, January 14, "for Emly"(W). "The whole of that district," he explained, "is under 'the plan of Campaign,' and I hope to help on the cause, quietly." "As you observe," Croke noted, "if + E.T. attends the next meeting of [the] Senate, he will have unmistakably lifted the banner of revolt." "Robert Carbery S.J.," Croke added, referring to a cousin of his, "who is here, tells me that about 3 months ago, Lord Emly, canvassed for + E.T.'s appointment." "Amongst others," Croke continued, referring to two of the more prominent lay senators of the Royal University, "he called on Ball, and on Palles — Ball refused, at first to countenance his appointment, on the grounds that he was an advanced Nationalist and recommended the appointment of Browne of Maynooth, instead." "But," Croke explained, "on being assured by Lord Emly that + E.T. was an orthodox loyalist, he fell in with his Lordships views, and in furtherance of them canvassed Palles — or rather spoke to him approvingly of the proposed appointment." "So," Croke summed up, "the thing was well managed and secured."

Walsh, meanwhile, had written Croke again explaining that the bishop of Limerick was not the only one among their colleagues who was raising difficulties. Walsh enclosed a letter from Laurence Gillooly, the bishop of Elphin, who was an influential member of the episcopal education committee. Gillooly had obviously protested that "equality" was too high a ground for the Bishops to take if they really expected the present government to do anything about University Education. "I need not say," Croke assured Walsh, in returning Gillooly's letter, on January 17, "that I shall be with you on the lines you have marked out for the educational reform, and on none other"(W). "Dr. Gillooly," Croke maintained, "mistakes his following as usual; and is entirely wrong when he says, that the 'majority of the Bishops are of his mode of thinking.'" "The majority," Croke declared, " — vast majority — will follow you. He may have four or five for his expediency Scheme. We must stick to principle." "If we are to meet," he then added, "it should be about + E.T."

Walsh obviously had not taken Croke into his confidence in his decision to write Rome about O'Dwyer's conduct, for on the very day, January 22, that Walsh was confidentially writing to Kirby, Croke wrote Walsh, asking — "What about + E.T.?" "He is keeping very quiet," Croke reported, "On the Limerick side of the Diocese, where I have spent the last few days I learned that [he] is 'a caution' already amongst the priests, and that they are afraid of their skin of him." "Tis well our fellows do not shiver before us," Croke remarked, and added, "It may come, however, to that when we lapse, if we ever do, into a second childhood." "You did not answer my question," Croke then complained, referring to Thomas Carr, recently translated from Galway to Melbourne, "about the departure of the Melbourne Boss." "I dare say," Croke surmised correctly, "he will move next week. I meant to take leave of him in writing."

On his way to Melbourne, via Rome, at the end of January, Archbishop Carr broke his journey in London, where he had interviews with both Beach and Cardinal Manning. Carr then wrote Walsh reporting that Beach had gone so far in their interview as to make an offer with regard to the proper financing of University Education for Roman Catholics in Ireland. Walsh immediately wrote Manning in order to keep him abreast of the negotiations. "As Dr. Carr writes that he has had a conversation with your Eminence," Walsh reported to the cardinal on February 2, "in reference to our Irish University Question, I think it well to let you know that in consequence of his Grace's letter just now received I write by this post to Sir M. Hicks Beach saying that the offer of a capitalised sum puts quite a new face on the question, and that he may take it from me, and as coming through me from the Bishops, that any measure giving us *equality of endowment, secured by means of a capitalised sum,* will be received in a way as far as possible removed from unfriendly or carping criticism on the score of any shortcomings of the measure in other respects"(M). "I ask him at the same time to take my view," Walsh explained, "that if our scheme is not to be one of a single University in Dublin, but of four Colleges, one in each province, 'equality of endowment' ought to mean 'equality' not merely with the endowment of Trinity College Dublin, but also with the sum total of all endowments existing, or to be maintained, for University purposes in Ireland." "An endowment equal to that of Trinity College," Walsh pointed out to the cardinal, "split up into four parts, would put us in a position of inferiority *everywhere.*" "One thing is clear," he assured Manning, "no

Government ever got such a fair chance of dealing satisfactorily with the Irish Education Question."

In the next few weeks, however, Walsh's negotiations with Beach appeared to take a turn for the worse. "Kindly tell Dr. Carr," Walsh informed Kirby on February 15, "that I have been in constant communication with Sir Michael Hicks Beach since H.G. wrote to me from London, and that my former faith in the chief secretary is somewhat shaken"(K). "I practically closed with his offer," Walsh explained, "after hearing from Dr. Carr. The next letter I received began with a statement that he 'had not made any offer!' " "At all events," Walsh maintained in conclusion, "I have now abundant evidence *in writing* that if this present negotiation breaks down, the fault does not lie at our side of the question." Not only, it appears, did Beach claim that he had not made any offer in his conversation with Carr in London, but it seems also in his reply to Walsh he had offered something less than "equality." "In reference to your letter of yesterday," Walsh wrote Beach on February 5, "I think it right to take the counsel of the three Bishops appointed to advise confidentially with me whenever an occasion for doing so should arise. It is well that we should be able to see how far my colleagues are prepared to go in the way of accepting an arrangement short of equality"(H-B). "I have throughout our conversations," Walsh maintained, "endeavoured to make what use I could of the obvious distinction between the position of a body, such as that of the Irish Bishops, when putting forward a statement of claim, and when dealing with an offer actually made by a responsible Minister." "But," Walsh argued nicely, "that distinction ceases to be of use, if there is to be beforehand a compact, or understanding, that an offer admittedly short of equality will be accepted 'as a satisfactory settlement of the question.' " "At all events, as I have said," Walsh then added, "I am now about taking confidential counsel with the other three representative Bishops." "I am quite sure," he concluded cordially, "their feeling in all this matter is identical with mine, — to meet your views in every possible way, so far as we can do so without any surrender of principle."

In his reply, however, Beach was extremely reluctant obviously to make an offer which might be rejected, not only because it would weaken his bargaining power, but might easily prove politically embarrassing to himself and his cabinet colleagues in the House and in the country. "All that I can say,"

Walsh responded encouragingly on February 9, sensing Beach's dilemma, "in reply to your hand letter just received is, that I think it, from every point of view (except indeed from the point of view of those if there by [sic] any such, who are unwilling to see a practical settlement of the question arrived at), a mistake not to frame a proposal"(H-B). "In this first instance," he suggested helpfully, "the general outlines would surely be sufficient." "I say all this," Walsh assured Beach, "knowing what I do know of your personal views in this matter, as indicating, on the one hand, the general character of the proposal that is likely to come from your Government, and knowing, on the other hand, quite enough of the views of my colleagues generally to justify me in fairly forecasting what their action in reference to such a proposal is likely to be." "I expect on Wednesday next," Walsh added, referring to February 16, "to have the opportunity of taking counsel confidentially with some of them in the way I already mentioned to you." "Is there any chance," he asked, hinting broadly, "that in the meantime some progress will be made?" "It is, as I have also said to you," Walsh pressed delicately in conclusion, "much easier to agree on a *modus vivendi* after an offer has been made, than beforehand."

Beach, it appears, had made no offer by the time the Bishops met, but had suggested a conference with Walsh after his consultation with his colleagues. The four representative Bishops were Walsh, Croke, Gillooly, and probably the bishop of Ardagh, Bartholomew Woodlock. Croke, meanwhile, had written Walsh on February 9, that a previous local engagement would prevent him from attending the meeting, but that he would, as Walsh had suggested, put his views on paper for "the Episcopal Triumvirate"(W). "I have written my views," Croke reported dutifully to Walsh on Tuesday, February 15, "on the question of Education"(W). "I hope," he added, "you may be able to get round Beach." "Dr. Gillooly," Croke reassured Walsh again, "thinks the bulk of the Bishops are with him. I think he has about 4 and himself." "Write me," Croke then concluded, "after the meeting." "I think," he added in a post-script, "I fairly represent your views — as well as my own." Once again, Croke had given one of those impressive virtuoso performances on paper of which he had now easily become a past master. His letter was at one and the same time an eloquent *apologia* for his own position, a rationalization for the attitude taken by the Irish Bishops for the past quarter of a century, as well as a justification for an accommodation of the ideal and real at that moment in the matter of Irish University Education. After regretting that he could not be present at the meeting, Croke explained to his brethren:

My views have undergone no change on the Irish Educational question for the last *five and thirty years* — for it is fully that length of time since I first publickly spoke on the subject in the City of Cork. Those views may be summed up in the one word — *"equality"* — that is to say, that I claim for the Catholics of Ireland such freedom of action, and such state support in the matter of *higher education* (for of that alone, I take it there is now question) as have been granted, and are actually enjoyed by the Protestant portion of our fellow countrymen.

I am not sure, indeed, at the same time, that *"equality"* in that sense is not rather low ground for us Catholics to take, inasmuch as, being the vast majority of the inhabitants of this country, we have a right to have state support and privilege extended to us in some such proportion as would fairly represent, and recognise our numerical superiority.

However, be that as it may, I for one, shall never be content with any state recognition, or be a party to any pecuniary settlement of the Education question, unless that recognition, and that Settlement, be of a nature to place us Catholics, on a platform of *perfect equality* with even the most favoured of our dissenting Brethren.

Having said this much on the general features of the case, I now descend to particulars, and come to consider the *two* practical questions, set forth in the latter end of your Grace's highly interesting letter just received, and which I return with this line.

1° "Should we surrender?" — I think too highly of my Brethren in the Irish Episcopacy to suppose for one moment that there is even one amongst them who after due consideration would be prepared to barter any portion of our people's birthright, or abate any of their legitimate educational aspirations, for either "love or lucre." And yet, I have been seriously assured, that there are some such amongst us. I have been told that some *five* to *six* of our body are ready to cry quits with the Government, and haul down "the flag" so steadily, if not triumphantly, upheld by the Bishops for the last quarter of a century. And more in consideration of such an endowment for the purposes of higher education as would be equivalent to that actually possessed by Trinity College — Trinity to maintain, however, all its present privileges of representation, and all its

faculties as a University, while no similar advantages would be
enjoyed by the Catholic body! Surely this is not *"equality"* and
with less than that, as I have already stated, I cannot be
satisfied.

But 2° if an offer substantially the same just referred to were
made to us by the Government, how should we deal with or
approach it.

Of course, as is plain, such a proposal if made would be a
step and a great step in the right direction; and it would be in
my opinion both unwise and impolitic summarily to reject, as it
would be faithless and fatal, on our part, unequivocally and
unconditionally to accept it. How then should we treat such a
proposal?

Such a proposal, if hampered by no utterly inadmissable and
compromising condition, should, and, no doubt, would be
jumped at by the Irish Bishops. But, as I can perceive from
your Grace's letter, and as may be inferentially gathered from
the antecedents of this and other British Governments in their
relation with this country it is far from likely that such an offer
would be made to us, without one, or other, or possibly both of
the following conditions. The Government may say —

a — We make you this offer, but, if you accept it, the
settlement must be final: or

b — We make you this offer, but you can have no Catholic
University, or anything like it, and your people accordingly
shall have to take their degrees in *Trinity* or the Royal. In either
case, what should we say? We should say, as a matter of course
— "non possumus" — it can't be done. We have a right to
"equality." We, therefore insist on getting it. You offer us
LESS; and we reject your terms.

But then there comes up for treatment the case as it *now*
stands. What is to be done? Beach says now, it appears, that he
has made your Grace *no offer?* He admits, however, that he
had suggested "a basis" on which negotiations with the Bishops
may be carried on. Well then I am for treating with him on that
basis, pinning him, if possible, to some specific engagement, but
committing ourselves, at the same time, to no final course(C).

"As for my part," Croke concluded this long letter by
delegating his authority unreservedly to Walsh, "I leave the
matter entirely in your Grace's hands, fully satisfied that you
are too high spirited to accept an unworthy compromise, and
too clever to be outwitted by Her Majesty's Chief Secretary for
Ireland."

"The consultation about which I wrote you," Walsh

informed Beach right after the meeting on February 16, "has resulted, I think, satisfactorily"(H-B). "I am now in a position," he came quickly to the point, "to confer with you as to a plan for effecting a practical settlement to the question on the basis of the Royal University." "The Bishop of Elphin," Walsh added, referring to Gillooly, "has kindly consented to remain here for a few days, in the hope of your being able to carry out your intention of coming over." "Otherwise," Walsh then offered, "I should arrange to go over myself to London to see you there, if you deemed it advisable." "My own opinion, however," he concluded, "is that such a course would not be advisable." While it does not appear that Beach crossed over to Dublin or Walsh crossed over to London, negotiations apparently continued, for John Thomas Ball, senator of the Royal University, vice-chancellor of Dublin University, and one-time lord chancellor of Ireland, replied to a letter of Beach's on February 19, the Saturday after the Bishops' meeting on Wednesday.

"As I understand your letter," Ball wrote, "Archbishop Walsh would let the Royal University stay with its present Constitution — without any religious character"(H-B). "If so," Ball declared, " — I argue that a settlement ought to be made of the Education question." "I think this should be done," he advised, "by endowing a College in Dublin, which in addition to the usual [curriculum], should be at liberty to give religious instruction according to the Roman Catholic system."

The College would of course have a President or Rector & teachers i.e. Fellows and Professors or whatever they might choose to call them. It is positively necessary that there should be a Medical school connected with it. The great bulk of the students for the Royal & at the Catholic University College, aims at this profession, & they can only be examined, and not taught at the Royal.

The government of the College should be vested in a Board mixed clerical & lay. It should not be left altogether to the former. Certainly not as regards the application of funds; and I would say also as regards the courses of study. Of course both lay & clerical to be Roman Catholics. I would be disposed to keep the appointment of a Visitor or Visitors in the Crown, just as it is, for the Queen's Colleges. Only Roman Catholics should be appointed & some should always be from the Roman Catholic Judges. I am a Visitor of the Queen's College Belfast

& my experience is that Visitations generally involve law points.

I would in order to make funds close Galway College —

I do not know whether the Roman Cath. Bishops would interfere with Cork College — but if they do, I do not see that much is gained by keeping it.

I could not in a letter go into the matter fully — I would go to London,if you were ready to enter on it for practical purposes = which I suppose might be in the Easter Recess(H-B).

"What I suggest," Ball recommended, "is what would please the Catholic laity." "They do not want," he added interestingly, "to have a mere Catholic University." "They think," he concluded, "a College, where the teaching is, should be Catholic, & then the University would oblige the College to keep up the standard of education."

Walsh, meanwhile, had written Croke asking his advice as to whether he should publish a Lenten Pastoral, and also mentioned some proposed modifications in the structure of the Royal University. "It would not do for *you*," Croke replied on February 21, "not to put forth a Pastoral at this time of the year, and you have a fine field before you in the Education question"(W). "Of course," he agreed, "if the Royal were thoroughly overhauled so as to give it a sound Catholic body and Complexion, together with the other changes to which you refer, we would be fairly well off, and should be fairly satisfied." "But," he added pessimistically, "I see no likelihood of any such concessions on the part of this Tory Government." "I see + E.T.," Croke then noted somberly, "has returned from London. He has been away for some time." By this time, however, the storm had already broken over Croke's celebrated letter on the "non-payment of taxes" to the *Freeman,* and he was naturally more preoccupied with political rather than educational matters. Walsh did publish a Lenten Pastoral of some thirty-five pages, and forwarded this prodigious effort to both Beach and Croke. "I have dealt," Walsh explained in a covering letter to Beach on February 26, "with practically *all* our grievances, and I have done my best to make it plain that the ridiculous fiction of our wanting any sort of 'ascendency' is utterly baseless"(H-B). "I have got," Croke reported the next day, "and read the Pastoral"(W). "It is very good," he complimented Walsh, "One would imagine that you were at such things all your life." "As regards the education question," he added discreetly, "in all its branches, it is almost exhaustive.

As you observed yourself, it is a trifle too long." "But," he concluded more encouragingly, "having regard to the weight and variety of topics treated of, it could hardly be made much shorter."

"I send your Grace," Walsh wrote Kirby the day after Croke wrote him, February 28, "by this post two copies of my Lenten Pastoral, in which, after some observations appropriate to the time of Lent, I set forth all our claims in the matter of Education"(K). "For the last six months," Walsh complained, "we have been hearing that no one can make out what the Irish Bishops want, so I thought it well to show that all this was explained years and years ago in Cardinal Cullen's time, and that all we want is to have the demands that were then made satisfied." "I will send a copy to Card. Simeoni, probably today," he added, "but I will ask your Grace to explain to H.E. and to the Holy Father how matters now stand." "My confidential communications with the Government," Walsh explained, "are still going on most amicably. They will do practically all that I have asked for in this Pastoral!" "Up to this," he noted, "there has just been one little hitch in the way, but it has, thank God, now disappeared. It had reference to the University question." "They will not give us a University of our own," he informed Kirby, "but they are willing to endow for us *in the Royal University* a Catholic University College in Dublin, and they will make it in endowments &c, *EQUAL TO TRINITY COLLEGE!*" "This, of course," Walsh acknowledged, "is far more than was ever dreamt of until a few months ago." "Still *in principle,*" he added, "it is not quite satisfactory, as we have a strict right to have ourselves recognised as a *University,* just as Trinity College is."

"Sir Michael Hicks-Beach," Walsh continued, "kept insisting that I should pledge myself that the proposed arrangement would be accepted 'as a *satisfactory SETTLEMENT*' of the question!" "This of course," Walsh continued, "I could not do. But I have at length succeeded in getting him to be satisfied with an assurance that we shall regard it as a satisfactory *modus vivendi.*" "He has now put the matter confidentially into the hands of a high Conservative authority," Walsh reported, and probably referring to John Thomas Ball, former lord chancellor of Ireland, "not a member of the government, who is now framing a scheme for the establishment of a Catholic College." "It will," Walsh assured Kirby, "be quite satisfactory." "Of course Yr. Grace will understand," Walsh cautioned Kirby, "that all these communications are *most strictly confidential*." "But it is a wonderful step in advance," he added enthusiastically, "to have the Government conferring with us at all." "I think I mentioned," he reminded Kirby, "that the Bishops appointed me plenipotentiary for the purpose." "All this," he reiterated in conclusion, "is strictly for Yr. Grace, Dr. Carr, Card. Simeoni, and the Holy Father."

Within a week, however, all of Walsh's patient negotiations over four months were in a moment turned into a bitter disappointment, for Beach resigned on March 7, as chief secretary for Ireland. What chance there might have been, moreover, for salvaging any part of Walsh's own high hopes, or of being able even partially to fulfill the great expectations he had raised at Rome, were further diminished by Lord Salisbury's choice of chief secretary to succeed Beach. In appointing his nephew, Arthur Balfour, Salisbury made it clear that he now intended to coerce rather than conciliate Irish Nationalists. This explains, for example, Walsh's extremely strong letter of March 9, to Kirby, enclosing Croke's "disclaimer," on the non-payment of taxes, in which Walsh had minced no words over the government's obvious intention of introducing coercive measures, and had also pointed out that the government would now certainly try to make their own way easier in Ireland by exerting pressure at Rome. Walsh had, in fact, crossed over to London at the height of the ministerial crisis, and had undoubtedly heard the sad news of the resignation from Beach himself. The former chief secretary had obviously attempted to console Walsh as to the future, for when Walsh wrote Kirby on March 23, explaining his disappointment, he had naturally tried to put the best face possible on the breakdown by holding out some hope. "There is, however," Walsh reported encouragingly, "one of the points that we had under consideration — that regarding the Training Colleges, as explained in my Pastoral — which he assures me *in confidence* he has so fully dealt with, that 'unless some unknown and wholly unforeseen difficulties, should arise' we shall see it settled almost immediately"(K). "I know that he has put the University Question," Walsh noted, "also in a fair way of settlement." "But," he added less confidently, "here a great deal will depend upon the views of the new Chief Secretary, Mr. Balfour." "Of course," he warned Kirby somewhat unrealistically, "you will explain to the authorities that all this is *most strictly* confidential. If the Protestant party came even to suspect what is going on, the Government should be forced to drop all that they may be inclined to do for us."

Kirby, meanwhile, had taken it upon himself to solve the problem posed by the bishop of Limerick's appointment to the senate of the Royal University. About the middle of February, Kirby wrote O'Dwyer attempting to persuade him to resign his place on the senate. "I will write tomorrow," O'Dwyer, who had only just returned from London, replied on February 22, "on the subject of your Grace's very Kind Confidential Communication"(K). O'Dwyer, it appears, did not write the next day, and, in fact, did not write until some two weeks later. "Having given the best consideration in my power," O'Dwyer politely began his letter of March 9, to Kirby, "to your most kind and affectionate advice I regret that I cannot see my way, at present, to take the course which your Grace has been so good as to suggest." "I do not think," he added more firmly, "that the interests of higher Catholic education, or the influence of the episcopal body would be served by an action which as regards myself personally should be marked by levity and fickleness, and would be accepted as an affront by the Government which meant to act fairly by the Bishops in the matter." "The difficulty in the case does not lie with me," he explained, "I am of opinion that a representative bishop chosen by his colleagues would be infinitely preferable to one chosen as I have been by Government, and I am satisfied from my correspondence with the Chief Secretary on the point that the Government will easily accept a practical understanding to give effect to such an arrangement and if the Bishops direct their negotiations towards this end, I shall gladly put my resignation at their disposal: but unless under the direction of Propaganda I will not throw up a place where as a Catholic Bishop there are immense and yearly growing Catholic interests to be protected, as a mere isolated act, without reference to some definite and reasonable policy."

"Dr. Walsh ought to be our representative," O'Dwyer argued with perverse ingenuity, "I have no doubt that the Government would gladly appoint him, and as a matter of course the Bishops would elect him, and if he consented to go on the Senate, or failing him, if any other Bishop is selected, I will resign my place, in his favour." "But the difficulty is,"

O'Dwyer added shrewdly, "that Dr. Walsh having left the
Senate of the Royal University on some side issue does not wish
I presume to go back, and consequently there is a deadlock."
"But the Royal University," he explained further, "counts its
Catholic students now by hundreds, and almost thousands and
cannot be allowed for any personal considerations to drift out
of episcopal influence." "Dr. Walsh," he reported to Kirby,
"hinted [?] to me some time ago that he had arranged with the
Chief Secretary for my successor, laying it down as essential
that he should *not* be a bishop, and it was the assumption of
such authority as regards myself and the mistake of such a
policy as regards the Bishops that determined me to retain my
place at least until the next meeting of the general body of the
Bishops."

"I wish to add finally," O'Dwyer pointed out for good
measure, "as Your Grace has honoured me with so Confidential
a communication that I fear that there is underlying this
pressure that has been brought to bear on me from many sides,
the spirit of general resistance to Civil Authority which has
been growing in Ireland and if encouraged will produce the
same results to religion that the revolution has produced in
every country in which it has triumphed." "In my humble
opinion," he further argued, "we are abandoning the principles
of obedience, of reverence, and of charity that were the
traditions of our predecessors, and for the sake of mere favour
allowing the people to follow methods of violence and
disobedience." "As long as the priests of the Church,"
O'Dwyer warned, "are useful political agents for the leaders of
this system, they will be applauded, and appear to hold in
influence: but when the time comes as come it must that we
can no longer pander to popular passions, I fear the reaction
will show that our power has been undermined." "I write this to
your Grace with great sorrow, and diffidence in my own
judgement," he concluded humbly, "but with the most intimate
conviction of its truth." "I am sure," O'Dwyer wrote Kirby
again some days later on March 13, "that it is unnecessary for
me to convey to Your Grace that my letter of last week was
entirely confidential, and written under the influence of the
extremely kind and affectionate advice which Your Grace had
been so good as to tender to me"(K). "I should be very sorry,"
he explained, and obviously referring to Walsh, "however
deeply I deplore a good deal that is being said and done in

Ireland, to express my views generally in [a] way that might seem wanting in deference to those who are charged with weightier responsibilities and are so well qualified to bear them." "But when I have to express my own opinions in confidence," he concluded artfully, "I can only feel regret if I find that in the attempt to be candid, I have to assume a tone of self sufficiency."

The timing of O'Dwyer's letters of March 9 and 13, to Kirby was masterful. Beach had resigned on March 7, and it was obvious that Walsh's negotiations with the government were in jeopardy. Walsh was, therefore, no longer dealing from strength in educational matters, and O'Dwyer's threat to refer his difficulties with Walsh and his brother Bishops on educational matters to Propaganda, if necessary, implied not only a most serious challenge both to Walsh's position as leader in the Irish Church and to the authority of the Bishops as a body in terms of majority rule, but it also meant that Rome would acquire some of that initiative in educational matters that had been the monopoly of the Irish Bishops for well over a quarter of a century. O'Dwyer's letters, moreover, arrived in Rome when the furor over Croke's celebrated letter was still at its height, and thus further impaired Walsh's credibility as an effective leader since he was apparently no better able to manage his critics among the Irish Bishops than his friends. If indeed, the bishop of Limerick could not be contained at home and at Rome by the Bishops as a body, the Clerical-Nationalist alliance might not only be weakened, but if any considerable number of O'Dwyer's colleagues began to follow his lead, it might even be eventually broken up. When to all this is added the mounting pressure by some English and Irish Roman Catholic laymen in recent months for the establishing of the pope's heart's desire with regard to England — diplomatic relations — it is easily understood that O'Dwyer's letters to Kirby in early March represented a good deal more than simply the self-righteous indignation of a calculating, difficult, and bumptious type.

II. Intrigue at Rome
December, 1886 - April, 1887

The attempt by an influential group of English and Irish Catholics to promote diplomatic relations between London and the Vatican in the midst of his difficulties concerning the Plan of Campaign, the Education Question, and the bishop of Limerick, certainly did not make Archbishop Walsh's efforts to preserve and strengthen the Clerical-Nationalist Alliance any easier. The threat presented to the Irish Church by diplomatic relations was not simply that the British government would increase its influence by accrediting a representative at the Vatican, but that the government would also acquire in the negotiations for such accreditation considerably more leverage in Irish affairs at Rome. What the Irish Bishops and politicians were really concerned about was the *quid pro quo* that would be demanded by the British government for accrediting a representative to the Vatican. If it was to be a condemnation by Rome of the Plan of Campaign, or worse, the Home Rule movement, and the Irish Bishops were obliged to enforce, or even acquiesce in, such a condemnation, the Clerical-Nationalist alliance would be wrecked, and the stability of the recently made *de facto* Irish State seriously impaired. In the break-up of the Clerical-Nationalist alliance, moreover, the very real political power and influence of the Irish Bishops would also be laid in ruins because it was now a function of that alliance.

When in early December, 1886, therefore, Walsh learned that a number of influential English and Irish Roman Catholics had been granted an interview with Lord Salisbury in order to promote diplomatic relations, he was naturally concerned. When he further learned, however, that the deputation to the prime minister included an Irish bishop, he was aghast. "I think it well," Walsh advised Kirby on December 12, 1886, "to write your Grace in reference to a very grave occurrence deeply

48

affecting the welfare of our Irish Church"(K). "I write," he explained, *"IN THE VERY STRICTEST CONFIDENCE."* "It is, I think," he declared, "important that the Holy Father should be made fully acquainted with what has occurred. But as I have recently had evidence that some important correspondence with the Propaganda was in some way or other revealed, probably through the indiscretion of a subordinate clerk or other official, I must take this way of communicating with His Holiness." "I may begin by saying," Walsh further explained, "that it has reference to the delicate question of diplomatic relations with the Holy See." "Now it is one of those questions that," he then warned, "if unjudiciously handled in England, may be the occasion of causing feelings of distrust to grow up in the minds of our poor people." "Certain English noblemen (Catholics)," he reported, "have taken to making speeches in which they boast that by means of the reestablishment of diplomatic relations they can crush out the present constitutional movement in favour of Home Rule." "Now the urgent difficulty," he then continued, "that has at present arisen in connection with this matter is this:

> The "Saturday Review" of London, a weekly paper bitterly anti-Catholic, and consequently bitterly anti-Irish, has the following: "It is no secret that a deputation has recently waited on the Prime Minister in reference to this matter — the diplomatic relations — a deputation of English Roman Catholics, headed by the Duke of Norfolk, and including *representatives of the Irish hierarchy*"(K).

"When I mentioned this," Walsh reported, "to our Bishops at a full meeting of our Episcopal Standing Committee held last week, the Bishops at first thought the statement too ridiculous to be worth notice. But I was able to tell their Lordships that from what I had learned, through an official channel of information *now* fully open to me, the statement, incredible as it seemed to them, was literally true — I could not, however, mention names." "They at once instructed me," he informed Kirby, "to write in the name of the Irish Bishops to Lord Salisbury informing his Lordship that no such representative was in any way authorised to speak for us, that if any persons had undertaken to appear as our representatives, his Lordship was to understand that we in the most formal way repudiated any views thus put before him, and that we trusted he would not allow himself, or his Government, to be drawn into any difficulty by acting on the assumption that our views had been represented to him."[1] "Even still," Walsh confessed, referring to the general body, "the Bishops are under the impression that nothing more occurred than that certain over-busy *laymen* undertook to speak as if they represented our views." "Now," Walsh then finally came to his point, after his thorough introduction, "the alarming information that I feel it my duty to convey to the Holy Father is this, that as a matter of fact, *one of our Bishops,* fortunately only a Coadjutor, *was a member of this deputation* — Dr. Healy, the Coadjutor Bishop of Clonfert." "I dare say," Walsh continued, "your Grace knows something of his extraordinary action in public affairs, his open partiality for the landlords, and his constant association with them to the great wonder of Bishops, priests, and people." "But no-one," Walsh confessed, "could have believed he would have gone so far as this, to go on a secret mission, behind the backs of all his colleagues, to the coercionist Prime Minister, and to involve this delicate question, in which the Holy Father is so deeply interested, is the greatest difficulty and danger." "The present position of the Coadjutor is such," Walsh advised, "that, with my present knowledge of the facts of this and other cases, I feel bound to suggest that the Holy Father should consider the advisability of communicating with the 4 Archbishops asking them to ascertain is there any truth in the statement that any Bishop has acted so, and giving them an order to speak their minds freely, in sending *CONFIDENTIAL* reports as to what they think should be done in consequence." "Ask for an audience"; Walsh concluded significantly, "and if H.H. approves, read this letter for him." "*DESTROY IT,*" he added, "*WHEN READ.*" Immediately on receiving this letter, Kirby secured the required audience, and quickly wrote Walsh to assure him all was well. "I received your Grace's letter this morning," Walsh replied to Kirby on December 19, exactly a week after his first letter, "It is amazing how promptly you were able to see the Holy Father"(K). "I have no doubt," Walsh added with satisfaction, "that your words to him will be productive of the greatest good just now."

Though Walsh had been obviously much reassured by Kirby's reply, the effort to re-establish diplomatic relations between London and the Vatican were far from over. The key figure in this effort was John Ross of Bladensburg. He had been

---

[1] W, Walsh to Salisbury, December 14, 1886.

for more than six months before the interview with Lord
Salisbury assiduously at work promoting diplomatic relations.
Though born in Italy, Ross was an Irishman with an unusual
combination of allegiances. He was a Roman Catholic in
religion, a Tory in politics, and a Captain in the Coldstream
Guards. In the latter capacity he had served on Lord
Carnarvon's staff in 1885 and 1886 when Carnarvon had been
the Irish Viceroy. Ross was also a close friend of the premier
English Roman Catholic peer, the duke of Norfolk, and had
numerous connections among the Roman Catholic gentry in
Ireland. After Carnarvon's resignation in January, 1886, and
the fall of Salisbury's caretaker ministry in the following
month, Ross proceeded to Rome where he made the
acquaintance, among others, of the influential secretary of
Propaganda, Domenico Jacobini, and Abbot Bernard Smith,
an Irish Benedictine long resident in Rome. After he returned to
London, Ross continued to keep in touch with Smith. On June
20, for example, Ross wrote Smith asking him if indeed the
pope had been prompted by a resolution sent by the archbishop
of Tuam and his clergy to Gladstone, applauding his recent
action with regard to the Home Rule Bill, to counsel "the Irish
Bishops to refrain from political strife."[2] "Can you tell me,"
Ross asked, "if this is true?" "We are," Ross then explained,
and referring to the impending general election, "in a critical
moment. The Anti Gladstonians are confident that they will
win, but it is an anxious time." More significantly, Ross also
reported that he had written two memoranda, which had been
sent "to two very important Statesmen," and which had been
well received.[3] The first involved the "*necessity*" and the
"*advantages*" of establishing diplomatic relations with Rome,
while the second concerned the question of University
Education for Roman Catholics in Ireland.

That summer, it appears, Smith spent part of his holiday in
England, where he had the opportunity to read Ross's
memorandum on diplomatic relations. Smith wrote Ross from
Paris on his return to Rome, asking him to forward a
translation of his memorandum, which he could present to the

---

[2] Smith Papers (S), Archives of St. Paul, Outside the Walls, Rome.

[3] Salisbury Papers (Sy), Hatfield House, Hatfield, Herts., Norfolk to Salisbury,
August 21, 1886: "Here are the two papers drawn up by Captain Ross which you
were so good as to say you would read. I wish I could at all properly express the
sense of the enormous importance of the two questions dealt with which we all
entertain."

pope. Ross promised on October 23, from "Vittoria Barracks," in Windsor, to send him the translation, and if it was worthy of being perused by the Holy Father, he would "naturally be *MOST* exceedingly gratified and made happy." In this same letter, Ross also enclosed two copies of his memorandum on University Education in English, and asked Smith to read it and give a copy to Monsignor Jacobini, the secretary of Propaganda.[4] "The question of education," Ross assured Smith, "is ripe for settlement." "Now you will observe," he noted carefully, "the object of the paper I am sending you, is not only to induce the Govt. to do what they ought for Irish Cathcs., but also to induce them to settle this question at Rome, instead of going to the Irish Bishops." "There would be," he argued, "a double advantage in this."

> *First,* the interests of the Church, of the Empire, and of Ireland would be best safeguarded, and the British Govt. by dealing at Rome would obtain that acknowledgement from the Pope which they would deserve, if as I sincerely hope, they will only be just. This recognition they would never get from the Irish Bishops. In the *second* place, I believe if this were done, diplomatic relations would be gradually and firmly established without shocking ultra-Protestant prejudice which all fear so much(H-B).

Only a few days before, Ross then pointed out, referring to Walsh's speech on the Education Question at the Christian Brothers' Schools in Dublin on October 17, the archbishop had maintained that the government would try to settle the problem through him and endeavor to drive a wedge in the Clerical-Nationalist alliance. "Then he says," Ross reported, "speaking as he believes he does for his Brethren, he will be no party to a 'corrupt bargain,' and that he does not think any English Government can settle this question any more than they can settle any other Irish question." "Does this not show," Ross. maintained, "the futility of approaching persons who one almost might say are political agents first & Churchmen afterwards?" He then enclosed an extract of Walsh's speech, as well as one of the bishop of Limerick's protesting against Walsh's speech, which he asked Smith to show to Monsignor Jacobini. Ross then turned to another and perhaps even more significant of his recent initiatives. "Now I would ask you privately," he

---

[4] H-B, "Memorandum upon Irish University Education" [printed], "Private and Confidential / Not for Publication," October, 1886.

inquired of Smith, "about our Memorial to His Holiness." "Will any thing," he asked, "come of it? Will the Holy Father send a Visitatore to us? Is there no chance of this?" "Surely," he prompted, "a Visitatore would be able to speak to Ministers here, and dispel the illusions regarding relations; and be able also to speak about Education & get that great matter satisfactorily settled."[5] "They say," Ross added encouragingly, "the Govt. will deal with the University Question & they decidedly must do so shortly."

Some days before, in fact, Ross's mentor, the duke of Norfolk, had written Salisbury to remind him of a promise earlier made. "You will remember," the duke wrote on October 18, "you very kindly said you would be willing to receive a small deputation of Irish and English Catholics on the two-fold subject of diplomatic relations with the Vatican and of Higher Education in Ireland"(Sy). "We should be," he then added, "I believe about half a dozen and it is wished that *the matter should be kept quite private*." "Those Lords & Gentlemen from Ireland," Norfolk reported nearly two weeks later on October 31, "whom you received yesterday are very anxious that you should if it be possible give Dr. Healy an opportunity of talking with you alone"(Sy). "They assure me," he assured Salisbury, "that he is a very remarkable man with great opportunities of appreciating what is passing in Ireland and that an hour's talk with him about Ireland generally would they feel sure be of great use to you and that you would not think the time wasted." "He is," the duke then further explained, "coadjutor Bishop of Clonfert which means that he has the right of succession without further election."

"I hope," Norfolk continued, turning to the subject of education, "there is no ground for a fear which something you said yesterday, put into my mind that perhaps you are going to do nothing about Higher Education after all." "I cannot at all say," he strongly maintained, "what dismay this would cause among those Catholics in England who have stuck to the Conservative cause." "Let me urge," he emphasized, "that the more Dr. Walsh repudiates all gifts from the British Government the more clear it is that he and the party he has espoused dread the result of such gifts being accepted." "He

---

[5] Since the "Plan of Campaign" was announced in *United Ireland* the same day that Ross wrote this letter, there was obviously no necessary cause and effect relationship, initially at least, between the "Plan" and the "Visit" of Monsignor Persico to Ireland on a fact-finding mission some eight months later.

and his friends have got this grievance," Norfolk argued
interestingly, "and it suits their purpose very well, but I am
assured that *many* of the Bishops would gladly welcome a
measure which, sanctioned from Rome, they could accept as an
opportunity for throwing off the yoke of Dr. Walsh and his
nationalist allies." "A full and generous settlement of this
question," Norfolk then summed up, "would undermine the
position now taken up by the Irish Bishops, would bring to our
side the sympathy and support of the Holy See in our struggle
with the Irish, and would bring to their senses the number of
English Catholics who are shaky about the Union." "I do
hope," Norfolk encouraged Salisbury in conclusion, "you are
not going to let the opportunity slip."

Salisbury then forwarded this letter to Beach for his opinion.
"If you *can* spare the time," Beach replied on November 4, "I
think it would be well for you to see Dr. Healy privately"(H-B).
"He is a man," Beach added, "worth encouraging." "The D. of
Norfolk forgets," Beach further explained, referring to Walsh's
decisive influence among the Irish Bishops, "that Walsh
commands the voting power." "But I admit," he confessed, "if
we proposed such a settlement of Irish University Education as
would be really agreeable to the Duke and his friends, it might
be impossible for Walsh to openly oppose it." "My fear is,"
Beach confided, "that he would do so secretly: and that we
should run serious risk of offending Protestantism, without
carrying our measure." The fear of "offending Protestantism"
always carried great weight with Salisbury, and soon after this
exchange at the beginning of November, Beach began to sound
Walsh confidentially on the possibility of negotiating a
settlement of the Education question. The negotiations, as has
already been noted, were well under way by the beginning of
December, but it does not appear the duke and his friends were
aware of them. "I do not like to be everlasting pestering you,"
Norfolk apologized to Salisbury, on December 7, "but I can
assure you our own anxieties are not less keen and our hope"
not less eager than when last I wrote." "Are there yet any
crumbs of comfort for us," he concluded abjectly, "I am
speaking less of relations with Rome than higher education."

What the duke of Norfolk and his friends were attempting to
do, of course, was perfectly obvious. They wanted to undermine
the ascendency of Archbishop Walsh in the Irish Church. Since
his appointment to Dublin in June, 1885, Walsh had not only

had the confidence of the Irish Bishops as a body, but the confidence of Rome as well. The efforts to re-establish diplomatic relations, to shift the negotiations for a settlement of the Education Question from a Dublin-London to a London-Rome axis, and to persuade the pope to send a "Visitatore" to discuss these proposals, all were designed to push Walsh from the center of power to its periphery. Walsh realized, of course, that his own power in the Irish Church was a function of both the confidence of the Irish Bishops and of Rome. That is why he viewed with such great alarm the defections of O'Dwyer and Healy from the episcopal body at home, and the efforts of the English and Irish Catholics to promote diplomatic relations with Rome. Still in early December, 1886, all these efforts on the part of the duke and his friends, and the untoward conduct of Bishops O'Dwyer and Healy, amounted to no more than the proverbial small cloud on the horizon. Walsh still retained, as Beach had reminded Salisbury, the voting power among the Irish Bishops, as well as the apparent approval of Rome, and as long as he retained both, his ascendancy in the Irish Church could not be shaken.

Lord Salisbury, on the other hand, was having and would soon have even more serious difficulties with regard to sustaining his power. His ministry was tottering. The earl of Iddesleigh, the former Sir Stafford Northcote, was proving incompetent at the Foreign Office, the Irish situation appeared to be deteriorating, and worst of all, Lord Randolph Churchill had resigned in a huff as chancellor of the exchequer several days before Christmas. Early in the new year, Salisbury reorganized his cabinet, asking a leading Liberal Unionist, and an economist of international reputation, G. J. Goschen, to accept the post of chancellor, while he himself took over the Foreign Office. Both in and out of Parliament, however, matters continued to go badly, and nowhere more so than in regard to Ireland. After the opening of Parliament at the end of January, the Nationalists resourcefully and stubbornly resisted and obstructed the proposed coercion measures for Ireland, and finally forced the government to take up procedural reform of the rules of the House so that they could eventually proceed with their Coercion Bill. Further, the government prosecutions against Dillon and his colleagues failed as the accused were acquitted at the end of February amidst Nationalist rejoicing. Then, too, the

Irish landlords were at the end of their tether as the Plan of Campaign continued to gain ground, and the archbishops of Dublin and Cashel were certainly not making the government's political way any easier with their interviews and letters to the press encouraging resistance. Finally, when Beach, then, informed Salisbury at the end of February that his doctors would no longer allow him to go on as chief secretary, the prime minister must have certainly believed that troubles came not in single numbers but rather in battalions.

In the months following their interview with Salisbury at the end of October, 1886, the duke of Norfolk and his friends had continued to attempt to redress the balance in Rome. They had complained again and again of the Irish clergy in general and of Archbishops Walsh and Croke in particular, but until Balfour succeeded Beach in early March as chief secretary, and Walsh's negotiations on the Education Question then broke down, their laments seemed to have had little effect. Early in December, for example, the coadjutor to the bishop of Clonfert had written the cardinal prefect of Propaganda complaining about the Plan of Campaign, and Archbishop Walsh's recent endorsement of it.[6] "Matters of great moment to our Church," Healy had explained to Cardinal Simeoni on December 6, "and of gravest peril to the State are taking place daily in Ireland; and, though they are not unknown to Your Eminence, I have considered it my duty briefly to explain them."

> The National League, as it is called, has notified the tillers of the soil through their leaders that the following method of warfare — the Plan of Campaign — is to be employed against proprietors: all the tenants in the different estates are to decide at a private convention what abatement they are to demand from their landlords. If the landlords agree to grant it, the balance is to be paid to them; if otherwise they are to be paid nothing. Instead, the money is to be handed over to secret trustees with the object of fighting the landlord by means of it, should he proceed to eviction for non-payment of rent. As a matter of fact, in many estates this has actually happened. On the other hand, the Government is prepared *vi et armis* to enforce the rights of the landlords. Hence a quasi-civil war seems impending.[7]

---

[6] P. J. Joyce, *John Healy* (Dublin, 1931), pp. 138-39.
[7] *Ibid.*

"Moreover, what is still worse," Healy complained to the cardinal prefect, referring to Walsh, "Dublin on the 1st of December, in a quasi-public interview with the editor of a daily paper called the *Pall Mall Gazette* formally declared that those tenants are not to blame for acting in this manner; for although at first sight it would seem that a contract may not be determined by one of the contracting parties, nevertheless, for reasons that I cannot understand, it ought not to be so in Ireland." "This view," Healy reported, "is now published in all the newspapers, not only as the teaching of Dublin, but as the teaching of the Bishops of Ireland; for none of them has spoke against this view, or rather, none of them has dared to speak." "A war," he warned the cardinal, "is accordingly coming — a war for every reason to be deplored." "That nefarious system," he added for good measure, "the Boycott — a social excommunication which disregards all justice and charity — almost everywhere obtains, especially in the South and West, and terrifies everybody, even the bishops themselves and the priests, who hardly venture to absent themselves from the meetings of the National League." "This system," he witnessed in conclusion, "we see daily in operation with our own eyes."

Sir George Errington, an Irish Whig, and former unofficial British agent at Rome between 1881 and 1885, who continued to correspond with his old friend and contact, Abbot Smith, was also scandalized by Walsh's "interview." Though Errington had to give up his seat for County Longford in 1885, and failed to win an English seat at the general election in 1886 running as a Home Rule Liberal, he still moved in influential political circles, and was full, therefore, of the latest political gossip. "Dr. Walsh," he informed Smith shortly after Christmas, 1886, "has gone far beyond Dr. Croke; indeed there is evidence that the latter does not at all approve the extreme action and opinion of his brother of Dublin."[8] Errington also reported that "Parnell's position in the Irish Party is shaken; Healy, Dillon & others are working against him, regarding him as too moderate." "Some of the Irish papers," he then noted, "are very angry about the reports of diplomatic relations between England and the Pope; but I do not believe the Govt. have the slightest idea of anything of the sort. ..." Some two weeks later on January 16, 1887, Errington reported to Smith

[8] S, Fragment, no date.

that he would be in Rome in about ten days, and that the "Govt. is getting daily more shaky"(S). He also explained that he hoped to see Gladstone's closest political colleague, and former foreign secretary, Lord Granville, before he left, intimating that there might be greater hope for diplomatic relations for Rome with an imminent Liberal ministry than a tottering Tory government.

Captain Ross, on the other hand, Errington's Tory *alter ego* in Smith's Roman intrigues, was naturally as depressed at this time as his Whig counterpart was hopeful. "I fear," he reported to Smith on January 3, 1887, "our prospects are not lively!"(S). "Never perhaps," he confessed despondingly, "has a year opened up with greater darkness & uncertainty before. Everywhere one looks in Ireland, abroad, in the Cabinet, things are uncertain & gloomy." In the next six weeks, Ross grew less depressed, and more and more angry at the course of Irish events. "I have no desire," he informed Smith on February 16, "to exaggerate. Times are very evil, Conscience in Ireland is becoming vitiated & degraded, casuitical arguments are being used to justify the Plan of Campaign"(S). "I don't think," he then warned Smith, "the usual sense of Englishmen will stand the Plan of Campaign much longer." "And if they break it down themselves without the help of the Church what will be said by Protestant England to the Church?" "I know only too well," he commiserated with Smith, "the difficulties in Rome. I know only too well the bigotted folly of Protestants here, who regard representation at the Vatican as a religious question instead of its having a real political aspect. It is too sad, but such I fear to a great extent is the truth." "Intelligent Protestants," he explained, "agree in these questions, none however like it, & none like to make the plunge themselves, being afraid to lose their influence." "We are therefore," he candidly confessed, "in this dilemma, there is little power in Rome to do much without this representation, & there is no power in England to effect it."

Ross was, however, as tenacious as he was determined, and in this letter he returned again to a subject that he had been resolutely pursuing for more than two and a half months — the securing of a promotion for his good friend, John Healy, the coadjutor to the bishop of Clonfert. In September, 1886, Thomas Carr, the bishop of Galway, had been translated to Melbourne, and he was instructed to arrange for the customary election of the three names, or *terna,* to be commended to Rome by the Galway clergy for their vacant See. When Ross opened the subject with Smith on October 31, he apparently believed that Healy would be one of the three names on the Galway *terna,* and strongly recommended Healy to the attention of Smith.

> He is a person we should all like to see in a distinguished place. He is learned, vigorous and religious, a man of whom it can truly be said he puts his religion first and everything else afterwards. He is and has been strongly opposed to the Irish movement, and thus you may be sure he has had difficulties to contend with. These difficulties he has treated as far as we outsiders can judge, with judgement and success(S).

"As Coadjutor," Ross had then explained, "he has no real status among the Bishops. As Bishop óf a diocese he would have this status." "I do not like to write to Mgr Jacobini on this matter," Ross had added, referring to the secretary of Propaganda, "although before I left Rome he was kind enough to say that if I were to do so on such a subject as this, that he would be glad to receive any information." "However I have no doubt," Ross had concluded, "that what appears to you to be proper in this letter, you would tell him of it, as you see him so constantly."

In his reply Smith undoubtedly explained to Ross that since Carr had asked to be allowed to wind up some necessary business in Galway before proceeding to Melbourne, the election of the *terna* for Galway would be somewhat delayed, and consequently nothing could be done with regard to Healy until the three names voted by the priests and reported on by the bishops of the Province of Tuam arrived at Propaganda.[9] Smith must have also explained to Ross, that any information bearing on the various names proposed for ecclesiastical office in Ireland would be greatly appreciated,[10] for in his reply of January 3, 1887, Ross had also referred to the recent election of

---

[9] See K, Carr to Kirby, December 2, 1886, explaining the arrangements, mainly financial, which Carr felt to be necessary before his departure.

[10] See S, Enrico Gualdi to Smith, December 3, 1886. Gualdi was *Minutante* to the secretary for Propaganda and usually handled British and Irish affairs: "Sua Eminenza desiderebbe avere qualche informazione sui candidati per il Coadjutore di Dromore . . . nel caso che potesse darla la preghieri di trasmettermi quanto prima volendosi se sarà possible mandare la ponenza nella prossima Congregazione." The decision about Dromore must have been postponed from the December to the January "Congregazione." The "Congregazioni" were usually held twice a month.

a *terna* on November 10, for a coadjutor to the aged bishop of
Dromore. Ross informed Smith that he certainly regretted that
the *dignissimus,* or first on the *terna* for Dromore, Thomas
McGivern, was not likely to be selected(S). "As far as I know
him," Ross assured Smith, "he is a person of the old type & not
given to politics." "There is a chance," he added, "of a
considerable body of the Bishops joining round another center
than that afforded by Dr. Walsh and Dr. Croke, so the
importance of this See can hardly be under-valued." "I myself
am anxious about it," Ross confessed, "because it is my
Diocese and as things are going now, a quiet and a pious man
might keep us clear of the horrors of the revolution which is
seething elsewhere."

There was also much talk, Ross reported, of the appointment
of Nicholas Donnelly, bishop of Canea, and auxiliary to the
archbishop of Dublin, as coadjutor to Dromore. Donnelly had
been appointed auxiliary under Walsh's predecessor, Cardinal
McCabe, and was accounted a conservative in the Irish
political spectrum. "He wd certainly," Ross assured Smith, "be
acceptable." "Lately," he explained, "since Dr. Walsh came to
Dublin he has apparently gone over to the Nationalist camp,
but I am sure this was due only to the difficulties of his
position. As an independent Bishop he wd be very different."
"Then you have," Ross continued, turning again to his favorite
candidate, "Dr. Healy Coadjutor Bishop of Clonfert."
"Perhaps it would be contrary to Etiquette that he should go
from the West to the North," he supposed, forgetting obviously
that the appointment to Dromore involved only a
coadjutorship, "but if it is not intended that he should go to the
See of Galway ... here is an opportunity in Dromore to
appoint him to a Diocese where he would be independent &
take his place among the Council of Irish Bishops." In
discussing the second and third choice of the Dromore clergy,
Ross assumed that the *dignior,* Father John O'Brien, had no
chance of being selected, and that the *dignus,* Father Henry
O'Neill, was, as he explained to Smith, reported to be "virtually
the nominee of a parish priest who although an excellent man, is
a *most* fanatical Nationalist and unwittingly the stirrer up of all
sorts of rows."[11]

[11] See K, Thomas McGivern to Kirby, November 11, 1886, for voting in
Dromore on November 10, 1886: Thomas McGivern (8); John O'Brien (5); Henry
O'Neill (2); A. C. Finnegan (1).

The reason why Smith had informed Ross in late December that McGivern's appointment to Dromore was not likely to be made was that McGivern had been reported to Propaganda as having a brother and a sister who were afflicted with insanity. McGivern, who was an alumnus of the Irish College in Rome, wrote Kirby on December 10, protesting that the charges were not true, and enclosing an exact copy of a letter he had sent to his metropolitan, Daniel McGettigan, the archbishop of Armagh, denying the allegations and explaining the circumstances which had led to the false charges being made(K). McGivern's explanation was obviously satisfactory for shortly after Ross had replied to Smith on January 3, McGivern was appointed coadjutor to Dromore. Given the concern and timing, therefore, how effective Ross and Smith's efforts on behalf of McGivern actually were is an interesting question, especially since Ross was consciously attempting to structure a more conservative minority within the episcopal body. Some insight is certainly gained with regard to McGivern's character and attainments as well as his attitude towards politics in reading the letter he wrote Kirby on November 11, announcing the fact that he had been placed first on the *terna* for Dromore by his fellow priests.

> Since I left College now 31 years I have abstained from all political excitement at the same time without offending others, judging my own Sacred duties required both my time and study, while these better suited my own tastes and habits.
> Then for the past 20 years I have been Confessor to two large Communities of Nuns in Newry (Poor Clares over 30 P. St—ʳˢ of Mercy nearly 30 Members) as *Ordinary* when in Newry parish, as Extraordinary, since becoming P.P. in this parish, since 1872. This I mention to satisfy your Lordship that same as when in College, I have given satisfaction to my Superiors: while with every priest of the Diocese old and young, I have maintained friendly relationship: but not too intimate with any as such generally slides into party.
> Same as when in College I continue still to act as Master of Ceremonies on special occasions.
> My Lord Archbishop begging your indulgence for sending this personal narrative.
> I respectfully remain your most humble obedient servant(K).

In his letter to Smith of February 16, Ross explained that he was delighted that McGivern had been appointed, for he was "an excellent person & a really good & holy Priest."[12]

In this letter Ross also returned to the subject of the appointment to Galway now that the clergy had commended their *terna* to Rome. John Healy, Ross's favorite candidate, however, had not appeared on the list. Instead the Galway priests had chosen Francis J. MacCormack, the bishop of Achonry, as *dignissimus,* and two Galway parish priests as *dignior* and *dignus* for their *terna*. "I know Dr. McCormack"; Ross explained, "personally I like him much but he has made himself unfortunately notorious in more ways than one." Not only, Ross complained, had MacCormack been one of the five bishops to contribute to the Parnell Testimonial Fund in 1883 before that Fund was condemned by Rome, but Ross had it on good authority that the bishop of Achonry had approved of the Plan of Campaign the previous December. "You may imagine, therefore," Ross observed, "that to translate a Bishop, however excellent he may be personally, from Achonry to Galway, would have the effect of at least expressing the idea that Rome approved of the Plan of Campaign." Ross then turned his attention to the second and third names on the Galway *terna*. Though he had not met the *dignior,* James Ronayne, who was parish priest of Ballinrobe, he had heard a great deal about him, and it was all in his favor. Father Ronayne, Ross reported, was not a Nationalist, was of conservative tendencies, and was opposed "to the utmost the lawlessness that prevails around him." "Protestants who know him," Ross added, "speak of him in the highest terms, and that means much since the Protestants I allude to are not the bigoted fools who inhabit the North of Ireland but those who have seen him & who are refreshed at the sight of a sturdy Cath. priest who resists the poison which revolutionists are seeking to swamp the ignorant Irish peasant with." Ross did not feel that he had to say much about the third name, or *dignus,* Jerome Fahey, who was the parish priest of Gort. "I have seen him," Ross noted, and "I don't think he is what would vulgarly be called in the running." "I must now remind you," Ross finally concluded, and referring to his letter of October 31,

---

[12] The opposition to McGivern, like a good deal of Irish clerical opposition, however, died hard. See K, Patrick O'Neill, Rostrevor, to Kirby, February 7, 1887, explaining that though one of Kirby's favorite maxims certainly applied, i.e., "Roma locuta est, res finita est," there was in addition to an uncle and a brother of McGivern's being insane, a nephew who was also afflicted — i.e., three generations.

last, "what I have already said to you regarding Dr. Healy Coadj. of Clonfert."

What Ross was attempting to do in influencing episcopal appointments in Ireland was made perfectly clear in a long memorandum dated March 10, to Arthur Balfour, who had only just succeeded Beach as chief secretary three days before. This memorandum, which was essentially an argument for re-establishing diplomatic relations with the Vatican, suggested a number of ways in which the pope's power could be usefully exercised in helping maintain law and order in Ireland. In the eighth and final section entitled, "The appointment of New Bishops in Ireland," Ross noted for Balfour that — "There is one question I have not touched upon viz: The importance of giving information in Rome when new Bishops are to be appointed."[13] "I did not do so," Ross explained, "because, while with official relations this matter would be regulated, yet even without them much may be done at least in this respect by private representation." "It is usual with Irish Bodies," Ross pointed out to the new chief secretary, "that minorities are not allowed to make their opinions heard." "This is a general feature," Ross asserted with much truth, "in the National Association, from the Body representing the Irish National Party in Parliament downwards. The Body of the Bishops are not without this characteristic." "Hence the importance," he maintained, "of strengthening the present minority by the best & most able men, till they become sufficiently strong to make themselves heard and to resist those who are aiding & abetting the Irish Agitators."

Ross was well aware, however, that bishops like McGivern were not the stuff out of which leaders are made, and that is why he was trying so hard to secure an Irish bishopric for Healy. He hoped, thereby, to provide that conservative minority among the Bishops, which he also hoped at the same time to increase through British influence at Rome, with effective leadership. He miscalculated, however, on two points. One, that bishops like McGivern, because they were pious and not given to politics, were necessarily conservative in their political outlook and second, that Archbishops Walsh and Croke and their Nationalist colleagues would not be able to take effective measures to block his attempts to have Healy

[13] Balfour Papers (B), British Museum, Add. MS. 49821. "Notes on the Action of the Pope in Ireland," October 10, 1887.

promoted. In fact, McGivern turned out to be a staunch, though moderate, Nationalist, and Walsh and Croke were early and well aware of the dangers posed by Healy being able to gain a place on the Galway *terna*. "I had a note this morning," Croke circumspectly reported to Walsh, and referring to the archbishop of Tuam, John MacEvilly, "from Dr. McE. on the matter." "He (Dr. Mac)," Croke assured Walsh, "believes that Achonry will head the list — and that our *friend* will be nowhere." MacEvilly's forecast, of course, was absolutely correct, for the Bishop of Achonry received thirteen out of the twenty-three votes cast for the *terna*, and Healy did not appear on the list. Not only did the Galway priests, it seems, do their best to prevent Healy's name from being forwarded to Rome, but the bishops of the Province of Tuam, in making their customary report to Propaganda on the commendation of the clergy, were unanimous in their recommendation that the bishop of Achonry be translated to Galway.[14] When the appointment had still not been made by the middle of March, however, Walsh obviously became uneasy, and wrote Carr who was in Rome on his way to Melbourne. "On Monday last," Carr replied on Wednesday, March 23, explaining the delay, and referring to the usual fortnightly "Congregazione" of the cardinals of Propaganda, "a long adjourned Meeting was held, but as Card. Gibbons was present, the American visit occupied most of the time"(W). "The appointment to Armagh," Carr further explained, referring to the translation of Michael Logue from Raphoe to Armagh, with the right of succession to the ailing archbishop, Daniel McGettigan, "from the beginning has been looked upon as a matter of course. Hence all the papers were printed."[15] "But in the case of Galway," he added, "the papers are not yet printed and hence there will be no appointment before Easter." "Dr. Croke's first letter on 'Taxes,' " Carr then noted significantly, "caused great surprise and dissatisfaction amongst the Authorities in Rome." "But the second letter," Carr reassured Walsh, "and the explanations given by friendly hands, have removed to a great extent the unfavourable impressions created by the first."

Croke's initial letter had indeed raised the temperature of the

[14] K, MacEvilly to Kirby, February 18, 1887.
[15] See W, Croke to Walsh, January 22, 1887, on the occasion of the election of the *terna* for Armagh. "Dr. Logue has has [*sic*] a great success. I suppose the Primate worked up the Oracle. However, we must have you a Cardinal before it falls to him to preside."

opposition to the Irish movement, which was already very high, to a fever pitch. Ross's monthly laments to Smith, for example, became weekly complaints immediately after Croke's imprudent letter.[16] On February 23, Ross not only forwarded Croke's letter, which he characterized as "a Plan of Campaign agst. Taxes," but also a letter from James Donnelly, the Nationalist bishop of Clogher, subscribing to the defense fund of John Dillon and those of his colleagues who were being tried for conspiracy, "in language which seems to me to be of a very extraordinary character"(S). "Dr. Croke's letter," Ross maintained, "has given rise to much comment & to considerable scandal." "If there is no good in showing these letters," he suggested, "at least they should be put into the Vatican Press." "Do they know," he indignantly asked Smith, "that Dr. Croke an Archbishop is advocating open rebellion & sedition? I should remind you that the persons I have alluded to who are now being tried for Conspiracy are those who have carried out the Plan of Campaign." "How long," he then demanded of Smith, in obvious exasperation, "is this scandal to last?"

The government was also driven to the point of exasperation by Croke's letter of February 17, and the further humiliation of seeing Dillon and his colleagues acquitted a week or so later, almost pushed Salisbury into prosecuting Croke. One of Beach's last acts as chief secretary was to persuade the prime minister to stay his hand. "Irish opinion," he advised Salisbury on March 1, "is against the prosecution now: English opinion does not expect it"(H-B). Salisbury had not only good reason to be upset with the Irish who were making his political life miserable in and out of Parliament, but he had also had, shortly before the appearance of Croke's letter, a rather disagreeable diplomatic exchange with the pope. On February 12, Salisbury had telegraphed the British ambassador in Rome, Sir John Savile Lumley, that the bishop of Malta, whose health was rapidly failing, had recommended to Her Majesty's government that Peter Pace, the bishop of Gozo, be nominated as his coadjutor with the right of succession in the See of Malta.[17] The difficulty was that in 1885, the pope had

---

[16] S. Another of Smith's more intermittent (semi-annual) correspondents on Irish affairs also increased his volume during this period. See Thomas Eyre to Smith, February 21 and 22; March 16; and April 5, 1887.

[17] Foreign Office Papers (F.O.), 170/385, Great Britain, Public Record Office, London.

appointed Antonio Maria Buhagiar as auxiliary to the bishop of
Malta. Though Monsignor Buhagiar had not been appointed
with the right to succeed, he had been since 1885 effectively
administering the diocese, and to appoint a coadjutor over his
head would certainly cast a shadow not only over his
administration, but his career. His predecessor at the Foreign
Office, Salisbury further explained to Lumley, and referring to
the late earl of Iddesleigh, had communicated privately with the
Vatican the previous October through the Italian chargé
d'affaires in London, and had been assured that there would be
no difficulty in setting Monsignor Buhagiar aside when the
proper time came. The Italian chargé d'affaires, however,
begged that his intervention be kept secret. Salisbury then
instructed Lumley to let the Vatican know through Edward
Henry Cardinal Howard, an Englishman, highly placed and
influential in the Papal government, that the appointment of
Monsignor Pace would now be very acceptable to Her
Majesty's government.

Lumley immediately contacted Cardinal Howard, who
promised to lay the matter before the pope. When the cardinal
did present Salisbury's request, the pope was both surprised
and annoyed, maintaining that he did not understand why
Monsignor Buhagiar should be removed. "His Holiness said,"
Lumley noted in the course of a long dispatch on February 17,
reporting Howard, "that he had no cause of complaint ags^t the
acting Bishop of Malta who had been regularly appointed by
briefs and Bulls, and that even were he disposed to remove him,
he could not do so in the absence of canonical reasons for his
being set aside."[18] Lumley further explained that Howard was
at a loss to understand who it could have been at the Vatican
that the suggestion that Monsignor Buhagiar could be
suspended had emanated from. Howard was also of the
opinion that even if it were possible to remove Monsignor
Buhagiar, the pope was not favorably disposed to the
appointment of Monsignor Pace. "His Eminence conjectured,"
Lumley finally concluded, "that the affair might possibly be the
result of local Italian intrigues at Malta & did not know
anything of the private negotiations bet^{wn} the Earl of Iddesleigh
& the Vatican in October last." An old and clever hand like
Salisbury must have been terribly annoyed and embarrassed at

---

[18] F. O.. 170/382.

thus finding himself diplomatically mousetrapped, and especially at Rome. Either Iddesleigh had been hoodwinked by an ambitious Italian chargé d'affaires in London, or the Vatican was patently taking advantage of an engagement negotiated through an unlikely third party. Given the late earl's general incompetence at the Foreign Office, the former was much the more likely, but even if the latter were actually the case, since dead men tell no details, Salisbury had no recourse but to allow the matter to drop.

Salisbury's difficulties continued to mount, however, and when Beach resigned in early March, it appeared that the government was about to collapse. "I hear the Govt.," Errington, for example, reported to Smith on March 11, "are getting weaker and weaker in Ireland and that Home Rule is certain"(S). Ross, however, in the face of the deteriorating political situation only redoubled his efforts. "I send you," he doggedly informed Smith on March 7, "two extracts from newspapers to which I beg your earnest attention."

> 1. Letter which appeared in the last issue of the Union signed Ecclesiasticus & headed "Mr. Davitt & Cardinal Simeoni."
> 2. Report from an American paper called "The Leader" of 21st ult. giving a proclamation of certain persons to their fellow workingmen. The persons who signed this manifesto have mainly Irish names, and one is the Editor of the "Catholic Herald." The principle passages are marked(S).

"I feel sure these documents will be important to you," he pushed Smith a little, "and that Monsignor Jacobini should see them all as well as His Holiness, if that were possible." "I cannot but urge," he insisted stubbornly, if incoherently, in conclusion, "the importance there would be if they were also noticed in the Vatican Press."

"I am exceedingly sorry to trouble you so often," Ross wrote Smith again within the week on March 13, "& yet I am sure you wd blame me if I had not kept you informed at the present most critical moment"(S). "I have now," he explained, "an important matter to lay before you." "I send you two cuttings," he added by way of explanation, "from Dublin papers." "One from the Freeman's Journal," he noted, "of the 8th inst. & one of the Irish Times of the 9th." "The facts," Ross reported, "are these apparently."

To defeat the Plan of Campaign proceedings are often taken in the Bankruptcy Court. The proceedings are effectual, the machinery of this Court being powerful enough to interfere materially in certain cases where robbery is perpetrated by the Plan of Campaign. Witnesses have to be cited before this Court, and since many of the witnesses are unwilling to attend, they have to be forced to do so by subpoena.

Now it appears Father Keller, a priest in the Ponsonby estate, lately afflicted by the Plan of Campaign, has been subpoenaed; he failed to attend the Court. His letter in the Freeman's Journal (cutting herewith) will show you how he has treated the legal summons which was issued for his attendance by a Court of Justice(S).

"However," Ross further explained, after this long peroration, "it is *not* of him I wish particularly to write you." "The point I wish particularly to bring before you," Ross then pointed out, "is the Bishop's letter to Father Keller, in the Irish Times cutting (herewith)." "The Bishop," Ross added, citing the culprit, "is Dr. McCarthy of Cloyne." "The case," Ross then summed up for Smith, "is clear."

The Plan of Campaign has invaded the Ponsonby estate. The proprietor is in his right to proceed against those who are defrauding him by an ordinary process of law. In the course of his process certain witnesses have to be examined & among them a priest. This priest will not attend, & his Bishop backs him up. If those, respecting whom the priest has been called to give evidence, have done nothing immoral; if the priest has done no harm & committed no immoral act, how can he and his parishoners be injured? The Bishop's letter not only gives the priest *carte blanche* to do what he likes but makes it plain he need not give evidence in extreme cases. In fact the Bishop appears to incite a priest to disobey the law.

Of course you understand me, there is no question nor am I even remotely alluding to the privileges a priest must have in the discharge of his sacred function. Of that there is no question here (S).

"I trust you will excuse me," Ross apologized again, "for all the trouble I am giving you." "I am sure you will not think," he reiterated, "I am abusing your kindness by writing so often in this critical moment." "I wish," Ross concluded, "the Authies could see the Bishop of Cloyne's letter."

"Again I trouble you," Ross pounded away some ten days later on March 23, "and I am sure you will allow me to do so"(S).

1. I enclose a cutting from the Freeman's Journal giving a letter from Dr. McCormack, Bishop of Achonry, subscribing to the defense fund of Messrs. Dillon and Co. who you know were prosecuted for the Plan of Campaign. You cannot well have a more formal announcement on his part to show his sanction of the Plan — now the foremost question in Ireland — than this letter. You will remember that Dr. McCormac [sic] is the Dignissimus for Galway See.
2. I also send a cutting from one of the London Morning Papers of last Monday 21st inst., giving an account of Father Keller's committal to prison for contempt of Court(S).

"His journey to Dublin under arrest," Ross then reported of Father Keller, "was only made the subject of several demonstrations in his favour in which Dr. Croke took part. Subsequently, as you will see by the enclosed cutting Dr. Walsh took part in showing sympathy for Fr. Keller." You will observe," Ross then advised Smith, "that another priest has been subpoenaed — namely Fr. Ryan. By today's paper it appears that he did not attend the Court, and so a warrant has gone to him to compel his attendance. He too I suppose will refuse to answer some questions in Court when brought there by force, and will also be committed for contempt. Others I dare say will speedily follow, and the crown of Irish martyrdom will not be wanting to many." "I believe," Ross further explained, "that Fr. Keller & I imagine also Fr. Ryan — but of him I don't know — are the trustees into whose hands tenants are pleased to pay the reduced rents they choose at the dictation of the Land League to offer their creditors (the landlords)." "This is evidently a not very reputable act," Ross argued, "and if now they (the priests) shelter themselves from the consequences of this civil act behind their sacred calling what are we to think of the proceedings?" "I should be very glad to think," Ross confessed, "that some impression is being made by all the private information I am sending you." "Alas," he lamented dramatically in conclusion, "were it only official! but there is blindness everywhere, among those that hate the Revolution & I fear among the Clergy who coquette so dangerously with that same terrible monster."

Meanwhile, two of those "coquettes" referred to by Ross were attempting to come to terms in their own way with that "same terrible monster." "I am perfectly certain," Croke reassured Walsh with a sublime assurance on March 18, "that Rome will think a long time before it meddles again in Irish affairs; and I am equally certain that, if it issued a Manifesto tomorrow, enjoining silence in politics on all Bishops and priests in Ireland, or restricting their interference substantially, such a Manifesto would do no harm whatever to anyone, except the authorities from which it emanated"(W). "One of my priests," Croke explained on a Friday, referring to the Father Ryan cited by Ross to Smith, "is to appear before Judge Boyd on Wednesday next." "I have advised him to be on the sod," he added, referring to the fact that a man had been killed in the effort to serve a warrant on Fr. Keller, "lest, if he were to wait to be arrested, something worse than the Youghal imbroglio might arise over it." "He is a most determined man," Croke assured Walsh, "and a thorough 'Campaigner.' He will refuse, of course, to give any information as to the whereabouts of the 'War Chest,' and will otherwise I apprehend kick up a big dust, and *rile* the Rhadanthine (not sure of orthography) on the Bench to a tremendous extent." "I may go up to Dublin accordingly," he reported, "on Monday or Tuesday. I shall let you know in due time." "The 'Campaigner' is here," Croke concluded jauntily, "as I write, and so I must shut up. We are holding a council of war."

The following day Saturday, March 19, however, a somewhat less assured Croke again wrote Walsh. "We are dreadfully puzzled here," Croke confessed, "as to the course which our 'Campaigner' should take"(W). "Our doubts," he explained, "range themselves round the following heads —

1-ºShould he obey the summons, and appear before Judge Boyd accordingly on Wednesday next?
2-º Should he, on the contrary, take no notice of the summons and have himself arrested as Keller was?
3-º When in Court, whether voluntarily, or otherwise, should he object, a, to the Protestant version of the Testament, b, to be sworn at all, or c, should he submit to be sworn — refusing, afterwards, of course, to give any information as to the "War Chest" or any other criminating point?(W).

"We are divided," he reported, "almost upon every point." "What do you say?" he asked Walsh, "Write, at once, on receipt of this." "The great difficulty in this case," he then confided, "is to keep the 'Campaigner,' who is a dreadful enthusiast, within becoming bounds." "Today's proceedings before Boyd," Croke concluded hopefully, referring to Fr. Keller's examination, "may throw some light on our position, and suggest the most desirable course for us to take." On receiving Walsh's reply early Monday, March 21, Croke wrote again the same day. "I telegraphed this morning early," he reported, "to my 'Campaigner,' to say that he was not to go to Dublin"(W). "I shall write him by this evening's post," he added, "giving him full instructions as to the course he is to pursue in the witness box." "I will get him," Croke assured Walsh, "to walk as much as possible in Fr. Keller's footsteps." "The conditions of poor Keller's imprisonment," Croke lamented, referring to the fact that Keller had received two months at hard labour, "are very severe." "I know him well," Croke then explained, "I fear greatly for his health." "I was immensely pleased," he added gratefully, "at your attitude through the whole case." "It was," he concluded, "splendid."

Walsh, meanwhile, despite Croke's assurances about what Rome could or would not do, was becoming more and more concerned about the effectiveness of English Catholic efforts at Rome, especially since the collapse of his own recent negotiations with the government on the Education Question. In order to check the pretensions of English Catholics with regard to Irish affairs in Rome, and to stabilize what he suspected to be a deteriorating situation with regard to his own power base in Rome, Walsh had recourse to another of his set "interviews" with W. T. Stead, the editor of the *Pall Mall Gazette*. In the "interview," published on April 4, Walsh particularly lamented the fact that English Catholics were being misled as to Rome's attitude towards Irish affairs, and named the *Tablet* as being chiefly responsible for the mis-understanding. "Great allowance," Walsh explained to Stead, "must be made for the Catholic body in England who are systematically kept in the dark as to many facts of the utmost importance bearing upon our present Irish move-ment."[19] "Do you mean to say," Stead asked, "that the *Tablet*, the organ of Catholics in England, actually deprives its readers of the benefit of such information?" "Yes," Walsh replied

---

[19] *Pall Mall Gazette*, April 4, 1887; quoted in *Walsh*, pp. 254-55.

unequivocally, "its policy on this point is one of most deliberate misrepresentation, effected by means of wholesale suppression of the truth."

"People of confused habits of thought," Walsh then added, "may have come to the conclusion that the *Tablet* is a sort of semi-official organ of the Holy See." "This bubble would very speedily burst," Walsh charged, "if the *Tablet* had the honesty to put its readers in possession, for instance, of the articles which form so prominent a feature of the editorial columns of the *Moniteur de Rome*." "The *Moniteur*," Walsh then asserted, "is in strong sympathy with our Irish cause. It has endorsed the Home Rule policy. It has condemned most emphatically Lord Salisbury's coercion policy." "The *Moniteur*," Walsh further charged, "as an influential organ of opinion in the highest ecclesiastical circles in Rome is ignored by the editorial management of the *Tablet*. Thus a gross deception is practised upon those readers who are simple-minded enough to regard the *Tablet* as a newspaper conducted on Catholic principles, and therefore fairly and fully representative of Catholic views." "It has been stated, too," Stead then prompted Walsh, "that certain instructions were sent to your Grace for the guidance of the Irish clergy as regards their interference in political matters." "Yes," Walsh replied, "and it has been furthermore stated that those 'instructions,' although they were intended to be communicated to the clergy, had been suppressed by me." "The statement," Walsh declared, "is untrue and wholly groundless." "The case of Ireland," he assured Stead confidently, "is thoroughly understood, and therefore thoroughly safe, in Rome." "What about," Stead then asked the crucial question, "the establishing of diplomatic relations between England and the Vatican?" "I do not propose," Walsh rejoined cautiously, "to discuss the matter in detail, but I am able to state with the very highest authority that, if any such relations should be established, such a step will not be taken at all events during the pontificate of Leo XIII without provision of the most effective kind being made to safeguard the interests of Ireland from any English interference at the Holy See."

The *Tablet* replied on Saturday April 9, noting that if Walsh had been anything less than God's anointed, "we should have known how to deal with him, and certainly our reply would have been very simple and very straight."[20] "We know that it is

---

[20] *Tablet,* April 9, 1887; quoted in *Walsh,* p. 256.

a journal," the *Tablet* then remarked about the *Moniteur*, "that usually has very trustworthy information upon Catholic and local matters." "We are also aware," the *Tablet* added knowingly, "that at intervals the views shared by the very active and patriotic colony of Irishmen in Rome have found expression in its columns." "About the last thing that would have occurred to us," the *Tablet* concluded contemptuously, "would be to have regarded these somewhat crude compositions as due directly or indirectly to the inspiration of the Holy See." In this same issue of the *Tablet*, Walsh replied to this article, which had been telegraphed before publication to him in Dublin. Walsh, who had always had a talent with his pen for making his case, and topping it off when necessary with a caustic and withering sarcasm, really excelled at, and certainly seemed to enjoy, this kind of journalistic rough and tumble. With his lawyer's gift for poking holes in an argument, Walsh immediately indicted the *Tablet* for its "imbecile pleading."

"The *Tablet*," the lawyer in Walsh summed up, "a Tory anti-Home Rule organ, sailing under the figurehead of an extract from a Papal letter, and persistently assailing Home Rule so as to imply that it may be at variance with Catholic interests, is charged with keeping back certain important facts." "Its defence," Walsh added, "is that neither the *Weekly Register* nor the *Nation* is any better." "Is the *Tablet* serious?" Walsh asked, "Does it mean to say that either the *Nation* or the *Weekly Register* may be fairly charged with dishonest concealment of facts tending to advance Home Rule?" The next day, Easter Sunday, April 10, Herbert Vaughan, bishop of Salford, and owner and publisher of the *Tablet*, remonstrated privately with Walsh. "I have read your Grace's words — may I say savage words," Vaughan complained, " — in this week's *Tablet*."[21] "I cannot but think it a little unkind of you," he protested, "not to have called my attention to the articles of the *Moniteur*, to which you attach so much importance. You had so frequently — and so kindly — in the past told me of matters which you thought it important to print in the *Tablet*, and I had always so gladly tried to meet your wishes that I am unable to account for the change." "I do not attach so much importance," he explained, "to the *Moniteur* as your Grace does. But it is a pity if we cannot differ on matters of opinion without the danger of

---

[21] *Walsh*, p. 257.

being considered dishonest. I should only be too glad to get a
fair statement of views or facts which you think should be put
before the Catholics of England, and if you write such a
statement yourself it shall have every prominence." "What I
now say I have always felt," he assured Walsh, "these
debatable questions should be heard on both sides." "However,"
Vaughan concluded his protest, "let me end by wishing you all
gaudia paschalia."

"The *interview,*" Croke had congratulated Walsh on April 4,
"is excellent. It will do a deal of good"(W). "The 'Tablet,'" he
noted approvingly, "gets its tea, anyhow." That same day
Walsh had forwarded Manning a copy of the *Freeman's
Journal.* "Kindly read the 'interview,'" Walsh asked the
cardinal, "and the article in reference to it"(M). "I made it a
point," Walsh explained, "to speak with the confidence that I
feel, of the safety with which we may rely upon the people of
England. As to our Catholic friends, I made the best excuse I
could for them." "I have some hope," he added somberly, "that
what I have said may set some of them inquiring, who have
hitherto taken too many things on trust." "Your Eminence I
hope," Walsh noted, referring to the debate in the House on the
Coercion Bill on April 1, "has seen Mr. Parnell's speech on
Friday night." "His appeal," Walsh concluded approvingly, "to
the Irish people was a noble one." Walsh had, indeed, taken up
Parnell's line in his "interview." Parnell had, in effect, advised
the Irish people, in spite of the provocation given by the recent
introduction of the Tory coercion bill, not to embarrass
Gladstone before the next general election when the Liberal
leader "will be able once more to appeal to the common sense
and the sense of justice of the people of Britain."[22]

"I have read the report in the *Pall Mall,*" Manning politely
replied the next day, Tuesday, April 5, "with great interest. You
have, I believe, rightly estimated the feelings of the English
people."[23] "They have been blinded and misled," he maintained,
"by a false tradition; but now for fifty years they have seen and
known, and grown familiar with and fearless of, the Catholic
Church, and they have so much in common with the people of
Ireland that they are in good-will towards it." "What I add," he
noted, and significantly neglecting to comment on Walsh's

[22] *Freeman's Journal,* April 2, 1887.
[23] *Walsh,* p. 258.

remarks about either the English Catholics or the *Tablet,* "is for you and the Archbishop of Cashel." "On Sunday I wrote to the Holy Father," Manning explained, and referring to the under-secretary for Ireland and his testimony before the royal commission set up the previous year to investigate the chief causes for Irish economic distress, "and I translated the chief parts of Sir Redvers Buller's evidence." "Moreover, I said that half the Irish bishops had been invited to Rome," Manning concluded, referring to the invitations that had been issued to attend the Jubilee celebrating the 50th anniversary of the pope's priesthood, "but that the other half, including the Archbishops of Cashel and Dublin, remained to be invited, and that the Irish people, as once before, would feel great confidence in such a representation of their State."

Reminded obviously of the Roman flank, Walsh wrote Kirby a long letter the next day, April 6, in order to boister a sagging Irish cause in Rome. While Walsh did not have a great deal to offer, it must be admitted that he made good use of what he had. He not only enclosed the "splendid" speech made by Parnell on the recent passing of the Coercion Act, but also a copy of his "interview" with W. T. Stead in the *Pall Mall.* Walsh explained that Parnell had appealed to the Irish people "to keep within the law no matter how they may be outraged by being deprived, as they now will be, of their rights under the Constitution"(K). In thus asking Kirby to bring his "interview" to the attention of the holy father, and especially those portions concerning diplomatic relations and the *Moniteur de Rome,* Walsh reported that Stead was not only a great friend of Ireland, but had the confidence of Cardinal Manning as well. In further explaining that Stead had also wanted to interview Croke, but that the latter thought it wiser to leave it all in his hands, Walsh was discreetly intimating that Croke would not be making any more embarrassing pronouncements in the press.[24] Finally, in concluding his long letter, Walsh informed Kirby in confidence that Edward Dwyer Gray, owner of the influential Nationalist daily, the *Freeman's Journal,* had approached him about the advisability of starting a "purely Catholic weekly paper." Gray had been prompted, it appears, by his gratitude for the advice that Walsh had given

[24] See C, for Stead's letter to Croke of March 26, 1887, explaining that he was on his way to Rome and would like to talk to the pope about Irish matters and requesting an interview with him as well as with Walsh.

him in the recent financial reorganization of the *Freeman,* which had turned out prosperously for all concerned.

All of Walsh's efforts, however, to shore up the Irish cause in Rome proved to be of no avail. Within a week of his writing his long letter to Kirby, Walsh had to inform Cardinal Manning that the Roman flank, if not already turned, was in very great danger. "From information that has come to me from Rome," Walsh reported mysteriously to the cardinal on Easter Tuesday, April 12, "I can assure your Eminence that misrepresentation is strongly in the ascendent there."[25] "More than this," Walsh added, "I am bound in the circumstances not to mention *to anyone.*" "Even this," he warned in conclusion, "I can mention only in the very strictest confidence." In replying the next day, April 13, Manning inquired if the Reuter's telegram reporting that the Irish Bishops had been invited to Rome for the Papal Jubilee were true? "I hope you will go again," Manning urged Walsh significantly, "if not, we shall all be misrepresented."[26] The following day, April 14, however, Manning's curiosity about the nature of Walsh's bad news from Rome led him into one of his few indiscreet probes for more information. "Does the misrepresentation," Manning asked Walsh, "affect Ireland?"[27] "The Bishop of Richmond in a letter just received tells me," Manning reported, referring to a letter he had just written on Ireland, "that the *Moniteur* published my letter without opposition or animus." "But it must," Manning probed more delicately, "displease some people." "I am all the more anxious," he confessed to Walsh, "that the remaining number of the Irish bishops should go to Rome." "It is," he concluded, "the only sure way to exclude officious persons."

Walsh, it appears, did not reply to Manning's probe for more information, and the following Sunday, the cardinal significantly decided to write directly to the pope. "Your Holiness," Manning began his long letter in Italian on April 17, "will certainly be interested in the report of a most numerous popular Meeting of Monday last in Hyde Park: there were

---

[25] M, April 12, 1887. This was most likely a letter from the pope to Walsh, asking Walsh to do what he could to lessen the general tension. See S, Errington to Smith, May 25, 1887: "I am afraid the Pope's letter has not done much good to either Archbishops Walsh or Croke." A search, however, of the Dublin Ecclesiastical Archives has not turned up this letter of the pope's, nor indeed did it turn up any other that would shed light on who Walsh's mysterious informant was.

[26] *Walsh,* p. 258.

[27] *Ibid.,* p. 259.

between 50 and 100 thousand people protesting against the Coercion law, as it is called, for Ireland"(M). "The immense multitude," Manning reported, "conducted themselves with the most perfect order and peace." "The importance is not great, if one does not understand," he pointed out to the pope, "that for the first time the English people are becoming united in sympathy with the Irish people, which produces optimum results in Ireland, and guarantees the Union of the two people better than Acts of Parliament: and more, since the turbulence in Ireland was the result of aversion and desperation, the new and benevolent dispositions which are manifesting themselves, although very late, in England, are notably tending to order and tranquility." "In some agitated parts of Ireland," Manning added, "agrarian crimes recur without doubt, but are few in number, and one can hope that the law proposed by the Government, although restricted in scope, will give help to the 169,000 tenants, and will protect them from the intolerable exactions of some landlords."

"It is impossible that the rectification of bad government over three centuries will be remedied without political conflict," Manning explained, entering upon a thumbnail historical sketch of Irish history for the pope, "but as I have seen for 50 years, and this has included all kinds of information, the state of Ireland, I do not hesitate to declare, that the condition is better ordered, more prosperous and more tranquil than it ever was."

In 1828 Ireland smoked in the certainty of civil war; from that period until 1848 was menaced by Secret Societies; in 1848 she was swept by rebellion; from 1848 to 1868 she was troubled by Fenianism, which was allied with French Sects; there were armed movements; at the beginning of the present agitation Fenians and American Sects menaced all Ireland, politics were the politics of violent means, or as they said themselves, of physical force; the Bishops were divided and their authority hardly manifested itself. Today all is changed. Politics are the politics of Constitutional means. There are deplorable crimes, criminal language, and imprudence also among the good, but comparing Ireland of today with the Ireland of my memory, I declare again that never in my life has that Christian and Catholic people been more orderly and peaceful, more steady and more sensible than today(M).

"For these reasons," Manning assured the pope, "I am not frightened; and I attentively hope that the paternal soul of Your

Holiness will not allow the fears that perhaps some permit themselves to inspire." "I personally know the Irish Bishops," Manning added significantly, "they are true Christians, true Catholics, true Pastors." "United to Your Holiness," he reassured the pope, "and united among themselves, they are the salvation of Catholic Ireland, and of the Union of our two people." "Pardon, Holy Father," Manning concluded, "the liberty of an old man that speaks of things which he has seen, and which he sees; and confer on me your Apostolic Benediction."

The day after he wrote this long letter to the pope, Manning had some reassuring news from Rome through Sir Charles Dilke. "Bodley saw the Holy Father on Thursday or Friday," Dilke reported to Manning on Monday, April 18, referring to his former private secretary, who was also an intimate of the cardinal's, "& heard from him as to the representation of the Vatican here, that he thought it best to let well enough alone, i.e. — best that it should be in the hands of your Eminence."[28] Some weeks later Manning must have been further reassured by a letter he received from one of his spiritual god-children who had just returned from Rome. "The Pope," Kathleen Omeara reported on May 6, to her "dear Lord Father," "was said to be very feeble, having suffered much from a feverish cold"(M). "When I entered the Presence Chamber," she continued, "he looked exactly like a dying man propped up to receive the last Sacraments; but several prelates told me that his vitality was wonderful, & that he looked much more exhausted often than he was." "He was just then overpowered with business," she explained, "& had to keep Cardinal Simeoni waiting several days for an audience. The German ambassador was constantly with him, that business alone occupied him hours every day."

"But la question brulante above all others at the Vatican,"Miss Omeara maintained, "is the Irish one." "I soon found out that in Rome," she added, "it was necessary to open your ears wide, & lock your mouth & throw the key out the window." "My dear Father," she confessed, "it was wonderful to hear the stories people had to tell of the Pope & his advisors!" "One thing all agreed on," she reassured the Cardinal, "(holeus boleus), namely that your Eminence *alone* had the ear of H.H. about Ireland."

[28] Dilke Papers, British Museum, Add. MS. 43896.

I was assured by a person who seemed well-informed that Cardinal Howard tried his best to enlighten H.H. on "the true state of things," as he sees them, but the effect of the Pope's interference about the Parnell Fund showed them at the Vatican where *good counsel* lay, & since then Cardinal Howard has been "put in the black hole," and is never consulted on Irish affairs.

The Cardinal himself told me that, finding it perfectly useless to try to open the Pope's eyes, he had drawn aside and ceased to interfere directly or indirectly. "I try now never to speak about Ireland, or even think about it." He told me that you were the only authority at the Vatican on that subject(M).

"Mgr. Kirby," she added, "is said to have the Pope's confidence also on that head." "At my audience," she informed the cardinal, "I had occasion to mention his name, when the H.F. exclaimed, 'Ah, Mgr. Kirby! Je l'aime beaucoup; je le vois toutes les semaines.'" "The dear old Archbishop," Miss Omeara noted, "assured me confidentially that the land question was going to be settled." "'The B. Virgin & S. Patrick,'" she quoted Kirby, "'will bring it all right, you'll see.'" "This was a safe prophecy," she added, "Otherwise he had no plan of campaign apparently." The day after Manning received this letter he wrote Walsh again a little more confidently. "I should like to hear more," the Cardinal confessed on May 8, "of the anxiety you had about Rome?"[29] "You will see perhaps some action of a handful of English Catholics," he advised, "don't notice it." "They, both in numbers and influence," he reassured Walsh, "are powerless."

---

[29] *Walsh,* p. 263.

III. Diplomatic Chess
March, 1887 - July, 1887

Though Manning was still obviously under the impression that his influence at Rome, and especially with the pope, was still paramount, Walsh's information, whatever its mysterious source, was certainly the more accurate. Rome was, in fact, involved in the slow and painful process of once again changing her diplomatic mind about Ireland. Since her previous reversal of policy, which she had begun immediately after the experience of the Parnell Circular debacle in May, 1883, Rome had to a large degree successfully reconstructed her influence if not her power in Ireland. Her tacit approval of the Irish Clerical-Nationalist alliance had contributed enormously to both the success and the effectiveness of that alliance; and the appointment of Walsh to Dublin in June, 1885 had given the Irish Bishops that leadership, direction, and unity which Rome had then appeared to value so highly. Now that Ireland was once again a serious embarrassment to the British government, Rome's diplomatic bargaining power was also naturally much increased. To expect that Rome, especially in the pontificate of Leo XIII, would not attempt to make effective use of that power was simply to be naive. The material point, therefore, was not really whether Rome would or would not use her power, but rather how she would use that power and for what ends.

To maintain, however, that the pope and the Roman authorities were motivated only by a desire for diplomatic relations in dealing with Irish affairs is to take too simplistic a view. They were also concerned, of course, about the moral implications of the rapidly developing agrarian agitation, and more particularly about the deepening role of the Bishops and priests in that agitation. Croke's letter in February, and the arrests, convictions, and prison sentences of Fathers Keller and Ryan in March seriously alarmed the pope and his advisers.

The reports they continued to receive, moreover, about Irish affairs in the next few months, though obviously partisan and often exaggerated, were of such a serious nature that their uneasiness began to harden into a conviction that something must be done. Indeed, it may be fairly argued that what the pope and his advisers thought was necessary for the moral well-being of the faithful in Ireland was really a question quite independent of that of re-establishing diplomatic relations. What action Rome might have to take in Ireland, therefore, had only to do with an imperative moral duty that devolved on the pope as the head of the universal Church, and if diplomatic relations were promoted thereby, that was only incidental to the taking of such action as might be necessary. The Irish, both clerical and lay, however, can hardly be blamed for being increasingly unable to appreciate a distinction which appeared to be more and more academic in the light of the curious diplomatic game that was being played out between London and Rome.

In any case, if Walsh's confidential information was correct, the crucial decision to attempt to effect a *rapprochement* with the British government was taken by the pope shortly before Easter. Since Cardinal Jacobini had died on February 28, and Leo XIII did not appoint a new secretary of state until early June, the decision was most certainly taken on the pope's personal responsibility. The first move was, in fact, made by the pope on March 15, when he informed the British ambassador at Rome through Cardinal Howard that he was willing to reconsider the position he had taken the previous month with regard to the British government's request about Malta. In effect, the pope intimated that he would be willing to remove Monsignor Buhagiar, if such a request were made directly by Her Majesty's government to the Holy See. "The Pope, however," Lumley further explained to Salisbury on March 15, and indicating that the pope preferred to negotiate rather than concede all, "declined to undertake to nominate Mg^r Pace as Coadjutor with promise of succession but in any case the nominee should be a 'persona grata' to H. M. Gov^t."[1] Lumley then noted in conclusion that the cardinal had been informed, and Salisbury must have enjoyed the diplomatic "tit-for-tat," that there had been no intention on the part of Her Majesty's

---

[1] F. O., 170/382.

government "to propose the immediate supercession of Mg–^{r} Buhagiar."

Meanwhile, Ross had been industriously attempting to persuade the new chief secretary as to the advantages of diplomatic relations with the Vatican *vis-à-vis* Ireland. "Among the numerous advantages," Ross pointed out to Balfour, in his long memorandum, dated March 10, "to be derived from relations with the Holy See, two only need to be enumerated."[2]

> 1.   The Irish agitation with [*sic*] various forms is destroying the moral forces that hold society together. The conscience of the people is becoming perverted. Civil Government can with difficulty maintain itself under such conditions, anything tending to restore these moral forces would be of use in the present crisis, & naturally assist Gov–^{t} in the struggle now going on with crime. Experience shows that the Irish clergy as a body, cannot or will not exert themselves on the side of order, nevertheless Catholicism is still a moral power in Ireland, and if the Head of the Church makes his influence felt, he will help bring about obedience to the Civil Authority, now so shamefully resisted by the masses.
>
> 2.   The political forces ranged now under the banner of Nationalism are not in real union with one another, they are at present working together — under strict discipline & under the control of a well organized Association, but their objects and their aspirations are not the same. Some are moderate, some less so, and some are extreme. If the Pope exerted his influence he would not convince all the various sections now united against the British Gov–^{t}; some would resist him but others would follow him. The result would be that these sections would fall out among themselves, that their alliance would be dissolved & that the present resistance to the Civil Power would be weakened(B).

Ross then noted that the three most formidable obstacles in the way of re-establishing diplomatic relations were the Irish Nationalist movement in Ireland and America, the Catholic Hierarchy and clergy in Ireland and England, and the "Protestant element" in the United Kingdom.

From these truisms, Ross proceeded to argue that the first of them could be undermined by confidential reports from the British government to the pope on the activities of the Irish movement at home and abroad, which would illustrate the intimate relationship between the agitation and crime, and

---

[2] B. 49821.

which the pope, as the guardian of Catholic morals, would be bound to condemn. The Bishops and clergy, Ross further argued, could be brought to heel, by the government entering into negotiations with the Vatican over the heads of the Bishops on the Education Question, which the Bishops and clergy, since education was a moral issue, would be bound to submit to the lead and direction of Rome. The final obstacle, Protestant "feeling," Ross recognized as the most difficult one of all. He tentatively offered, therefore, an imaginative *coup de main* as a solution. "It is a question perhaps worth considering," Ross suggested in military metaphors, "as to whether Protestant prejudice might not be disarmed, if simultaneously with the appointment of an agent to the Vatican a direct attack was to be made by the Pope upon the unusual methods now adopted by the people of Ireland." "I believe," Ross had maintained, in prefacing this proposal with an interesting German precedent, "Prince Bismarck did not establish relations with the Holy See, until he had ascertained confidentially what the Pope would give in return." "Having ascertained," Ross added significantly, "that a positive advantage would accrue to the Gov—^{t} by the Pope's action in Poland[,] M. de Schlözer was sent to Rome officially." "Since then," Ross assured the chief secretary, "Germany has felt the benefit of this step, in Poland, in the affair of the Caroline Islands and in the late elections." In a word, Ross proposed a Papal condemnation of the Plan of Campaign as the proper *quid pro quo* for re-establishing diplomatic relations with the Vatican.

Soon after Ross had written and presented his memorandum, the under-secretary for Ireland, Major General Sir Redvers Buller, also raised the question with the chief secretary of securing Rome's aid in the good governance of Ireland. "Has it occurred to you," Buller asked Balfour on April 4, from Dublin Castle, "to consider whether it might not bear well for the Gov—^{t} to send someone to Rome who would be authorised to try and get the Pope to use his influence to bring Dr. Walsh & Croke to good behaviour."[3] "I do not see," he confessed, "how without this we are to get out of the Father Keller difficulty well." "The subject of a mission to Rome," Balfour replied from London on April 6, "has been much discussed, and personally I am strongly in favour of it."[4] "There are, however," he

---

[3] B, 49807.
[4] B, 49826.

explained to Buller, "very strong arguments to be argued against it, one of which is that it would alienate or shock a good deal of the Protestant feeling in Ulster." "I suppose we may say," Balfour added ruminatingly, "that Ulster is more bound to us by community of religion than by anything else; and though I have little sympathy with their views in this matter, we are bound to respect them." "Undoubtedly, however," Balfour concluded, inviting a rejoinder, "the inconvenience of allowing the whole Romish Hierarchy in Ireland to ally themselves with the forces of disorder is so great, that I would readily run some risk, if I saw a chance of obviating it."

"I feel so strongly about the advantages of a mission to Rome," Buller rejoined obligingly on April 8, "that I cannot refrain from pursuing the subject a little."[5] "Granted," he admitted, "that such a mission would shock the Protestant feeling of Ulster." "Irishmen are notoriously an ungrateful race," Buller observed, not distinguishing interestingly between Protestants and Catholics, and referring to the Land Bill about to be introduced in Parliament, "but still I cannot but believe that the direct and immediate benefit which Ulster obtains by the admission of the leaseholders to the advantages of the '81 Act will hold Ulster to the Gov^t for the present." "If this is so," he proposed shrewdly, "the present is eminently a convenient time for the Gov^t to disregard somewhat the feelings of Ulster and to make a bid for those of the other 3/4 of Ireland."

> It will be hopeless to attempt to govern Ireland unless we get some of the people on our side. How are we to get them. We must have intermediaries. The only intermediaries possible I can see are the priests. Moreover, if you intend a general measure of land purchase, its effect must be to make the Gov^t the landlord in the congested districts. In that case, more than ever we shall never be able to remedy the evils of those districts by emigration, public works &c — look at the malign influence the priest now exercises in Achill — it must I think be specially recollected that the Gov^t have no mouthpiece in Ireland(B).

"Think what a social revolution would be effected," he argued further, and somewhat unrealistically, "if all the priests were suddenly to take in the 'Irish Times,' instead of the 'Freeman' and instruct their flocks accordingly — and something of this

[5] B, 49807.

sort must it seems to me be brought about before it can be said that we have commenced to restore peace in Ireland." "I cannot see," he confessed in conclusion, "how we are to get this without the aid of the Vatican. For this reason, I venture to urge its immediate importance most seriously upon the consideration of the Gov-^{t}."

When early in May, therefore, the pope made another diplomatic gambit, Salisbury, knowing that both Balfour and Buller were in favor of some accommodation with the Vatican *vis-à-vis* Ireland, was much more amenable than he had been some months before with regard to the Malta affair. The pope proposed, through the duke of Norfolk, to send a representative to congratulate the queen on the occasion of celebrating the Golden Jubilee, on June 21, of her accession to the throne. The duke, who had consulted with Salisbury on May 8, about the pope's most recent initiative, had somehow neglected to explain what the pope really had in mind in proposing such a visit. In writing Salisbury the next day, May 9, however, Norfolk pointed out that since this was also the pope's Jubilee (the 50th year of his priesthood) he supposed the pope would want the queen to reciprocate by sending him an envoy as well(Sy). Since he was about to leave for Rome, and the pope was sure to question him on this point, the duke wanted to know if it would be all right to tell him that the queen would reciprocate. Salisbury, however, was not to be so easily persuaded. He obviously replied immediately that the political risks were too great in the light of Protestant prejudice, for Norfolk responded on May 10, that he certainly saw the difficulty, but the real point for consideration was "whether the extra risk entailed in sending someone to Rome should outweigh the advantages to be gained by getting the Pope to make the first move"(Sy). "The Pope may not care about a return visit," Norfolk argued, "but I think it very likely he will say that while he quite sees the difficulty he still cannot but feel that it would be a political mistake on his part to pay the Queen a compliment if she cannot return it especially when an excellent opportunity offers in the same year — an opportunity moreover from which other non Catholic courts do not shrink of availing themselves."

Salisbury, however, was not to be moved on the question of reciprocity. The official letter forming the pope's intention of sending a representative was received from Cardinal Howard on May 16, and Salisbury had it privately printed for

discussion in the cabinet the following day.[6] In his reply to
Howard on May 20, he noted that the queen would be pleased
to receive the papal emissary but that she insisted that the envoy
should not be a British subject.[7] The duke, meanwhile, had left
for Rome the day before, May 19, taking Ross with him.[8] On
arriving in Rome he had to wait some days before he received
an audience with the pope. The pope, he advised Salisbury on
May 29, the day after his audience, had decided to send as his
envoy Monsignor Ruffo Scilla, archbishop of Petra, and

---

6. F.O., 45/661, May 17, 1887.

7 *Ibid.*

8 S, Ross to Smith, May 7, 1887. Some further gloss is given to the origins of the
duke's visit to Rome in a long and interesting letter from Wilfrid Ward, friend and
biographer of Cardinal Newman, to Lord Emly. "I had a long talk with the Cardinal
last night nearly an hour & three quarters;" Ward reported to Emly on April 21,
1887, and referring to Newman, "& he was most interested in the whole question.
He said very much in the way of suggestion which I must reserve until I see you.
Without committing himself to a strong opinion as to the consequences of the present
state of things in Ireland (in this he seemed unwilling to speak decisively one way or the
other) he was very emphatic in this point — that the facts referred to in the draft
petition which you saw ought to be pressed on the Holy Father's attention. Also he
was very clear in saying that the laity were well within their rights in conveying to the
Holy Father their sense of the gravity of the crisis. His difficulty is how this can be
done in such a way as to be effectual. He thinks that the Pope *might* take such a
position as I sketched embodying Bishop Healy's notes with [?] or modified in
accordance with your suggestions, as 'lecturing' him; — if he were not first sounded
as to how far it would be acceptable to him to receive it. But he added that if the
Pope were willing to receive a petition & attend to it the one I read was substantially
complete & satisfactory. The great object being to induce the Holy Father really to
give his mind to the matter all risk must be avoided, he says of anything which wd
lead the Holy Father to put the thing aside as he seems to have put aside the private
memorial. His opinion was very definite that someone should see the Holy Father,
and he suggested that the Duke of Norfolk (if his recent sorrow did not put that out
of the question), Lord E. Talbot, Lord Denbigh & yourself shd. go to Rome with all
such documents & facts as would explain the state of things, commissioned to do so
by those who according to the present notion wd. sign the petition. He thought that
personal representatives could ensure a hearing & avoid the appearance of lecturing
the Pope or bishops better than a written petition. Then if the Pope seemed willing
also to receive the petition it might be produced. Such a deputation would, he thinks,
have the more influence if some foreign Bishop who feels in the same sense were to
countenance them & give an 'Ecclesiastical flame' as he called it to the movement.
He ... seemed to think that a personal deputation could find out how much
necessary, how much the Holy See knows, how far it may even now be intending to
act wh: he suspects in consequence of a letter he has had from some Cardinal (who is
going to visit England), & how far it knows the state of Catholic opinion. If the Holy
See is now intending to act it might be only irritated at what would appear to be a
reproach, — unmerited considering its difficulties. In view of the Pope's letter on the
Parnell fund the C. says it is clear that he does not shrink from strong action in such
matters if he sees it to be advisable. But he dwelt strongly on the fact that while the
British government ignores him & treats him (in some sense) with contempt it is very
difficult for him to do much . . ." Monsell Papers, 3818(14), National Library of
Ireland.

recently appointed papal nuncio at Munich(Sy). "As the Nuncio at Munich has really to deal with Germany," the duke further explained, "I had hoped that we had got a man coming of great diplomatic standing and ability who might discuss Irish affairs with you in a way that might lead to some result." "I am told however," Norfolk added, and obviously disappointed, "that Monsignor Ruffo Scilla is not looked upon as a man of great ability and that people wonder why the Pope is sending him to Munich. He seems however, to be a very pleasant man, a thorough gentleman, and with plenty of common sense and no nonsense about him. He speaks French well but no English. His views on Ireland appear to be what we should call sound and he does not take snuff." "Just as I was leaving the Pope, after a good deal more rigamarole about who should or should not accompany the 'Envoy Extraordinary,' " Norfolk then noted, finally coming to his point, "he said that perhaps now he had taken the initiative the British Government might send some [one] to him to discuss Ireland, perhaps the Queen would return what he was doing by sending some one for his Jubilee who might remain on." "This was said," Norfolk pointed out, "quite hypothetically and needed no answer but I ought to mention it."

At the same time that all these subterranean machinations in the interest of re-establishing diplomatic relations between London and Rome were going on, the London *Times* had been publishing a series of articles, beginning in early March and continuing through early June, on "Parnellism and Crime." The most notorious of these articles included the publication, on April 18, of the famous facsimile letter, allegedly written by Parnell, condoning the murder of T. H. Burke, the under-secretary, who had been assassinated with Lord Frederick Cavendish in the Phoenix Park in May, 1882. The letter, which was later proved to be a forgery, was published, significantly enough, on the day of the crucial second reading of the Coercion Bill. Since the government was now determined to attempt to break the Irish National movement, it was essential that English public opinion should be provided with the necessary moral justification for the policy of coercion, and the *Times* by equating Parnellism with Crime was doing just that. Naturally, the Irish Church, as the moral component of the Clerical-Nationalist alliance, came in for a large share of the abuse, and the denunciations of the Irish clergy both at home and in Rome by the English Catholics and their Irish allies, were simply fierce. Typical, perhaps, of the effect that the anti-Irish propaganda was having in Rome was the reaction of Cardinal Manning's godchild, Kathleen Omeara. "I was several times deeply pained & shocked," she had explained in her letter to the cardinal of May 6, reporting on her recent visit to Rome, "to see the impression produced on souls by the conduct of the Irish clergy"(M). "People kept asking," she complained, " 'but why does not the Pope order the Bishops to denounce murder and boycotting?' " Miss Omeara then proceeded to tell the cardinal a long story about a family who had converted to Catholicism some eight years before, but who had reverted to "heresy" because they claimed the "scandal of the Irish Bishops has shaken the very foundation of their faith." While admitting that this might not indeed have been the real reason for their apostasy, Miss Omeara confessed — "All the same I do wish the Bishops would denounce crime."

During May the rumors and counter-rumors, the charges and counter-charges both increased and became more ugly in tone. Ross naturally continued to attempt to influence the course of events in Rome. Interestingly enough as the crisis deepened, Ross's charges became even more extravagant. In his last letter to Smith, prior to his apparent departure for Rome with the duke of Norfolk, Ross had become almost hysterical about Archbishop Croke's conduct. The occasion for Ross's tirade to Smith it appeared was Croke's praising the Manchester Martyrs as patriots. The Martyrs were three young Fenians, Allen, Larkin, and O'Brien, who had accidentally killed a policeman while attempting to rescue several imprisoned Fenian leaders. They were hanged for their crime in 1868, and had been for nearly twenty years part of the Nationalist martyrology as well as the heroes of the unofficial Irish national anthem — "God Save Ireland." "Dr. Croke as Archbishop," Ross complained to Smith on May 7, "glorifies the memory of men condemned to death for murder"(S). "But what is more extraordinary," Ross went on to explain, "on the flimsy pretext that according to him — who seems to know more than judge & jury who actually heard the case — the verdict was unjust, he says that the three 'martyrs' died for 'Faith & Country!' This cannot be the case, unless Dr. Croke believes that the outrage which cost a human life was perpetrated for the Faith, & was therefore justifiable by whomsoever committed." "The Archbishop could never pretend," Ross maintained, with his temper obscuring his logic, "that a man died for the Faith, if he was hanged in error, the offence being murder committed during an ordinary drunken brawl or for purposes of plunder." "It is really," he concluded more simply, but no less passionately, "a very sad state of things."

On the same day, May 19, that the duke of Norfolk and his entourage set out for Rome, the London *Daily Chronicle* published a most irresponsible report from its Roman correspondent. The report claimed that a memoir, "Ireland as it is," "has just been drawn up by the Irish College in Rome; that the Memoir goes straight against the Parnellite Party, and hails with joy the passing of the Crimes Act."[9] "In the Memoir," the *Chronicle*'s correspondent continued, "the connection is clearly traced between Parnellism and crime, and the Holy Father is informed from a source of unquestioned and unquestionable sympathy with the cause of constitutional freedom in Ireland, that the present national movement deserves the reprobation of every honest and law-abiding man." That same day, May 19, Ascension Thursday, Walsh wrote Kirby enclosing the *Chronicle* report. "It is absolutely essential," Walsh instructed Kirby, "I should have *ON MONDAY,* and *AS EARLY AS POSSIBLE,* a full and flat contradiction of the enclosed." "Kindly telegraph to me," he concluded, "First make inquiries of all priests in the College." Kirby telegraphed that Monday morning, May 23 — "The Memoir attributed by the *Daily Chronicle* to the Irish College is entirely and absolutely false."[10]

"I am sure," Kirby wrote Walsh at length that evening, "you have before now received my telegram of this morning declaring the statement of the *Daily Chronicle* a falsehood."[11] "Concocters of absurd fables," Kirby explained rather naively to Walsh, "should not put forward such nonsense which, they could not but see if they reflected for a moment, would drag on them the shame of immediate exposure." "For the rest," he concluded piously, but not very helpfully, "we should not much disquiet ourselves about such things, but after doing our own part rely on the protecting hand of Divine Providence on our humblest efforts for His cause, and say with confidence:

---

[9] *Walsh,* pp. 259-60.
[10] *Ibid.,* p. 260.
[11] *Ibid.,* p. 261.

'Libera me, Domine, a labiis iniquis et a verbo mendacii.' "
Walsh was both furious and almost despairing in his reply by
return of post. "The famous 'Irish College' document," he
reported to Kirby on May 27, "is given in full in to-day's *Irish
Times*"(K). "It is," he declared, "a most libellous and lying
document. There runs through it from first to last the
assumption that the Irish movement is aimed (1) at the
subversion of the authority of the monarchy, and (2) at the
'Separation' of Ireland from England. Of course, the author
knows all this to be absolutely false." "You ought to tell H.H.,"
Walsh advised Kirby, 'the whole story, and say to him that we
have over and over again, in the most public manner protested
against such statements."

By the end of May the rumors had shaken even the
confidence of even so indomitable a warrior as Cardinal
Manning. "I hope you and Monsignor Kirby," Manning
cautioned Walsh on June 1, "are active in Rome, for there are
mischief-makers abroad."[12] "Have you seen a paper in English
and Italian," Manning asked, referring to the "Memoir,"
"which has come to me from Rome?" "Our handful of English
Catholics," he warned, "are also busy here." "It is," the
cardinal concluded ominously, "the hour and power of
darkness just now." Walsh, who replied the next day, was
obviously in a very grim mood. "I can well understand," Walsh
assured the cardinal on June 2, "your Eminence's anxiety. As
for me, I am not taking action of any kind in reference to the
present unhappy proceedings in Rome. If, as there seems but
too much reason to fear, the Holy Father is now in imminent
danger of being led into a grave mistake, I must take care to
keep myself clear of all share in the terrible responsibility that
will be incurred by all who may have a share in the
transaction." After explaining to Manning that he had not been
consulted by Rome, Walsh confessed that — "I cannot indeed
believe that the Holy Father will act without some previous
reference to us in Ireland." "If my opinion is asked," Walsh
then declared, "I will at once reply requesting permission to
confer with the other Archbishops and with the newly-
appointed coadjutor to the Primate. I can answer for it that we
five may be counted upon to act in solid unity."

---

[12] *Ibid.*, p. 263.

In discreetly alerting Walsh on June 1, Manning had undoubtedly been told in confidence by the pope that he was sending Monsignor Ruffo Scilla to congratulate the queen on her Jubilee. Walsh, who obviously sensed there was something more in the cardinal's letter than met the eye, immediately forwarded it to Croke for his opinion. "I return the Cardinal's note," Croke replied on June 3, "— there is no doubt that there is something up"(W). "But I believe," he added, anticipating Walsh's own reply to Manning, "it would be the height of meaness [sic] on our parts to take any steps in the matter as it now stands." "We are here, the National hierarchy," he maintained, "and, if the Pope wants to know how things are in Ireland, or to be advised as to the course he should take, at the present Juncture, he should consult us, and not take his information from our deadliest enemies." "As for me," Croke declared, "I would not go across the road to prevent the publication by Pope or Propaganda of another anti-Parnellish pronunciamento. I always believe that the Roman authorities got too quietly out of the Parnell tribute blunder, in the sense that they should have been forced to acknowledge their mistake openly, instead of simply admitting the fact by implication, and in private interviews. And I further believe, that if they repeat the blunder, they will not find it easy, or possible to wriggle out of the difficulty in the same way." "No National Church in the world," he then emphasized, "is treated like ours. See still how our rights are periodically threatened, if not invaded." "I'll write no more," he concluded angrily, "it only vexes me."

Three important points emerge from these letters of Walsh and Croke in early June. First of all, they were certainly much more concerned about a Roman condemnation of the Irish agitation than they were about diplomatic relations. Second, they had not been consulted by the pope or the Roman authorities. And finally, since they had not been consulted, they were determined not to be the first to initiate discussions with Rome. The three points, moreover, are logically connected by the interesting premise that a Roman condemnation would only shake papal power and influence in Ireland and not their own. This had indeed been the case when Rome issued its famous Circular, referred to by Croke in his letter to Walsh, condemning the Parnell Testimonial Fund in May, 1883, and Walsh was certainly aware of it. "Even the famous 'Circular,' " Walsh explained to Michael Verdon, vice-Rector of the Irish

College, on June 2, "has done no permanent harm. It has, of course, shaken the strong feeling of confidence that existed before it was issued. But beyond that no trace of its influence remains"(K). What Walsh was saying, of course, was that while Irish Catholics had learned to be wary of what might come from Rome, their confidence in their own Bishops and priests was still unshaken. That is why Walsh pointed out to Manning that since he had not been consulted, he was not going to incur any responsibility, for what was certain to be a politically disastrous move on the part of Rome, by initiating discussions in the present crisis.

From an Irish point of view, however, the situation in Rome in early June continued to deteriorate. On June 3, the Reuter's News Agency announced not only that the pope had decided to send a special delegation to congratulate the queen on her Jubilee, but even more significantly, that Cardinal Rampolla had been appointed to succeed the late Cardinal Jacobini as papal secretary of state. With the duke of Norfolk still in Rome, encouraging the pope, the appointment of Rampolla was certain to result in greater activity on the part of Rome in matters diplomatic. Walsh's reaction to the threatening situation was characteristic. He redoubled his efforts in order to see that Rome was supplied with the proper information. He still refused, however, to bend in the matter of forwarding the information directly to either Propaganda or the pope. He wrote instead another long letter to Kirby on June 9, asking him to bring the detailed report he had sent on earlier to the attention of the pope. The report concerned the charges of the Irish judges at recent assizes testifying to the fact that in the greater part of Ireland there was very little crime and outrage. "We know here," Walsh assured Kirby, referring to the pope, "of the unscrupulous efforts that are being made to mislead him. When the anti-Gladstonian newspapers at home do not shrink from mis-statements of the grossest character, although they know that whenever it is deemed worthwhile to contradict them, they cannot escape, we all feel that they are sure to make the fullest use of the opportunity of making false statements, pretended quotations &c. &c. in a place like Rome where they count on their statements never seeing the light in any way which they could be checked or contradicted"(K).

As was often his habit, Walsh left this letter open in order to add what might be important before post time, for he suddenly asked Kirby — "Could you see the Holy Father *AT ONCE*?" "It is really of *URGENT* importance," Walsh added excitedly, "he should hear that our affairs are really in a critical condition." What had happened was that Michael Davitt, prominent Nationalist and radical agrarian reformer, had made a most provocative speech at Bodyke in County Clare.[13] Davitt had maintained that since the tenants who had been evicted at Bodyke were in a wretched and destitute state, and since Parnell, who was apparently ill, had not offered any advice or guidance in the crisis, he was free to advocate any policy he thought applicable as a member of the National League. Timothy Harrington, secretary of the League, and undoubtedly prompted by Walsh, immediately protested that Davitt had no such right, and further maintained that such a claim could only lead to anarchy in Nationalist ranks. Walsh, it appears, had overreacted to Davitt's speech, and was having Harrington's protest translated into Italian and printed, as well as issuing a public protest of his own. Harrington's protest, Walsh then explained to Kirby, would be ready in a few days. "But," he insisted, "I would ask your Grace to see H.H. *AT ONCE*. When it reaches Rome you can see him again, bringing it to him." "I have written a letter," Walsh added, "to calm the public mind, which is *dreadfully agitated* by rumors from Rome. In the latter, I strongly back up the action of the Central League, and say that so long as our people keep from violence &c, their enemies can never succeed in depriving them of the sympathy of the Holy Father." "If you can," Walsh concluded, *"read this letter for him."*

The pressure on Walsh over the past six months had indeed been incredible, and it was becoming quite obvious from his letters that the strain was finally beginning to tell on him. He had been, in fact, under constant attack, especially at Rome, since he had approved of the Plan of Campaign in early December. English Catholics and their Irish allies, lay and clerical, had kept up a sustained barrage. Both critics and friends within the Irish hierarchy, moreover, had embarrassed him at Rome. The coadjutor to the bishop of Clonfert and the bishop of Limerick had both questioned his judgment in crucial matters, and Croke by his enormous "gaff" in February had only increased Walsh's difficulties at the Vatican. Rome

---

[13] For a calmer account of this episode, see M, Walsh to Manning, June 26, 1887.

had held her hand for mainly two reasons. In the first place there was not much sense opening negotiations with a ministry that appeared to be on the verge of collapse, and second Walsh's own negotiations with the government, by his own account at least, seemed to be bearing fruit. When the government, therefore, not only managed to sustain itself, but appeared to be growing stronger, and Walsh's negotiations broke down, Rome decided that it was the opportune moment to take Irish affairs more into her own hands. The pope's offer to reconsider the Malta affair and his sending Monsignor Ruffo Scilla as his representative to the queen's Jubilee were his opening moves in the new diplomatic chess game. Leo XIII's real problem, however, was how to play this new game without forsaking the confidence of Walsh, who after all, as the arch-exponent of the Clerical-Nationalist alliance, had become the pope's most important piece on the board. Since Walsh, moreover, had a very able mind of his own, the pope would need to handle him very delicately if the archbishop of Dublin was to be moved at all.

The pope, however, was soon to prove that he played technically, at least, an excellent game of diplomatic chess. Shortly after receiving Walsh's letter asking him to see the pope, Kirby had his usual weekly audience. "Yesterday," he reported to Walsh on June 17, "I had the honour of an audience with His Holiness, and I took with me the famous document ('Ireland as it is') against the Irish movement, with some written observations of mine to confute, as well as I could, its false statements. Of what I had written I gave a verbal summary, which His Holiness was pleased to listen to with great attention."[14] "I also brought to him," Kirby added, "your most useful collection of the charges made by the judges at the late Assizes, with a brief analysis showing that of 39 judicial charges thirty-two proved the favorable state of the respective districts whilst only seven were of a contrary nature." After assuring Walsh that His Holiness had showed the greatest interest, Kirby then turned to what was really on the pope's mind. "He spoke to me," Kirby explained, "about the Queen's Jubilee and said, notwithstanding the present hostile attitude of the English Ministry towards Ireland, it would be becoming if something were done in Ireland complimentary to the *Queen*

---

[14] *Walsh*, pp. 265-66.

personally on the occasion, as she represented the principle of authority which comes from God, and 'as she is a woman.' "
"But His Holiness," Kirby then emphasized," did *not* give these observations any form of *command,* nor did he charge me to communicate them to your Grace. But if your Grace and even our good friend of Cashel would see your way to do anything in that line, as of your own accord, I think it would be most useful and would make our cause stronger, as indicative of that generous spirit of Christian forgiveness and charity which has always happily animated the Irish Catholic heart."

Kirby then turned to another and equally painful subject for Walsh. "I think," he insisted once again, "you should write to Propaganda often during these times. They receive 'whole files' of accusations against us, and not a word scarcely coming to them from the episcopal body in our own defence. Collective letters from the episcopacy at periodical occasions do not, I think, produce the desired effect, as they are not followed up by private, frequent confidential communications." "Here," he added reasonably in conclusion, "the authorities are most anxious to receive information favorable to us. So write often and confidentially, and make Cashel, Tuam and Dr. Logue do the same. *Se la compana non suona, nessuno andra alla messa.*" Before he had received this letter of Kirby's of June 17, however, Walsh had already written him explaining that he had decided to write to the authorities if they but would indeed officially request him to do so.[15] What had prompted Walsh to bend a little was undoubtedly a very sober and sensible letter from Kirby's vice-Rector, Michael Verdon. Verdon had written Walsh on June 9, thanking him for forwarding the charges of the Irish judges at the assizes, and explained that they had given him the opportunity which he seldom got of speaking with the authorities at Propaganda about Irish affairs(W). He had long conversations with both Monsignor Jacobini, the secretary of Propaganda, and Enrico Gualdi, the undersecretary responsible for English and Irish affairs.

Monsignor Jacobini, Verdon reported, had assured him that there was no truth in the rumor that another Parnell "Circular" was about to be sent to Ireland. Jacobini was very anxious, moreover, to receive information, Verdon assured Walsh, for he had told him, "I get no information from the Irish side and the

---

[15] M, Walsh to Manning, June 26, 1887. See this for an account of the original Walsh letter to Kirby which does not appear to have survived.

Holy Father frequently asks me about Ireland when I go to
him." Padre Gualdi also seemed very well inclined, Verdon then
observed, "but he is thoroughly made up on the Irish question
according to the English view of it." Gualdi had told him,
however, that they received at Propaganda "piles and piles of
letters and documents sent by private persons and the enemies
of our cause and that they scarcely ever get an official
document from any reliable source explaining matters
according to our view of the case." "From what I have heard,"
he further reassured Walsh, "I believe that the Authorities of
Propaganda would be greatly pleased if your Grace would
often send them information of the State of affairs and I am
certain it would do a great deal of good." In finally making his
point about the need to write, Verdon warned Walsh that in the
last four months there had been a great change in the opinions
at Propaganda about Irish affairs. "I do not think," he added,
"that I ever before saw them so uneasy about Irish affairs. The
English party undoubtedly have been making desperate efforts
of late to get some condemnation from the authorities. The
worst of it is that they have the field almost entirely to
themselves here in Rome."

In advising Kirby that he had modified his views about
writing, Walsh suggested that the annual General Meeting of
the Irish Bishops scheduled for the following Wednesday, June
22, might provide Propaganda with the occasion to intimate
officially that he should write the authorities directly about Irish
affairs. In this way, Walsh explained to Kirby, he could bring
the matter before the assembled prelates in an open and above-
board way, so that they would understand in writing Rome he
had been requested to do so, and not without their knowledge.
Walsh further suggested that if indeed this was Propaganda's
desire he might send him a telegram before the Bishops met,
and Kirby responded by advising Walsh on June 20, that —
"Authorities wish you to write full information."[16] Walsh
replied the next day, June 21, to both Kirby's letter of June 17,
in which he had told him of the pope's guarded request
about the queen's Jubilee, and his telegram(K). After promising
Kirby that he would lose no time in writing to the authorities,
Walsh turned to the delicate question of the pope's request,
remarking that it was indeed deplorable that the Irish Bishops
could take no part in it. The difficulty, Walsh explained, was

[16] *Walsh*, p. 277.

HIS HOLINESS POPE LEO XIII. BLESSING THE WORLD.

that the government and its supporters had turned the celebrations into a political demonstration. On the day the Dublin Jubilee Committee was formed, Walsh reported, the chairman of it announced that the demonstration was not only to be a loyalist but a "Unionist" one. To make matters worse, the London *Tablet,* he noted, had announced that the celebration meant thanksgiving on the part of the people for the blessings of good government brought to them by the Queen's reign. "This being so," Walsh further explained, "it is plain *we* could have nothing to do with it." "But," he pointed out, even more significantly, "it is also important to observe that even if *we* took a different view, the people of Ireland would not do so. We should forefeit all their confidence and lose all the influence by which we have up to this succeeded in keeping them out of secret organizations." "P.S.," Walsh then added reassuringly, "our meetings have just closed. Everything, thank God, went on with most marvellous unanimity."

Before closing this letter, however, which he had kept open until Friday, June 24, in order to report on how the Bishops' meeting had gone, Walsh had received not only another very disturbing letter from Kirby, but a most alarming one from Michael Verdon. The day after his audience with the pope on Thursday, June 16, Kirby had written Walsh, but he had obviously not told him all that the pope had told him, because he wanted some time to think about how best to break his disagreeable news. In writing again the next day, Saturday, June 18, however, Kirby decided to come straight to the point. "His Holiness," he explained, "told me that he is considering the entire Irish question."[17] "The re-establishment of diplomatic relations," Kirby then warned, "between the English Government and Rome seems most likely. If it takes place, God may draw great good out of it even for our country, if we all do our duty to God and His Holy Church. For *Si Deus pro nobis, quis contra nos*?" "Indeed," he noted solemnly, "it may be that the Pope in his own quiet way may induce the Government to secure as much or even more for Ireland than the 86 Irish members were able to obtain, and perhaps on a more safe and durable basis." "I am *a priori*," Kirby reassured Walsh, "most unfavourable to the establishment of such relations. But if God, in the ways of his adorable providence, so dispose. . . ." "The

---

[17] *Ibid.,* p. 276.

present, Pontiff," Kirby finally concluded with an act of faith, "seems to have a special mission from God to governments and sovereigns, and great victories for the Church and the salvation of souls may, and let us trust will, be the happy result."

On that same day, Saturday, June 18, and unknown to Kirby, his vice Rector, Michael Verdon, also wrote Walsh. "I have just heard — very privately — from one of the Under Secretaries here," Verdon reported, "that it is in contemplation to send Monsignor Persico accompanied by F. Gualdi as Ap. [Apostolic] Visitor to Ireland. The question was discussed at Congresso in Propaganda yesterday"(W). "My informant," he explained, "did not know what was the result of the discussion at Congresso yesterday — but if it has been decided that he is to go I shall soon hear about it and let your Grace know." Verdon wrote Walsh again the next day, Sunday, explaining that he had told Kirby about the Visitation project, but not that he had written to him, and asked Kirby to prevent it if possible. Verdon thought that Kirby might at least be able to delay it, and thus give Walsh and the Irish Bishops enough time to attempt to prevent it. For once, however, Rome did not procrastinate. Verdon telegraphed Walsh two days later on Tuesday, June 21, that the Visitors mentioned in his letters would certainly start for Ireland that week(W). The next day, June 22, Verdon covered his telegram with a letter to Walsh announcing that Persico and Gualdi would leave for Ireland the following day(W). "They have their mission," he further reported, "immediately from the Holy Father, but as yet no one seems to know precisely what instructions they have received. It is said that they are to remain in Ireland about a month visiting various parts of the country and seeing and examining things as far as they can." "I had to tell Dr. Kirby," Verdon explained, "that I sent information for he asked me about it in a way that left me no escape."

Kirby had, in fact, in his letter of June 20, covering his telegram advising Walsh that the authorities wished him to write regularly to Propaganda, also informed Walsh that Persico and Gualdi would soon leave for Ireland.[18] Gualdi had told him, Kirby explained, "that the Holy Father wished to remove from the minds of the Irish prelates any apprehensions that his envoy to compliment the queen on her Jubilee had

---

[18] *Ibid.*, p. 278.

anything whatever to do with Irish ecclesiastical matters (his information on which he wishes to receive from the proper source of information, the Irish prelates themselves)." "On that account," Kirby added, "he has deputed the two above-named ecclesiastics to go to Ireland directly as a proof of this his intention. This will afford the bishops an occasion of making known to the envoys the true state of the country and the religious feeling of the people, and the consequent falsehood of the calumnious reports continually spread against our country." "Their communications with your Grace," he advised shrewdly, "will be of immense utility even for further occasions. Tell our friend in Cashel and your other episcopal friends that the cordial reception which they will give to these worthy ecclesiastics and the information they will afford them, will, D.V., be productive of great good for Ireland." Four days later, on June 24, Kirby wrote Walsh again confirming that Persico and Gualdi had left Rome for Ireland the previous evening.[19]

The effect of all this disconcerting news from Rome on Walsh, in the midst of all his other preoccupations, may be easily imagined. "The announcement of the intended mission to Ireland," Walsh informed Kirby on June 27, "has naturally caused much ferment of mind among our people"(K). "The explanation which Y.G. gives of it," he acknowledged, "fits in perfectly with what I know from the Holy Father himself as to his determination to keep Ireland safe from English intrigues. But it is not easy without imprudence to make use of this knowledge so as to calm the minds of our people. It is difficult to make any public use of it at all. I must, I think, try to devise some way of saying a pacifying word. If not, I fear that a great damper will be thrown on our collection of next Sunday for Peter's Pence as a Jubilee offering to the Holy Father." "Everyone is asking me," he then explained, "for information. I have to say I know nothing about what is being done. Then they say it is plain the Irish Bishops are being badly treated. No other hierarchy in the world would be treated so. How different this is from the present mission to England; from former missions to Canada, to India, &c. &c. &." "We must only pray," Walsh concluded darkly, "that all this may not turn out badly. For my part I have the gravest fears about it."

---

[19] *Ibid.,* p. 279.

Walsh was not the only one among the Irish Bishops, however, who was deeply troubled by the news from Rome. "Possibly," Croke informed Walsh, on June 27, "the Roman delegation may do good; but I do not like the appearance of it. It is based on the supposition that the Irish movement is still held in Rome to be of a doubtful character. That is to say it supposes, that not withstanding the unanimous and reiterated statements and assurances of the Irish Bishops that the movement was strictly Moral and Constitutional, and that Religion was never in a more flourishing condition here, the English faction has been able to raise such doubts about the facts in the mind of the Holy Father as to warrant, and, in fact, coerce him to send out a delegate to test and report on the real state of the case." "This is nothing short of an insult to the Irish Episcopacy," Croke declared, and realizing that he had gone too far, added, "though, of course, it is not meant as such." "I see by today's Freeman," he concluded dryly, "that Persico's visit has been postponed — Maybe So —."

Meanwhile, Cardinal Manning had written Walsh on June 25, to assure him that both Persico and Gualdi were "intimately" known to him.[20] Gualdi, who hero-worshipped the cardinal, had been one of Manning's priests for fifteen years before his return to Rome. He not only knew English well, but he was "thoroughly good and decent." Manning had known Persico for thirty-six years. He too knew English well, having translated a book of Manning's into Italian for Propaganda, and served as a bishop in both British India and the United States. He, therefore, knew the English-speaking world well, and Manning thought also that his heart was "with the poor." Persico, the Cardinal also noted, was a Capuchin. "It now all depends," Manning then shrewdly advised Walsh, "upon his relations and contacts in Ireland. He will be (I take it for granted that he will be) in immediate contact with you and the bishops." The cardinal further suggested that Persico see with his own eyes those estates, like Glenbigh and Bodyke, where the tenants had been reduced to destitution by the cruel evictions of the landlords, for this would provide the best answer to "certain whisperers" in Rome. In a final reassurance, the cardinal pointed out that the selection of Persico and Gualdi certainly implied impartiality and a desire to know the truth. "If they

---

[20] *Ibid.*, p. 280.

come to London," he added in conclusion, "you may trust me to give them an outline of inquiry."

Walsh replied promptly the next day.[21] He had to make the embarrassing admission that as yet he had received no "official announcement" from Rome. Kirby had, however, Walsh confessed, written reporting Gualdi's explanation of the pope's purpose in sending the mission, and that was quite in accord with what the pope had told him when he had been in Rome for his consecration some two years before. "He knows," Walsh assured the cardinal, and referring to the pope, "that *our* only difficulty here in Ireland in reference to the re-establishment of diplomatic relations is that we should be placed at the mercy of a possibly unscrupulous, and probably hostile, English representative in Rome. His view then, as I have already told your Eminence, is that the Irish Bishops should have an officially recognized representative of our own, with the recognized function of checking all statements made about us or affecting our interests." "Well," Walsh added, and somewhat unconvincingly, "H.H. having now sent an Envoy to England sees that some distrust may spring up at our side of the water. He meets this by sending us an Envoy to get from the Irish Bishops as the most trustworthy sources of information, the state of things in Ireland." "Mgr. Persico," Walsh noted, echoing the cardinal, "as is most important, is to see as much as possible with his own eyes. What an exposure it will be of the tactics that some have been working against us!" "Coming to a country," he pointed out, "that is represented as on the verge of anarchy and civil war, he will find himself among the most peaceful people in the world." "A great effect," he finally assured the cardinal, and crowing a little, "has been produced at Propaganda by a paper which I compiled (and a copy of which I enclose) giving the statements of the Irish Judges in their charges at the last Assizes, as to the presence or absence of crime in the country. In his reply to this long letter of Walsh's, the next day, June 27, the cardinal confessed that he was much relieved, for he had been "full of fear about Propaganda and Rome," because they were so easily misled, and "inculpably, so unable to understand the state of Ireland."[22] He then assured Walsh that the Ruffo Scilla mission had no bearing on Irish affairs, and that the archbishop would

---

[21] *Ibid.*, p. 281.
[22] *Ibid.*, p. 283.

be doing him a real service and kindness by keeping him well informed. Manning then concluded by noting that he had already sent "the testimony of the judges to the Holy Father three weeks ago."

The same day that the cardinal was thus writing Walsh, however, the London *Times* commented editorially on a Reuter's News Agency telegram from Rome dated June 27, which maintained that "in consequence of the representations made by Cardinal Manning and Archbishop Walsh of Dublin upon the inexpediency of an intervention of the Vatican in Irish political affairs at the present moment, and the bad impression it would produce, the pope today ordered the suspension of the mission to Ireland with which Mgr. Persico and Fr. Gualdi were to have been entrusted."[23] Walsh immediately denied that he had any hand or part in advising Rome about the Persico mission, while Manning took the *Times* to task for its editorial remarks. "In your leading article of this morning," the cardinal wrote on June 27, "you express your regret that the mission of Monsignor Persico has been revoked 'at the instance apparently of Cardinal Manning and Archbishop Walsh,' adding, 'the active promoters of Separatist intrigues are hardly the persons who should have a determining voice in the Councils of the Church.' "[24] "On this I have two remarks to make:

1.   The word "apparently" will not clear the *Times* of the grave responsibility of sending all over the world a statement which is false. A contradiction in the name of Archbishop Walsh and in my own is to be found in the *St. James Gazette,* and in the *Pall Mall Gazette* of this evening.

2.   My other remark is of a graver kind. You describe Archbishop Walsh and myself as "active promoters of Separatist intrigues." No gloss or evasion can explain this away; for you fix the meaning of the terms by describing us as having "a determining voice in the Councils of the Church." This can apply to no layman, and the Archbishop of Dublin and myself are the text of this comment.

I gladly unite myself with the Archbishop of Dublin. He is but slightly known in England, except in the descriptions of those who are fanning the flames of animosity between England and Ireland. I am known in England, both to the Ministers of the Crown and the leaders of the Opposition. I leave to them who well know my mind to answer for me; and I who know the

[23]   *Times* (London), June 27, 1887; quoted in *Walsh,* p. 283.
[24]   *Ibid.*, June 29, 1887; quoted in *Walsh,* pp. 284-85.

mind of the Archbishop of Dublin answer for him. We are neither intriguers or Separatists.[25]

"If sir," the cardinal concluded eloquently, in high dudgeon, "I have written with unusual warmth I will confess to you that I hold resentment sometimes to be a duty. And this is such a time, when your words touch our highest responsibility and inflame more and more the heated contentions between the two peoples whom justice and truth still bind in peace and unity."

In publishing the cardinal's very able and clever letter, the *Times* wisely decided to focus its editorial comment on Walsh rather than on Manning. "Archbishop Walsh," the *Times* pointed out, in shifting to the more vulnerable target, "is a good deal better known in England than Cardinal Manning would have us believe; he is known, not by the invectives of his enemies, but by his own spoken and written words."[26] "He is," the *Times* declared, "in the very strict sense of the word, a Separatist. He is working for the establishment of an independent Irish Parliament and Executive." "In pursuing that policy," the *Times* claimed, moving to safer ground, "he has identified the Irish Roman Catholic clergy with the cause of the National League, he has given his public approval to the Plan of Campaign, and his conduct has tended during the last eleven months to embarrass the Government and paralyse the enforcement of the law in Ireland." "This is a course," the *Times* stoutly maintained in conclusion, "which Archbishop Walsh may be legally entitled to pursue, but it is in our judgment rightly described as a Separatist intrigue."

Walsh, however, who was usually quick to take offense at such editorial comment, had the good sense to leave very well alone. He was not only grateful for the cardinal's very able defense, but pleased because Manning had finally and irrevocably identified himself with the Irish cause. "I cannot attempt," he explained to the cardinal on June 30, "to thank your Eminence for your noble letter. All Ireland will thank you for it yet"(M). "It has produced," he assured Manning, "an extraordinary sensation here. Few knew how thoroughly your Eminence has been with us all through this trying time." "Your Eminence," Walsh then noted, and underlining the tactical importance of the cardinal's letter for both Rome and English

[25] *Ibid.*
[26] *Ibid.*

public opinion, "will, of course, have observed that you have driven the *Times* to confess that what it means by 'Separation' is Home Rule in the shape of a legislative body." In dropping Walsh a short note that same day, however, it was Croke who perceptively put his finger on the political lesson implicit in the cardinal's letter. "Nothing could be more opportune," Croke noted shrewdly, "nor nothing more satisfactory. . . . It identifies the Cardinal *publickly* with the Irish cause *and with yourself*"(W).

In Rome, meanwhile, Cardinal Rampolla, who had only recently succeeded the late Cardinal Jacobini as secretary of state, had a long interview with Kirby. "He told me," Kirby informed Walsh that same day, June 27, "that he called me by order of His Holiness who wished me to know the spirit and terms of the Commission confided to Monsignor Persico in Ireland."[27] "The instructions," Kirby then reported, which had been given in writing to Persico, "stated that this was intended to be one of sympathy and deference to the Irish episcopacy in the troubles and afflictions in which their country was at present placed. The Cardinal called my attention to the words *'simpatia e deferenza'* as a proof of the spirit which impelled His Holiness to send this message of paternal affection to his Irish children through their sacred pastors." "I gave the Secretary of State," he then assured Walsh, after several pious observations, and referring to Walsh's recent pamphlet — *L'Irelanda nella sua condizione attuale* — "three copies of your *Monita* — which arrived most opportunely — one for the Holy Father, another for himself and his office, and the other for his other office, that of *Affari Ecclesiastici*. The others I will distribute to Cardinal Simeoni, and in other influential quarters. Drop me a line after your first interview with Monsignor Persico, and give me your view and feelings, thereon." "For the rest, my dear Lord," he concluded piously, "let us not fear anything. When we act with a pure intention for God's glory and keep, as ever, well united with the Rock of Peter, we may smile at all the howling of our enemies throughout the world."

Three days later, on Thursday, June 30, Kirby again wrote Walsh explaining that he had just had his weekly interview with the pope that morning. "At the end of the audience," Kirby reported, "he told me to go to the Secretary of State as he had something to communicate to me on the part of His Holiness,

[27] *Walsh*, pp. 279-80.

who was too hurried then to mention the matter in detail to
me."[28] "I went accordingly," Kirby added dutifully, "to His
Eminence who kept me a good while. He said that the son of
the Prince of Wales was about to visit Ireland very soon —
Prince Victor. He said that it was the wish of His Holiness that
your Grace should show him the usual acts of courtesy due to
the members of reigning royal families, as, he added, to fail
therein might be prejudicial to the country, and in the eyes of
Europe might be considered as not creditable to the dignitaries
of the Irish Church. He spoke a good deal on the subject, all
tending towards the same point — to show that we ought not to
mix up the question of our general rights, which are strong on
their own merits, with the received usages of personal courtesy
to the members of the reigning sovereign family — that not
lacking in such courtesy will render our cause and ourselves
more strong and respected." "So he charged me," Kirby added
pointedly, "to write at once to your Grace in this sense, adding
that you would kindly try to interest the other bishops through
whose places the prince would be known to pass, to mention to
them confidentially the wish of His Holiness on the subject. I
replied that I would at once fulfil his Eminence's commission,
adding as my own personal feeling that from what I know of
your Grace, I am sure you would only be too happy to carry
out the wishes of the Head of the Church on this and every
other point to which His Holiness attached importance."
"Ecco," he good humoredly lapsed into Italian, *"tutta la mia
comissione!"* "Drop me a line," he advised more seriously in
conclusion, "as they will be most anxious on the subject."

"Your Grace's letter," Walsh replied by return of post on
July 3, "has just come to hand in due course"(K). "The
proceedings to which it refers," Walsh reported dryly, "came to
an end three or four days ago. The visit lasted only three days.
Dublin was the only part of the Country visited, or intended to
be visited. Fortunately, all passed off quietly — without any of
the unpleasant rioting that formerly characterised such
gatherings." "It was, of course," he explained, warming to his
subject a little, "very trying to our people — for from first to last
it was an anti-Gladstonian, or anti-Home Rule, demonstration.
This was distinctly avowed by the Chairman of the Committee
of Reception on the very opening day of its meetings. It was

---

[28] *Ibid.,* pp. 286-87.

just as well that Y.G.'s letter did not come sooner, as I should then have been obliged to write some statement of all the reasons why it is impossible for me, or for the other Bishops, to fall in with such movements. If we were to do so, the result would be to drive our people from their attitude of respectful silence to one of hostile demonstrations; for they would then feel themselves called upon to show that they at all events had not joined the ranks of the Tories." "The present Lord Lieutenant," Walsh continued, adducing his reasons, "with whom the Princes stayed is an offensive political partisan."

> Even in his office of Viceroy he has made open profession of his antagonism to Home Rule!
> This, of course, is very different from the action of either of his predecessors, Lord Aberdeen or Lord Carnarvon.
> It is simply impossible that I could have any relation with him.
> He has not even sent the ordinary formal invitation to a State Banquet, always sent to Card. MacCabe (though of course H.E. never accepted it) and sent to me by the two former Viceroys(K).

"All this," Walsh testily concluded, "is very hard, practically impossible for people outside Ireland to understand. But to us here, the situation is unmistakably clear."

Indeed, if Kirby had any doubts about the appropriateness of Walsh's response to the pope's request, he certainly must have been disabused when he read the reply to a similar suggestion he had made to the bishop of Down and Connor, Patrick McAlister, who resided in Belfast. "With respect to the Princes," McAlister informed Kirby on July 7, "they are not coming to Belfast — They have returned to England — I beg to assure your Grace that any suggestions from the authorities in Rome shall always be received by me with the greatest deference and respect; but I consider I would be wanting in a conscientious duty, if I omitted to frankly state, that while we never fail to teach obedience and submission to the civil authorities; to seek opportunities to pay court in our present circumstances — seeing the terrible treatment our poor people have and are receiving and the still worse treatment with which we are threatened by the Tory Government now in power, would beyond all doubt lead our people to look on us as sympathising with their oppressors and withdraw their confidence from us." "The result would be sad indeed," McAlister warned Kirby, "for it is only the love of our people for their Holy Religion & the confidence they have in the sympathy & good advice of their clergy that give them patience and courage to sustain their trials."

"I am quite certain," McAlister argued, "if the venerable authorities of the Holy See saw our good priests exhorting our poor people to patience in the midst of an eviction scene . . . and entreat[ing] their poor people for the sake and love of the Crucified to submit to this barbarous treatment, they would I am sure make allowances for our circumstances." "And these terrible and inhuman scenes," he maintained, "are continually occurring throughout Ireland and are legalised and carried out in the Queen's name."

The present Queen's reign has been to Ireland the most disastrous since that of Elizabeth. During her reign there have died of Famine in Ireland 1,228,000 persons; the number of Emigrants was 4,186,000; there were evicted 3,667,000. The number of evicted equals 75 percent of the actual population. In 1885, there were 15,423 persons evicted; in 1884, 20,025 persons evicted; in 1883, 17,855 evicted; in 1882, 26,836 evicted and so on, for the last half century(K).

"I entreat your Grace," McAlister concluded, "to explain to the authorities our trying circumstances and to ensure them of our entire devotion to the Holy See and everything emanating from it."

Not every Irishman, however, was either endowed with so tender, or had even acquired so acute, if inaccurate, an historical memory. "Since I wrote to you," Sir George Errington had reported to Smith on July 3, the very day Walsh had written Kirby about the Royal visit, "much interest continues to be taken about Msgr. Persico, and I have heard some strange things"(S). "Msgr. Ruffo Scilla," Errington informed Smith, "wrote a few days ago to Father Klein the *Jesuit* professor of Natural Philosophy at the Royal University of Dublin telling him that he ought to take part in the reception of the Princes in Dublin last week as a Royal professor, and thus do honour to the Grandsons of the Queen to whom the Pope had sent a special Envoy: he added that he spoke from himself, but that he was sure he expressed the views of Rome on

the subject." "Father Klein (as bound in obedience)," Errington
explained, "went to consult the Provincial (Father Brown) who
took the letter from him & forbid [*sic*] on any account to follow
the Nuncio's advice!!!" "Father Klein," Errington added, "is a
very distinguished & learned *Alsatian* Father, of moderate loyal
views. The Irish Jesuits are strange to say very advanced, but in
this case the Provincial is supposed to have acted out of fear of
Dr. Walsh." "This is *quite certain* & true," Errington assured
Smith, "and I thought it right you should know it. I write in
haste to catch the post." "P.S.," he added hurriedly, "Would
you advise me to go over to Ireland to see Msgr. Persico?"

Kirby, meanwhile, it appears, had also written Croke as well
as Walsh in an effort to dispel any false impressions that might
have been created by rumors about Monsignor Persico's
Mission, for Croke replied on July 4, that Kirby's letter was
"most valuable and most satisfactory"(K). "I hold my annual
Diocesan Synod, today"; Croke explained, "and I shall read for
the assembled clergy such portions of your admirable letter as
bear on Msgr. Persico's Mission and the public affairs generally
of this country. It has taken a weight off my mind; and it will
when contents are made known to them, have a similar effect
on our Clergy many of whom were under the impression that
the mission of Msgr. Persico was a proof that the H. Father had
given credence to the reports of the English enemy rather than
to the published resolutions and representations of the Irish
Bishops." "I see now," he assured Kirby in conclusion, "the
real drift of the business, and can explain it accordingly." How
sincere Croke was in his protestation to Kirby about
understanding the "real drift" of affairs is a moot point, but
there is no doubt about how Walsh understood the trend in
Irish ecclesiastical affairs over the past six months.

In fact, no one appears to have understood better than
Walsh, except perhaps Manning, at this stage exactly what was
at stake. "By this post," Walsh informed Kirby on July 4,
"there goes to Card. Simeoni the first of the series of 'relationes'
that I intend to send him. This regards exclusively the
proceedings of our last meeting in Maynooth. It will show the
Cardinal the unanimity that exists"(K). "I take the opportunity
of explaining a point that Y.G. mentioned to me as not fully
understood at Propaganda," Walsh noted, raising the extremely
significant question as to where the initiative should rest with
regard to Irish educational matters, " — the necessity of dealing

in a confidential way with the Government in the present (or rather *recent*) stage of the negotiations on the Education Question. I say *recent* because for some time past, the Government have practically given up even the pretence of wishing to settle the question." "At all events," he advised Kirby, plainly pointing out who was still the focus of power in the Irish Church, "all that was done has been fully and *unanimously* approved by the meeting of Bishops." "In such a statement," Walsh observed, obviously referring obliquely to his recent difficulties with the bishop of Limerick, Edward Thomas O'Dwyer, "it is not easy to draw the line as to how far one should enter into details. I have, I hope, hit off the proper medium. But I will ask Yr. Grace to see the Cardinal, and ask whether this is so." "I understand," Walsh added, turning to a subject where his initiative was more appreciated, "that the organisation I set on foot for working up the Jubilee Peter's Pence Collection yesterday has turned out *very* successful. In many Churches the usual amount was more than doubled. But, the people are greatly disturbed in mind. Only for my letter in Tuesday's Freeman, and an article I had inserted on Saturday, the result would have been simply disastrous." "They fear," Walsh concluded, referring again to the people, and not mincing his words, "that English influence has once more prevailed, and that the Pope in sending Mgr. Persico has given way to the representations of the Duke of Norfolk, and of the Bishop of Salford, that the Irish Bishops are not to be trusted."

The pope had certainly made up his mind, in conjunction with his new secretary of state, Cardinal Rampolla, about his new Irish policy by the time of his audience on June 16 with Kirby. The core of his new policy, however, was not that the pope, as was assumed by Kirby and reported to Walsh after his audience, was reconsidering the question of diplomatic relations. For as Walsh well understood, that question only concerned the Irish in as far as it affected them, and both he and the pope had agreed in 1885 that it could easily be managed if the Irish had their own representative in Rome who would officially review, if not indeed be responsible for, all Irish business at the Vatican or Propaganda. What was really novel in the pope's policy, then, was that he had decided to send Monsignor Persico to Ireland to collect the required information about the condition of the Irish Church and not depend, as he had been doing since he appointed him archbishop of Dublin two years before, on Walsh and the witness of the Irish Bishops as a body through their accredited representative in Rome. The fact the pope did not authorize Kirby, if indeed he mentioned it to him at all in their audience, to report the intention of the Persico mission, and Kirby's further humiliation in being apprised of the mission by his vice rector, indicates that Kirby's position as the official representative of the Irish Bishops had in recent months, to say the least, become very tenuous. The pope had, in brief, presented Walsh and the Irish Bishops with a *fait accompli,* though he had somewhat softened the blow by carefully choosing two emissaries who were *personae gratae* to Cardinal Manning.

IV. The Persico Mission

July, 1887 - December, 1887

"The 'mission,' " Walsh informed Manning from Dublin on July 8, "has arrived. It has been most industriously circulated that Mgr Persico was to stay with his religious brethren, not with the Bishops. It will rather disturb the minds of certain friends of ours to find that I am to have the honour of his staying with me here while he is in Dublin." "The Mission," Walsh further reassured the cardinal, "is to the Bishops. The Holy Father is naturally troubled at the representations so freely made to him as to the state of things here. He has given the best possible means of letting him know the truth." *"Both our visitors,"* he added, and referring to the cardinal's recent letter to the *Times, "are loud in their praise of your Eminence's letter.* The 'Separatist' cry is one that evidently had told in Rome." "My view of the whole case," Walsh characteristically summed up for the cardinal, "is that I should put before them in fullest detail an exposition of the present state of Ireland under the following heads:

1°   The *political* movement; not revolutionary, but thoroughly constitutional in its aim and in its means. / This to be shown (*a*) from the nature of our demand viewed in itself, (*b*) from the fact that we have Mr. Gladstone, Lord Spencer, Sir G. Trevelyan etc. etc. with us.

2°   The *land* movement; not communistic etc. etc., but a just and reasonable demand, to save the people from eviction so long as they pay a really *fair* rent (reference to Cowper Commission).

3°   Comparative freedom of Ireland from crime (Judges charges etc.).

4°   All that is satisfactory in the preceding, the result of the guidance of the movement by the Bishops & priests / Contrast with time when Fenianism was the only line of action in Ireland designated as "Nationalism"(M).

"I know Your Eminence will be good enough," Walsh hinted in conclusion, "to send me any suggestions that occur to you."

"Your letter," the Cardinal replied on July 10, "was very acceptable, and I thank you very much for it."[1] "The heads you have drawn up contain everything;" Manning assured Walsh, adding characteristically, "and in working them out much will arise."

1. — I hope Monsignor Persico will go to Glenbeigh and Bodyke, and see with his own eyes the people and the ruins.

2. — I will send certain information about Kerry where he can examine with the Bishop and the parish priests.

3. — No doubt the "Separatist" outcry has had its effect in Rome.

4. — And also the charge that the bishops have not spoke out strongly enough, or often enough, against outrages and atrocities. Under this head let me know whether there is any case in which moonlighters have abused wives or daughters. I ask this because a friend of Home Rule has been led to believe it. If I could refute it much good would be done.

5. — Also the apparent solidarity of the bishops and the Irish members, and of these with Chicago is always used here and in Rome.

6. — I hope that Mgr. Persico will go and see the next eviction with his own eyes. *"Summum jus summa injuria."* By English law a man for forging a shilling was hanged, a woman was burnt — as late as 1776. A theft of 5s. in a shop was capital-hanging. All these executions were *legal*. But they all cried to Heaven. I hope Mgr. Persico will master this distinction well.[2]

"You will do me a great service," Manning concluded, "by keeping me informed."

Walsh had also written Croke about the arrival of the "mission" on July 8, for the archbishop of Cashel also replied in characteristic fashion the next day. "I have no fancy for Persico and Co.," he confessed to Walsh on July 9, "but, still, of course. I shall do all I can to make their Mission a success"(W). "I have nothing to add to your programme," he explained, "only, I think it essential that he would tell us precisely and on every point what are the charges made against the Movement, the men connected with the Movement, and the

[1] *Walsh*, p. 291.
[2] *Ibid.*

results of the Movement. Let us hear all — *once for all*. We are able to smash it up." "How," he asked Walsh, "do they (P & Co) intend to proceed? How are they to get the knowledge they seek? Will they go round to the Bishops, or what?" "Write me," he concluded imperatively, "all the news." The following day, July 10, Walsh also wrote Kirby, explaining that the visitors had arrived, and what their itinerary had been and would be. "We shall go over," Walsh informed Kirby, "the whole case of Ireland, social, political, moral, &c &c &c. They seem quite willing to stay with me any time that may be requisite to make themselves up in everything. Then they will go through the country"(K). "This morning," Walsh explained, "Mgr Persico at my suggestion said the 8 oclock Mass in the Capuchin Fathers Church in Church St. After breakfast I drove him round to visit six or seven of our City Churches — including the Cathedral — that he might see the people in the ordinary way hearing Mass. I need not say how edified he is at all he has seen. As yet, of course, he has seen only two or three of our institutions, but what he has thus seen has filled him with wonder." "Of course," Walsh noted testily, "he will hear any number of lies, but I told him it would be folly to waste our time contradicting each fresh falsehood as it arose. The proper course is for me to give him in writing a full statement of the Irish case in all its bearings. This can be referred to whenever information is wanted." "Of course," Walsh reassured Kirby in conclusion, "I am very much occupied, working both night and day, but I did not wish to leave your Grace without some little information as to how things are going on."

When Walsh replied to Manning's letter of July 10, he explained at greater length and in more detail than he had to Kirby exactly what line he would take with Monsignor Persico. "Your Eminence's letter," Walsh acknowledged politely on July 12, "is, I need to say, most valuable. As regards Glenbeigh etc., I will press the matter on Mgr Persico"(M). "But, of course," he added, referring to the ineffective bishop of Kerry and the aged coadjutor to the bishop of Killaloe, "much will depend on the local authorities of each place. And Kerry and Clare seem to be simply drifting; there seems to be no energy and no care for anything. I have picked out a few instances of the most absolutely baseless statements, made in the most fully circumstantial way, about myself. I shall use these by way of caution. They fully bear out my view that no weight whatever is to be attached to any statement made against anyone who is in sympathy with the tenants, by those who are on the landlord side."

> As for denunciation of outrages, I have a statement made out. There is no defending the Bishops of those few districts where the outrages occur. But do they occur in Dublin, for instance, or in Cashel? My only opportunity for uttering a word of denunciation was in my replies to addresses received in country places: these (the addresses) always contained a passage denouncing outrages: I could then speak out on the subject, as on such occasions I never failed to do.
>
> This, and other questions about the imprudent action of priests are strictly *local* questions. My advice to Mgr Persico will be to deal with them as such, and to note carefully where any need for dealing with them exists. In this diocese, for instance, but one case came under my notice of a priest's using unbecoming language. The case occurred during the election contest of 1885. All I had to complain of was a rude personal reference to the family history of a prominent Catholic gentleman. Next morning the priest in question had a letter from me putting an absolute restriction upon him against taking any further part in political affairs, either by writing or speaking in public. I have repeatedly told him that I have full confidence in him in a way that is well understood. But as he has shown that he is wanting in prudence, I have felt myself bound to keep him safe(M).

"As regards the Kerry moonlighters," Walsh argued, returning to his earlier remarks about agrarian disorder and crime in the West, "instead of trying to defend them, I should try to collect all possible evidence against them. They have no claim upon us for protection or sympathy of any kind." "Monsignor Persico," Walsh noted finally in concluding this long report to Manning, "sees everyone who comes to call on him. Consequently, I have as yet had but little opportunity of talking with him, and only indeed on the Education Question as yet."

Walsh had also apparently written Croke asking him to put his views on paper. Croke's considered and carefully worded reply was obviously meant to be shown to Monsignor Persico by Walsh in order that the papal envoy might have no doubt about where the controversial archbishop of Cashel stood on the critical questions of the day. "There does not appear to me," Croke declared categorically in his letter to Walsh dated

July 15, "to be any difficulty whatsoever about Home Rule, Land, or Education, any more than about the religious condition of the Country and our devotion to the H. See. We do not ask for any system of Home Rule that would trench 'on the Supremacy of the Crown' or on 'the Unity of the Empire' — and as for *'Separation'* from England, I would oppose it by all means in my power preferring vastly the English Connection to a French or American one" (W). "In one word," he reasserted emphatically, "we all think *Separation* impossible, and, even if possible, I for one would oppose it." "I never heard," Croke added for good measure, "even one rational man, or reasonable politician, *no matter how advanced,* going in for *Separation.* On that head there is no room for doubt."

"The land question," he then declared just as dogmatically, "admits of just as little doubt. We are prepared to pay *fair rents;* but will never consent to pay more." "What are fair rents?" he asked rhetorically, and replied — "Rents comparable with the decent support, clothing, and education of the tillers of the soil according to the standard of England, Scotland, and other countries, and in proportion to the price of agricultural produce and the annual yield of same. Let these things be fixed by an *impartial* tribunal — not by *Landlord*– or *tenant.*" "In 'Education,' " Croke summed up simply, "we want 'Equality.' " "Our Centenary at Ursulines," Croke then reported, turning to local rather than national preoccupations, "was a wonderful success. I was able to hand £1200 to Revd. Mother on the celebrating day. Since we have got close on £200 more. I would have given anything to have his Excellency and Signor Gualdi present." "Schools and College," he added regretfully in conclusion, "closed here now when he comes to us — should he so honour us — we will be in a confused state — in many respects."

Before and since Persico's arrival in Dublin, meanwhile, Walsh, in concert with officials of the National League, had been busily gathering statistical ammunition in order to be able to make a case for amending the government's proposed Land Bill in the interest of the tenants. The Bill, which had already been passed by the House of Lords, was introduced by Arthur Balfour on July 11, in the Commons, and was immediately assailed by nearly everyone as being unsatisfactory. Walsh joined in the general assault by publishing his findings in two long letters of July 16 and 19, in the *Freeman's Journal,* which he immediately forwarded to Manning.[3] What Walsh was really attempting to achieve was that if the judicial rents, which had on the average by 1886 been reduced some 25 percent, by the Land Courts set up by Gladstone's Act of 1881, were to be further revised by amending the present Bill, that the revision would have some basis in statistical fact and not be arbitrary, especially since the Bill proposed to include 100,000 leaseholders not previously covered. Walsh also argued that since a general settlement of the Land Question seemed imminent, all evictions should be suspended. "But as usual," he confided to Cardinal Manning in his letter of July 20, covering the copies of the Freeman, "I fear that the Government will spoil their concessions by petty and undesirable restrictions." "However," Walsh concluded optimistically, "this may be all the better in the end: their own supporters may not stand by them very enthusiastically if any strong opposition is shown to these on any point." "The Freeman," the cardinal replied promptly the next day July 21, "has not yet reached me."[4] "Lord Salisbury," Manning reported hopefully, "seems to have made certain concessions, but as yet we have not got certain knowledge." Salisbury had, indeed, made concessions, and agreed, under extreme pressure from his Liberal Unionist allies, to a revision of the judicial rents. The rents, moreover, were to be valid only for three years, instead of the fifteen under the Land Act of 1881, and were to be fixed by the courts in terms of local price and labor schedules. The amended bill was returned to the Lords, who were very unhappy with it, but eventually agreed, and the bill became law on August 18. The government had, in fact, been severely shaken by the various concessions it had been forced to make in order to survive.

"Will Mgr Persico," Manning shrewdly inquired of Walsh, returning to the paramount issue in his reply of July 21, "see the Lord Lieutenant before he leaves Dublin?" "I see two sides," the cardinal hedged delicately, "of the question for you — but Mgr. Persico is a stranger to all local conditions and embarrassments. He represents the Holy See and is neutral beyond question." "The Government here," he warned, finally coming to his point, "are making it a test of his impartiality, and so, I

---

[3] Freeman's Journal, July 16, 19, 1887.
[4] Walsh, p. 295.

hear, is Sir Redvers Buller, who is certainly no adversary. My own opinion is that it would be an act of simple courtesy due to the representative of the Crown, if he were to write his name in the book, or even to see Lord Londonderry. It would also stop the mouths which complain of his being under your roof." "This is confidential," the cardinal then assured Walsh in conclusion, "and no one knows of my writing it."

Several days later, Sir Redvers Buller reported to Balfour in London from Dublin Castle that — "I think the Persico business is going alright."[5] "When I got home last night," he explained on July 24, "I found that both he and Archbishop Walsh had called upon me as well as having written their names in the Lord Lieutenant's book." "So far as I can make out," Buller concluded, "Lord Emly has been the inspirer of the visit of his Ex." The following day Buller received a most interesting letter, which he forwarded to Balfour, from Colonel Alfred Turner, who was responsible, as a special commissioner of the Royal Irish Constabulary, for the most troublesome and difficult area in Ireland — Kerry and Clare.[6] "I am just off," Turner explained hurriedly to Buller on July 25, "I had a great opportunity last night with Mons. Persico and his Secretary Gualdi — and I told them fully about the priests in Kerry & Clare."[7] "The Bishop of Limerick (R.C.)," Turner then reported of Edward Thomas O'Dwyer, "had already told them that the parts of Limerick near Clare were made a perfect Hell through boycotting & intimidation & that had made a great impression on him, which I added to by telling him that all Clare was in the same state, & that most of the priests helped in producing that state of things." "They go to Limerick," Turner added, "tomorrow & then proceed to Kerry & Clare."

The Roman "mission" did indeed leave the following day, July 26, for Limerick. When Croke, however, learned that Persico had proceeded to Limerick, to visit a See in his ecclesiastical province before visiting him, and had further added to the discourtesy by staying with Lord Emly at Tervoe, he was very annoyed. "It would, I think," Croke complained to Walsh in a letter marked *"PRIVATE"* on July 31, "be more in order

---

[5] B, 29807.

[6] *Ibid.*, Buller noted in forwarding Turner's letter to Balfour: "I thought that the first awakening would come to Persico better from Turner than from me. I ought I think to come in later."

[7] *Ibid.*, July 24, 1887.

and look better in the public eye, if instead of going to Lord
Emly, and passing Thurles by, his Excellency came to visit the
Archbp of Cashel." "However," he added, obviously in a huff,
"I do not busy myself much about that. Duty of one kind or
another will detain me at home until the middle of August, and I
shall then most assuredly pack up my effects, and seek a little
rest whether Mgr Persico has visited me by that time, or not.
Indeed, I have very little to tell him. The Country is as quiet as
possible — is, I believe *too* quiet. That's all I have to say about
my own place. The people are good, and we need no inquisition." "As regards the Country at large and the agitation,"
Croke observed, his temperature rising, "the best proof that the
latter is Constitutional, and not revolutionary, is that a savagely
hostile Government cannot successfully grapple with it: and he
has had enough proof in Dublin alone, that we have the faith
and morals, also. I wonder would his Excellency feel called upon
to salute, if he met him, the late General Garibaldi, or Signor
Mazzini, or any one of the numerous *nice* fellows, his
countrymen, who pollute at present the Italian soil." "Charity,"
Croke boldly maintained, "cannot compel any one to touch or
deal with, much less to feed a monster that means, if possible, to
devour him —. 'Tis all bosh. England has deprived us of arms —
the right of every free Citizen. We have invented a weapon that
serves our turn instead. It is called 'boycotting.' " "If we have
no means of shooting our enemy," Croke concluded defiantly,
if indiscreetly, "we may have the privilege of leaving him
'severely alone.' " Four days later Croke was still seething when
he wrote Walsh again. "Great indignation," Croke reported
from Thurles on August 4, "loudly expressed here, and generally felt in South, at Mgr Persico's extraordinary manoeuvre in
passing me by here, and going to meet Lord Emly and his gang.
I have not time to say more now on the matter"(W). "When,"
Croke then asked Walsh irritably in a post-script, "is his Excellency to come here — if at all?"

"I hear very conflicting accounts," Errington accurately informed Smith from London on August 6, when the mission had
been in Ireland for a month, "about Msgr Persico"(S). "Some
say," Errington reported, "he is entirely in the hands of Dr.
Walsh; others tell me that he is quite alive to the attempts being
made to impose upon him, & that he sees through the
Nationalist pretences, & this [*sic*] dangers to the Church. I shall
know more in Dublin & write you thence." "The Gladstone

Party & views," he then added hopefully in a postscript, "appear to be regaining influence in the country." At the end of August, Errington, as he had promised, wrote Smith a long and interesting letter about the peregrinations of Monsignor Persico. Errington was staying at the time at Castle Forbes, the home of his old friend and neighbor, the earl of Granard, a prominent Irish convert to Catholicism, and a substantial landlord in County Longford. "Msgr Persico," Errington reported to Smith on August 30, "is going actively about the Country. I have not seen him as yet. My fears that his Mission was a very imprudent step and that he is almost entirely in the hands of the violent Clergy are I am sorry to say confirmed"(S). "He has been asked to many of the best houses Catholic & Protestant;" Errington explained, noting that Lord Emly had been the lone exception, "so far he has only been to Tervoe, & only pays an occasional afternoon visit to the others as he goes round. Now considering that he lives night & day with the clergy, it is absurd to suppose that this influence can be counter-acted by an occasional conversation with laymen, though he professes himself most ready to receive everybody & listen to all." "Msgr P. promised at first," Errington then picked up his theme again after a long digression on a misunderstanding that had arisen between the envoy and Lord Granard, "to visit several Catholic & other houses. Now I understand he is rather backing out of his engagements, on the grounds of time &c; but the appearance & effect will be bad. My opinion has always been that Lord Denbigh & other busybodies who brought about this Mission have much to answer for." "The Gov't. are much weakened;" Errington then assured Smith, referring to his own political star, "I think they will go out in February, & we shall have Elections in March, Gladstone returned & Home Rule carried."

Croke, meanwhile, was still on tenterhooks. "I am in a dreadful state of incarceration here," he complained again to Walsh on August 22, "waiting for the advent of the Papal Envoy"(W). "If not here in a day or two," Croke warned, "I shall drop him a line to say that I had remained at home for him, more than a month, though I sadly needed a little run, but that I could not remain any longer, and so steered off." "I see," Croke wrote Walsh the next day, August 23, "the Monsignor has gone to Tuam. His gyrations are somewhat eccentric"(W). "In his address to the Tuam Clerics," Croke noted, "published in this days Freeman, he makes the extraordinary statement 'that if there has been a growth throughout Ireland of religious feeling, it is in no small measure due to the Clergy of this (Tuam) Diocese.' " "Was there ever anything so preposterous?" he asked Walsh irritably, and concluded dolefully — "I am in an ugly fix." That same day, however, Persico had written Croke that Thurles was to be his next stop after Tuam, and then followed this up with another note a few days later(C). "I had a note, this morning," Croke reported to Walsh on Saturday, August 27, "from Mgr. Persico saying he would be here on Monday evening next, at 8 1/2 oclock"(W). "'Tis time," Croke noted dryly, "I suppose he will remain a few days. Tuesday will be occupied with sight-seeing here. Unfortunately, things are in a state of Confusion in both the Convents and College, pupils being absent from both, and a general washing and cleaning up going on. However, his Excellency must be satisfied. We shall have no addresses or demonstrations of any kind, here, or elsewhere. I will go a good deal in[to] generalities with him, in rebus land, Home Rule, boycotting, and so forth." "I am still puzzled," Croke confessed, "as to the object of his visit. I hear from some that he has been sent simply to ascertain whether Religion *still* holds sway in Ireland, or whether it has not been washed away, wholly, or in great part by the waves of Agitation. Others say he is in quest of political information. We shall see." "It will be hard on you," Croke finally concluded, referring to the fact that Monsignor Persico planned to end his trip as he began it, in Dublin, "to have to meet him again after his sojourn in Yr. department. But, as you observe, you will be able in that way, to wind him up well."

"The Envoy," Croke reported promptly to Walsh four days later on Friday, September 2, "has come and gone"(W). "He is a nice man": Croke added, obviously impressed, "and, I think, friendly in a high degree — So, indeed, is Gualdi. We received him warmly, and, of course respectfully here: We we [*sic*] made no displays, following Yr. example, either in demonstration, or address. We parted, last evening on the best of terms." "I leave this for London on Monday next," Croke explained, "I mean 'to cross over' that night — weather permitting — and so far as I can now see, will not be home until after the October meeting of the Bishops. I find that I want a *long* change and rest. Sleep very bad." "Will you be home," he then asked Walsh, "on *Sunday?* For, if you were, I might go up to Dublin on that day, and spend the evening with you. There is a deal to be said."

During the summers in Rome, Kirby usually only wrote Walsh intermittently because he generally accompanied his seminarians to the Irish College's farm near Tivoli to escape the worst of the heat. "I saw His Holiness," Kirby informed Walsh from Tivoli on July 26, "and Cardinals Simeoni and Rampolla before leaving Rome. All feel greatly anxious about Ireland. But the observations were general. His Holiness told me that he wished Monsignor Persico not to be in a hurry to leave Ireland, in order to be able to know well the condition of the country, and the state of religion, etc., in the several localities."[8] "From what the newspapers say," Kirby observed shrewdly, "the impression made on him seems to be most favourable to us, and I am sure he reports according." "Your Grace's letter," Kirby noted, referring to Walsh's recent communications to the *Freeman,* "directed to obtain a Bill of protection for the tenants from being evicted till the passing of the Land Law, will, please God, do good." "It seems," he further commended Walsh, "to have had a useful influence in the late discussions in Parliament."

Three weeks later, Kirby, who had returned to Rome for the pope's Feast Day (St. Joachim), reported to Walsh again. "I saw Cardinal Simeoni," Kirby explained on August 16, "I also communicated to him that the Australian Government had awarded 600,000 acres for whatever Catholic Congregation will devote itself to the civilising of the natives in the new vicariate of Kimberly."[9] "The Pope," Kirby added, "held his levee this morning."

All the Cardinals, bishops, prelates, and other ecclesiastics and lay dignitaries attended. The conversation touched on several religious subjects, many of which showed the progress of Catholicity in different countries. As an additional proof of this, Cardinal Simeoni mentioned the above fact regarding Australia, and mentioned my name as his latest informant. This brought me on my legs and I detailed the circumstances briefly. His Holiness asked me was the above gift of land made by the English Government. I replied in the negative — that it was the gift of the Colonial Government; because I added, Australia

---

[8] *Walsh,* pp. 297-98.
[9] *Ibid.,* pp. 298-99.

divided into several territories has a separate Parliament of its
own for each — a fact which accounts for the marvellous
progress of the country in arts, commerce, etc. "And this Holy
Father is what Ireland demands for itself — the right to make its
own laws, retaining its subjection to the English Crown, but
with its own Parliament."[10]

"All the Cardinals listened, with the other dignitaries present,"
Kirby noted, somewhat naively, "and not one uttered a word of
contradiction or dissatisfaction at what I said. After the meeting
one of them said to me: 'It was well for you that Cardinal
Howard was not present, as he would have jumped up *con
fuoco* to assail you.' I know your Grace will be glad to get this
piece of news which, I hope, will not get into the newspapers, as
this might hurt my usefulness on future occasions."
"Monsignor Persico," Kirby assured Walsh finally, "reports
favourably. I hope your Grace continues to write often to
Cardinal Simeoni." "Let not Monsignor Persico's reports,"
Kirby advised in conclusion, "prevent you. He will have his
say, but you can have yours also."

Walsh was only able to reply to this letter some ten days
after he received it because he was overwhelmed with work.
"Mgr. Persico, of course," Walsh explained to Kirby on August
29, and lamenting the fact that he would have no holiday that
year, "does not wish me to be away when he returns to Dublin
after his round of the Country"(K). "Your Grace's remark
about Australia," Walsh then added, "was a most happy one.
Our Lady of Good Counsel must have helped you. Curiously,
after a little visit to her shrine in the Augustinian Church, where
I presided at High Mass yesterday, it occurred to me to take a
step in reference to a possible friendly settlement of the Land
Question, the result of which is a letter of mine which you will
see in this days Freeman's Journal," "The same paper," Walsh
concluded "contains a most interesting essay by Sir Chas.
Gavan Duffy. Y.G. will see how much use can be made of the
fact that he, an Australian Prime Minister, is so strong an
advocate of Home Rule here as well as there." In his letter to
the *Freeman,* Walsh had proposed a Round Table Conference
of representatives of the landlords and tenants, at which the
issues and grievances could be reasonably discussed and
worked out to the mutual advantage of all concerned.[11]

[10] *Ibid.*
[11] *Freeman's Journal,* August 29, 1887.

Both friend and foe, however, not only questioned the practicality of the proposal, but also whether Walsh was really serious, or merely using the proposal as a tactical ploy to influence Monsignor Persico. "As regards your 'Round table Conference,' " Croke candidly confessed on September 2, "the proposal will, I believe, do some small good, but hardly in the direction intended by you — that is assuming that you meant such a 'Conference' to take place at all"(W). "It will serve to show, anyhow," Croke explained, "that you desire nothing but even handed justice on all sides, and believe, moreover, that it should be meted out by Irish hands. But I regard such a Conference as an absolute impossibility." "The bulk of the brigands," he maintained, referring, of course, to the landlords, "would never submit to it — and those that do so would not be disposed to yield up a tithe of their plunder." "Continued pressure alone," Croke declared pugnaciously in conclusion, "can strangle them; and tis only when fairly choked that they will cry out for quarter — and give it."

When Errington read Walsh's proposal for a "Round Table Conference," he also wrote to the *Freeman*. "Though I should rather have left to others," he confessed to the editor and the public on August 31, "the task of duly appreciating the interesting proposals contained in the Archbishop of Dublin's recent letter, the occasion is one of such importance that you will perhaps allow me as an Irish landlord, to say how cordially I, for one, welcome any approach to a policy of mutual understanding and forebearance."[12] Errington, who was well aware on whom his political future, if any, depended, forwarded a copy of this letter on September 10, with a long and interesting explanation to Mr. Gladstone. "I hope," Sir George began characteristically, "you will not disapprove of it."[13] "It would indeed be a happy thing," he observed shrewdly, "if the land question could once enter the stage of friendly discussion, but too good I fear to be possible. A conference to be practical implies some preliminary basis for agreement, and can this be hoped from people so foolish as the landlords, and so hotheaded as the tenants' advocates. At least however the landlords should have the sense to meet friendly overtures, & should see the importance of pinning Archbishop Walsh to proposals from which he may be tempted to back out; for it is

[12] *Ibid.*, September 1, 1887.
[13]. Gladstone Papers, British Museum, Add. MS, 44501.

no secret that the Nationalist leaders look with no sympathy on
his advances to the landlords, and are I am told determined to
thwart them should should they come to anything."

"Everything here," Errington, who was writing from the
West of Ireland, reassured Gladstone, "I am happy to say
seems to confirm the growing prospects in England of an early
settlement by you of Home Rule, and its urgency is more than
ever evident. What daily comes home to me here the most
however is the enormous and varied difficulty offered by the
land question, but at the same time the necessity of its
preliminary solution not only for the establishment but for the
subsequent successful working of Home Rule." "After all," he
noted in interesting Whig fashion, "much as we deplore the
policy of the landlords, it must be admitted that the struggle for
them is one for existence far more than it is for the tenants. The
latter, though not so well off as they were a few years ago, are
infinitely better off even in these bad years, than they were in
the good years before 15 years back. Whatever happens, I hope
your original plan will not be departed from, of making Home
Rule & Land Settlement dependent one on the other, & this not
least in the interest of the future success of Home Rule, the
greatest and most difficult problem with which perhaps your
name has ever been associated." "I remain here a week,"
Errington then reported, "& on my return to Dublin on my way
to England I hope to see Msgr Persico the Papal Envoy, of
whose mission we hear a great deal. What will be the result it is
hard to say." "The thing is certain," he observed perceptively of
Persico, "that he has the Italian gift of making the people whom
he sees on both sides believe that he is firmly convinced that
their views are the right ones: a useful gift I suppose for a
commissioner in search of information." "I have always
thought," Errington added interestingly in conclusion, "that
those who urged this mission on the Pope (people chiefly
unconnected with Ireland) made the greatest mistake, especially
from a religious point of view; for I can conceive no good it is
likely to do, while it is almost sure to greatly embitter feeling."

Meanwhile, after leaving Thurles, Monsignor Persico had
slowly made his way to Kerry *via* Cork.[14] On September 10, he
and Gualdi dined with the earl of Kenmare in Killarney. Shortly
after, one of the other guests, Samuel H. Butcher, professor of

---

[14] K, T. O'Callaghan to Kirby, September 5, 1887; John Coffey to Kirby,
September 12, 1887.

Greek at Edinburgh University, wrote his old friend Lord de Vesci, an Irish landlord, giving him an account of the dinner party. De Vesci, in turn, forwarded Butcher's letter to his old friend, Arthur Balfour, asking him to regard it as private.[15] "I have had my talk with Persico," Butcher wrote de Vesci on September 13, "who has now left Killarney."[16] "I am sorry you cant now meet him," Butcher explained, "as he still needs to be instructed, though I think facts, which rather amaze him, are beginning to penetrate the ecclesiastical barrier within which they are attempting to keep him. I sat near him at dinner at Killarney House on Saturday, & thanks to Lady Kenmare had an almost uninterrupted conversation with him. He strikes me as a thorough man of the world, most observant, but less inscrutable than one had expected. Making all allowances for his being an Italian & a diplomat I still think he spoke his real sentiments upon the main questions." "There was evident sincerity," Butcher noted significantly, "in the way in which not once but several times he declared that the land question is at the root of all others — that it *can* be solved if reasonable men will give their minds to it, & that no *pretext for Home R. will then be left.*"

"I gathered more from his private secretary (who is as cute as possible) than from himself," Butcher further informed de Vesci, "that he is horrified at the political part that is being played by the priests. As for the Plan of Campaign, he threw up his hands over it himself. He expressed a hope in modest & guarded language, but still a good hope, that his visit w[d] lead to some results. We talked about other subjects than Ireland — continental politics, American &c. I think it was *apropos* of Germany & Bismark that he observed with much emphasis: One thing I see & know better than I ever did before: — there is no country in the world where the Catholic Church has such freedom as it has in Ireland. This must be said for English Statesmanship." "Walsh's proposal," Butcher then alerted de Vesci, after his digression, "is clearly meant to impress Persico. And so far it has succeeded. Persico told me that he wrote to commend him for it & said it was the wish of his heart that the question s[d] be settled. Even before this interview, I had been strongly of opinion that the Irish landlords s[d] meet Walsh's

---

[15] B, 49821. De Vesci's letter to Balfour is dated July 15, 1887 — but this is an obvious error.
[16] *Ibid.*

proposal in the assumption that it is a *bonâ fide*. Probably nothing will come of it, but that's not the point. The landlords will put themselves in the wrong if they stand aloof & appear to be irreconcilable. Let them meet though its pretty certain that Dillon OBrien & Co. will wreck any conference after the first sitting." "I forgot to mention," Butcher then added in conclusion, "that I explained to Persico my position & that I was not a representative of landlords."

Monsignor Persico continued his visitation of the various Irish dioceses through the rest of September. Meanwhile, the representatives of the landlords continued to react coolly to Walsh's proposal for a Round Table Conference. At the end of September, however, Walsh still remained optimistic. "My 'Conference' project," he reported to Kirby on September 29, "is still attracting a good deal of attention"(K). "Many leading landlords," Walsh explained, "— such as Lord Monck, the Lord Lieutenant of Co. Dublin — are indignant with their 'delegates' for their folly in throwing cold water on my suggestion. A letter of mine written to a very prominent landlord, will be published by him with my permission in tomorrow's newspapers." In the next few days, however, when it became obvious that his proposal for a Conference had all but collapsed, Walsh naturally became more and more preoccupied with the effect this might have on Monsignor Persico who was about to return to Dublin to wind up his mission. In reply on October 4, for example, to a letter the same day from Cardinal Manning asking for news of the Monsignor, Walsh's preoccupation was self-evident. "The landlords," Walsh complained to Manning in the course of his reply, and referring to Persico, "will make a dead set on him, I am sure. But I have given him a test question for any landlord who comes to him to talk of the dishonesty of Irish tenants. Have any of your own tenants submitted the question of the fairness or unfairness of your rents to the decision of the Court? And what was the result?"(M) "For 99 out of every 100 landlords," Walsh assured the cardinal, "the only answer would be a confession that the decision went against them. My project of a Conference on the Land Question is sure to come to the front again. I have full information of what went on in the landlords councils. They made up their minds, that by holding back they would secure some further advance from me, meaning better terms for them in the end. Now that they see the mistake they made in tactics, they are looking about for the best means of repairing the mischief." "But I really fear," Walsh added grimly, "that they have lost their last chance of having the question settled in any way that will not bring about the ruin of their class."

Walsh's preoccupation with the Land Question and the effect it might have on Monsignor Persico and his report to Rome continued to deepen in the next few weeks. Several days after he had written Manning, Walsh learned, probably through his contact in the "landlords councils," that an Irish land agent on one of the Plan of Campaign estates had asserted, on the alleged authority of the promoters of the Plan, that though it was ostensibly designed to effect a reduction in rents, the Plan was really only "the first step in a general measure of confiscation of all the land of Ireland!" In explaining all this to John Dillon, one of the originators and chief promoters of the Plan, on October 8, Walsh pointed out that it was "just now of vital moment that I should be in a position to give my informant a definite assurance on the following points:

1. · that the real object of the "Plan of Campaign" as put in operation under responsible guidance on any estate does not differ from that which the author of the calumny in question describes as the ostensible object of this policy, namely, to obtain a reasonable reduction of the rents of the holdings, to which it is applied.
2. that the ulterior project of confiscating those holdings is a fiction without a particle of foundation. So that
3. it would be altogether superfluous to add a further repudiation of this fiction in reference to its extension to all the land of Ireland!(W).

All that it would take, Walsh assured Dillon in conclusion, to "sweep out of existence the ridiculous, but mischievous, hobgoblin that has been conjured up," was one word from him, for there was not "a landlord in Ireland who will hesitate in accepting your statement as absolutely conclusive in the case."

Dillon, who had obviously been previously consulted by Walsh, replied to this set piece two days later. He assured the archbishop on October 10 that there was no foundation for the statement mentioned in his letter as having been made by an Irish land agent(W). "It is of course impossible," Dillon went on to explain, "for me to tell what statements may or may not have been made to this gentleman — but I can answer confidently and I may say with some authority — as to what the "real objects" — aimed at by the policy of the Plan of Campaign were and are:

> the objects of that policy can be stated in a very few words — it was to place at the disposal of the tenant farmers of Ireland a method by wh. they could obtain just and necessary reductions in rent from landlords who refused to listen to reason. And by which they could protect themselves from the ruinous consequences of eviction for the non-payment of unjust and impossible rents(W).

"It was," Dillon added more significantly, "essentially a temporary policy — designed to meet a terrible emergency — to supply that protection to the Irish people which the ignorance and class prejudice of the London Parliament had refused to give them." After this indictment of the competence of Parliament, Dillon then challenged the gentlemen mentioned in Walsh's letter or anyone else in Ireland to point to a single instance in which a fair offer was made by a landlord to his tenants, and in which the Plan of Campaign was continued in the face of such an offer. "So far from this," Dillon declared flatly, "we have always been most anxious to promote settlements when it seemed possible to do so consistently with every just regard to the position and future of the tenants — and as a matter of fact — in the case of more than 3/4 of the estates in which the 'Plan' had been put in force, settlements have been arrived at — and the rents paid." In emphasizing his own conciliatory attitude, Dillon assured Walsh in conclusion that before the Plan had even been originated by his colleagues and himself in October, 1886, he had publicly stated in the September issue of the *Nineteenth Century,* if the general body of Irish landlords followed the example which had been set by a few of the large landowners in Ireland, he "would answer for it that the winter would be a peaceful one."

During the whole of October, Walsh worked very hard to revive his Round Table Conference, and the letter he elicited from Dillon was designed to reassure the landlords that the representatives of the tenants were indeed reasonable men. Walsh also undoubtedly realized that a general settlement of the Land Question, or even the opening of negotiations for such, especially while Monsignor Persico was still in Ireland, would not only be a very formidable demonstration of his own power and influence, but would certainly temper Monsignor Persico's upcoming report to Rome. The obstacles in the way of reviving the Conference, however, appeared to have been insuperable. Walsh not only had to deal with suspicious and stubborn landlords and their agents, but both Dillon and O'Brien were reluctant to come to terms on the part of the tenants. Walsh made serious efforts to persuade Dillon and O'Brien to soften their terms, but failed.[17] Why Dillon and O'Brien refused, of course, was that they felt that they now had the landlords at a serious disadvantage, and that by keeping up the pressure they would eventually force the great mass of them to reduce rents even further and eventually to sell out at a good purchase price to their tenants. But if Walsh found both the representatives of the landlords and the tenants difficult to deal with, he had even greater trouble with his good friend and colleague, the archbishop of Cashel. Croke, who obviously agreed with Dillon and O'Brien, was, in fact, adamant in his refusal to negotiate. "My views," he informed Walsh unequivocally on October 29, "about the 'Round Table' are unchanged"(W). "It cannot possibly succeed," he declared, "according to your original purpose, or indeed, to any appreciable extent; and its success just now would be little short of a National disaster." "De Freyne and such fellows," Croke further insisted, "who are perfectly hunted may, no doubt, grasp at it, because they would grasp at anything that would delay the day of doom for them; but the big men amongst the gang of Landowners, and who have yet a shot, or shots in the locker only ridicule the idea of conference and are not yet prepared to enter it, or give it any practical countenance whatever." "Besides," Croke added conclusively, "I know full well that the general feeling throughout the country is against it."

In the months following Persico's return to Dublin and his eventual departure from Ireland, rumor was perhaps never more rampant in Irish Church affairs, with the possible exception of the period which preceded Walsh's own

---

[17] W, Dillon to Walsh, Friday, October 21, 1887: "It gives me the greatest pleasure to accept your invitation for Wednesday . . . I hope it is unnecessary for me to renew my assurance to you — that nothing for a long time gave me greater pain than what occurred last night. I feared that it might appear to you that O'Brien & I were wanting in a desire to respect & defer to your views — wh I can assure you both of us feel in the strongest manner."

appointment to Dublin. Once again secrecy, maneuver, and intrigue were the order of the day, and almost everyone seems to have been affected by the rising tide of insecurity, which rumor is bound to produce. When Persico's secretary, Father Gualdi, returned to Rome, ostensibly for health reasons, and Persico decided to stay with his brethren, the Capuchins in Church Street, on his return to Dublin in early October, rather than as previously with Walsh, many eyes and ears not only began to see and hear more than usual, but tongues began to wag even more wildly than before. Sir Redvers Buller, for example, who had just resigned as Balfour's undersecretary, wrote his former chief a letter full of interesting, and generally inaccurate, "ifs" and "ands." "If it is true," Buller advised Balfour on October 20, referring to Cardinal Rampolla and an English Catholic bishop of Tory persuasion, "that the Cardinal Secretary has written to Bishop Patterson a letter intended for Lord Salisbury to see, suggesting that Mons–ʳ Persico should be left in Ireland, you probably will have heard of it ere this and I need not go into particulars on this chance, but I thought I would write one line to say that I hear that a definite proposition was made on the part of Mr. Gladstone to Mons–ʳ Persico in the presence of Walsh by John Dillon & some Englishmen that if the Pope would take Mr. Gladstone's side, Mr. G. would open diplomatic relations with the Holy See."[18]

"I am told," Buller continued his hearsay, "that the letter to Bishop Patterson is the result of this and it really means that Rome thought the offer too good to lose, but that they would rather take it from the Conservatives, than from the Socialists, but still if the former refuse, they are not adverse to being able to say — you refused us don't blame us if we try the gentiles." "I am also told," he further reported to Balfour, referring to the Jesuit College in Dublin, "that the management of the Stephen's Green College are going into debt at the rate of £2000 a year, and are desperate, they see no hope from the Gov–ᵗ and their only hope is from Gladstone. It is suggested to me that it would be an opportune time to try some offer." "I cannot say how this really is," Buller confessed, "as having left Dublin I have only information on one side but the appointment of a Dominican and an Austrian to teach ethics at Maynooth seems to show that Persico has done something, & it may be true that the opposition would see advantages in being bought at this

18 B, 49807.

moment." "Probably you know all this if true," he added in conclusion, "— or possibly it is not true, but I send it on the chance."

On the other hand, the news being received on the Nationalist side does not appear to be any more accurate. "If, as I learn from Rome (strictly confidential)," Monsignor Bernard O'Reilly, an ecclesiastical journalist and social gadfly, reported to Kirby from Dublin on October 24, "Monsignor Persico's report is to be unfavourable to the Irish cause, I fondly & firmly trust that such influences as your own will prevent the Holy Father from acting upon it"(K). "Were he to do so," O'Reilly noted with alarm, "God alone knows what fatal consequences might ensue." "I have, as you know," he assured Kirby, "done my very best to give his mission the most favorable interpretation." "But I must say," O'Reilly confessed in conclusion, "that from the beginning the way he went to work made me fear he was not the right man to send here. God save Ireland!" Even Cardinal Manning, perhaps the best informed person in either England or Ireland, was caught up in the contagion of rumor. "Reuter tells me," the cardinal informed Walsh on October 25, referring to the News Agency, "that Mgr Persico is in Rome."[19] "But," he noted shrewdly, "that is a reason for believing he is still in Dublin." "Still," Manning added, reflecting the general uncertainty, "I should like to know whether he is on the Tiber or the Liffey." "Abbate Gualdi's conclusions," the cardinal reassured Walsh, and referring to a visit made by Gualdi while passing through London on his return to Rome, "about Ireland were essentially sound. He read what I have written to the Holy Father and confirmed it from his own experience." "This gives me reason," he assured Walsh again in conclusion, "to believe that his witness in Rome will be in the main useful." The day before, meanwhile, in the midst of all the rumors, Errington wrote Smith a long, insightful, and generally well-informed report from his English country residence at Wiltshire.

"I saw Msgr. Persico in Dublin," Errington informed Smith on October 24, from Lackham near Chippenham, "just before I left, & was much pleased with his manner"(S). "He impresses everyone he sees," Errington observed cautiously, "with the idea that he agrees thoroughly with them; in this he is a

[19] Shane Leslie, *Henry Edward Manning* (London, 1921), p. 422.

thorough Italian. I am sure he is a conscientious man, & he has seen & heard a great deal; considering however that almost all his time he has lived amongst the advanced section of the Clergy & saw everything through them. I can hardly think an occasional half hour with moderate men can counter-balance such such [sic] constant intercourse, & that even unconsciously his impressions must reflect what he has heard so constantly impressed on him. My conversation with him was very interesting."

> I said I came merely to compliment & not to trouble him with news of which he had already heard so much. He was very anxious to impress on me how careful he had been to hear all sides; I said that the opinion of all who had the honour of seeing him were unanimous as to his patience and the courtesy & attention with which he listened to everyone. We spoke about diplomatic relations: I gave him my American interview to read, for I gathered that he had heard many stories against me. On my 2nd visit to him (at his request the 1st having only lasted a few minutes) he told me he had read the interview with much pleasure, and he expressed himself *strongly in favour* of diplomatic relations; we talked of India & Goa, & I explained how matters stood with regard to me in that question: & I informed him (which he did not know) that Govt intend to send a *Complimentary* return Mission to the Pope(S).

"I suppose," Errington added, referring of course to the compliment paid to the queen by the pope in sending Monsignor Ruffo Scilla, "they will send the Duke of Norfolk."

"He then spoke of & asked me," Errington continued, "about Ireland; I said there was only one point I wished to notice viz. that I felt we should not express any opinions as to the *objects* of the present agitation; all I regretted were the unchristian means into which its supporters were drawn & that this seemed to be a great danger for the future of the Irish church:

> I added that so long as the struggle against England was as in O'Connell's days for *religious* liberty no one could blame clergy for taking part, on the contrary their action was useful & necessary, but now absolute religious equality had been obtained, & the present was purely political with a strong revolutionary tinge. He asked me what would be the effect if

Clergy withdrew from politics now; I replied that it would be an advantage to their spiritual position in the future; that the real danger of the Clergy losing their legitimate influence came much more from their following the popular to extremes inconsistent with their clerical character, than by withdrawing from prominent action in an agitation which everyone saw had nothing in common with religion, but on the contrary like all revolution would one day turn against the Church: I then quoted Cardinal Cullen's strong words about Home Rule(S).

"I invited Msgr P. to come here on his way to London to meet Dr. Clifford": Errington added, referring to the local Roman Catholic diocesan, the bishop of Clifton, "he said he would if he could, but of course he will not." "Things are going," Errington concluded, "from bad to worse in Ireland."

Smith, meanwhile, had written Errington that the situation in Rome as far as the Persico mission was concerned, was not very encouraging. "What you tell me," Errington noted dryly on November 6, "of the result of his Mission does not surprise me . . . and I have said from the beginning that the busybodies who induced the Pope to send a Visitor had much to answer for"(S). "I enclose you now," he continued, "a remarkable letter in strict confidence; please return it to me. It is from Mr. Dease late M.P. for Queens Co., a great friend of mine, Cousin to Lord Kenmare &c &c. He is a Commissioner of Education, & he supplied full reports to Msgr. P. of the many cases of Boycotting in Schools, also an admirable Memorandum on the Clerical & religious aspect of the agitation in Ireland. The letter enclosed gives the result of his interview; let me know what you think of [it]." "In the face of all this," he then asked Smith, "is it possible Msgr P. will report in that things are in a satisfactory condition as regards the position of the Clergy in politics?" After discussing the pros and cons of his proposed visit to Rome for the pope's Jubilee, Errington finally turned to the subject of parliamentary politics. "It is very hard to say," he noted, "how Electoral matters are going here. The Gladstonians say the Country is turning round in their favour, others deny it. Balfour (Lord Salisbury's nephew) is showing ability in Ireland." "Pray let me know soon," Errington added in conclusion, "what you hear from M^{sg} Gualdi & others about Ireland & the Mission."

Whichever way the country was turning politically, Errington was certainly correct in his estimate of Arthur

Balfour. In his eight months in office, Balfour had slowly but surely won the confidence of his colleagues in the cabinet, and put some nerve into the Irish administration. By November, 1887, he was no longer being derisively dismissed by the Irish Party in the House as "Fanny," but was instead being bitterly denounced by them and their friends in the country as "Bloody Balfour." The Coercion Act had been passed in July, and under its terms the National League was "proclaimed" as a dangerous association on August 19, the day after the new Land Bill became law.[20] The government could now selectively suppress the most troublesome branches, especially in Kerry and Clare, and still escape the charge of political suppression. This tactic was, of course, the result of the need by the government to conciliate the civil libertarian sensibilities of their Liberal Unionist allies on whose votes they depended for survival. Balfour also insisted that no distinction would be made between ordinary and "political" prisoners, and all prisoners would be obliged to wear prison garb. In November, William O'Brien was convicted and sentenced under the Crimes Act to serve a year in Tullamore Jail, the first of twenty-four Irish members and some half-dozen priests, who would serve prison terms over the next two years.

Indeed, the question of prosecuting priests was discussed at the highest level of government. The occasion for the discussion was that a priest of the Killaloe diocese, which included chiefly County Clare, had rendered himself liable to prosecution under the terms of the Crimes Act. In writing to his uncle on October 27 from Dublin, Balfour wanted to know whether before prosecuting, it would be wise to write to the bishop of the offending priest and whether the enclosed draft of the intended letter to the Bishop was appropriate(Sy). "The objections," he pointed out to Salisbury, "are obvious — (1) you cannot be quite sure where a correspondence will land you (2) it may be interpreted as indicating that we are *AFRAID* to prosecute Priests. On the other hand, it puts the Bishop very much in the wrong if he does nothing or practically nothing: it shows also that we desire no insult to the R.C. Church: — and it might be appreciated at *Rome*." "Let me know," he asked his uncle, "what you think of it." Salisbury replied the next day, Friday, October 28, from London by cipher telegram. "Have

---

[20] B, 49826, Balfour to Londonderry, August 12, 1887.

just heard from Smith," he advised Balfour, referring to W. H. Smith, first lord of the treasury and leader of the House of Commons, "who is rather against consulting the Bishop. If you have taken no step in that direction you had better keep the question for Cabinet on Thursday"(Sy).

Balfour was, however, not to be so easily put down, for he replied to his uncle's telegram that same day with a most revealing and characteristic letter. "W.H.'s views hardly seem to me," Balfour complained to Salisbury on October 28, "to bear on the question"(Sy). "I am so far from taking objection to them," he explained, obviously referring to the view that no negotiations should be entered into by the government with the Irish Bishops on any question, "that I have always regarded the opinion which they somewhat clumsily embody as the corner stone of our ecclesiastical policy. But the real point is *what* action are we to take, subject to this limiting principle?—" "The English R.C.'s," Balfour pointed out, "practically suggest in the Memo, which I forwarded to you

(1) No direct dealings with Walsh
(2) Direct dealings with Rome
(3) No direct bribe to the Irish Catholics to alter their way of going on
(4) A direct bribe to Rome (in the shape of a Catholic College, endowed by the State, & governed in the first instance by the nominees of the State) to be given when, by the efforts of the Holy Father, the Irish Priesthood shall have learnt the ten Commandments.—(Sy)

"What we shall have to decide," Balfour concluded with inexorable logic, "is how far we mean to adopt this policy, and to the solution of this question, Smith has not materially contributed!"

When Balfour crossed over to London for the cabinet meeting, however, he found that he would have to compromise. "We decided in Cabinet," he explained to his new undersecretary, Sir Joseph West Ridgeway, on November 6, "*not* to write a special letter to the Bishop before prosecuting a priest, but to write a general letter of warning to the Bishop saying that we had reason to believe that some of his priests were breaking the law, and expressing a hope that he would put a stop to such a practice. After which we would go straight at any priest against whom we could get a case. I will draft a

letter of the kind I mean."[21] Three days later Balfour wrote
Ridgeway again, enclosing the promised letter. "The only
objection I see to sending the letter," Balfour explained on
November 9, "is that it may provoke that very conflict with the
Church which we desire to avoid, and that it may compel the
Bishop or Bishops to issue a kind of manifesto against the
Government practically encouraging their Clergy to resist the
law."[22] "If this result were likely to occur," he added, "it would
probably be the better course simply to go ahead and prosecute
Priests like anybody else in cases where they render themselves
liable." "Just think over the matter," Balfour advised, and
referring to Peter O'Brien, the Irish solicitor general, "and
consult with O'Brien and other persons who know more about
the temper of the Catholic Hierarchy than I do before putting
the letter in the post."

But once again Balfour had to modify his attempt to serve
notice on the bishops of offending priests as Ridgeway opted
not to send the letter. Nearly three weeks later, on November
27, Balfour lamely had to inform his uncle that the plan finally
adopted was to have the divisional magistrate write a private
letter to Monsignor Persico complaining of the priest in
question(Sy). Why Balfour was thus forced to dilute his good
intentions even further was that his subordinates in the Irish
administration were reluctant to take any strong action against
the clergy. "It is a curious fact," Balfour further explained to his
uncle, "that it is always the R.C.'s among those whom I have
talked to who wish to prosecute: the Protestants are all afraid."
"The only point," Balfour then confessed, somewhat naively,
"about which I am at all nervous is the Priest prosecution
business, is that it *may* tend to heal the existing breach between
the Clerical & Fenian element." "But on the whole," he
concluded firmly, "I am of the opinion that we had no choice."
The day before he wrote this letter to Salisbury, Balfour, who
was again in London, had also had a long talk with the duke of
Norfolk about the problem of prosecuting Irish priests. The
duke, who had finally secured Salisbury's approval for a
reciprocal mission to Rome to congratulate the pope on his
Jubilee, and who was just about to leave for Rome as the head
of that mission, asked Balfour to supply him with the necessary
information about the troublesome priests which he could

---

[21] B, 49808.
[22] B, 49826.

present to the pope. Balfour agreed and immediately instructed Ridgeway to prepare the information. In assuring Balfour on November 27, from Dublin, that the material was being collected, Ridgeway also noted that Persico sent the divisional magistrate an evasive reply to their letter, and that Father Matthew Ryan, Croke's "Campaigner," would be soon tried again.[23]

Balfour's ultimate goal, of course, was to kill Home Rule. His immediate objective, however, was to break up that consolidation of power that had so recently made Parnell and his Party masters in Ireland. Since the cornerstone of that Parnellite *de facto* power was the Clerical-Nationalist alliance, Balfour was determined to undermine it. He intended, therefore, to bring as much pressure to bear as he could legally muster as Her Majesty's chief secretary on those priests and politicians who supported the alliance. To do this he proposed to enforce all the rigors of the Crimes Act, making no distinction between priests and politicians, or between them and common criminals. Balfour was prepared moreover, not only to use the legal remedies at his disposal, but also those extra-legal means, such as the influence of the duke of Norfolk and his friends at Rome, to force the clergy to forsake the alliance, or at least assume a more modest posture in Irish politics. By raising the legal pressure to an appropriate level, Balfour hoped that he could so weaken the Clerical-Nationalist alliance that when the Roman wedge was finally driven, the effect would be to split the alliance. The wedge, of course, was to be a condemnation of the Plan of Campaign, by which the pope was to teach the Irish clergy the meaning of the "ten Commandments," and for which the pope's reward would be an Irish Catholic College, or perhaps even diplomatic relations. Such a condemnation would certainly place a severe strain on the Irish clergy's Roman, as against its Nationalist allegiance, as well as sow the seeds of suspicion between them and their lay allies if they temporized in their Irish allegiance. Even if the alliance did not actually break up under the combined British and Roman pressure, Balfour could at least expect that it might be so impaired that his efforts to liquidate Parnellite *de facto* power and control would be made that much easier.

---

[23] B, 49809.

Balfour's policy of coercion was obviously taking a very heavy emotional toll of the Irish clergy in general, and of Walsh and Croke in particular. The clergy, both high and low, were especially fearful that they would not be able to contain the violence of their people in the face of Balfour's provocative policy, and that the whole constitutional agitation would be thrown into the hands of the Fenians. In their attempt to preserve the Clerical-Nationalist alliance, Walsh and Croke, however, were not only being generally pressed hard by both the government and by the Fenians, but they were also threatened with internal disruption on the clerical side by the patent disloyalty of several of their episcopal colleagues. On top of all this, there was Monsignor Persico's impending report to be considered, as well as the action Rome would presumably take in the light of that report. Moreover, the fact that the duke of Norfolk was going to Rome as the official representative of Her Majesty's government at the pope's Jubilee could not have contributed much to either Walsh or Croke's peace of mind.

"The strain on the Country," reported the bishop of Cork, T. A. O'Callaghan to Kirby on November 5, "at the present moment is simply terrible but it is looked on as necessary for experience has taught us there is no other way to reach a better state of government"(K). "We fear the struggle will be long," he explained, "as the present Government has thrown aside all restraint and excited a determined opposition which no coercion can suppress." Several days later, Kirby received another letter in the same vein from one of his former students, Patrick O'Neill, the parish priest of Rostrevor. O'Neill had little doubt, in fact, who was on the side of law and order in Ireland. "I sincerely hope," he informed Kirby on November 7, "our people will continue quiet during these three final months of winter until Parliament meets. Balfour's object is to provoke the people into acts of violence, that he may have some pretext for shooting them"(K). "He justifies the massacre at Mitchelstown," O'Neill further explained, referring to an incident on September 8 in which the police had fired on the crowd, killing three and wounding two, "and encourages the police to do so again. The imprisonment of O'Brien without a fair trial, and his cruel treatment in prison has created the strongest feeling of indignation in Ireland, but still I hope the people will be quiet. There is scarcely any crime in Ireland save those committed by the paid agents of Balfour." "The farmers

of Ireland," O'Neill finally reported, and going to the heart of
the matter, "will have a very hard winter. The price of every
kind of produce and of cattle is now so low that the farmers will
not be able to pay their rents, and the rack-renting landlords are
bent on exterminating them."

Meanwhile, Walsh was faced with a perplexing situation. He
was of course expected to be in Rome to head the Irish
delegation in celebrating the pope's Jubilee, but Monsignor
Persico, it seems, was to remain in Ireland to finish his report,
and given the state of his health that would take even longer
than had been anticipated. To leave Ireland, therefore,
especially when Balfour's policy of coercion seemed to be on a
deadly collision course with what were soon to be the inevitable
consequences of a rapidly deteriorating agrarian situation, and
allow Persico to witness such a catastrophe without proper
safeguards, might perhaps result in an even greater disaster. In
an obvious effort to settle his own itinerary, Walsh wrote Croke
asking him what his intentions were with regard to his visiting
Rome for the Jubilee celebration. "I have nearly made up my
mind," Croke replied on November 5, "*not* to go to Rome. I
don't see what I want there. Every visit I made to Rome for a
series of years, has been more or less, a painful one"(W). "The
contemplated one may not be painful," he admitted, "but it
would be perplexing in diverse ways, and in so far, unpleasant.
Still the final decision has not as yet been taken." "I have asked
H.E.," Croke then changed the subject, referring to Persico, "to
come here for a few days. I wrote him yesterday, to that effect.
I do not think he will come" "As Cardinal Manning said to me
in our last interview," Croke explained interestingly, "talking of
his Excellency's possible visit to his Eminence, when the Envoy
would be on his way to Rome, and passing through London, 'he
may not visit me as he may think me *a very wicked person.*' "
"So be it," Croke commented somewhat petulantly, "I shan't
cry. But I should like to show him our schools and colleges in
operation, as they now are."

"I have had," Croke finally confided, turning to what was
depressing him, "a deal to think of since I wrote you last. I have
passed through a financial crisis to begin with. Then the Dean,
whom I liked and prized greatly, is dying. Further, Rev. M.
Ryan, the 'General' attended a *public* meeting in Limerick
without leave. So +E.T. wrote me."[24] "Apropos of +E.T.,"

---

[24] For a more "technical" discussion of this matter, see W, Croke to Walsh,

Croke then noted, "see what an insidious and, indeed, thoroughly dishonest speech he made, yesterday in Limerick, in reference to Educational Affairs. One would imagine that Religious Education was neglected in Ireland, and that our youth, in consequence, were going straight to perdition. His trickery and treachery will soon be shown up or I am very much mistaken."[25] "I have not time — or rather space — to speak of the G.A.A.," Croke apologized, coming finally to the end of his tribulations, and referring to the Gaelic Athletic Association, "but there is a deal to be said on that matter." "I shall retire," he concluded despondingly, "very soon anyhow."

In his reply to Croke's letter, Walsh obviously explained that Persico was not indeed well, and consequently that it was unlikely that he would accept Croke's invitation.[26] Walsh also wrote Manning informing the cardinal of the envoy's indisposition. "Monsignor Persico," Walsh reported on November 9, "is still in Dublin, and your Eminence will regret to hear that he is now confined to bed. I trust the illness is in no way a serious one. But when I saw him, yesterday evening, he seemed very low indeed. This mornings account is not a very favourable one." "The confusion in our public affairs is," Walsh then added, "as was fully foreseen, is increasing from day to day. Mr. Wm. O'Brien has practically beaten the administration on the question of his treatment in prison. Mr. Balfour and his subordinates seem incapable of doing anything without bungling. But it is hard to see how an end can be put to their mischievous policy. Mgr. Persico has great faith in Parliament. He frequently deplores that it is not now in Session. But so long as the Liberal Unionists feel that a General Election must result in their exclusion from Parliament, they will of course vote with the Ministry on every critical question. I cannot see any ground for hope except in one direction." "Lord Hartington," Walsh noted in conclusion, referring to the leader of the Whig section of the Liberal Unionists, "it seems to me, is keeping a door open. He has more than once declared that he feels bound to give the present policy a fair trial. It is always open to him to say that the trial has been full enough and that the result has been a disastrous failure."

November 9, 1887, in which Croke explains the Provincial regulations governing the attendance of priests at political meetings.

[25] See *Freeman's Journal,* November 5, 1887, for O'Dwyer's speech on the distribution of prizes at Sacred Heart College, Limerick.

[26] See W for Croke's reply to Walsh, November 9, 1887.

Several days later Croke again wrote Walsh reporting that he and the Gaelic Athletic Association, of which he had been a founder, had come to a parting of the ways. "Their meeting here was disgraceful," Croke explained on November 11, "It was packed to the throat with Fenian leaders and emissaries. The Chairman is a notorious propagandist. The Killaloe priests present made a bold, but not a very effective stand."[27] "Freeman prints my few lines dreadfully," Croke complained to Walsh, "Things are not going on right, I'm afraid, in that office." "I have just written," he added, referring to the Editor of the *Freeman,* "to Byrne to say so." "I wonder," concluded Croke politely, "how is the Monsignor." Persico had, in fact, recovered to the extent that he was ready to leave Dublin for Cork where he would write his report for Rome in the Capuchin convent there. When Walsh wrote Kirby to explain that the envoy's mission was coming to a close, he took advantage of the opportunity to express in no uncertain terms what he thought would be the result of the government's policy of coercion.

"I have a farewell dinner this evening," Walsh informed Kirby of Persico, on November 17, "in his honour, as it may be some time before he dines in Dublin again. H.E. will meet a strange assemblage. We shall have a number of the principal Catholic judges, including the Lord Chief Justice, and the Chief Baron, and with them the (Nationalist) members of the City including of course the Lord Mayor"(N). "Last week," Walsh explained, and referring respectively to Christopher Palles and T. D. Sullivan, "the Chief Baron delivered an elaborate judgement deciding a critical law point against the Lord Mayor — the effect of which, if other points cannot be successfully raised, as we trust they can, will be to send the poor Lord Mayor to prison to be on a 'plank' bed, and to live as well as he can on bread and water for punishment if he refuses, as of course he must refuse, to wear the clothes of a common criminal."

"There is very little room for doubt," Walsh further maintained, drawing the moral from his parable for Kirby, "that the present Government are pursuing a deliberate plan to drive the young men of the country back into the old lines of

---

[27] W, November 11, 1887. See also Croke to Walsh, November 23, 1887, for an interesting discussion of Croke's role in attempting to restructure the G.A.A. to check the Fenian influence in that organization.

secret societies. By making all agitation or political combination illegal, they break down the strong position we were able to take up against the secret organization system. It has an attraction for enthusiastic young men. And they are now able to say to their more moderate companions, who were determined to give Parliamentary action another good fair trial, that there is no longer any difference of legality between one line and the other. When the constitutional ranks are well broken, and the ranks of the secret organization well filled, the government can make a swoop by means of the informers of whom it is said they have simply an army now in their pay." "At all events," Walsh concluded, "it cannot be said that the Irish Bishops neglected to sound a warning note in time."

Several days later Walsh learned that Father Gualdi had died soon after his return to Rome, and immediately informed Persico who had proceeded to Cork to write his report. "I have received your Grace's letter," Persico acknowledged on November 23, "conveying the mournful news of good Father Gualdi's death. I must confess that, though half prepared for it, the news has terribly affected me. He was indeed a good priest, and an able official, and the Propaganda has lost one of its best officers. My own health is more or less the same."[28] "Your Grace," he advised Walsh, in reference to his own report, "need not write a memorandum on Home Rule or on the Land Question. A memorandum on the Education Question will be sufficient." Walsh, who had finally decided to set out for Rome in early December, obviously worked at fever pitch on the proposed memorandum, and kept Persico informed as to his progress. "I am interested to hear," Persico wrote Walsh again on November 29, "that your Grace has reached page 40 of the Memorandum on Education. It will be a volume in folio."[29] "This is not surprising," he added admiringly, "You can write so easily."

Meanwhile, Walsh had written Kirby advising him that he planned to leave Dublin within the week and would arrive in Rome shortly after Christmas. "Great difficulties," Walsh reported on November 28, adding yet another aggravating problem to his already long list, "have arisen about the new *Chiesa di S. Patrizio*. It seems there are legal difficulties in the way of its being built except it be made the private property of

[28] *Walsh,* pp. 300-01.
[29] *Ibid.,* p. 301.

the Augustinians. The Irish Bishops cannot recognise such a Church as a National Church. So we have to stand aside"(K). "This is indeed a pity," Walsh concluded, somewhat ironically, "but it is only another illustration of the intolerable situation created for the Catholic world by the Italian occupation of Rome." Walsh had also written Croke on the subject of the Church of St. Patrick in Rome, and enclosed a letter from the prior of the Augustinian convent there, Father Glynn. Croke, who after having made his decision not to go to Rome, seemed to have recovered from his depression and replied to Walsh's letter in characteristic fashion.

"Our position is clear," Croke declared on November 29, "— We are not going to build a Church for the Augustinians, but we are going to build a Church for Ireland, to be 'run,' if it must be by Augustinians"(W). "As I write," he reported, "bands and banners are passing here, as we are to hold immediately a Monster Meeting in the Square (a dirty spot) at which our English Cousins, six in number, are to speak. I entertain the gang afterwards at dinner in the Palace." "Our Dean died yesterday," Croke further reported, "He was a worthy man, and a fine Pastor. I wrote a few lines on him in this days Freeman. I said 'earnest in his Sunday discourses' -- they made me say '*learned* in his discourses' — which he was not — and so much the better." "When are you off," he then asked Walsh, and noted, "I wrote my ultimatum to Glynn. It is to the effect that I cannot go to Rome, and cannot therefore, preach there. I should, if I went be hobnobbing with, and paying court to, certain dignitaries who handled me roughly when I was alone, and supposed to be vulnerable. This would not suit my democratic turn of mind, and so, I stop at home. I will, I suppose, send my money, *£1000,* by you to his Holiness." "I must stop," he concluded abruptly, "Clerics approaching [word illegible] all round."

Walsh was unable to leave Dublin until Monday, December 5, and, as he explained to Manning in a note from the Charing Cross Hotel, his arrangements were wretched and all out of order. "It puts me about very much," Walsh explained, "to be in London without being able to call on your Eminence"(M). "I had counted," he then added, "on being in London last Saturday and seeing your Eminence to-day. But, a rather heavy work that I undertook for Monsignor Persico — a Memorandum on the *whole* Education Question — kept me

144   THE ROMAN CATHOLIC CHURCH

back." "I was unable to leave Dublin until this morning,"
Walsh concluded apologetically, "I did not like to pass through
at all events without writing to your Eminence." In all the hurry
and last minute preparations, Walsh's secretary also neglected
to forward a copy of the Memorandum to Persico. "There must
be some misunderstanding," Persico wrote Walsh, on
December 5, "about your Memorandum on the Education
Question which I have not yet received. As I told you, I had
been charged to ask the opinion of every bishop — which I did.
Though I remember very well the substance of your Grace's
views, I should like to have your opinion in your own words."[30]
"In the Report I have to send to Rome," he advised Walsh, "I
must write a special chapter on the Education Question." The
oversight was soon remedied, however, and the envoy thanked
Walsh for the Memorandum, which extended to 79 folio
pages.[31]

Even before Walsh had set out for Rome, the information
which Kirby had been receiving about the general economic
and political state of Ireland was not encouraging. The
archbishop of Tuam, John MacEvilly and the coadjutor to the
bishop of Waterford, Pierce Power, for example, neither of
whom could certainly be called an "advanced" man in politics,
both reported that the country was in a deplorable state. "We
have," MacEvilly informed Kirby on November 27, "rather
troubled times for our poor country. I fear the Tory governmt.
are bent on crushing everything like free opinion, even in
defence of our downtrodden tenants. But of course, our
bounden duty is to inculcate patience and above all the
avoidance of all outrage, which would throw us back for half a
century"(K). "The times are very depressed," he further
explained, "I myself am trustee for charity money, and cannot
get the rent. They have not it to pay as the prices of all
commodities are so low." Two days later, from the other end of
Ireland, the coadjutor to the bishop of Waterford also wrote
Kirby independently confirming the report of the archbishop of
Tuam. In explaining to Kirby on November 29, that he had had
a recent visit from Monsignor Persico, and that he had
answered him frankly in everything, Power added that — "Our
poor country is indeed in a deplorable state at present. Poverty

[30] *Ibid.*
[31] *Ibid.*, p. 302, Persico to Walsh, December 17, 1887. See also for contents of
Memorandum by author.

surrounds on all sides. All agricultural produce is lower in the markets at present by 50 percent compared with 2 years ago. There is no circulation of money"(K). "However," he observed more hopefully, "there is no fear of scarcity or want among the poor as the potato is all that could be desired." Power then concluded by remarking that since Waterford had sent £1200 to Rome when the Jubilee was announced the previous year, they thought it best to wait a year before making another collection.

Several days later and two days before Walsh left Dublin, Daniel McGettigan, archbishop of Armagh, who had been ailing for some time, died, and was immediately succeeded by his coadjutor, Michael Logue. "The good Primate of Armagh," the bishop of Down and Connor, Patrick McAlister, reported to Kirby on December 4, "passed to his reward yesterday"(K). "He was a man," McAlister noted, unconsciously writing the primate's epitaph, "with a *big & good heart* whom everybody revered & loved." "The funeral," the new archbishop of Armagh, Michael Logue, informed Kirby on December 10, "was a wonderful display"(K). "The Protestants even," Logue reported in wonder, "came in crowds to the Cathedral, and the Protestant Primate walked bare headed in the procession after the Bishops. There is universal mourning among all classes and all creeds." "The poor Primate," Logue explained, "was his own executor. He left three small legacies to the poor schools of three Convents, a small annuity to his old servant and his books, furniture and pontificals to me." "This was his whole will," Logue concluded somberly, "and whether there be means to meet even these little legacies is not certain."

The succession of Logue in Armagh tended to create another focus for power, even if as yet only formal, in the Irish Church. As primate of *All* Ireland, the archbishop of Armagh took precedence over the archbishop of Dublin as the primate of Ireland. Since McGettigan had not been well in recent years, Walsh by right had presided at episcopal meetings in his absence because Logue was still technically only the primate's coadjutor. In all future meetings, however, Logue would now take the chair, and while he was a Nationalist, he was certainly not as "advanced" as Walsh and Croke. Further, while Logue was, at one and the same time, curiously enough, as pliable and as dextrous as he was stubborn and shrewd, he was not to be compared with his more "advanced" brethren either in intelligence or in administrative capacity. In any case, Walsh, who was slowly making his way to Rome to face what would be the supreme crisis of his episcopal career, certainly had more substantial and pressing problems to ponder on than the recent succession of Logue to the primacy.

V. Roman Interlude

December, 1887 - April, 1888

One of the problems which must have given Walsh very serious cause for reflection on his way to Rome was the implicit threat in the recent announcement that the duke of Norfolk would officially convey the queen's congratulations to the pope on the occasion of the fiftieth anniversary of his priesthood. Since Lord Salisbury, however, insisted that the compliment by the queen was to be paid to the pope personally and privately, the protocol involved in the duke's special mission became incredibly complicated. The duke, for example, was instructed to leave Rome before December 31, the day appointed for the public celebration of the pope's Jubilee, in order to avoid the embarrassment of having Her Majesty's envoy participate in the scheduled religious ceremonies. Norfolk, however, was not only his Protestant Sovereign's subject and envoy, but he was also the top-ranking English Catholic layman, which further complicated matters. "I wish to join," the duke formally requested the Foreign Office on November 8, "the Deputation of Catholics of Great Britain which will be received by the Pope on January 10"(Sy). "Would Lord Salisbury," Norfolk inquired, "wish me to leave Rome between my official visit and this deputation." "Or could I remain," he suggested, "in Rome from the one to the other and during that time carry out my instructions from Balfour."

"In reply to your queries of yesterday," Eric Barrington, undersecretary at the foreign office, informed Norfolk on November 9, "Lord Salisbury desires me to say that he would certainly wish you to return to this country at the conclusion of yr. Mission rather than that you sh^d remain at Rome for the arrival of the British Catholic Delegation. As regards your instructions from the Chief Secretary, they will only be verbal, & it will probably be advisable that they sh^d be carried out on the occasion of your first visit but you will hear again on this

point"(Sy). "Lord Salisbury," Barrington then reported to the
duke, "will be happy to provide you as is usual with an official
Sec[y] from the staff of the F.O. or the Diplomatic Service. You
may take anyone else you like besides, but the Treasury object
to a large suite unless they pay their own expenses." "Lord
Salisbury wishes to know," Barrington finally inquired in
conclusion, "whether you think it wd. be an advantage for yr.
Sec[y] to be a Roman Catholic." In fact, Le Marchant Gosselin,
a secretary at the British Embassy in Brussels, and a Roman
Catholic, was assigned to the duke's mission.

The preliminaries to the departure of Norfolk would have
been ludicrous if the whole situation was not so very serious.
"The Queen," Sir Henry Ponsonby, her private secretary,
informed Barrington on December 1, from Windsor Castle,
"says the Duke of Norfolk cannot go at this moment"(Sy).
"You say he is going," Ponsonby observed good naturedly, and
knowing Her Majesty, "I await further developments." "After
what Lord Salisbury told me," Ponsonby noted, "I went to the
Library and asked for the most valuable book there. This was a
Psalter worth £10,000, so I asked for some smaller work." The
Librarian, Ponsonby then pointed out, "suggested Gould's
Birds of Europe — but wont let his copy go — & can get me
another for £140. It is the most important book published in
the Queen's reign — and being ornithological — is neither
political nor religious." "But the Queen," he added, "will not
have it. She says it w[d] be absurd to give the Pope a book on
birds. And she suggests a piece of tapestry from the Windsor
works." "I rushed there last night," he explained, "& have got 5
pieces upstairs for her to choose from." "I trust," Ponsonby
concluded, and still obviously in good humor, "that 'Summer
with Nymphs battling' will not be chosen."

In his reply the next day, Barrington reminded Ponsonby
that a date must not only be settled for Norfolk's formal
audience with the queen before his departure, but that a letter
from the queen to be presented by the duke to the pope was in
order. In thanking Barrington on December 5, for stirring them
up about the duke's audience, Ponsonby explained that the
problem was that the queen was not very keen about it(Sy).
There was also a question in Her Majesty's mind, it seems, about
how the pope should be addressed in the letter to be presented
by the duke. Ponsonby readily agreed that the expression
"Holy Father" implied "a sort of subserviency," but noted that

the queen also objected to the alternative formula, "Eminent Sir" as being inappropriate. At this point, the whole matter of the duke's departure was further complicated by the death of his uncle, Lord Lyons, the British ambassador in Paris. The duke reported to Barrington on December 5, that the funeral would be held on the 10th, and that he could leave for Rome as soon after that as was compatible with being received by the queen(Sy). In forwarding the duke's letter to Salisbury that same day, Barrington explained how complicated the situation was becoming(Sy). Even if the queen received the duke on the 12th, he could not arrive in Rome before the 15th, and since the 16th and 17th were Ember days and probably unsuitable for an audience with the pope, he would only have the week of the 18th to complete his business before the Jubilee commenced. "There are," Barrington suggested further, "two other alternatives: either to defer his departure until the end of January in which case he w^d excuse himself from accompanying the English Catholic Deputation, or to go out as soon as possible in order to be formally received as Envoy, and do his business secretly when he returns to Rome as a private individual." "From Ponsonby's letter," Barrington informed Salisbury in conclusion, "it is evident that the Queen has not understood your objections to the Duke's being at Rome during the Jubilee."

The duke did indeed have his interview with the queen the following week and immediately set out for Rome. He was also informed by Ponsonby that the queen had finally decided to present the pope with a plate copy of an old silver piece at Windsor, and that it would be sent on after him as soon as it was ready.[1] Before he left, however, Balfour wrote the duke to keep him informed about the latest developments in Ireland. "I hear that Persico's line at present," Balfour explained to Norfolk from Dublin, "is to say that the Crimes Act is a mistake — but that as it is the law of the land the Holy See will not countenance any disobedience to it. In his report he is going to say that the Land Question and the Education Question are at the bottom of the Irish difficulty, and he is going to lay before the Pope his own solution of the latter. I do not know whether all this is true, but I have it from a good source; and it seems to me intrinsically probable, and in any case you ought to know of

---

[1] Sy, Ponsonby to Barrington, December 14, 1887.

it."[2] "In your conversation with me," he reminded the duke, "you seemed to think that the Pope would not rate at any very high value a liberal Education project. Persico's attitude, if I am rightly informed is not quite the same." "By the way," Balfour inquired, "are you aware (I should think not, for few Englishmen are) of the Extraordinary Educational system which exists in Ireland, under which practically the whole cost of Education is borne by the State, while the chief local management is in the hands of the priests?" "The central Government, which provides the funds," Balfour wryly pointed out to the duke, "is rewarded by finding the National School Teachers among its most strenuous opponents, and most assuredly the experience derived from the working of the Elementary Education and the Maynooth scheme is of evil augury for the future of any new Educational project. *Absit omen.*"

The duke and his entourage arrived in Rome on December 16, and were received by the pope the following day. "Our audience came off to-day," Gosselin reported privately to Barrington on December 17, "— and all went very satisfactorily — you will in due time receive a long account of it w[h] the Duke is now composing, so I need not enter into details"(Sy). "It struck me," Gosselin added, "that we looked like 4 19 Century blots in a medieval picture — surrounded as we were by Swiss guards & chamberlains in Henri IV costumes, & a lot of English & Maltese Monsignori in purple & lace." "H.H. was very pleased at the Mission," he informed Barrington, "& said (so I heard on entering the Throne Rome) 'questa é una gran giornata.'*"[3] "Il duca wants to know," Gosselin then inquired, and referring to the two other members of the Duke's suite ". . . whether the F.O. have any objection to Ross & Hastings remaining on here after his departure from Rome?" "I think that Hastings," he then noted interestingly, "will probably end by returning with us, but Ross & his wife want to stay on in Italy." Gosselin also asked Barrington "what is to be done if the queen's present is to be indefinitely postponed?" "If the present," he posed, after explaining that he and the duke planned to leave Rome the day after Christmas, "has not arrived by that time, are we to wait for it?" "The Pope said the

<hr />

[2] B, 49821, no date.
[3] Asterisk was Gosselin's noting: "*Can't remember whether this sd be gràn or grande forgotten all my italian."

Queen alluded to it in her private letter," Gosselin reported, "&
he seemed especially gratified at the present — (This quite entre
nous), but I do not think it would do for us to hang on here — &
leave only the day or 2 before the Jubilee on the 31st." "It
would look rude," he added, "to His Most Eminent Sir. Please
let us hear Lord Salisbury's wishes as soon as possible." "The
Duke proposes," he finally concluded, "to refer to negotiations
in *private* letters only —. . . ."

In his official dispatches to the Foreign Office the duke
confined himself to simply reporting what the Roman press
were saying about his Mission. His excerpts and translations,
however, were hardly examples of diplomatic disinterestedness.
"I have the honour," he informed Salisbury on December
19, "to enclose a copy and translation of an article published in
yesterday's 'Opinione' one of the leading organs of public
opinion in Rome commenting on the objects of the Mission
with which I have been entrusted by Her Majesty and drawing
attention in no unfriendly terms to the line recently adopted by
the 'Standard' newspaper with regard to the relations of
Her Majesty's Government with the Vatican."[4] The duke's
translation of the leading article in *L'Opinione* of December 18,
read:

> The Duke of Norfolk, chief of the English Catholics has been
> charged, as all are aware, with the Mission to present to the
> Pope the congratulations of Queen Victoria. But there is reason
> to believe that the Duke of Norfolk will not confine himself to
> this, and it is supposed that he has also been charged to enquire
> whether the moment has not come for England to establish
> regular diplomatic relations with the Vatican. Hitherto English
> traditions have furnished an unsurmountable obstacle to any
> scheme tending to establish official relations between Great Bri-
> tain and the Holy See. It will be remembered that some years
> back the English Government made some timid efforts to ap-
> proach the Vatican and sent Sir George Errington to Rome on
> a secret mission. But on the very first question being asked in
> the House of Commons, Sir George Errington was so to speak,
> disavowed.
>
> Even now the old leaven of Protestant feeling and Puritan in-
> tolerance, and the prejudices and antipathies against
> Catholicism exist in England, although less strongly than

---

[4] F. O., 45/661. See also *Ibid.*, December 22, 1887, for enclosure of
L'Osservatore Romano of December 22, 1887.

formerly. The English press have need of great caution in admitting that England might usefully establish diplomatic relations with the Holy See. The "Standard" which has had the
courage to touch this burning question, is only able with many
a circumlocution to say that England should not fear to follow
Germany's example, to receive in London a Pontifical Nuncio &
to send to Rome an English diplomat. . . .

The Irish Question is the only motive which can induce the
English Government to approach the Holy See.
Notwithstanding the Coercion Law, the situation in Ireland remains always disturbed and bristling with difficulties. Lord
Salisbury probably hopes to take away from the Nationalists,
by means of the Vatican, the help of the Irish clergy. Everyone
admits that the Pope sent Monsignor Persico to Ireland to examine into the part taken by the Irish clergy in the political
agitation in their country but it does not appear that the conclusions at which Monsignor Persico has arrived are such as
would meet the wishes of the English Government.

Meanwhile some English Catholics who belong to the Liberal
Party, & in regard to the Irish Question are partisans of the
views of Mr. Gladstone, are striving to upset the work of the
Duke of Norfolk. Lord Ripon, Lord Ashburnham & certain
other English Catholics are circulating amongst their co-
religionists an address to Mons^gr Persico, which is a sort of
Manifesto. Lord Ripon and the other signatories of this letter
clearly inform Mons^gr Persico that the group of English
Conservative Catholics have undertaken the task of publicly
running down the Irish & specially the Irish Episcopate &
clergy, adding that they deplore the acts of certain lay
members of the Catholic Church in England who have
adopted an attitude of bitter & implacable hostility towards
Ireland.

They also protest against the insults directed against the
venerable Episcopate & Irish clergy, and they express their
conviction that no false reports, — no matter how high may be
their origin, will be able to induce the Holy Father to cease from
supporting and trusting the Irish people.[5]

"We leave Rome tomorrow night," Norfolk informed
Salisbury on Christmas day, in a note marked *"Private and
Confidential,"* "and are due in London at 5. on Thursday
afternoon the 29th"(Sy). "I ought to start again," he explained,
referring to his return to Rome, "on the following Wednesday
the 4th. I hope very much you will let me see you between these

⁵ *Ibid.*

TWO JUBILEES.—A HARMONY IN BLACK AND WHITE.

St. Peter's and St. James's face to face,
Exchanging, with a more than courtly grace,
    Their mutual gifts and greetings!
A sight to stir the bigot; but the wise
Regard with cheerful and complacent eyes
    This pleasantest of meetings.

Queen, fresh from fifty years of glorious sway;
Pontiff, in the great Headship strong, though grey;
    A world's good wishes gather,
From gentle hearts of all the creeds, to dower
With love the two chief types of high-placed power,
    Good Queen and Holy Father.

Two Jubilees! Patriot *Punch* is nothing loth
In line and verse to celebrate them both.
    True freeman he, unfettered
By servile fear, or hate's poor purblind heat.
When such great opposites in friendship meet,
    Wit and the world seem bettered.

The willing bow of mutual respect
Leaves individual honour still erect,
    And liberty unshaken.
What bulwark fails because across the lands
Two diverse Sovereigns their illustrious hands
    In amity have taken?

dates." "I should also," Norfolk concluded, "like to see Balfour to whom I am writing." In his letter to Balfour the same day, also marked *"Private and Confidential,"* Norfolk extended himself a little. "I think it would be a most important thing," he suggested to Balfour, "if you would furnish me with the names of such Priests as you would wish to see nominated as Bishops to the vacant Dioceses. Propaganda is in communication with Monsignor Persico (this is quite private) on the subject and I think what I suggest is of first importance. Ross says he has not sufficient information with regard to localities with which he has no connection to give you information on this point."[6] "He leaves Rome with me tomorrow," Norfolk noted in conclusion, "but does not come back to England."

"Your letter has just arr^{d}," Balfour explained to Norfolk on December 30, from Dublin Castle, "— and I send just a line in reply: — I shall probably have to trouble you again."[7] "I fear that I shall not be able to get away from here," he apologized, "during your stay in England: — my time is fully absorbed. This is a bore as letters are a very imperfect substitute for oral communications: but I dare say we will be able to manage. I do not at this moment see my way clearly anent the *Priests*. I have as Secretary for Ireland absolutely no means of learning the qualifications of the good priests in the Country. Of the *bad* priests I hear enough. But I know of no one to whom I could turn and ask for the information you desire with the slightest hope of getting the information, or keeping the application secret." "The course wh speaking off hand & no time for reflexion," he advised, "strikes me as the best under the circes is that Ross should write to Emly to consult Bishop Healy: and possibly Bishop ODwyer: I do not advise him to write direct to the Bishop: and Emly should of course ask for the information without hinting that he had heard from Ross." "It appears to me," Balfour added in conclusion, "that it is only from one of themselves that he really can learn something about the personnel of the Clergy, and no other way suggests itself to me of finding out privately what the well disposed among them thinks."

The duke also wrote Salisbury on Friday December 30, thanking him for his invitation to spend Monday night at Hatfield House, while at the same time begging to be excused

---

[6] B, 49821.
[7] *Ibid.*

(since he was still in deep mourning) if there was to be a large group, and suggested instead an interview at the foreign office(Sy). Indeed the duke was excused and spent that Monday composing a long memorandum for Salisbury marked *"Strictly Private and Confidential"* on Rome *vis-à-vis* Ireland. "The following notes," Norfolk advised Salisbury on January 2, "are for your consideration before I see you when I will amplify them in conversation. The Vatican expresses a full readiness to enter into the question of the pacification of Ireland as far as action of the Church is concerned."

> It submits that for this it is necessary to have mutual understanding and interchange of ideas with the British Government.
>
> It admits that the conduct of the Clergy requires to be checked.
>
> It hesitates as to the possibility of doing this publicly.
>
> It is disposed to make use of a Synod to be held in Ireland early in this year as a means of recording directions from Rome to the Bishops for their guidance and the direction of their Clergy.
>
> It is extremely anxious (in order that its own dealing with the Bishops may be made easier) to grasp at anything which it can induce the British Government to do in the form of concessions.
>
> This being so it especially welcomes the Education scheme and urges that there may be further means of showing a conciliatory spirit — e.g. the financial position of Training Colleges; more frequent employment of Catholics in Irish Government posts &c. &c.
>
> It is clearly most anxious to make all these matters a basis for official diplomatic discussion. I think it would accept something of this sort in a temporary sense, as for instance, some one specially sent to Rome to discuss the Education scheme(Sy).

"The above notes," Norfolk further explained to Salisbury, "represent the conclusions to which I have come. They are not declarations on the part of the Vatican." "I submit," he concluded, "that the present moment is one which the British Government ought on no account altogether to let slip owing to the two important facts of the Papal delegate having been six months in Ireland; and of the approaching Synod."

A number of rather important points appear to emerge as a consequence of the duke's brief visit to Rome before Christmas. First of all, the pope and his advisers were obviously agreed that something would have to be done about Ireland, and more particularly about the conduct of the Irish clergy. Secondly, that they were not at all certain about either what should be done or how it should be done. Thirdly, that Monsignor Persico's preliminary reports were evidently not providing the Roman authorities with the patent justification they would have liked for taking action in Ireland. Finally, that whatever policy was to be decided on by Rome for Ireland should provide the basis for those discussions with the British government which hopefully would result both in meaningful concessions to Irish Catholics and in the restoration of diplomatic relations. The most material of these points for Rome in early January, 1888, of course, was the second — what should be done to effect the pacification of Ireland and how should it be done. In the last analysis, however, the real problem for Rome was not so much the declaring of her will in Ireland, but the making of that will effective there. If the duke was correct in his assessment at Christmas-time, the Roman authorities appeared to be leaning in the direction of a Synod to be called in Ireland early in the year. Given the explosive nature of the Irish situation in the winter of 1888, and the dangerous consequences that might result from precipitate action, what Rome needed, therefore, was more time, and none perhaps were better versed in the art of procrastination than the Roman authorities.

Prior to and during the duke's stay in Rome, the British and Irish newspapers were full of rumors about the meaning of his Mission. Walsh, meanwhile, who was taking a long deferred holiday by leisurely making his way to Rome, did not neglect to keep either in touch with Persico, or up on the latest news from London and Dublin. He had, in fact, written Persico explaining his apprehensions about the rumors currently being circulated by the *Tablet*. "I beg to acknowledge," Persico replied to Walsh on December 22, "your note of the 16th wherein your Grace apprehends the danger that the educational question may be settled with the English Government in view of diplomatic relations that would be established between the Holy See and England, and that they may be effected independently of the bishops."[8] "As to the probability," Persico confessed, "or

[8] *Walsh*, pp. 305-06.

rather the possibility of diplomatic relations between the Pope and England, I have nothing to say, as I am a perfect stranger to all these things. But as to the settling of the education question, that is a thing which I cannot believe: and if the *Tablet,* or other British papers say it, I say that they only give expression to their own wishes, and not that they can have a real foundation for asserting it." "For on what basis," he asked Walsh, "could the Court of Rome have entered into this settlement, not having as yet received my report on the Education Question?" "And yet," he assured Walsh, "the Holy Father was desirous to ascertain and to know the views of the bishops in the matter." "Again," he then reassured Walsh, with an interesting qualification, "I have not received any *intimation whatever* on this special subject, so I shall be really surprised if anything be done without the necessary elements." "As your Grace will soon be in Rome," Persico noted appropriately, "it will not be difficult for you to know something about it."

The ultra-Nationalist weekly, *United Ireland,* meanwhile, had made matters worse by reporting on December 15, that the *quid pro quo* offered by the British government to the Vatican for its support in the pacification of Ireland was "(1) to endow richly a Catholic University in Ireland, and (2) to receive an Envoy from His Holiness, and to send an ambassador to the Vatican."[9] The next day, Friday, December 16, the Liberal *Pall Mall Gazette* added fuel to the fire with an extraordinary series of insinuations. "The Government," the *Pall Mall* charged, "wish to checkmate Home Rule by Rome Rule. They have decided to strike up an alliance with the Pope of Rome."[10] "It has for some time been an open secret," the *Pall Mall* declared, presumably for the benefit of its non-Conformist readers, "that Lord Salisbury contemplates some such concordat with the Vatican, and in this he was strongly encouraged by the Duke of Norfolk."

When Father Gualdi died and Monsignor Persico, leaving the healthy atmosphere of the arch-episcopal residence of Dublin, had made his way southward to the diocese of Limerick, the shattered hopes of the Unionists began again to revive. The Bishop of Limerick, like the Coadjutor Bishop of Clonfert, and

---

[9] *Ibid.,* p. 302.
[10] *Ibid.,* pp. 302-03.

one or two other prelates who could be named "Landlord Bishops," regards the national agitation with undisguised dislike. At the same time the word was given in Tory circles that the Papal Envoy had to be taken in hand, and that every effort should be made to nobble his Excellency by profuse hospitality and the most deferential treatment.

Monsignor Persico was given the hint that the Castle intended locking up the priests who took part in the meetings of the suppressed branches of the National League, but that if his Excellency put the screw on the priests through their bishops the Government would gladly refrain from taking so extreme a step. Willingly or otherwise, Mgr. Persico seems to have fallen into the trap. The way the thing is done is very simple. The Monsignor gives the hint to the Bishop. The Bishop nothing loth — for the game is tried on in dioceses where the bishop can be relied on by the Castle — dispatches private and confidential communications to the clergy warning them of what is in store for them.

Delighted with the success of this manoeuvre the Government have now further undertaken to endow a Catholic University in Ireland for the benefit and welfare of Irish Catholics.[11]

"In the midst of the commotion," the *Pall Mall* concluded, and referring to Balfour, "caused in Ireland by the discovery of the extent to which the astute intriguers of the Castle had been able to use the Papal Envoy as a coercionist cat's paw, Archbishop Walsh has been suddenly summoned to Rome by the Pope."

When the *Freeman's Journal* reprinted the *Pall Mall's* charges the following day, Saturday, December 17, the result was a public furor in Ireland. In a speech the next day, for example, John Dillon was not only furious, but bitter and explicit in his warning. "If Mr. Balfour imagined," Dillon declared on Sunday, December 18, "he was going to better his position by applying for the Pope's assistance, he misjudged the Catholics of Ireland."[12] "These very men who were now calling in this strange assistance to the back of the English government in Ireland," Dillon ironically pointed out, "were the men who only a short time ago used to say to Englishmen that Home Rule meant Rome Rule." "What kind of rule," he asked pointedly, "meant Rome Rule now?" As an Irish Catholic,

---

[11] *Ibid.*

[12] F. S. L. Lyons, *John Dillon* (1968), p. 92; *Freeman's Journal,* December 19, 1887.

Dillon then boldly maintained, that although the Irish people "revered the Pope in Rome as the head of their religion, they would no more take their political guidance from the Pope of Rome than from the Sultan of Turkey." John Dillon, however, was not the only aggrieved party reported the next day in the *Freeman's Journal.* The bishop of Limerick also wrote the editor of the *Freeman* a burning and bristling letter. O'Dwyer indignantly denied that he was an "intriguer," a "Unionist" or a "Landlord Bishop."[13] He further declared that he considered the Plan of Campaign to be "unjust," and "boycotting" to be irreligious. He also added for good measure that he thought "the guidance of the agitation was not only politically stupid but morally wrong."

The charges and countercharges naturally were most embarrassing to Monsignor Persico. "Out of the great respect I entertain for your Eminence," Persico explained to Manning on December 21, from Cork, "I write to tell you that *as far as I am concerned* there is not a word of truth in all that has been lately published in the *Pall Mall Gazette* and other newspapers about my league with the Government and so on."[14] "My intercourse with the bishops," Persico then assured the cardinal, "has been straight forward and loyal, and nothing underhand has passed between me and them. I have strictly confined myself to the object of my mission — to observe, to study, to know — and in due time to make my Report. Beyond this I have done nothing, and I even safely defy anyone to prove the contrary. Your Eminence will understand that I must remain silent before these attacks; but I have been deeply pained at the language of some newspapers in Ireland, specially two articles in the *Freeman's* on the 17th and 19th instant. I am afraid that the enemies of Ireland will take advantage of that." "Of course," he added, turning to his own views on Ireland, "there are things to be corrected and certain inconvenients to be removed; and when I have the honour of seeing Y.E. I will freely mention them to you. But I may even now tell Y.E. that in submitting my *subordinato parere* to my Superiors I have said that whatever is deemed necessary or useful for Ireland must be done *with* and *through the Bishops.* That any other mode of acting or a different procedure may have deplorable consequences. I hope and trust they will abide by my humble

13 *Walsh,* p. 304.
14 *The United Irishman* (Dublin), April 23, 1904.

proposals." "In fact," Persico maintained, obviously aiming to please the cardinal, "I would like to see the four Archbishops and one Bishop for every Province in Rome, and *there* prepare and settle things; and this might be a preparation for their National Synod. Again, I do not see why I am to prolong my stay here, as it is causing comments and suspicions." "The object of my temporary mission," he concluded finally, "has terminated, hence I ought to retire. I hope they will allow me to do so."

In his letter the next day, responding to Walsh's note of December 16, Persico also attempted to scotch the various rumors with an emphatic denial. "In a word," he summed up for Walsh on December 22, "everything that has been published is false and calumnious and I repudiate it most emphatically."[15] The controversy, however, continued to rage in the newspapers and Persico felt called upon, *motu proprio,* to write Walsh again. "No doubt," he explained to Walsh on Christmas day, "your Grace must have seen the publications made in the *Freeman's Journal* for the last eight or ten days and how my name has been dragged along, etc."[16] "Now in justice to myself," Persico added, "and also in justice to the Bishop of Limerick, I deem it proper to let you know, *privately* and *confidentially,* the following particulars:

At a dinner given by Mr. Moran of Lucan, at which your Grace was also present, we met a Major or Captain Turner, R.M., if I mistake not, of Ennis. I was simply introduced to him, but he talked a good deal with poor Fr. Gualdi, and told him that he would write to him now and then. In fact from time to time he sent Fr. Gualdi either complaints or copies of reports against the action taken by priests, etc. The only reply that was ever given him was that we had received his communication and taken cognisance of it. I need not say since my arrival in Ireland I received hundreds and hundreds of such communications in different shapes — to which the same reply has been invariably given.

Your Grace also remembers that a few days after my arrival in Cork, I begged the Bishop of Limerick to pay me a visit, and I wrote to your Grace to say that he had come and I also informed you of the result of my conversation with him. Now, it so happened either the day before or the morning of the day

15 *Walsh,* p. 305.
16 *Ibid.,* pp. 306-07.

that Dr. O'Dwyer called on me I had received a communication
from this Major Turner, in which he complained against three
or four priests of the Killaloe diocese, adding that he had
written several times to the Bishop without any effect; that he
should be sorry to send summonses against priests, and would
be glad if the Bishop took matters into his own hands, etc. I had
thought of sending that same communication to the Bishop, Dr.
Ryan, but availed myself of Dr. O'Dwyer's visit to beg of him
to give it to the Bishop. Dr. O'Dwyer promised to do so, adding
that if the Bishop, Dr. Ryan, was unwell he would either give
the letter or speak to the Vicar-General, who, he said, was a
friend of his. I did not hear anything more about it, nor have I
heard a word either from Dr. O'Dwyer or any one else on the
subject. Yet reading the articles of the *Pall Mall Gazette,* and
the way in which they insist on the same thing, it strikes me that
either that the Vicar-General must have acted imprudently, or
the priests who were warned resented it, and so, what was done
for good and with good intention has been misinterpreted and
given an odious sense altogether.[17]

"This, my dear Lord Archbishop," Persico concluded his long
apologia to Walsh, "is the fact whereupon may have been built
all those imputations against me and the Bishop of Limerick —
that I have been cajoled by the Government, and become their
agent, and commenced my operations in one diocese through
Dr. O'Dwyer, etc., etc."

Walsh was, indeed, as Persico suspected, very disturbed
about the reports reaching him from London and Dublin. In
fact, he wrote Kirby from Florence on Christmas Eve to
explain the disastrous consequences that might ensue if there
was any foundation to the rumors. "There seems to be a very
unpleasant agitation of mind in Ireland," Walsh informed
Kirby, "since I left home, about some suspected Government
intrigues. As Mgr Persico contradicted anything, he is certainly
called upon to contradict all this. If he does not do do so, it will
be impossible to eradicate this notion from the public mind"(K).
"I have thought it right," Walsh explained to Kirby, "to write
him on the subject, not directly suggesting that he should
personally contradict it, but pointing out the disastrous
consequences that cannot fail to follow, if the story be
believed." "Our people," Walsh warned Kirby, "who have

---

[17] *Ibid.*

hitherto stood so loyally by us in the cause of religious education will be simply turned against that cause and thrown bodily into the open arms of the English Radicals. In fact, I do not know any other way in which it would be possible to turn the present Irish movement into a movement like the modern revolutionary ones of Italy and France, over which neither priests or Bishops nor the Holy See itself can even pretend to exercise the faintest control." "But we shall have time enough," Walsh concluded, "to talk over all these topics when I have the pleasure of seeing Y.G. in Rome." The continuing newspaper reports, however, caused Walsh to write Kirby again from Florence three days later. "There seems to be," he noted on December 27, "great confusion in Ireland"(K). "All the Tory papers," Walsh observed, "are exulting over what they regard as the split among the Bishops. Of course, there is nothing new. Everyone knew, or ought to have known, that there is in Ireland a small minority in every class and in every body, prepared to take the Government side." "The difference now," Walsh maintained, "is that, as regards the Bishops, the body is so solidly united that no harm can come of any individual crotchets, no matter how skillfully paraded at a critical time."

The following day Persico wrote Walsh from Ireland answering the letter Walsh had alluded to in his letter to Kirby on Christmas Eve. "I have duly received," Persico acknowledged on December 28, "the registered letter of the 20th inst., which your Grace sent me from San Remo. It contains a cutting from the *Scotsman* newspaper, which proves what your Grace says about the fabrication (so to say) of news, etc. This, of course, is an instance of what we find every day in the newspapers. You may depend on it that I shall not fail to make this known at the proper quarters."[13] "Regarding the publications," Persico then argued, referring to Walsh's suggestion, "that have recently taken place, I do not think we ought to take any notice of them. For, if we begin to contradict we ought to do so every day; or every day you find something either in Unionist or Nationalist papers which we ought to contradict or rectify." "In my humble opinion," he further explained, and declining to act on Walsh's suggestion, "the most effectual way of dealing with certain publications is either not to admit them (that is republishing them) or to treat

---

[18] *Ibid.*, pp. 307-08.

them with the utmost contempt." "Y.G.," he added in a
postscript, "can now know things much better than I can here."

Manning, meanwhile, who with Walsh on his way to
Rome, was attempting to cover the vulnerable home front,
did not neglect to take advantage of the recent correspondence initiated on December 21 by his old friend
Monsignor Persico, for he replied the following day. "I duly
received your letter of the 22nd," Persico gratefully responded
to the cardinal from Cork on December 28, "which afforded
me great comfort, and which reveals your excellent qualities of
mind and heart. While I thank you very much for the same, I
deem it proper to inform Y.E. of a letter I have received from
Cardinal Rampolla in reply to a letter of mine in which I
mentioned that my mission might now be brought to a
termination, since I had all the information required &c."[19]
"His Eminence," Persico alerted Manning, "tells me plainly
that it is the will of Our Holy Father to prolong this mission
indefinitamente, so that if I could not remain on account of the
climate, they would appoint a successor. At the same time he
urges me to remain,and adds that I can reside anywhere in the
British Isles during this winter, where the climate is milder. It
must, however, be understood, his Eminence says, that the
mission continues, and that this should be known. Again that I
must not reside in London, so as not to give the least suspicion
that I have anything to do with the British Government."
"Now, my dear Lord Cardinal," Persico added, "I must
mention that the dampness of this climate is against me, and the
doctors say that I should spend two months, from the middle of
January to the middle of March, in a much healthier and milder
climate. I have been thinking of spending said two months in
some quiet place in England where the climate is comparatively
milder." "So to prevent my applying to be recalled," Persico
then explained, "I would try to spend two months, as I have
said, somewhere in England. Steamers leave Cork regularly for
Bristol, Liford, Liverpool, Cardiff, Newport, and Southampton.
May I beg of your Eminence to have the great kindness to
mention which of the said places would be better for me to go."
"As to the going of the four Archbishops and four suffragans to
Rome," Persico informed Manning, turning to a suggestion in
the Cardinal's letter, "I had already proposed it, and have
repeated the same thing. I shall have occasion to write again on

---

[19] *The United Irishman,* April 23, 1904.

the same subject, when I shall urge the thing most earnestly. Your Eminence understands the Irish question thoroughly; I wish others in Rome understood it as Y.E. does." "As far as I am concerned," he reassured the cardinal again in conclusion, "I shall not fail to make a proper exposé of things."

The cardinal again lost no time in replying the following day as soon as he received Monsignor Persico's letter, and suggesting not only Teignmouth in Devon as the best place in England to spend the winter, but also introducing the one subject the monsignor had refused even to enter on a discussion with Walsh earlier — diplomatic relations.[20] "I had the pleasure," Persico reported on January 6, "of receiving Y.E.'s letter of the 29th ultimo, and thank you for the very great kindness in giving me the required information about some place in England where the weather is comparatively temperate."[21] "I have read and re-read your Eminence's letter," he then assured the cardinal, "with an ever-increasing interest and sincere satisfaction, for I find therein the confirmation of my deeply-settled convictions on the subject of diplomatic relations." "I agree fully with your Eminence," he again assured the cardinal, after explaining what his own experience had taught him on the subject, "that 'the true Nunciatura for England and Ireland is the Episcopate. If the Bishops do not know the state of the country they are not fit to be Bishops. If they do, what more can *una persona ufficiosa o ufficiale* do for the Holy See?'" "And again," he agreed, "I fully understand, what your Eminence adds, 'The English people tolerate the Catholic Church as a spiritual body. The first sign of a political action [on the part] of the Government would rekindle all the old fears, suspicions, and hostility.'" "It is a great pity," he further lamented, "that they do not realise this in Rome. And it is also a great pity that English Catholics do not understand all this!" "I am sure that His Holiness understands it well," Persico observed politely, "but I share your fears that those about him may harass him with the fickle and vain glory that would accrue to the Holy See by having an accredited representative from England also." "I may assure Y.E.," he again reassured the cardinal, "of course, *in a most confidential way,* that even in my humble position I do not fail to represent my views to the Holy See. Above all, I have informed the

---

[20] Leslie, *loc. cit.*
[21] *The United Irishman,* April 23, 1904.

Secretary of State of the way in which such a thing would be felt in Ireland." "I hope that when in England," Persico then concluded, "I may have the opportunity of seeing your Eminence. I recommend myself to your Eminence's prayers, as I am tried by the continuous attacks of the newspapers, and therefore I need great patience."

Walsh, who had finally arrived in Rome on December 29, was even more appalled by the rumors he encountered there than he was by those he had read in the English and Irish papers while on his way. He almost immediately wrote Croke to place him on the alert, and especially with regard to Monsignor Persico. In replying on January 7, that he had just received his letter of December 30, Croke assured Walsh that it was most welcome"(W). "It did not surprise me in any way," he confided, and referring to Persico, "either as regards the disorganisation prevailing all round the holy places or the revelations about our diplomatic friend." "He is coming on a visit to me," Croke explained, "on Monday next! — I will be on my guard and shall let you know my views soon after his arrival." "You know all about the Country," he then assured Walsh, "as well as if you were at home. Trials, and imprisonments, and releases from prison, and rejoicings there/at, are the order of the day." Croke, however, did not write Walsh until Persico had finally left Thurles to return to Cork. "He remains," Croke reported on Thursday, January 12, "in Cork until Tuesday next, and then leaves for Torquay *via* Bristol, 'for the benefit of his health' "(W). "He is to remain there for about a month," Croke added, most significantly, "when he will return to Dublin! Such is his programme. During his stay here, I had several exhaustive interviews with him in reference to the situation generally. If he is to be believed, he is '*ipsis Hibernis Hibernior.*' He *is* the friend of Ireland, and always has been, and he never wrote a line to Rome, and never will not be favourable to all her legitimate aspirations, including Home Rule. The rumours that come from Rome are, according to him, the merest tittle tattle, such as was going on in the Eternal City during that Vatican Council, and such as is sure to go on whenever large gatherings of English people are in Rome." "He denounces," Croke then explained, giving an interesting example of Persico's ability to say the same thing with differing shades of emphasis, depending on whether the ear was English or Irish, "the English Catholics most vehemently for their hostility to Ireland, and their shameless and flagrant ingratitude for the blessings of freedom won for them by Irishmen." *"Nominatim,"* Croke noted with obvious satisfaction, and referring to Herbert Vaughan, owner and publisher of the *Tablet,* by his episcopal title, "he is death on Salford."

"The Pope, he has *solemnly* assured me, 'will never issue any repressive legislation as against Irish Ecclesiastics high or low,' " Croke quoted Persico, "— though he may *'with* and *through* the Bishops' do something to check the impetuosity, and moderate the political rhetoric of young priests." "He is," Croke noted further, referring to Healy and O'Dwyer respectively, "perpendicular on the 'Pet' — but undisguisedly favourable, *on the whole,* to +E.T., whom he regards as honest and honourable, though somewhat conceited, and imprudent." "He told me of his interview with him," Croke added, and referring to the reason why Persico had asked O'Dwyer to visit him in Cork, "in reference to the Limerick Education Speech; and was greatly pleased at the manner in which he received his advice and instructions on that occasion. As regards his stay in this country, he cannot say to what length it may run, and he has no desire whatever to return to Italy, as he would vastly prefer to stop here!" "He may be at the National Synod to be held this year;" Croke alerted Walsh, "but he supposes if so, that he will be there not as president, 'but as a friend,' — this I extracted from him with difficulty, and by a ruse. But he has let the 'cat out of the bag' in so far —."

"I gave him," Croke advised, and Walsh must have winced, "my mind very plainly. I told him that we distrusted everyone and everything Roman; that we did not understand his Mission, or himself; that we feared English influence as against Irish Nationality — and that the rumours that were afloat in Rome and elsewhere, though possibly groundless, were awakening suspicion, if not creating alarm just now in Ireland." "I added," Croke declared, "that if the Pope sought to substantially check the action of either priests or Bishops in Ireland, the Irish race over the world would resent such interference and disregard it — and that so far as I individually was concerned, I would resign the See of Cashel on the very day on which such legislation would come into force." "Our friend," Croke summed up finally on Persico for Walsh, "is plausible, slippery, and self-contained a party as ever I met — He can talk much and say nothing." "Still," Croke added, "I can hardly believe he is the rogue and hypocrite he would be, were he unfavourable to the Irish cause, instead of being, as he says he is, most friendly to it." "Persico has urged me earnestly," Croke then explained, "to go to Rome. But I cannot." "Someone of influence," he then added, "should be in Ireland at this critical time." "Paper out," he concluded peremptorily, ". . . Write."

When Persico returned to Cork after his visit with Croke, he found a letter from Walsh of January 7, waiting for him. Walsh had enclosed a cutting from the *Irish Times* which asserted that the late Father Gualdi had been recalled from Ireland in disgrace to Rome. In his letter Walsh had obviously suggested again that the monsignor publicly contradict the reports in the press. Persico immediately wrote Walsh to assure him once again that all the various rumors at Rome and in the newspapers were simply not true, and that he was determined to ignore them. "The people," he explained to Walsh on January 12, "who are said to have got hold of Fr. Gualdi's papers are quite welcome to publish them. As I mentioned in my last, Fr. Gualdi had written more than once, on account of his health, and towards the end, *most urgently* to be allowed to return to Italy."[22] "The idea of his having been recalled," Persico maintained firmly, "is the offspring either of malice or ignorance. As to myself, I must tell Y.G. plainly that I have now made up my mind not to say one word either to correct or to contradict any statement that may be published about me." "I am now the representative of the Holy See," he pointed out to Walsh, "so that everything that has public reference to my mission must be taken up by the Holy See and not by myself. The time may yet come when I shall be in a position to speak for myself; but for the present I must be silent, and rest satisfied with the will of God and my own conscience." In concluding his long letter to Walsh, Persico then finally clinched his arguments for silence by invoking the authority of Cardinal Manning, who had also advised him not to pay any attention to the newspapers.

Persico did leave Cork the following week for England, and a few days later he again wrote Manning. "I am happy to let Y.E. know," he reported to the cardinal on January 21, from Teignmouth, "that my superiors have received favourably my

---

[22] *Ibid.,* pp. 310-11.

poor suggestions and seem to agree with the expediency of the relative proposals. For the present they cannot give much attention to the Irish [sic], but will decide on the mode of treating them the moment they are free from the present celebrations"(M). "I know that Y.E. will be pleased to hear this," Persico added, "so I have hastened to *confide* said news to Y.E. At the same time I am most anxious that certain disciplinary points should be properly settled for the good of Religion and the dignity of the Priesthood. Of course, I always mean that whatever is to be done, must be done with and through the Bishops. It is absolutely necessary that the Bishops should be thoroughly persuaded of the necessity of introducing those things, so that by their acceptance the observance may be secured." "My love for Ireland and the sacred duty attached to my present mission," Persico noted finally, "make me doubly anxious on this subject."

Monsignor Persico was obviously a very able man, and his abilities are yet another testimony to the nervousness with which the Roman authorities viewed the situation in Ireland. In choosing the envoy for the queen's Jubilee, for example, Rome wasted little talent in sending Monsignor Ruffo Scilla to London. Persico's gifts are apparent in his letters, and especially in those to Cardinal Manning. Besides an impressive fluency in English, he had a quick and perceptive intelligence informed by a considerable experience in the Roman diplomatic service. But more important than all these, perhaps, he was not in the least confused about his role in Ireland. He well understood that his was essentially a passive role, and that ultimate responsibility for whatever might be decided did not rest with him. Still, as a sensitive and honorable man, he was appalled at the things that were being said about him in the press, and hence his confessional correspondence with Cardinal Manning. The criticism was all the more painful to Persico because it was unjustified, for the outlines of his report to Rome that emerge in his correspondence with the cardinal reveal that he was on the whole sympathetic to the Irish cause. Though he was apparently both upset by the conduct of some of the Irish clergy and disturbed by the moral implications of the Plan of Campaign and Boycotting, he also quickly perceived that the real question was less *what* should be done than *how* it should be done.

Persico certainly appreciated the fact that Rome had only two alternatives in dealing with whatever was to be done in

Ireland. She could authoritatively command the Irish Bishops
to do her will, or she could attempt to persuade them as to her
will. Persico, in effect, advised the second course by
recommending to Rome that whatever was to be done "must be
done *with* and *through the Bishops*." Given the character and
the abilities of the archbishop of Dublin, however, and his
apparent ascendency over his brother Bishops, a considerable
amount of pressure would have to be exerted on him and his
brethren in order to persuade them to conform to Rome's will in
Ireland. That is why Persico recommended a preliminary
meeting in Rome of a representative body of the Irish Bishops
to prepare for the calling of a National Synod. In that way
Rome would retain the initiative over the crucial matter of the
agenda for the proposed Synod because the cardinal prefect of
Propaganda would naturally preside at any meeting of the Irish
Bishops in Rome. Once the agenda had been settled to the
satisfaction of Rome, however, the real problem would be how
to control the Synod after it was convened in Ireland. All would
depend, of course, on who presided, and it was evident that it
would have to be a Roman invested with Apostolic powers.
That is why Cardinal Rampolla insisted that the mission was to
be continued, and requested Persico to remain on in Ireland.
From Rome's point of view, Persico was the logical choice to
preside as apostolic delegate at such a Synod. He was not only
a reliable and able servant, but he had also already taken the
measure of all the Irish Bishops, and he now knew more about
Ireland than anyone in Rome's service. In any case, the pope
and his advisers would soon have to face up to Monsignor
Persico's recommendations, for the archbishop of Dublin had
finally arrived in Rome.

The first week of Walsh's stay in Rome was comparatively
hectic. He had finally arrived on December 29, and stayed with
Kirby in the Irish College. The following day he was received at
the head of an Irish deputation by the pope with marked
cordiality, and that evening he was a guest at a banquet in
honor of the prefect of propaganda, Cardinal Simeoni. On
December 31, of course, he assisted at the celebration of the
pope's Jubilee in St. Peter's, and was himself the guest of
honor on New Year's Day at a dinner in the Irish College
given by Kirby. Later in the week, Walsh presided at a meeting
to arrange the details for the laying of the foundation stone of

the new Irish National Church of St Patrick in Rome, when it was arranged that Cardinal Parocchi, the pope's vicar general, would represent his holiness, and Walsh would bless the foundation stone on February 1, the Feast of St. Brigid. Walsh then proceeded to mobilize his four episcopal colleagues, who had also come to Rome to celebrate the Jubilee, in order to be able to present a united front on Irish affairs. A strong joint letter was sent to Propaganda, and an agenda was prepared for the coming expected private audience with the pope. Walsh reviewed the whole situation in Rome for Croke on January 18, in an interesting series of observations.

"The information contained in your letter," Walsh informed Croke, referring to his account of Persico's visit on January 12, "was most useful"(C). "It helped me," Walsh explained, "in the interpretation of many puzzling rumours here, and also in the shaping of a line of practical action. I have worked up the Bishops here to send a strong letter to Propaganda — pointing out the extremely critical character of the present time as regards religious, as well as political affairs in Ireland — dwelling in detail on the uneasiness and alarm caused by the persistent circulation of unfriendly rumours by the Roman correspondents of the London papers — and referrring especially to the circumstantial statement of the *Times* correspondent that 'two English Bishops have sent to Propaganda a translation of the Bishop of Limerick's letter with their own comments thereon' etc. etc." After making particular reference to some offensive reports in the *Tablet* and its owner, the bishop of Salford, Walsh then assured Croke again — "The letter is a strong one. It goes in signed by myself, Tuam, Elphin, Cork and Galway." "Elphin especially," Walsh noted for Croke, referring to the most conservative of his colleagues, Laurence Gillooly, "is doing his work well here, speaking out like a man to everyone concerned, from the Cardinal Secretary of State down." "Cork, too," he also noted, referring to T. A. O'Callaghan, O.P., "is most useful: his free command of the Italian serves us in many ways."

"We applied," Walsh pointed out, "for a collective audience four or five days ago. As yet we have not had it, but it is only to-day that the regular audiences are received. I am most anxious to get away, but there seems to be a general impression that it will be necessary for me to stay on here for some time, as they say, the Pope wants to hear all about the Irish question in detail. We have arranged our programme for the audience. We intend to note down the heads on which we shall try to dilate, and at the end we shall ask H. H. to allow us to write out for him a full statement of our views, to come, if possible, from a meeting of the Irish Bishops." "We shall insist," Walsh maintained, alluding most significantly to the mode suggested by Persico in his Report in reference to any action to be undertaken by Rome, "on the necessity of his moving only 'with and through the Bishops.' Apart from all other considerations, this will mean an important gain of time. Even a few months now may be of importance in bringing about changes in the political situation. Lord Salisbury's despondent tone seems to show there is some strong undercurrent of opposition at work." "I have not heard a word," he noted briefly and significantly, referring to Kilmore, Raphoe, and Achonry, "about the vacant Irish Bishoprics at home." "The great topic with us in the College," Walsh reported, referring to the various displays set up in Rome by the Catholics of the different countries of the world for the Jubilee, "is the Exhibition. . . . We have routed the English 'all along the line.' They are indeed an insolent and aggressive lot." "As regards Propaganda," Walsh then reassured Croke in conclusion, "it is well to know that both the Prefect and the Secretary are most emphatic in their assurances of support." "The Secretary," Walsh added, referring to Monsignor Jacobini, "is especially outspoken."

Several days later Walsh reported to Croke from Naples, where he had gone to nurse a cold, about the collective audience he and the other Irish bishops had finally secured on Friday, January 20, with the pope. "I had some difficulty," Walsh explained on January 23, "in getting away from Rome. H. H. mentioned to several people that he wished to go over the whole case of Ireland with me, and although we (the Irish Bishops) had put in an application for a collective audience, there seemed to be no prospect of our getting it within any reasonable time as we heard several references of his anxiety to have a long talk with me. However, Dr. Gillooly, who was practically obliged to leave, pushed matters on, and had an audience fixed, on Thursday last, for the next morning"(C). "After the usual formalities," Walsh then noted, coming to the actual audience, "Dr. Gillooly introduced the Irish question in the usual business fashion. 'We have now to leave Holy Father,' said he, 'but we leave behind us the Archbishop of Dublin and the Bishop of Cork, so our going makes no difference: your Holiness has in these Bishops two most faithful exponents of what we all wish for and think.' "

"On this," Walsh informed Croke, "H. H. took up the running, and, certainly in a most impressive way, spoke of the great glory that it would bring to the Church and the Holy See if he could now use his influence so as to bring about the final pacification of Ireland. He spoke of the difficulties of the task, but these, he said, did not deter him. Nothing should be impossible to God. He did not see then why he should not make the effort." "The main concern of the Church," he added, continuing to paraphrase the pope, "is of course the spiritual welfare of man. But the Church has also a secondary mission, to promote the temporal well being of the various peoples. So, he said, we must try whether we cannot succeed now in having the difficulties of the Irish people settled 'sub auspiciis nostris et archiepiscopi Dublinensis.' He then said to me that we should agree about a time for conferring on the subject. I said, of course, that I was at his disposal." "But (having my eye on the prospect of a week at Naples)," he confided to Croke, "I added that H. H. could not possibly take up such weighty business at a time of such pressure, and that, I supposed we might leave it off until after the 1st of February — the day fixed for the general Irish audience and the laying of the foundation stone (I must write again about this: everything possible has been done)."

"Thus the matter stands, then," Walsh assured Croke, "until the 1st of February." "In the meantime," he advised Croke, "write to say what line I should take." "I think," he suggested, "the following a pretty safe outline:

1° Pacification possible only on the basis of a concession of all our just demands on the Land question and the question of Home Rule and constitutional government for Ireland (legislature and administration).

2° No disorder or tendency to disorder, except in connection with these: (Evictions and arbitrary conduct of officials under Coercion Act.) Consequently (a) Education Bills, though most desirable in their way, can have no effect on social order; and (b) necessity of a Suspensory Bill stopping evictions pending the settlement of the question: This, of course, should be surrounded with all due safeguards(C).

The day before he wrote this long and matter-of-fact letter to
Croke, Walsh had written a long letter from Naples to Manning
as well. The tone of Walsh's letter to the cardinal, however, was
not nearly as encouraging as that to Croke, for he was both
doubtful about Persico and pessimistic about the pope's new
policy. What Walsh did not dare tell Croke, or even mention to
Manning, however, was that he had heard a document had
already been prepared, and was ready to be published
condemning the agrarian agitation in Ireland. One of the
Roman cardinals had, in fact, informed Walsh's auxiliary
bishop, Nicholas Donnelly, that the publication of the
document had only been "deferred to an opportune and
psychological moment."[23] Walsh obviously preferred not to
trust this information, which if it got out, would prove
disastrous in Ireland, to paper, and more especially since the
cardinal would soon hear it all from those Irish bishops who
had been in Rome and would soon pass through London on
their way home. "I did not care to write your Eminence," Walsh
explained on Sunday, January 22, "until I had some definite
news, satisfactory or unsatisfactory as it might be, to send
you"(M). "Rumours," he reported, "have been in circulation by
the dozen — all of the most unpleasant character. But, as your
Eminence knows, there is nothing in all this to disturb one. The
only rumour that seemed to give solid ground for uneasiness was
one about Fr. Gualdi. It was and is very generally believed." "I
thought it right," he advised Manning, "to let Mgr Persico
know of it as it made very free use of his name. He writes as if
there was nothing in it, but, any reference to his having
contradicted it only sets peoples heads and shoulders going in
the way recognised as a very emphatic indication of
incredulity."

The story is that the Mgre. made up his mind that Fr. Gualdi's
strong feeling of sympathy with the Irish cause was an element
to be got rid of from the "mission" and so represented to the
Vatican the advisability of recalling the obnoxious individual.
Fr. Gualdi's known delicacy, and also his known wishes to be
taken out of an unpleasant position being taken into account as
sufficient ground to put before the public for what was done. It
is even said that representations were made as to the

---

[23] *Irish Times*, May 5, 1888. See for Donnelly's interview with a French
journalist, Arthur Dumesnil.

advisability of removing him from the office of Irish *minutante* at Propaganda. On all hands one is assured here that the poor man died simply from the affects of the communications made to him on his return here. Not withstanding the contradiction to which I have referred, I must continue to believe what has been so circumstantially stated to me especially in one quarter in Rome. It leaves no doubt in my mind that Fr. Gualdi (R.I.P.) regarded himself as being "in disgrace," and took it very heavily to heart. Of course it is possible that he may have been the subject merely of a delusion on the subject. As one most important part of the story was told to me, it included the statement of a series of incidents which, at all events as they occurred were known only to Fr. Gualdi, to Mgr. Persico, and myself!(M)

"The whole affair," Walsh summed up, "has made me in the highest degree distrustful of the way in which the 'mission' is being worked out."

"The Pope now thinks," Walsh then reported to the cardinal, "he can settle the Irish question. I am to play some important part in the transaction. The details are reserved for some conference or conferences to which I am to be called after the 1st of February. All this may mean something practical, but unless I can see my way very clearly into what the Holy Father means, it will, of course, be my duty to tell him of the serious risk that is run by mixing up the Holy See in so uncertain a transaction." "If he is prepared," Walsh maintained, laying down his *sine qua non,* "in communicating with the Ministry, to put forward as essential bases of a settlement the two unchallengeable requirements of Home Rule and a thoroughly satisfactory reform of our Land system, all may be well. These points are essential. No influence in the world could move our people, either at home or abroad to abandon either one or the other." "If things are to enter upon a course," he solemnly advised the cardinal, "in which the Holy See may be made to figure as claiming an influence to secure the abandonment of either, we must see that the Holy Father is sufficiently forewarned to have himself to bear the full responsibility of any disaster that may follow." "The Archbp of Tuam, and the Bishops of Elphin and Galway," he then alerted the cardinal in conclusion, "left Rome on Friday. I assume they will call on Y. Em. before the end of the week."

As soon as Croke received Walsh's "welcome and interesting" letter of January 23, from Naples, he responded in characteristic fashion. "The Pope, of course," Croke declared flatly on January 28, "is well disposed; but he overestimates his influence greatly, if he supposes for a moment that he can settle the Irish question in a manner satisfactory to the Irish people. . . . But, still, we must not put any obstacles in his way so that his experiment may be tried under favourable circumstances"(W). "Your programme is all right," he assured Walsh, "We simply want to manage our own affairs, stock, lock, and barrell. We are satisfied to live for evermore under the sceptre of Englands King or Queen, yielding all due obedience to the same, provided that the Irish administration be in the hands of the sons and friends of the Irish people." "Voilà tout —" Croke summed up, "We have a right to that, and we are bent on that. Short of that we will not be satisfied. Any compromise of that right we will not accept. When that right is conceded, all other good things will in due course, come to us." "Im afraid, though," Croke noted, echoing Walsh in his letter to Manning, "that his Holiness either misunderstands our needs, or miscalculates his own ability to supply them." "As things go," Croke observed, turning to the home front, "the Tory Government appears to be greatly shaken. It has not left us a vestige of liberty. Every day reveals some fresh excess of despotism. Where it will end nobody can tell. Tis hard to bear it; but any uprising against it would be worse than a crime." "There is a warrant," Croke then reported, "out for the re-arrest of O'Brien. He has made tracks out of the Country, so as not to be 'run in' at once. 'Tant mieux.' " "You will drop me a line, no doubt," Croke then suggested, "after the memorable 1st of Feb."

Walsh, it appears, did not write Croke about the pope's reception of the Irish delegation in Rome. Why Walsh neglected to do so, is, perhaps, best explained by a dispatch to Salisbury from the British ambassador in Rome. "My Lord," J. G. Kennedy reported to Salisbury on February 4, "I have the honour to inclose in the original Latin text as well as a carefully made translation of the reply of Pope Leo XIII to the Irish deputation received by H. H. at the Vatican on 1. inst."[24] "The reply," Kennedy explained, "has been much appreciated by

[24] F. O., 170/393. See also *Ibid.*, for Ross's translation from the Latin of the Pope's reply taken from *L'Osservatore Romano,* February 2, 1888.

prominent English, Scotch & Irish Catholics in Rome & is generally considered a lecture read to the Irish priesthood." "The chief points are," he summed up for Salisbury, "the references to the mission of Mgr. Persico as a 'means' of learning the true state of affairs & of ascertaining what would be most to the advantage of Ireland — also the advice to take as a safe rule of conduct the letters formerly 'addressed to the Archbishop of Dublin' and again the reference to the Catholics of Germany who drew themselves successfully out of a very difficult position by adherence to that moderation & that respect for the laws which were the result of our counsel & authority." "Capt. Ross of Bladensburg," Kennedy added, "to whom I am indebted for the enclosed translation informs me that the letters to the Archbishop of Dublin must be public letters as H. H. was addressing the laity as well as the clergy." "The address to the Pope of the Irish deputation," Kennedy concluded, "was I am informed simply one of congratulations & of submission & the fact that H. H. should have chosen the occasion of Jubilee congratulations in order to preach moderation to Irishmen constitutes an important event."

One interesting aspect of the pope's reply, which Kennedy overlooked, was a reference to the role of the Irish Bishops *vis-à-vis* the Irish people and Rome. After referring to the Catholics of Germany, the pope had said — "Therefore we put full hope in the authority & wisdom of the Irish Hierarchy & also in the fidelity of the people, whose respect for the Apostolic See & whose obedience to their Bishops has always been a matter to be praised."[25] The real significance of the Pope's remarks, of course, was that he chose to repose his "hope" rather than his "confidence" in the Irish hierarchy. This lack of confidence was certainly further manifested both in the pope's reference to the Persico mission as a "means" of finding out what the "real state of affairs" in Ireland was, and in his recommendation that his letters to the late archbishop of Dublin, Cardinal McCabe, be read as a reliable guide to Irish conduct and action. Moreover, in his reference to the Catholics of Germany, the pope raised the one issue the Irish Bishops almost unanimously viewed as a menace — diplomatic relations. Both Croke and Walsh, and those who agreed with them, therefore, might be forgiven, if they thought the pope's reply was an implicit criticism of all that they had stood for and still recommended.

---

[25] *Ibid.*

Undoubtedly Walsh's cautious and careful letters to Croke, as well as his reticence about the pope's recent reply, were intended not to irritate or to excite the archbishop of Cashel any more than was necessary. For no one realized more than Walsh how critical the situation really was in Ireland, and no one knew better than he how much political and social order in Ireland depended, especially in view of his own absence, on Croke's enormous moral influence. In any case, the news which must have reached Walsh through Kirby from Ireland was certainly disquieting. This was all the more disturbing because none of Kirby's clerical correspondents at this time could be described as holding to "advanced" views. "We want distributive justice," the venerable dean of Dublin, Walter Lee informed Kirby firmly in the course of a letter on January 8, "and nothing more nor less"(K). "Our excitable people are keeping wonderfully quiet under great provocation," he noted further, and added with unintentional ambiguity, "let us pray that it may not be of long duration." A short time later, the new archbishop of Armagh, Michael Logue, also wrote Kirby that one of his former priests in the diocese of Raphoe had been arrested at the railway station in Armagh, when he arrived to attend the month's mind Mass in memory of the late primate, Daniel McGettigan. The arrest, Logue maintained, was extremely provocative, since the priest could have been just as easily arrested at home in Letterkenny *and secured bail* there "without making his attendance at month's mind the occasion of a scene." "And these are the men," Logue declared indignantly to Kirby, "who are trying to secure the alliance of the Holy Father in crushing Irish Catholics!" "Poor Ireland!" exclaimed one of Kirby's former students, and still more conservative correspondents, James Hasson, a week later on January 27, from Derry, "it is consoling she stands well somewhere — above all at Rome, for at home she gets but kicks and blows from this stepmother government"(K). Finally, several days later, and shortly after his return to Ireland from Rome, the archbishop of Tuam, John MacEvilly, reported in a most gloomy vein to Kirby about conditions in Ireland. "It is hard to say anything," he confessed on February 1, "of the Political Atmosphere which is darkening more & more every day"(K). "There seems to be," he further noted, "little or no liberty left. The people [are] greatly exasperated at the treatment." "Of course," he added, in a most interesting, if unconscious slip in punctuation, "there is no fear, Rome will side with our enemies." "I have said all I could at Rome," MacEvilly explained to Kirby in conclusion, "on the subject of the irreparable evils to religion and spiritual fealty of the Irish race at home & abroad, if such a thing occurred."

Walsh and Croke, however, were not the only ones concerned with the turn Irish affairs were taking at Rome. "When I wrote last," Persico explained to Manning on February 9, and referring to his letter of January 21, "I had received letters from Rome wherefrom I could gather that they had accepted my proposals and also my views. I have not heard anything since, and the return to Ireland of the Archbishop of Tuam and other Bishops that had gone to Rome makes me believe that no meeting of the Bishops is to take place in Rome. This makes me very uneasy, as in my humble opinion, if anything was to be done, it could only be done in that way. It is only by discussing quietly, and coming to certain decisions that some practical result may be obtained. I may assure your Eminence that on my part I have done my duty in exposing things and giving my humble opinion."[26] "If they deem proper," Persico concluded passively, and in the diplomatic tradition, "to adopt other ways and to act otherwise I shall have no remorse whatever." Manning, who was neither passive nor a career diplomat, obviously wrote Persico by return of post stressing the critical nature of the situation in Ireland. "I am entirely of your Eminence's opinion," Persico reassured the cardinal again on February 12, "that the people of Ireland have had no defenders but the priests, and I firmly believe that the clergy in Ireland must be the guides and protectors of the people."[27] "It would be an evil day for Ireland," he further agreed, "to separate the clergy from the people. I have shown this important fact in my reports to Rome, and I hope that they are persuaded of its necessity."

"While on this point," Persico then added most significantly in the course of this letter, "I must *confide* to your Eminence my impression about the Archbishop of Dublin."[28] "He has most eminent qualities and can do an immensity of good," Persico noted, "not only in his own diocese, but for the whole of Ireland. I would like to see him a little more spiritual and more

---

[26] Leslie, *op. cit.*, p. 424.
[27] *The United Irishman*, April 23, 1904.
[28] *Ibid.*

attached to his *pastoral* duties. I am in hopes that he will do so in time, for he is young, and has been only a professor all his life." "To Y. E. also I must *confide*," Persico added revealingly, "that this is the opinion of *many* Bishops in Ireland." "My intercourse with all the bishops," he assured Manning, "has been of a most friendly character, and so it has been with the Archbishop of Dublin. He has written to me constantly, except for the last month. On his arrival in Rome, he heard (as he himself wrote to me) many things about me. Among others, that I had caused Fr. Gualdi's recall and similar things, and from the tenor of his letter, I could see that he had doubts about me." "The Archbishop of Dublin," he then remarked to the cardinal, after denying there was any truth in the Gualdi story, "does not know Rome with regard to rumours and reports." "Y. E. knows it well," he noted politely. "Often a word from a writer or underwriter of a Sacred Congregation is given as a fact, and goes round Rome. Again at the evening conversazioni, comments are freely made from unknown sources or from personal feelings, and these comments are given out as certain facts the next morning." "I am sure Y. E. remembers well," he reminded Manning, "what was going on in Rome during the Vatican Council! I am also afraid that the Archbishop of Dublin and the majority of the clergy of Ireland take me for a man *ligio al governo inglese*. They are greatly mistaken in this." "I had forgotten to tell Y. E.," Persico then informed Manning, "that there is another point about which I have given my *negative* opinion in my reports, and that is against the appointment of a permanent Apostolic Delegate for Ireland. Such a thing would not only humble her, but wound the feelings of both clergy and people." "Again I thank you very much for the patience you have with me." Persico then observed significantly, "and I shall be very much obliged if Y. E. will write to the Holy Father on the subject of a Council of the Irish Bishops in Rome." "I have full confidence in Y. E.," Persico finally concluded, "and I thank Y. E. for telling me that our correspondence is sacred, and that you will keep perfect silence about it."

Manning must have been considerably shaken by Persico's confidential remarks about Walsh, since he certainly appreciated the fact that now that he was identified unequivocally with the Irish cause, any undermining of Walsh's position in Ireland would have very serious consequences with regard to his own power base in England. The cardinal, therefore, not only took, it seems, what was for him an unusual amount of time to reply to Persico's long letter of February 12, but the monsignor's immediate response was obviously intended to reassure the cardinal that he had not been indiscreet in his reports to Rome about the archbishop of Dublin. "With reference to the person alluded to in my last," Persico came straight to the point on February 29, "I beg to assure Y. E. that I fully agree with you as to the character and aptitude, nay, I acknowledge his eminent qualities."[29] "If I opened my mind to Y. E.," he explained, "upon one thing only, I did it from my wish for the greater good. But we must take into consideration his being taken from college life and other circumstances. Above all, I am decidedly of Y. E.'s opinion that it would be a great disaster if the confidence of His Holiness in him should be shaken. On this point, I may also assure Y. E. that, as *far as I am concerned,* I have shown the necessity of *hearing* and *acting in concert* with him about everything. And, writing to Cardinals Simeoni and Rampolla, I have insisted on their showing and placing *in him* great confidence." "I am, indeed, happy to see that the whole of the Irish clergy have great veneration and love for Y. E.," Persico finally exclaimed, "and oh! how I wish that Y. E. would be entrusted with everything."

By the time that Walsh had been in the Eternal City for a month, his confidence in Roman good will was much shaken. He had not only lost faith in the honesty of Monsignor Persico and distrusted the Roman authorities, but he had even become doubtful about the pope's judgment, if not his intentions, in Irish affairs. Whatever may be said about his attitude towards the pope and the authorities, however, Walsh was certainly doing Persico an injustice in assuming that the monsignor's reports were the reason why there had been a change in Roman attitudes about Ireland. Some time about the middle of January, the pope and his advisers decided not to take Persico's advice of only working *"with* and *through the Bishops"* by convening a National Synod in Ireland. Persico immediately realized this when he learned that those Irish Bishops who had been in Rome with Walsh had returned to Ireland, and that the preliminary discussions so necessary for the summoning of a Synod, therefore, had not taken place. Why the pope and his advisers did not opt for Persico's recommendations, of course,

---

[29] *Ibid.*

is the crucial question. Once they had decided, however, to condemn the Plan of Campaign and Boycotting, and Persico's reports undoubtedly tended to justify that decision as much as the exhortations of the duke of Norfolk and his friends prompted it, the formidable question of how to proceed really depended on whether the Roman authorities could work "with" and "through" the Irish Bishops.

In the preliminary conversations with Walsh in early January, the Roman authorities undoubtedly came to the conclusion that he and those bishops who had accompanied him to Rome were not to be easily persuaded as to what needed to be done. The authorities must have also been as interested as Manning was appalled by Persico's intimation that the ascendency of Walsh among the Irish Bishops was perhaps something less than it appeared in Rome. They might be forgiven, therefore, for thinking that the convening of a Synod might result in an embarrassing split among the Irish Bishops, especially if, as it appeared likely, Walsh and Croke refused to endorse Rome's proposed condemnation. From Rome's point of view, then, the wiser and more prudent course would be to present the Irish Bishops with a *fait accompli* by an authoritative condemnation, which would preclude discussion by commanding obedience. The real difficulty for the pope and his advisers in effecting all this was how to contain the archbishop of Dublin. The pope began his very clever game by taking Walsh into his confidence. The difficulties of the Irish people, he had told Walsh and his brethren in Latin at their collective audience on January 20, was to be settled "under our and the Archbishop of Dublin's auspices." Why did Walsh, who was both a man of spirit and no fool, submit so tamely to playing the Roman game? In the first place, he could hardly ask the pope to explain himself as he was being taken into his confidence. But more importantly, Walsh realized that if the condemnation had already been decided on, the only course left open to him was to play for time in the hope that Lord Salisbury's government, which was reported to be very shaky, would soon collapse and the *quid pro quo* of diplomatic relations for the Roman condemnation would evaporate with that collapse. In a word, Walsh needed time even more than did the pope and his advisers.

When Walsh did not write after "the memorable 1st of Feb."

Croke did not press the matter for he undoubtedly appreciated the reasons for Walsh's reticence even if he had not heard the latest news from those bishops who had returned from Rome. On hearing from one of his priests, James J. Ryan, who was visiting Rome for the Jubilee, that Monsignor Verdon had resigned as Kirby's vice-rector to take up the rectorship of Cardinal Moran's new seminary in Sydney, Croke took occasion to drop Walsh a short note. In reporting to Walsh on February 11 that Ryan, whom he humorously referred to as his "Envoy," had asked him for a letter of recommendation to Kirby for the post, and that he had complied, Croke asked, "When are you arriving home?"(W). "I may go to London," he explained, "for a few days. Write here, however. No news that would be news to you." "How did," he finally inquired discreetly in conclusion, "audience (*private*) come off?" Croke's letter, in fact, crossed Walsh's, who wrote him the next day giving him a full report of the audience. "All arrangements," Walsh explained on Sunday, February 12, "had, it seemed, been made for Thursday evening, but owing to some bungling, I got no notice til next day"(C). "To day, 10 a.m. was then fixed": Walsh noted, "Cork to come with me. Cardinal Rampolla was present."

The Pope asked us to explain fully the Irish question. We went exactly on the lines I indicated to Y.G. insisting most emphatically on the absolute necessity of stopping evictions by a temporary Bill, as the only possible means of putting a stop to the only element of trouble in the country. I made most successful use of the omission to deal with arrears, thus knocking the benefits to be derived from the new scale of reductions into a cocked hat. Of course I had the point that the Crofters got this very thing that was refused to our poor people, and when the Pope fully endorsed my view as to the fairness of our demand, and of the necessity of having it attended to in the interests of peace, he asked what explanation there could be of the inconsistent attitude of the Government. I gave him several answers, but I began by taking out of my pocket a number, which I fortunately picked up yesterday, of the Illustrated London News (Jan. 21) showing a most spirited picture of the way in which the Crofters do *their* business. He showed it to Card. Rampolla, with the words, "Ah. ecco, una vera insurrezione." I said, yes, and unfortunately the lesson taught our people by the whole transaction was that they lose everything by being too orderly and quiet, and that, in my opinion, it would now very speedily become impossible for any influence to keep them from taking up more vigorous measures(C).

"All this told well," Walsh added. "The fact that we had just received the Queen's Speech, showing that practically nothing was to be done for Ireland, and absolutely nothing in this one essential point, helped us on wonderfully."

"Times are surely changed," Walsh reassured Croke, referring to Croke's own encounter with the pope five years before, "since the famous audience of 1883." "Today," Walsh reported, interestingly, "the Pope anticipated us in almost everything, and fully endorsed, I may say, everything we said. We told him that if he felt in a position to help our people, he might perhaps try whether he has influence to get the evictions temporarily stopped until the whole question can be fairly dealt with." "We also got on the Plan of Campaign and Boycotting," Walsh observed more gingerly, "distinguishing as well as we could between the uses and abuses of both. He seemed really impressed with all we said and then, he said, now you must set to work and give me a full relatio on the whole of this Land question that we see how we stand, and what can be done. Home Rule came on, and he asked would we be satisfied with an arrangement somewhat like that in Germany." "Of course," Walsh assured Croke most significantly, "I told him we never think of going so far, that Bavaria for instance, has a King of its own."

Yes, said he, but it is politically united in the Empire, having its own national Parliament for its own affairs. I said, of course, that this was all right. Card. Rampolla referred to Austria-Hungary. No, said the Pope, that system of dualism has difficulties in it, the German illustration is better. I, of course, explained the full provisions in Gladstone's Bill as safeguards against separation(C).

"I then came out," Walsh informed Croke, "on the lies in the London papers, and he was both amused and indignant." "The policy of lying," he then added, "is going on to a most fearful extent. But we shall soon, I hope, be in a position to disregard it. I am not at all well. I feel quite sick tonight with a heavy cold, the result, I suppose, partly of the nervous depression brought on by the prolonged stay here." "I will try," Walsh then promised in conclusion, "to get a *relatio* printed so as to show Y.G. and others what I have done."

"Yours of Sunday," Croke replied at once to Walsh's long letter on Tuesday, February 16, from London, "reached me *here* this morning. It afforded me the greatest pleasure, as far as regards the audience"(W). "Tis an ease to us to know," Croke then remarked, "that the Pope is all right." "But," he added unrepentantly, referring undoubtedly to the recent public rather than private audience, "he ought to manage to keep so. There is no good in being Irish today and English tomorrow." "His position," Croke admitted, "is a difficult one, he hears so many conflicting stories. Still, one would imagine the Irish Bishops ought to be the best judges of the situation and, on Irish affairs, the most reliable advisors of the Pope." "I shall be anxious" Croke confessed solicitously, "to hear you are all right. I can easily understand how you are knocked up. Such tension as yours must be terrible. But, your success will have a soothing influence." "I believe," Croke then observed, and referring respectively to Walsh's auxiliary and the bishop of Cork, "Dr. Donnelly has returned. Dr. Callaghan is expected." "Great bishop meeting," he hurriedly assured Walsh in conclusion and referring to the recent meeting of the Standing Committee, "Delighted about O'Donnell. Do not know the other parties. Partially distrust the *Sligo* man."

What Croke was referring to, of course, at the end of his letter, were the appointments which had been just made to the three vacant Irish sees. Appointments to Irish bishoprics were generally a very good indication of the way the diplomatic wind was blowing in Rome, and though little had passed between Walsh and Croke on the subject, there is little doubt that they must have been somewhat anxious. Two of the appointments, Kilmore and Raphoe, could hardly have caused Walsh or Croke any serious concern, since the vacancies had only respectively occurred in early November and early December, and the Jubilee celebrations had, in effect, resulted in the postponement of nearly all ordinary ecclesiastical business. The third appointment to Achonry, however, had not only been pending for over nine months, but Propaganda had taken the most unusual course of rejecting the original *terna* commended by the clergy, and reported on by the bishops of the province of Tuam. The general impression abroad about why Propaganda had then ordered a new *terna* was that the *dignissimus,* Denis

O'Hara, was reported to be an "advanced" Nationalist and the *dignior* and *dignus* were not episcopal material.[30] "I dare say," the archbishop of Tuam had written Kirby on November 27, 1887, "that you are aware that the H. See has ordered a *nova terna* for the diocese of Achonry"(K). "*More consueto,*" MacEvilly had added obediently, "*Roma locuta est. Causa finita est.*" "The Vicar Capitular," MacEvilly explained to Kirby, "raises a question as to the eligibility of any of the former three. I wrote back giving it as my opinion, from the reading of the Propag. Documents to me, I could draw no other conclusion than this, *ne unus* of the former was eligible that the "nova terna" meant *novi tres*. However, on writing last night to his Eminence, I asked him graciously to correct me if I was wrong." "Might I ask Y. Grace," he requested "to ascertain it from his E. and save him the trouble of writing. 2^{ly} I informed him that before receiving the letter of Propag. regarding Achonry, Dr. Gillooly, MacCormack and myself had fixed on leaving for Rome to be present at the Jubilee celebrations, which could hardly be done if we were to wait till the 10th day for a meeting of the Bishops." "They asked me to write," he further explained, "for permission to have a meeting in Rome, as we constitute the greater part of the Province and have the recommendation of the two others in writing." "This was done," MacEvilly reminded Kirby, "on the occasion of the Killala coadjutor at the Vatican Council."

Kirby replied that MacEvilly's interpretation of a "*novi tres*" was the correct one, and that the bishops of the province of

---

[30] Monsell Papers, 3818(14), National Library of Ireland, Dublin, John Mulhall to Emly, August 3, 1887, Vice Regal Lodge, "With reference to your question as to the action taken by the Rev^d F^r O'Hara with reference to the events that led up to & followed the murder of Constable Armstrong in 1881 I have searched the file from which I take the enclosed statement bearing on the case. I have also ascertained that Mr Forster, the then Chief Secretary, intimated to the Bishop of Achonry that he would arrest F^r O'Hara unless his action was modified, and I have been informed that this caution produced the desired result. On the other side of this page I have written an extract from a letter of a high official in whose judgement I have the greatest confidence. I applied to him for his confidential report & obtained this answer / *Extract from letter* / 24 June 87 / 'Canon O'Hara is a man of highly nervous temperament, he is impulsive & emotional, honest in his intentions, but wanting calm judgement. He holds very extreme views and when crossed in any way I believe he would proceed to dangerous lengths. He is sympathetic & generous in his disposition and responds readily to generous treatment. I do not regard him as a safe counsellor or a wise leader of men.' . . . ' / Canon Staunton is not so clever or so quick a man, but he is prudent & cautious, has a great deal of tact, and possesses that firmness of character which would command the respect and secure the obedience of both Priests & people.' "

Tuam could make their report on the new *terna* to Propaganda when in Rome. The bishop of Elphin, Laurence Gillooly, was especially anxious, however, for almost immediately on his return to Ireland he wrote Kirby asking him to let him know as soon as possible about the new appointments to the vacant sees. "The Cardinal Prefect," Gillooly explained on Monday, January 29, "told me before I left that they would be considered at the Congregation of *Monday* last"(K). Gillooly was not only concerned because both Raphoe and Achonry bordered on his own diocese of Elphin, but also because one of the candidates for Achonry, John Lyster, was a protegé, and taught in his local College of the Immaculate Conception in Sligo.[31] When Lyster, therefore, was appointed to Achonry, and a favorite of Walsh's, Patrick O'Donnell, the *dignissimus,* to Raphoe, while Edward McGennis, vicar capitular and *dignissimus* succeeded to Kilmore, it must have appeared to Walsh and Croke that Rome had no real intention of interfering with the customary procedure in appointments to Irish Sees. "I am delighted," one of Kirby's former students, James Walker, for example, reported from the diocese of Raphoe on February 12, "at the choice of Dr. O'Donnell made by the Holy Father as it will save possible unpleasantness which would, had any other selection been made, probably ensue particularly as he had such a sweeping majority of votes"(K).

Both O'Donnell, who was only thirty-two years old, and McGennis were Nationalists, while Lyster, like his mentor Gillooly, was more conservative in politics. The political spectrum, however, in which these terms now found their meaning, had moved considerably to the left in Ireland in the last ten years. What Walsh and Croke, perhaps, did not understand was that Rome had recently endorsed the customary procedure in the appointment of Irish bishops not because of any real appreciation of the point of view they represented, but rather because Rome's sources of information with regard to the fitness of the various candidates were extremely limited. Norfolk's request to Balfour at Christmas, for example, for information about the political complexion of candidates for Irish sees, was an attempt to provide for Rome's deficiency in this matter. Not even Persico's recently acquired

---

[31] S, Errington to Smith, January 24, 1889: "From all I can learn there seems to be no chance of Lord Salisbury venturing in diplomatic relations. Many thanks for your interesting private information about the Bishoprics: the person mentioned for Clonfert [*sic* Achonry] I hear highly spoken of. He is the protegé of Dr. Gillooly."

information, which according to Norfolk had also been solicited, was apparently equal to Rome's needs. Balfour's own inability, however, to supply such information proceeded as much from similar lack of resources, as from a fear of the political consequences of such action on English public opinion. Until Rome's resources with regard to Irish information could be improved, therefore, she would only have an ineffective veto power, and those commended by the clergy and reported on by the bishops would continue to be generally, if discreetly, representative of the dominant Nationalist strain in the Irish Church. As long as Walsh and Croke, then, retained the confidence of the vast majority of their episcopal colleagues, Rome could only have her way in the Irish Church by acting independently of them.

The reports from Ireland, meanwhile, which Kirby received, could only have resulted in strengthening Walsh's conviction that both the country and clergy were one in their determination to resist, by every constitutional means in their power, the government's patent attempt to break the agrarian agitation. "Two of our priests," James Walker had also reported to Kirby in the course of his letter of February 12, from the diocese of Raphoe, "have been arrested under the Crimes Act one a P.P. and the other a C.C."(K). "The former," Walker explained, "got 3 months imprisonment but appealed & the trial is to come off in April, is out on bail. The C.C. is to be tried by a Coercion Court in a few days." "Their only crime," he remarked bitterly, "is that they advocated the cause of a miserably poor and downtrodden people." Three days later, Michael Logue, the archbishop of Armagh, wrote Kirby an interesting account of the trial of Father McFaddin, the parish priest of Gweedore, in Donegal, referred to by Walker. "Of course he has appealed," Logue also explained, "but that only puts off imprisonment to April"(K). "The Police in Donegal," he further charged, "are rampant. Before the trial of Fr McFaddin I telegraphed to the Chief Secretary that if he kept the Police quiet, I would get the priests to keep the people quiet." "He assented to this," Logue added, "and the result was, that although it was estimated there were twelve thousand people assembled, there was not even an angry word." "About twenty priests gathered," he noted with obvious satisfaction, "and kept the people under such perfect controul that a military officer present said he never saw such an immense multitude so quiet before. He said the people seemed more afraid of the umbrellas of the priests than of the rifles of his men."

"Notwithstanding this," Logue complained, "the police have been going about in the dead of night, every night since, and dragging out of their beds the poor people who assembled to show sympathy with their priests. When the police caught a batch of them, they hauled them off in the cold and storm to the nearest town, brought them before a magistrate and put them under bail to stand their trial." "The trials commence tomorrow," he continued, "and will continue for a week at least. Of course these poor people will all get a month at least now in the Spring when they should be preparing their little holdings for cropping." "Apart from anything else," he concluded indignantly, "anyone who knows how our poor people live in the mountains will feel the terrible inconvenience of a number of policemen visiting their little houses at dead of night when families are in bed with very little means of securing privacy." Logue was not the only one, however, with a story to tell about the iniquities of government under the Coercion Act, for the indomitable bishop of Meath, Thomas Nulty, also wrote Kirby two days later explaining how he had brought the local authorities to heel. "In spite of coercion," Nulty reported from Mullingar on February 17, "this country is wonderfully peaceable and orderly"(K). "The Gov^t," he added, "took it into its head to send nearly all the political Prisoners to Tullamore Jail in this Diocese. At first, the Authorities refused to let me visit them or any other prisoners in that Jail. But, I wrote a few public letters against them that soon brought them to their knees and I have just returned from visiting that Jail." "I lectured political and other prisoners there publicly," Nulty noted with obvious satisfaction in conclusion, "saw them all in their cells alone, and the authorities were as officious now as they were insolent before."

In the south, conditions were very much the same as those reported from the north and the midlands. "We are passing," the bishop of Cloyne, James McCarthy, informed Kirby from Queenstown, on February 23, "thru a very critical time at present"(K). "The Government," he maintained, echoing both Logue and Nulty, "are enforcing with unnecessary harshness a Coercion Act passed principally for the purpose of preventing the unhappy tenants of this Country in this disastrous year, from agitating against the payment of rents which the tribunals appointed by the Government itself have pronounced to be urgent, & which they have reduced in many cases below the reductions claimed by the tenants. Thank God however, except in one or two districts in Clare & Kerry where moonlighting exists, the tenants are conducting their struggle against the payment of excessive rents without having recourse to crime or outrage of any kind." "Indeed," he concluded firmly, "the only crime, if it can be so called, that exists in the country at present is that created by the Coercion Act, & consists in the refusal of the people to give up their meetings and their combinations against the payment of rents, which owing to the fall in prices, & the bad harvests of the last few years it is impossible for them to pay." From the West, the archbishop of Tuam reported to Kirby that since his return to Ireland from Rome he had been doing yeoman work in upholding the pope's reputation. "On our return home," MacEvilly confessed on March 3, "there were very ugly rumours about Rome & Ireland"(K). "I took every suitable opportunity," he assured Kirby, "of proclaiming from the *house tops,* 'that Ireland had not a greater friend on Earth than Leo XIII.' I repeated it and repeated it as I always like to say '*multum in parvo.*' " Noting then that he was on his Lenten visitations, MacEvilly concluded by adding that his flock were tranquil in the hope that they would soon have their own legislature. The real significance of MacEvilly's letter and those of the other Irish bishops to Kirby, of course, was that with the passing of winter and the coming of spring the worst of the crisis was over. They had, in effect, been able to contain the agrarian agitation in the face of extreme provocation on the part of the government, and had been able to do this, moreover, without compromising either the pope's or their own authority with the Irish people.

In Rome, meanwhile, immediately after his audience, Walsh set to work on the *relatio* on the Land Question requested by the pope. He retired to the Augustinian Convent at Genazzano, and for seven weeks labored unceasingly, producing a volume of sixteen chapters and an introduction totaling 329 pages. Some idea of Walsh's abundant energy and his remarkable ability to focus and concentrate is evident in an account of his daily routine at this time given by a then young Augustinian seminarian, John Condon, many years later to his biographer.

At 6:10 each morning the Archbishop was in the convent

oratory ready to say Mass. He had already shaved — and by that time he had also finished the recitation of Matins and Lauds. After Mass he made his thanksgiving and then recited the Small Hours of the Divine Office. At seven he and Mr. Condon took their coffee together. The Archbishop then went at once to his room and worked without a break until he joined the little community at the midday meal. An hour was devoted to dinner and a walk in the cloister. He wrote again from one till half past five, when, in company with Mr. Condon, he took a short walk and paid a visit to one of the neighbouring churches. Three-quarters of an hour was devoted to supper and conversation, and at half past seven the Archbishop retired to his room to continue his labours till about midnight.[32]

"I have been daily," Croke finally wrote Walsh on March 25, "expecting to hear from you, and, very likely, you were similarly looking out for a line from me" "Of news," he confessed, after a long and amusing account of the St. Patrick's day celebrations in Thurles, "I have none. Dr. O'Callaghan of Cork called here yesterday and in a very disjointed way, partly in Italian and partly in English, gave me a sketch of the Roman campaign and of your hard work. I could never go to any such length to satisfy Roman authority as regards Ireland. If they budge, they will only hurt themselves." "Drop me a line," he then concluded, "saying how and where you are."

On Easter Monday, April 2, Walsh finally found some time to bridge the gaps in his correspondence, and wrote both Croke and Manning. "I know how anxious your Eminence must have been all this time," Walsh apologized to Manning on April 2, "about the progress of affairs here. But I was so dreadfully hard pressed for time, working against time as I have been for the last month or six weeks, that it was really impossible for me to write"(M). "I have now a little breathing time," he explained to the cardinal, "as for the first time, I have got fairly ahead of my printer. Your Eminence will wonder how I have come to be in the printer's hands, but you will I know, be glad at hearing how it came about."

The Holy Father undoubtedly has a strong conviction that he can get something very substantial done for us in Ireland. So he asked the Bishop of Cork and myself to go to him one day, and

[32] *Walsh*, p. 326.

> to tell him fully how the whole case stands. It was most marvelous to see how he entered into everything, one would think that outside the shores of Ireland there was nothing in the world that he took the smallest interest in. We were with him for nearly two hours, and his sole anxiety at the end seemed to be whether there was anything else we wished him to understand. At the end he charged us to draw up a *relatio* on the whole question of the Land(M).

"Home Rule," Walsh noted significantly, "he understood fully, and needs no information about it — but I may say the Home Rule of which I expressed myself in favour, and which he at once took up with evident earnestness was something more like the state legislature system of the United States, or the federal arrangement of the German Empire, than that proposed by Mr. Gladstone." "As for Education," Walsh added interestingly, "we could hardly get him to notice the question at all. He sees very clearly that it is not, as he said, 'la questione attuale.' "

"Now coming to the *relatio,*" Walsh then informed the cardinal, "I decided on writing a *historical* statement, giving all the prominent incidents, including the various Bills and Acts of Parliament, for the last 30 or 40 years. This seems to me the best way of showing that the people want nothing but common justice, and that the great obstacle in the way of their getting it has been, and is, the Tory party. The work grew on my hands, and at a most critical moment my translators, for I had two at work, failed me." "I was then driven to the expedient," he explained, referring to a synopsis of his *relatio*, "of making up the enclosed, which was in the Holy Fathers hands last Wednesday. I do not expect to have the fuller exposition ready for about a fortnight. Your Eminence of course understands that the enclosed is *most confidential.* I have only a few copies, so I must ask you to let me have this one when I see you on my way home." "The Duke of Norfolk," Walsh then observed most pointedly in conclusion, "it seems, leaves to-day. He has been a most frequent visitor at the Vatican while here. His visits to the Secretary of State have been most numerous and most prolonged."

Three days later, the cardinal replied immediately by return of post from London. "The 'opusculo,' " he reported to Walsh on April 5, "I have read with great interest."[33] "It is clear and

---

[33] *Ibid.*, p. 328.

firm," Manning observed succinctly, "The Holy Father has already detailed knowledge to supply its brevity." "I will carefully keep the 'operazione' for you," he promised, reminding Walsh good humoredly of his lapse when on his way to Rome in December, " – as a pledge of my seeing you, when you return." "I hope," the cardinal concluded cordially, "you are well, and up to your work." The next day, Croke also replied to Walsh by return of post. "I got your letter," he informed Walsh on April 6, "and the dissertation on Irish affairs that accompanied it. The latter I have read over pretty carefully, but mean to re-read it tomorrow or after again, so as to be able to appreciate it fully"(W). "Then as you direct," he promised, referring to the bishop of Cork, "I will send it on to Dr. O'Callaghan." "The dissertation," Croke then noted, "must do a great deal of good." "It is very clear, well knit together," he assured Walsh, and unlike the cardinal, appreciating its *substance* as well as its form, "and manfully outspoken where it was needed to be so." "Persico," Croke added approvingly, "gets a rub or two, and by all accounts deserved it."

In the course of this letter, Croke had also explained to Walsh that he was just then in the midst of negotiations about the new management of the *Freeman's Journal*. The sudden death, at the end of March, of the owner and publisher, Edmund Dwyer Gray, had precipitated the crisis. Since the paper had, in the last seven or eight years, virtually become the organ of the Irish Parliamentary Party as well as the National journal, the question of what was to be done was of crucial concern to all who had hand or part in the National movement. "I am to have an interview, tomorrow," Croke had reported to Walsh, "with Ambrose Plunkett, in reference to the Freeman's Journal. Shares are considerably depreciated, and great speculation is going on concerning poor Gray's successor as Managing Director." "What do you think should be done?" he asked Walsh. "The post is sought for by Davitt, Harrington (T.), Sexton, and I believe by T. P. O'Connor. Plunkett has been co-opted by the Directors to fill the place of Moore deceased. That is a good move. He is a great friend of the Grays, and otherwise I hear, a pretty capable and far seeing man." "Young Gray," Croke noted, "is coming home. Everyone speaks well of him. He has, they say, all his father's best qualities as a man of business. He will be of age soon. Some think, therefore, that it would be well to work the Freeman till then by the present staff, placing the youngster on it, and in due course to put him, if found fit, in his father's place." "Plunkett and I," he assured Walsh, "will discuss and diagnose the situation tomorrow." "I will," he promised, "write result."

Three days later Croke was as good as his word, "Just a line," he informed Walsh on April 9, "to say that Plunkett has been here and that we were quite of the same opinion as to the course which should be pursued in reference to the vexed question of the managership of the Freeman"(W). "We will have no Managing Director just now," he explained," MacSweeny [?] will do the Editor and Plunkett will have a sharp look out upon the plant generally. There will be weekly meetings of the heads of the Staff, at which the present aspect of things will be discussed, and an agreement come to as to the topics to be treated of in the Editorial Columns generally during the subsequent week. This, fortunately, was initiated by poor Gray, and, it appears, with the happiest of results." "Suitors for the place," Croke noted, "will be sadly disappointed, especially, I fear Davitt who alone has formally applied for the post." "I send off document," he then reassured Walsh in conclusion as to his *relatio,* "to Dr. O'Callaghan today, or tomorrow." "I send by this post," he added in a postscript, "the usual £100 to Card. Simeoni for the foreign missions — I am afraid I won't have much merit for it."

In his two letters to Walsh of April 6 and 9, however, Croke neglected to mention that his agreement with Plunkett had, perhaps, been influenced by other considerations than simply the good governance of the *Freeman.* Parnell, it appears, was also very soon and very much concerned as to what was to be done, and wrote an exceedingly interesting letter to the most important of the Directors, Alderman Kernan, a copy of which was forwarded to Croke. "The sudden and untimely death of our dear friend Mr. Gray," Parnell explained to Kernan from the House of Commons Library on March 31, and coming straight to the point, "makes it necessary for us to consider the question of providing a successor to him in his post of Managing Director of the Freeman's Journal Company"(C). "A suitable person to fill this position," Parnell acknowledged, "will be difficult to find, and I am sure you fully recognise the great responsibility which devolves on you as a Director of the Company in the matter." "For myself," he observed, "I regard the subject from three points of view, or rather I consider that the person to be chosen should have three qualifications." "He should," Parnell maintained, "as the manager & editor of the national journal of Ireland, possess the confidence of the Irish people as a whole, he should from his judgement, talent, moderation & business capacity commend himself to the class from whom the shareholders are largely taken and to the shareholders themselves, and lastly he should have that experience, journalistic capacity and prudence for the successful conduct of so important an undertaking as the Freeman." "I do not know," Parnell confessed, "whether the choice will devolve on the Directors or upon the Shareholders." "Perhaps," he added in conclusion and ensuring a reply as well as finally explaining to Kernan what was really on his mind, "you will kindly inform me on this subject, also whether you have considered whether it might be desirable not to reconstitute or rather to abolish the office of Managing Director, and appointing an Editor simply [to] manage the concern through the Board of Directors." In this remarkable letter, Parnell once again demonstrated his very real political astuteness. By imposing as a first condition that the new managing director must have "the confidence of the Irish people as a whole," Parnell was simply asserting that he had a veto on the appointment. Since he was obviously the Leader because he possessed that "confidence," who then could succeed to the management of the *Freeman* without his approval? Further, in suggesting that the office of managing director be abolished, Parnell was serving notice that such power in the hands of another individual was not compatible with his being Leader. In effect, then, by his letter Parnell had, by presenting both the directors as represented by Kernan and Plunkett, and the Bishops as represented by Croke, with a *fait accompli,* further consolidated his political power base.

Indeed, this very astute move on the part of Parnell was but the climax of a situation which had been developing for more than a year. Since the previous March, when the pope had finally decided to take a new line with regard to Ireland, the Clerical-Nationalist alliance had been under very great pressure. The worst effects of what was essentially a deteriorating situation for the Clerical component of the alliance were contained for a time by Walsh's enormous personal influence, and his timely efforts to reassure Nationalist opinion both in the press and by initiating the Round Table

Conference. All this was possible not only because of the availability to him and his designates of the columns of the *Freeman's Journal* and his mastery of the intricacies of the Land Question, but also because of his presence in Dublin. When he set out for Rome in early December, therefore, the situation immediately began to worsen, and the press in general, and Dillon in particular, actually accused Rome of a bargain, in which the pacification of Ireland was to be the *quid pro quo* for diplomatic relations. As the government continued to mount its pressure on the Clerical-Nationalist alliance in the early new year by proceeding to prosecute priests as well as laymen under the Crimes Act, and British influence at Rome appeared to be in the ascendency, especially after the official visit of the duke of Norfolk, the effectiveness of the Clerical component of the alliance was correspondingly diminished. The diminution was, moreover, seriously aggravated by the pope's insistence that Walsh remain in Rome, for in leaving the Irish Bishops and clergy virtually leaderless in what was obviously a critical situation, they were in great danger of being reduced from equals to mere auxiliaries in the Clerical-Nationalist alliance. While such a transformation in the political role of the Irish Bishops and priests might not immediately wreck the alliance, it would certainly further impair its effectiveness. In the last analysis, then, the greatest danger to the political power and influence of the Church in Ireland was not simply that Roman action should render them vulnerable, but that their lay allies would unilaterally take advantage of their vulnerability to modify their role in the alliance in a fundamental way.

Part II

THE DECREE

VI. The Decree
April, 1888 - June, 1888

While Archbishop Walsh was diligently working away to finish his full *relatio* for the pope, Norfolk and Ross had returned to Rome and were just as busy on the other side. The very day, in fact, that Walsh was having what was, in his opinion at least, his very satisfactory audience with the pope and Cardinal Rampolla, Norfolk wrote Balfour a "Private & Confidential" note which indicated that Leo XIII was once again involved in a very deep game of diplomatic chess. "Supposing the Pope," Norfolk suggested on Sunday, February 12, from the Hôtel de Rome, "were preparing some letter or manifesto on Irish questions dealing especially with the moral aspect can you give us any points that would be of practical importance to be noticed by him *at the present moment.*"[1] The duke then listed the general headings that might be considered:

1.   Plan of Campaign
2.   Debtors (with the land court in existence) constituting themselves judges in their own cause.
3.   Boycotting
4.   Boycotting at schools (corruption of youth)
5.   Land League Courts
6.   The "unwritten law," being itself devoid of authority, being enforced by self-constituted judges.[2]

Walsh had in his audience, however, obviously provided the pope with more room for maneuver, for Norfolk wrote Balfour another *"Private and Confidential"* letter ten days later. "Can you let me have," he asked Balfour on February 22, "the information asked for on the enclosed paper."[3] "It is of great importance to me," Norfolk explained, "to have it and as

---
[1] B, 49821.
[2] *Ibid.*
[3] *Ibid.*

197

quickly as possible. Our object is to get accurate and speedy information so as to show the utter falsehoods which are reported to the Vatican in the endeavour to found the belief that the people in Ireland are being driven from their homes in thousands." "Absurd and grotesque as these representations are," Norfolk observed, and referring to Walsh, "I fear they have an effect and it is most important that we should not only show them to be false but also expose the source from which they come. I hope my two former letters reached you safely." "We should of course be grateful," Norfolk further suggested to Balfour in a postscript, "for anything bearing on the enclosed or any other points which you may think it well to inform us of."

The day before Norfolk wrote Balfour, the British ambassador in Rome, J. G. Kennedy, had informed Salisbury that the pope had received three addresses from the Scottish Roman Catholic deputation, and enclosed the pope's reply. "The language of H.H.," Kennedy had reported on February 21, "as Y. L^P will perceive was affectionate towards the Scots & conveyed no advice as on the occasion of the reception of the Irish deputation reported in my despatch. On this occasion H.H. confirmed to Scotland the title of special daughter of the Apostolic See & conferred on the much esteemed Rector of the Scots College in Rome the title of prelate."[4] "Dr. Campbell," Kennedy concluded, alluding to the rector of the Scots College, and one of Norfolk's and Ross's important contacts in Rome, "was foremost amongst the R. Catholics in Rome in guidance of loyalty towards the Queen on the occasion of·the celebration last year of H.M.'s Jubilee." Three days later Kennedy again reported to Salisbury on Irish affairs. "I hear on good authority," he assured Salisbury on February 24, "that Mg^r Persico has written to his friends in Rome in a desponding tone in regard to the results of his mission to Ireland. He is now it seems in the South of England & does not wish to return to Ireland."[5] "On the other hand," Kennedy informed Salisbury most significantly in conclusion, "I hear that the Pope is preparing a letter to the Irish Bishops enjoining them & through them, the Parish Priests to keep aloof from the Nationalist Party in Ireland."

"As you may sometimes receive letters from people in

F.O., 170/393.
Ibid.

Rome," the duke pointedly warned Salisbury some ten days later on March 3, "with reference to Irish matters, I think it well to let you know that no one who may write to you does so at my suggestion or in order to communicate anything I do not like to write myself"(Sy). "Ross and I are working away here," he assured Salisbury, "communicating information and doing what we can to check the false information sent in from the other side. I really believe we are doing important work. I can report nothing yet of a definite nature and must warn you to receive with caution any facts that may be communicated to you. Ross is the only person in Rome besides myself who has means of really knowing if any action here is decided upon and we cannot yet report anything with absolute certainty." "I enclose you a pamphlet," he explained, "drawn up by Ross on the Agrarian question. It has been corrected by a legal expert in Dublin and carefully looked over by Lord Selborne. We are sending it out to the Cardinals and others, and taking care it is mastered at headquarters."[6] "It is particularly well calculated," the duke observed, alluding again to Walsh, and even more discreetly to the utility of diplomatic relations, "to clear away the false and wholly mistaken impressions which closed men's minds here and which it is terribly hard work to dispell as our opponents have been able so long to pour their side of the story into the ears of the Vatican unchecked and without being answered in any authoritative way." "Lord Selborne," he further noted, referring to the former Liberal lord chancellor in Gladstone's first and second ministries, "has written a similar pamphlet on the Crimes Act which we are getting translated and shall distribute." "It is important," the duke stressed in conclusion, "that the fact of these papers emanating from us should be kept secret for the present."

Meanwhile, one of those reports which Norfolk had warned Salisbury about finally reached the prime minister. On March 16, Balfour forwarded Salisbury a letter from the son of the earl of Denbigh to the Irish lord chancellor, Lord Ashbourne. Denbigh, who was a prominent English Roman Catholic peer, was also an old and close friend of Leo XIII. "You will perhaps be glad to know," Denbigh's son had informed Ashbourne on March 12, "that my father writes from Rome, on the *very best authority,* that the Pope has quite made up his mind to go

---

[6] B, 49821, "La Question Agraire en Irelande, Résumée d'apres les Documents Originaux (1860-1887)."

against the Plan of C. & boycotting & to refuse preferment to
every priest who goes in for being more of a political partisan
than a priest."[7] "He says," young Fielding added, "the Pope
and his advisors have taken the correct measure of our worthy
Archbishop, who is kept there to supply information (?)." "A
supply of salt, however," he concluded, "is always kept handy."
"If the news is true," Balfour warned his uncle in his covering
letter of March 16, "(and Fielding is by no means such an ass
as his father:) His Holiness may think he has earned his *quid
pro quo* in the shape of a University or —."[8] "Thanks,"
Salisbury initialed this cover in reply, "We will talk of it in
Cabinet."

The duke returned to London from Rome on Easter Tuesday
evening, April 3, and wrote Salisbury the following day asking
for an appointment. "I have to go into the country today," he
explained on Wednesday, April 4, "for a funeral and shall come
back on Friday"(Sy). "If it would be possible," he suggested to
Salisbury, "for you to see me in London on either the 7th 8th or
9th for from half an hour to an hour I should be very glad. I am
fully occupied the whole of the three following days but shall be
free again by 13th." "If you thought it well," the duke concluded
efficiently, "that I should see you and Balfour together it might
perhaps be well as a saving of your time and his." What is most
interesting, perhaps, about this rather laconic letter is that there
is certainly no sense of urgency in it. If Norfolk had anything
very positive to report about Irish affairs, he would have most
certainly pressed harder for an interview with the prime
minister and his chief secretary for Ireland.

Norfolk's return from Rome, however, did increase the
speculation about Irish affairs. "I hear that in his address to the
Irish Bishops," Errington wrote Smith from Dublin on April 8,
referring to the audience of February 1, "the Pope spoke *very
strongly* about the conduct of the Clergy in supporting
resistance to the law; the Bishops of course have been anxious
to suppress this fact. There seems to be no doubt that Msgr
Persico has taken a very serious view of the dangers with which
the attitude of the Clergy towards this revolutionary movement
threatens Religion. They say he is to come back to Ireland with
executive powers; this will do good"(S). "In spite of what some

---

[7] B, 49689.
[8] *Ibid.*

newspapers say," Errington assured Smith, "I do not think Govt. will venture on diplomatic relations with Rome. I hear the Duke of Norfolk's mission did good, and that Lord Emly is very busy at Rome. The Govt have been so far successful, & they are stronger than they were. If steady Govt. here could be kept up for a few years, the revolutionary portion of the agitation would be put down, & the Country being quiet a fair measure of local autonomy might safely be tried; but home Rule NOW would mean anarchy in Ireland, and disruption of the Empire." "In 1885," Errington observed in conclusion, and justifying his own developing political metamorphosis, "things were different, & home Rule might then have been safely tried, not so now."

The rumors and speculation, which had been stimulated by the return of the duke of Norfolk from Rome, were greatly increased when the London *Times* reported on Thursday, April 19, that the Holy See had finally condemned the Plan of Campaign. When the *Times* entered into the details of the condemnation the following day, and maintained that the condemnation would be soon made public, the duke's mission certainly took on the appearance of having been successful. Still, when no authoritative condemnation came in the next few days, the Irish Bishops, and especially Walsh, who was just seeing the final pages of his *relatio* for the pope through the press, must have breathed a great deal easier. On Monday, April 23, however, Walsh received, and the other Irish Bishops some days later, a circular letter of that date, from the prefect of Propaganda, covering another letter, or "Decree," issued by the Holy Office of the Inquisition, under the signature of R. Cardinal Monaco, and dated April 20, 1888. This remarkable document deserves to be quoted in full:

My Lord, — Whenever the affairs of their country seemed to require it, the Apostolic See has frequently addressed to the Irish people — towards whom it has always shown special affection — seasonable words of warning and counsel with the object of enabling them to defend or to assert their rights without prejudice to justice or to public tranquility. At the present moment our Holy Father, Pope Leo XIII, fearing lest right notions of justice and charity should be perverted amongst that people in consequence of that mode of warfare called the *Plan of Campaign,* which has been employed in that country in disputes between letters and holders of lands or farms, as also in consequence of a form of proscription in connection with the same contests known as *Boycotting,* commissioned the Supreme Congregation of the Holy Roman and Universal Inquisition to make the matter the subject of grave and careful examination. Accordingly the following question was submitted to the Most Eminent Fathers who share with me the office of General Inquisitors against heretical error, etc., viz.: In disputes between letters and holders of farms or lands in Ireland, is it lawful to have recourse to those means known as the *Plan of Campaign* and *Boycotting?* – and their Eminences having long and maturely weighed the matter, unanimously replied: *In the negative.*

Our Holy Father confirmed and approved this reply on Wednesday the 18th of the present month.

How equitable this decision is any one will see who reflects that a rent fixed by mutual consent cannot, without violation of contract, be reduced at the arbitrary will of the tenant alone. This the more, since for the settling of such disputes courts have been established which, allowance being made even for failure of crops or disasters which may have occurred, reduce excessive rents and bring them within the limits of equity.

Again it cannot be held to be lawful that rent should be extorted from tenants and deposited with unknown persons, no account being taken of the landlord.

Finally it is altogether foreign to natural justice and to Christian charity that a new form of persecution and of proscription should ruthlessly be put in force against persons who are satisfied with and are prepared to pay the rent agreed on with their landlord: or against persons who in the exercise of their right take vacant farms.

Your Lordship will therefore – prudently but effectively – admonish the clergy and people in reference to this matter, and exhort them to observe Christian charity, and not to overstep the bounds of justice whilst seeking relief from the evils which afflict them.

Your devoted servant in the Lord,

R. Cardinal Monaco[9]

Rome 20th April, 1888

When Walsh received Cardinal Monaco's letter on April 23, he certainly must have been stunned. After his initial shock,

---

[9] *Walsh,* pp. 331-32. See also pp. 329-30 for the Latin text. See also F.O., 170/394, Kennedy to Salisbury, April 27, 1888: "My Lord, / I have the honour to enclose copy of a Decree just issued by the Inquisition (Holy Office) condemning the Plan of Campaign and Boycotting."

however, he must have also realized that he had only four days to decide what action he should take before the news was published in Ireland. At the end of three days Walsh decided to play for more time, and on April 26 he telegraphed his fellow Irish archbishops and the *Freeman's Journal*.[10] The substance of Walsh's telegram may be gathered from the *Freeman's* editorial reaction the next day. "The Irish people," the *Freeman* noted benignly on Friday, April 27, "will receive the decree of the Pope or the Propaganda with respect the most profound." "They will await," the editorial added, "the propounding of it by the prelates whom they love and trust as ever heretofore with anxiety but with courage." No one, however, realized better than Croke that Walsh's opportune telegram had only secured a little more time. For when the text of the Decree was published, as it must soon be, the Irish Bishops would be then obliged to give a lead in order not to forfeit their considerable influence in the political and agrarian agitation to their more militant lay colleagues. On Saturday, April 28, therefore, Croke had an interview with the most influential of the lay leaders, John Dillon. As Croke later explained to Walsh on May 1, Dillon was "quite cool over the matter"(W). "We understand each other fully," Croke assured Walsh as to Dillon, "and the course determined on was to agree with Inquisitors in condemning 'Plan' and 'boycotting' where they were, or are, attended with the conditions referred to in the so called 'decree.' "

Croke also remembered to cover the English as well as the Irish front, for he wrote Cardinal Manning the following day, Sunday, a most interesting letter, given the fact that he had already decided on his course of action with Dillon. "You have seen, of course," Croke observed on April 29, "the last Roman pronunciamento"(C). "We are placed by it," Croke explained, "in a great fix here." "What," he asked Manning tactfully, "is to be done?" "Two courses," Croke suggested, "are open to the people. Either to ignore the document altogether, as was done in the Parnell Testimonial case, and to allow things to go on as if it had never been issued, or to grapple freely and fully with the reasons assigned as a basis for the Decree, and thus to show, as easily may be done, that it rests on no solid foundation." "The Archbishop of Dublin," he further informed

---

[10] C, April 29, 1888. See Walsh to Croke for mention of the telegram.

the cardinal, "never heard of the document until after the Pope's approval of it, and was meanwhile, and for months before that, busily engaged in making a report on the Irish question generally, at the special request of his Holiness." "In a few days more," Croke assured Manning politely in conclusion, "I shall see my way clearly before me and asking your blessing and advice I remain. . . ." Croke was, of course, more interested at this stage in the cardinal's blessing than his advice. In offering the cardinal two seemingly viable alternatives, Croke was really presenting Manning with a *fait accompli*. An astute tactician as his eminence must have certainly realized that Croke had already made up his mind what was to be done, since the proposed alternative of ignoring the Decree, given its explicit terms, was no choice at all for a prince of the Church, and the only other really viable alternative, submitting unreservedly, was not even mentioned by Croke.

While Croke was thus writing the cardinal, Dillon was explaining to the tenants of one of the Plan of Campaign estates in Herbertstown that the Decree did not apply because there was no freedom of contract, the land courts were landlord run and, therefore, not impartial, and the Plan was furthermore not run "by force and intimidation."[11] That same Sunday evening, April 29, Walsh also wrote Croke from Rome. "I hope to hear from you," he explained anxiously, "in a day or two as to the state of feeling in Ireland"(C). "The telegrams announce to-day," Walsh then noted, "that J^n Dillon has opened the campaign against the new Decree. It is hard to say what ought to be done. For the sake of the Holy See it is a deplorable business. It is well that the *reasons* were added, for this suggests a line — which Dillon seems to have adopted — of passing by the Decree without questioning in any way the Pope's authority in judging moral questions." "At all events," Walsh further observed, "the thing which the Decree practically announces that it condemns does not exist." "Should any action," Walsh asked Croke, "be taken by the Bishops?" "Would it be worthwhile," he added rhetorically, "to hold a meeting?" "I should think not," he answered. "It seems to me," he further maintained, "that someone — and I dare say I will do it myself, if no one else does — should submit a case, setting forth that at all events in his diocese the events were not fixed by contract in any true sense of the word, but were simply imposts, put upon the people by the landlord — also that the tribunals are in many

---

[11] *Irish Catholic* (Dublin), May 5, 1888.

cases not open to the people at all as an effective protection against eviction for the non-payment of the most excessive rents." "The case, then," Walsh asserted, echoing both Dillon and Croke, "might ask whether the Decree applied to such cases." "But then," he added plaintively, realizing that he had been "mousetrapped" by Leo XIII, "all this has been explained already, as clearly at all events as I could explain it." "The whole thing is deplorable," Walsh summed up again for Croke in conclusion, and asked finally, "Ought anything to be done?"

Croke had also wondered about the advisability of summoning a general meeting of the Bishops, and wrote the archbishop of Armagh, who as primate of All Ireland, took formal precedence among the Irish archbishops. "The question Your Grace asks," Michael Logue confessed on Monday, April 30, "has been puzzling myself and it is difficult to find a satisfactory answer. It is evident we are required to publish the decision, but how this can be done prudently and without leading to mischief is another matter"(C). "It strikes me," Logue declared rather obviously, "we have arrived at a very momentous crisis, and that a meeting of the Bishops should be at once called to determine what is the most prudent course in the circumstances, and to put the true state of the case *plainly and boldly* before the Holy Father." "It has always appeared to me," he added, somewhat naively in the light of Walsh's efforts in Rome, "we have been too timid in this respect, and I fear our timidity has led to serious dangers. Indeed, I can see now that a general meeting of the Bishops should have been called much earlier, and probably I will be blamed for not having taken action. But such blame would be very unjust." "Though there were two of our body in Rome," he complained, "I have never received a line or a hint to indicate what was going on. I have been left to rumour, conjecture and the newspapers for any suspicion I have formed that there was something in the wind." "I write to Dr. McEvilly by this post," Logue explained, more helpfully, referring to their archiepiscopal colleague of Tuam, "and if your Grace and he think that a general meeting should be held, I will request the Secretaries to convene it." "Meantime," he warned Croke more pointedly, "I have some fears lest imprudent pronouncements on the part of the lay Nationalist leaders may do harm. Mr. Davitt is especially dangerous." "Their mistake," he then added, referring to the lay leaders in general, "is that they regard this as a question of politics, which it is not, but a pure question of justice upon which the Pope has every right to pronounce and to be heard. If the decision has been given on any wrong grounds, we may blame our supineness for it." "If Your Grace," he finally assured Croke in a more docile vein, "kindly sends a line by return of post or a wire, I will act on any suggestion you may make."

The rumors, meanwhile, were simply sensational. They ran from the very disturbing news that the pope had actually ordered the sacraments to be refused to members of the National League,[12] to the even more unnerving report that Walsh had resigned the see of Dublin.[13] "Your letter of 29th, just to hand," Croke declared on Wednesday, May 2, "was an immense relief to me. I could not account for your silence"(W). "You will have seen before this reaches you," Croke then noted, referring to the Decree, "the admirable 'expose['] on the whole affair that appeared in yesterday's Freeman, presumably from the pen of Dr. McGrath of Clonliffe. It is quite clear and conclusive." "If I have a warrant," Croke argued, "in my possession for the arrest of a man with red hair, heavy beard, no teeth, black eyes, protruding stomach, a lame leg, and six feet high, and that I arrest a man in whose person all the above qualities are wanting, I surely should liberate the supposed culprit, on seeing my mistake — and make an apology to him besides. Sat verbum." "I had a letter this morning," Croke reported, referring to the cardinal's reply to his letter of Sunday, "from Cardinal Manning. He says he has written to you for information. We all want that. He says 'inter alia,' 'I always thought that "Plan" legally untenable but morally just.' " "I wrote to Dr. Logue, yesterday," he further reported, "*half* recommending and *half* suggesting a general meeting of the Bishops. But, I see great difficulty in that course. So I wired him this morning not to summon it; and I add that you do not appear to be favourable to it."

"As regards the feeling through the country," he informed Walsh, "all that can be said is, that no public notice has been taken of 'decree' at all yet — the people don't seem to mind it —

[12] See letter from Ripon to Manning, April 30, 1888, quoted in Shane Leslie, *Henry Edward Manning* (London, 1921), p. 426.

[13] See K, O'Connell, Press Gallery, House of Commons, London, to Kirby, May 1, 1888: "Kindly say whether Archbishop Walsh has resigned reply prepaid."

Everything goes on as usual." "The Freeman," he explained, "at my suggestion, is looking up campaign cases through the Country and means to give reliable statistics to show that 'contracts' were not free, that 'courts' (impartial) were not accessible in numerous cases (if at all) and that money was paid into the 'war chest,' most freely by the campaigning tenants, and not 'extorted' from them. So also of boycotting." "I met the priests," he further observed, "here at Conference, yesterday. We talked over the '*decree*.' I issued no instructions, except, of course, to discourage hasty and irreverent language addressed to the Holy See, and to condemn the 'plan' and 'boycotting' when the 'decree' *applies*." "Have you seen the Pope," he asked Walsh, "since '*decree*[']— was issued? If so, what had he to say for himself? When did you get official intimation of existence of decree? Did you present your report? What are you at? Why don't you come home? What is the good in wasting and worrying yourself over this matter any longer?" "I shouldn't care," Croke declared warmly, "to live amongst the Philistines an hour longer than I could help it." "O'Brien in the dock daily," he then finally concluded in his usual telegraphic style, "Dillon preparing for same. Weather wet and boysterous [*sic*]. Write immediately in detail. Give some facts instructive, or interesting, in the case. God bless you."

Immediately after he had received Croke's letter of Sunday, April 29, Manning had indeed written Walsh. The cardinal, however, not only wanted more information, as he informed Croke, but he also had some advice to give. "Pray without delay," he advised Walsh on Monday, April 30, "let me know the history of the Decree."[14] "Had you any knowledge of it?" Manning asked, "Had Mgr. Persico?" "1. While it stands," the cardinal declared categorically, "all must submit." "2. But the reasons," he suggested, "may be analysed and laid before the Holy Office." "Mgr. Jacobini of Propaganda and Cardinal Schiaffino," Manning further suggested, "would probably advise best." "I am glad you are well," the cardinal concluded pointedly, "and I am glad you are in Rome." "I have really nothing to add," Walsh replied immediately on May 3, Thursday, "to what your Eminence has seen in the papers"(M). "The condemnation of boycotting," he pointed out to the cardinal, "does not seem to be objected to by anyone. As for

[14] *Walsh*, pp. 339-40.

the Plan of Campaign, it is obvious that some misleading statement of its nature was set forth in the case dealt with by the Holy Office. The three reasons set forth in the Decree are unassailable as statements of truths. They are equally satisfactory no doubt as reasons applying to the case that was in hand. But manifestly, they have no bearing upon what we know as the Plan of Campaign in Ireland." "If the Holy Father," Walsh maintained, "had waited for another week when my information would have been in his hands, the Decree could not have been issued in its present form. But then, I should have felt some responsibility in the matter. As things stand, I am quite clear."

"Now that the Decree has been issued," Walsh rationalized, coming to the first of the cardinal's points, "I see great advantages in what has been done." "The Holy Father," he explained further, and Manning must have been relieved, "in clearing away from our cause those things that were, honestly or dishonestly, put forward by our adversaries as reasons for leaving our case undealt with, has done us, I think, an enormous service. He meant all this, and if he is able now to carry out the rest of his programme, his Jubilee Year may yet bring us a satisfactory settlement of our difficulties." "Feeling as I do upon the whole question," Walsh assured the cardinal further, "I should be sorry to see any move made for an interpretation or explaining away of the Decree. We should leave things as they are, thus our case is an immensely strong one." "If, however," Walsh warned Manning in conclusion, "nothing is done for us, and the people are left without help to face another winter, we must give them a free hand."

"Your letter," Manning responded three days later on Sunday, May 6, "reached me late last night, and gave me much relief."[15] "Our papers," he reported, "have been full of folly, and I could not tell what might be passing. It is strange — but nothing surprises me — that you were not consulted, and that no one verified the reasons alleged for the decisions as to rents. Boycotting, I said five years ago, begins in horseplay, but may end in bloodshed. The Plan of Campaign is a true reflex of the whole Irish Question. 'Legal right and moral wrong' — *Summum jus, summa injuria.*" "I have written these words," Manning further reminded Walsh, and referring to the pope,

15 Leslie, *op. cit.,* pp. 427-28.

"long ago — you know to whom. For the moment, worldly influence has prevailed. My daily fear is that some word or act may exceed the limits of faith or morals." "At first," he confessed, "I wished that this decision had been sent in private to all you Bishops as private direction. But then I saw that you might have been embarrassed, and the brunt would have fallen on you. Now it comes over your heads from the highest source, and you are all sheltered, and have the pastoral and peaceful office of guiding and guarding your people in submission. But I hope the Plan of Campaign will be fully explained and understood as an abnormal but moral equity. Parliament has recognised this in the areas of the crofters of Scotland." "Try to convince," he advised Walsh, "Cardinal Monaco and Cardinal Mazzella. The former is very acute; the latter knows the English and Irish outer world well. If you can gain them, and Mgr. Jacobini of Propaganda, they will guide the rest." "One thing more," the cardinal added, obliquely referring to the rumors of Walsh's resignation, "do not let pain, or uprightness of heart, or any self-renouncement, lead you to offer to leave your post of duty, difficulty or danger." "God," he concluded magisterially, "has chosen you to fill it, and to stand there till you die."

Almost immediately after he wrote Manning on Thursday, May 3, Walsh finally made up his mind about what was to be done in the crisis created by the Decree, and his decision was a good deal more in line with the cardinal's advice of April 30, than it was with the action Croke had decided on. On Saturday, May 5, Walsh wrote Timothy Harrington, secretary of the National League, offering his advice on the forthcoming fortnightly meeting of the central branch of the League in Dublin, which functioned unofficially as the executive committee of the League, and at which Harrington would preside. "I mark this letter 'confidential,'" Walsh explained to Harrington, "in the sense that it is not to be published, and that its contents should not in any way be used as coming from me."[16] "I write for your own guidance," he added, "as I think there will be a meeting of the League on Tuesday; and I am, of course anxious that nothing should be said or done to give a handle to its enemies." "I have," Walsh informed Harrington categorically, "practically no doubt of the following:

[16] *Walsh,* pp. 342-43.

1st. — That for some time past a very complex machine has been at work to obtain a condemnation of the Home Rule movement if possible, *but at all events of the League.* This, if successful, would of course make it necessary for ecclesiastics at once to withdraw from all connection with it.

2nd. — That the points dealt with in the Decree, Plan of Campaign and Boycotting, were taken up by the opponents of the movement with the view of obtaining a condemnation not of these things only but of the League itself.

3rd. — That the clear limitation of the Decree — to say nothing of the general words of encouragement — has been a source of bad disappointment to the originators of the intrigue.

4th. — That the Pope saw through the whole affair from the beginning, and took the very best way of countermining the plans of the intriguers. He simply referred a case stated to the Holy Office, which in the discharge of its duty examined that case and decided it.

5th. — That the chief hope of the intriguers now rests on the chance that the League may commit itself by some imprudent action which will bring it under the condemnation of the Holy See.

6th. — That the business of the hour is to take every possible precaution on this point. Not only should the Central League keep its hands clean, but it should act, as it has always acted, in condemning the excesses of any local branches that may be guilty of them.[17]

"All this being so," Walsh asserted, "you may ask what I think should be done on Tuesday. I should make the following suggestions:

1st. — Pass a resolution declaring that any political organisation would be out of place in a Catholic country such as Ireland, which would fail to receive not only with respect, but with profound submission, the teaching of the Holy See on a point of morals.

2nd. — Pass another resolution saying that in the present case *as questions have been raised as to the precise meaning and extent of the Decree,* you await whatever instructions may be issued regarding it *by the bishops.*

3rd. — And a third, that you impress earnestly upon all who have the success of the National movement at heart the necessity of abstaining from anything in discussions, whether oral or written, that could be construed by the enemies of the

---

[17] *Ibid.*

movement as a questioning of the authority of the Holy See on matters of faith and morals.[18]

"I am strongly of opinion," Walsh further suggested to Harrington, "that, as a matter of *politics* or *tactics,* an opportunity should be taken just now to drop the Plan of Campaign as quietly as possible. It did splendid work for the tenants. But there is no doubt it led recently to much embarrassment. Mr. Parnell never liked it. Of course the same must be said of Gladstone and the other Liberal leaders who have given such splendid help for the last year or two." "As regards its justification from a moral point of view," Walsh added, returning for a moment to safer ground, "a great deal could be said about the Plan in abstract, which could not be said of it in actual operation. At all events waiving the theology of the matter, and looking at it as an affair of *practical politics,* I can see no room for doubt in the matter."

"Not only the Government," Walsh argued, now adducing *his own* reasons for the condemnation of the Plan, "but the 'Unionist' people generally, would find themselves in a most serious difficulty — in fact, I don't see how they could justify any further inaction — if the excuses on which they have so long been relying were suddenly cut away from them." "I take it for granted," Walsh maintained, noting undoubtedly the restrained pronouncement of the special correspondent in London of the *Freeman's Journal* on May 4, as to what Parnell would say in his forthcoming speech to the Liberal *élite* at the Eighty Club on May 8, "that Mr. Parnell would in no way incur the responsibility of advising the continuance of the means in question, in the face of the new state of things that has arisen; and this being so I don't see how the responsibility is to be incurred." "I write, I need to say," Walsh concluded finally, "altogether from myself; and also altogether to yourself, merely that you make your own use of the ideas that occur to me." "P.S.," he added, "— Of course I include any two or three confidential persons you may think it necessary to consult."

Why Walsh decided to take a stiffer line on the Decree between May 3, when he wrote Manning, and May 5, when he wrote this long and revealing letter to Harrington, had undoubtedly to do with the developing situation in both Rome

---

[18] *Ibid.*

and Ireland. In Rome Walsh found the attitude of the authorities was hardening over the reception of the Decree in Ireland. Walsh was, as were Logue and Manning, obviously alarmed that the lay National leaders could not be contained. Indeed, Walsh's suspicions were fully justified for the lay leaders, with John Dillon in the vanguard were mobilizing for action against the Decree. After his speech in Herbertstown on Saturday, April 28, Dillon spoke again on the following Thursday, May 3, at Kilmurray in Clare. His speech was certainly provocative, since he was reported as having "dealt especially with the recent Papal Circular, and set forth in very strong terms what he conceived should be the attitude of the Irish people towards it."[19]

> He said that, after having studied the document, and having consulted those who are learned in the law of the Church, it was his opinion that the Rescript was not binding on the conscience of any Irishman at all. Every people, he said, who had ever enjoyed the smallest degree of liberty, or who had any self-respect, should object to be ruled in temporal concerns by men who did not understand the circumstances under which they lived. While yielding unqualified obedience to the Church in spiritual matters, people should preserve absolute independence in temporal matters.[20]

Before he read the reports of Dillon's effort at Kilmurray, Croke had written to compliment him on his speech at Herbertstown. In his reply, Dillon proceeded to lay down the law as far as the lay National leadership was concerned. "I have been out of town," Dillon explained to Croke on Sunday, May 6, "and only returned last night — or I would have written before now. I was very glad though to learn that you approved of what I said at Herbertstown and I trust that nothing that I have said since will appear to be too strong or to be disrespectful to His Holiness"(C). "You will have heard," Dillon added significantly, "that it has been decided to have a meeting of the Catholic Members of the Parliamentary Party. Parnell has approved — and I feel confident that it [is] the right thing to do." "Altho'," Dillon admitted, parrying obviously one of the arguments made by Croke, "the Circular may have no serious effect on the movement — it is impossible to shut our

[19] *Irish Catholic,* May 12, 1888.
[20] *Ibid.*

eyes to the spirit it gives evidence of and I feel perfectly confident that if not met with some unmistakable demonstration this would be followed by other & more effective measures." "It is certainly hard for Irish Catholics," Dillon pointed out to Croke most effectively, "to endure threats particularly that Mr. Ross of Bladensburg & Lord Emly should be the accepted counselors of the Vatican whilst the Irish Archbishops & Bishops & the Catholic Members of Parliament should be treated with studied contempt." "So far as I have been able to gather," Dillon observed pointedly, "— the feeling throughout the country is first rate. And the priests and people are only waiting for a lead to shew in an unmistakable way what their feelings are. I *never* saw a finer spirit than was shown by the priests and people in West Clare. The Coercion Act & the Papal Circular seem to have acted as an excellent tonic mixture on the National spirit. I don't believe such enthusiastic meetings could have been held at any previous period of the agitation." "William O'Brien," Dillon finally informed Croke in conclusion, "is going over tonight to see Mr. Parnell."

That Croke was either unaware of or unconcerned about the rising lay tide, at least before he received Dillon's notice of a "tonic mixture," was made evident in a letter he had written to Walsh the day before Dillon had written to him. "I take it for granted," Croke assumed on Saturday, May 5, "that though I have not much to tell you beyond what is had in the papers you will like to get a line from me. Everything is quiet here. All the National, or semi National priests, take substantially the same view of the Irish situation. It is not materially changed. On goes the cause: 'decree' or no 'decree' "(W). "I had a good deal of difficulty," Croke explained to Walsh, "in preventing Dr. Logue from calling a meeting of the Bishops. I should hardly have succeeded had I not so opportunely got your letter discountenancing it." "As you would naturally expect," Croke added, referring to Bartholomew Woodlock, one of the two Secretaries to the episcopal body, "Ardagh was anxious for it and so wrote the Primate. But just as he had written he got word of the serious illness of his Sister, Mrs. Mahony of Blarney, and proceeded South — calling here. I changed his mind: and we wired conjointly to the Primate our united opinion — that and other considerations conveyed to him by me in letter determined his advice; and there is now to be no meeting." "Had it taken place," Croke maintained, referring undoubtedly to the differences of opinion amongst the Irish Bishops themselves, "it might have been most embarrassing, as is pretty plain to anyone."

"I met all the Cashel priests at Conference," Croke informed Walsh again, expanding on what he had written in his last letter, "and laid down the line for them there. They are, of course, to prevent as far as possible, and discountenance all expressions of opinion on part of respective flocks, at all irreverent to Holy See; and, if asked for information respecting 'decree,' they are to say, that the 'plan' and 'boycotting' as described by the Inquisitors, and vested under the conditions laid down by them, is condemned undoubtedly, and *rightly* condemned. As to the question of *fact*, it will be for the Clergy in any place where the 'plan' prevails to pronounce on that — No further promulgations. I think that is the course which will be taken everywhere, or nearly so." "Tell me how matters stand in Rome," Croke then demanded, "and what is thought of our attitude towards the 'decree.' " "I don't know about stating a case," he advised, "What would we do if they gave an adverse decision." "Things are very well," he maintained, "as they are. They left us what Ardagh calls a 'back-door' for escape, by assigning reasons. Only for that we were done." "I had a letter yesterday," he added dryly, "from Cardinal Simeoni acknowledging receipt of my £100 — the last he'll ever get from me." "Don't fail," Croke finally concluded, "to write *fully*."

When he received Croke's letter of the 5th, three days later in Rome, Walsh not only replied *"fully"* about the "situation" in the Holy City, but authoritatively about what action he thought should be taken by the Irish Bishops. "As far as I can gauge the situation," Walsh explained to Croke on Tuesday, May 8, "it now stands as follows:

    1.   The Decree, which would be manifestly a dead letter if taken as limited by the reasons stated, is now regarded here as *not* so limited. A distinction (which no doubt exists) is pointed out between the act of the Holy Office and the letter of Card. Monaco La Valletta. The *decree* seems to be absolute.

    2.   Action, then, taken in the direction of working the *Plan* and *Boycotting*, is looked upon as a public resistance to the *Decree*.

    3.   It seems now to be openly acknowledged that the condemnation is based on the reports of Mgr. Persico. This *seems* to mean that he has committed himself to the statements

relied on as reasons in the Cardinal's letter — for it is not easy to conceive that when giving reasons at all the Cardinal would not give the best he had — but care is taken to point out that the Decree is there, and that the reasons are not.

4. The distinction drawn between politics and morals is (no doubt most fairly) objected to. A line of politics may be morally wrong(C).

"It is not easy," Walsh further explained to Croke, "to state in this way the results picked up in conversations and all sorts of ways. But I think the foregoing sums up the situation here accurately, and as fully as needs be."

"Now," he added, "for what should be done. I believe that [the] most essential point to look is the saving of the National League. If it takes the line which is regarded here as setting the Decree at defiance, it will be condemned next. I have written to Harrington on the point. Of course the Leaguers may say they will go on never minding the Decree, but this would mean an open public resistance which would give rise to all sorts of trouble about admitting people to the Sacraments etc. etc. Besides it would involve the withdrawal of the priests. And possibly it might give a handle for condemning the whole National movement. In all this I am taking things at the worst." "I have no doubt indeed," he argued somewhat unconvincingly, and referring to the dissident Irish bishops, "that the line taken by the Pope is a total upset to the plans of the 'faction'. Their denunciation of the *means* was simply used to secure a condemnation of the *organisation*." "If the League does anything authoritatively," he suggested, as he had to Harrington, "it should be done to express confidence in the Bishops as expounders of the Decree. This would make its position perfectly safe. It seems to me a very ill-advised proceeding to have individual members of the Party going about the country speaking, as they are, at such a time." "I read the affair about Parnell," Walsh noted, referring to the *Freeman's* forecast of what Parnell would say at the Eighty Club dinner to the Liberal *élite,* "in Friday's paper as a quiet hint from him to keep them quiet at all events for a few days. It seems in this respect to be a failure." "John Dillon's speech in Clare," he further complained, "and the presence of so many priests, are most embarrassing just now."

"I think," Walsh declared finally, "the course of the Bishops is clear.

1.   Let it be ascertained whether it is generally regarded as
advisable from a *tactical* point of view that the Plan etc. should
be kept up. (As matters stand, *I* look on it as almost essential
that they should be quietly *dropped:* Parnell never liked the
Plan: and it is no doubt a great embarrassment to Gladstone
etc.: it would I think be a very serious step now to try to keep it
on without having the responsibility of the step fully assumed
by Parnell i.e. if he is to continue as leader.
2.   If the Bishops are not something like unanimous for
letting it go on, I think this should settle the question practically.
3.   If they are anything like unanimous, they should apply
Benedict XIV's principle about withholding the publication of
Papal Acts, and communicate at once with the Holy See,
sending forward an authorized representation to present a
carefully drawn up document. This document should point out
that the whole affair was evidently the result of an attempt to
mislead the Holy See: the very foundation being cut away by
what the Bessborough Commission reported as to freedom of
contract &c. &c.(C).

"Harrington, the League," Walsh then hurriedly warned Croke
again in a postscript, "is in danger if it does not keep clear of
imprudence." "I have written a letter for Friday's Freeman,"
Walsh added, softening a little, "which put the best face I can
on the whole business." "It may indeed," he concluded
hopefully, *"end well."*

"I can only write you a line," Croke explained to Walsh post
haste on Thursday, May 10, "I am off on visitation"(W). "I have
just got yours of 8th," he acknowledged, "and read yours of 7th
in this days Freeman. I understand the 'Situation' fairly. It does
not look well." "Dr. Murphy wrote you, on Wednesday night,"
he further informed Walsh, referring to the latter's secretary,
and to the meeting of the Irish Bishops obviously held against
his advice on May 9, "about result, in brief, of our proceedings
at Clonliffe. They were fairly satisfactory. We have forwarded
letter to propaganda. We await result." "I have written to
Dillon, and spoken to him," Croke added, "urging on him the
necessity of keeping himself quiet, and of not denying the
Pope's competency to deal magisterially with this question,
which differs 'toto caelo' from the veto, or Parnell's tribute. Tis
hard to manage him." "Dr. O'Callaghan," Croke further
explained, referring to the bishop of Cork, "has told us that in
his last interview with the Pope, his Holiness said 'that he was
determined to support the Tory Government, and that he had

no fancy for Gladstone whom he looked upon as a dangerous revolutionist.' This is dreadful." "I am sure," he added, referring to the meeting of the Irish Catholic M.P.'s scheduled for Thursday, May 17, "the members will talk strong next week." "I hope you are quite well," Croke then noted solicitously, "Leave as soon as you can. I would recommend a fair rest in via." "Had two letters," Croke then reported in a postscript, "from Dr. K. They urge as you do, quiet acceptance of *decree*."

In his two very long and revealing letters to Harrington and Croke, Walsh was evidently attempting to preserve the Clerical-Nationalist alliance, which he had done so much to sustain in recent years. In terms of the British parliamentary equation, as long as the Liberal and Clerical-Nationalist alliances were maintained, Home Rule was inevitable. The immediate danger to the Clerical-Nationalist alliance, however, lay not simply in any Coercion Act enforced by the British government, for that could only make Irishmen, lay and clerical, even more conscious of how different they were from Englishmen in mind as well as in place, or even in the recent Decree, but rather in another rescript from Rome, which would certainly be designed to force the clergy out of the National movement and break up the alliance. Since Rome could only proceed against the National movement in terms of morals or discipline, Walsh attempted to block Roman action by insisting on both the dropping of the Plan of Campaign as well as the containing of lay criticism regarding Rome's authority to pronounce on such questions. Moreover, Walsh was faced with another very serious problem, since it was obvious that Croke and he were not fully in accord as to what to do about the Decree. In his letter to Harrington, for example, Walsh significantly did not recommend that he and his colleagues consult Croke. Furthermore, Walsh not only insisted that his line was entirely his own, but that it was authoritative as far as he was himself concerned. Croke must have immediately realized the cogency of Walsh's remarks to him in his letter of May 8, especially since he had just received Dillon's remarkable manifesto, and the announcement that the Catholic M.P.'s would pronounce on the Decree. At the meeting of the Bishops on May 9, which Croke reported to Walsh on May 10, as being "fairly satisfactory," he neglected to mention that he had had some difficulty in preventing a motion of censure being passed on

Dillon, and further confessed to the English Catholic Home
Ruler, William Scawen Blunt, that if the Catholic M.P.'s at their
forthcoming meeting on May 17, passed a resolution against
papal interference, he was afraid the attitude he represented
would be disavowed by the other Irish Bishops. By the time he
wrote Walsh on May 10, therefore, a chastened Croke had
pulled in his horns, and was loyally prepared to take his lead
from his friend and colleague, the archbishop of Dublin.

The reaction of the Bishops and the lay Nationalist leaders to
the Decree, and their consequent reaction to each other, was
yet another testimony to the functioning of the Clerical-
Nationalist alliance. Under the terms of the alliance, it will be
recalled, the Party and the Leader were jointly responsible for
the Home Rule and Land Questions, while the Bishops were
responsible for the Education Question. The Bishops were also
responsible, however, for dealing with Rome, and the intrusion
of the lay Nationalist leadership with regard to the Decree
resulted in a good deal of initial resentment on the part of the
Bishops. A similar resentment, for example, had arisen on the
part of the Party the previous September, when Walsh had
initiated his Round Table Conference in an attempt to settle the
Land Question. What was at stake, in the first instance, at least,
as far as the Decree and the Conference were concerned, was a
question of jurisdiction. Walsh might have argued, and
cogently, that since Monsignor Persico was in Ireland
representing Rome, his Conference initiative in September was
appropriate to the Bishops' jurisdiction under the terms of the
alliance. When it became obvious, however, that such a
Conference would cost the Irish tenants a good deal more than
they could possibly gain in Roman good will, the jurisdictional
priority clearly rested with the Party. That is why, of course,
that Walsh encountered real difficulties with Dillon and
O'Brien, and even his good friend and colleague, Archbishop
Croke, did not encourage him to persist. Walsh then very
wisely allowed the matter of a Conference to drop. In the case
of the Decree, however, the Bishops patently thought that
jurisdiction belonged to them. Walsh had, in fact, insisted on
that jurisdiction immediately in his telegrams of April 26, by
enjoining the laity to await loyally the expounding of the Decree
by the Bishops. Dillon and his colleagues, however, were
determined to take action. Essentially, their argument was that
since Rome had acted unilaterally, the question of the Bishops'

jurisdiction in the matter was irrelevant. In ignoring the Bishops, Rome obviously refused either to accept the conventions of the Clerical-Nationalist alliance, or to acknowledge the existence of a *de facto* Irish State. Rome's untoward action in issuing the Decree, therefore, was not a question of jurisdiction at all, but a matter of State, and matters of State demanded the concurrence of the Leader and the Party as well as the Bishops. That is why, for example, the Party, or at least the Catholic members of it, insisted on calling a meeting to pronounce on the Decree. That is also why, moreover, Parnell as Leader not only sanctioned the calling of the meeting, but decided that he would make his own position clear in his forthcoming speech to the Eighty Club.

Those like Walsh, who hoped Parnell would do something to rescue them in his forthcoming speech to the Liberal *élite* at the Eighty Club on Tuesday, May 8, were sadly disappointed. Parnell not only declared that the Decree was bound to be "a disastrous failure," but pointed out that the discussion of it was better left to his Catholic colleagues. As far as the Plan of Campaign was concerned, he further maintained, though he had never been enthusiastic about it because of its bad effect on English public opinion, and had been for some time past working out a means by which it would be replaced, all that would now have to wait upon the present crisis. In effect, Parnell had declared that both the Decree and the Plan were politically irrelevant as far as the great end of the National movement was concerned, and that end, Home Rule, could best be served by relying on the alliance with the Liberal Party of England, "men who have never ultimately been beaten." The Bishops who met the following day, May 9, at Clonliffe College in Dublin, must have realized that Parnell had delivered them up to the tender mercies of his Catholic colleagues. Since the Plan would not be dropped, and the Bishops would have to find their own means of containing lay criticism of the Decree, the responsibility for any strain put on the Clerical-Nationalist alliance would fall on them. Hence their extreme annoyance at Dillon, and their fear that the resolutions that would be passed at the meeting of the Catholic Members would force their hands. Moreover, Parnell's equivocal attitude about the Plan certainly antagonized the agrarian wing in the Party led by Dillon, O'Brien and Harrington, and they would obviously be in no temperate mood on Thursday, May 17, when they finally convened.

Cardinal Manning, meanwhile, did his best to calm the Catholic M.P.'s. *"Confidential,"* he wrote William Scawen Blunt on Friday, May 11, which the cardinal meant to be shown to the Irish M.P.'s, "I hope Mr. O'Brien and the Catholic members will wait before they enunciate any irrevocable matter, and I may add my belief that Monsignor Persico has had no part in this late event."[21] "I do not," the cardinal insisted, "say this lightly." He further advised them not to contest the pope's general right to interfere in politics. Several days later, on Sunday, May 13, the cardinal's good friend, Michael Davitt, noted in the course of a speech in Liverpool that he "thought the action of the Catholic Members in holding a conference in Dublin on this rescript was a mistake. In his opinion too much was being made of the same rescript." When the Catholic Members met on May 17, in Dublin at the Mansion House, with the Rt. Hon., the Lord Mayor, Thomas Sexton, M.P. in the chair, they deliberated for nearly three and a half hours, after which they announced "that a sub-committee had been appointed to draw up resolutions on principles agreed to."[22] The composition of the sub-committee was an ominous sign for those who hoped the Catholic Members would show some restraint regarding the Decree, for it was dominated by the most militant spirits of what had become the agrarian wing of the Party.[23]

---

[21] *Leslie, op. cit.,* p. 428. See also *The United Irishman,* April 23, 1904, for Persico to Manning, dated May 19, 1888. This date is obviously incorrect and I have taken May 9, 1888, as more likely though indeed it may have been May 7 or 8, 1888. In the course of his letter, Persico maintained: "You are a Cardinal of the holy Church, and one I deeply esteem and respect; hence, I feel that I can speak as I would before the whole Church, and before God Himself. Now, it is known to Y.E. that I did not expect at all the said Decree, and I was never so more surprised in my life as when I received the circular from the Propaganda on the morning of the 28th ultimo. And fancy, I received the *bare circular,* as I suppose every Irish Bishop did, without a letter or a word of instruction or explanation. And what is more unaccountable to me, only the day before I had received a letter from the Secretary for the Extraordinary Ecclesiastical Affairs, telling me that nothing had been done about Irish affairs, and that my report and other letters were still *nell casetto dell' Emo Rampolla!* And yet the whole world thinks and says that the Holy Office has acted on my report, and that the Decree is based on the same! Not only all the Roman correspondents, but all the newspapers *avec le "Tablet" en tete* proclaim and report the same thing! Hence I must incur and bear the whole odium of the act with all the disagreeable and painful circumstances."

[22] *Irish Catholic,* May 19, 1888.

[23] *Ibid.* The sub-committee consisted of Dillon, O'Brien, Timothy Harrington, John Redmond, T. M. Healy, T. D. Sullivan, and the Hon. Secretaries to the meeting, Dr. J. E. Kenny and J. J. Clancy.

THE DECREE 221

The resolutions drawn up by the sub-committee and
endorsed eventually by some sixty Catholic Members of the
Party were very strong indeed.

We, the undersigned Irish Catholic members of Parliament,
being aware that the Circular recently issued by the Holy Office
of the Inquisition is being employed by the unscrupulous
enemies of the Holy See and of the Irish people as a political
weapon to prejudice the Irish cause, to create misunderstanding
and estrangement between the Irish people and their spiritual
guides, and to increase the dangers which threaten the liberties
and even the very existence of our people at this moment, and
being gravely mindful of the nature of the obligation which in
common with all Catholics we owe to the Holy See, and,
moreover, of the extent of our duty to our country arising out of
the responsibility inseparable from our public trust as the
constitutionally elected representatives of the Irish people, have
deliberated together upon the Circular of the Holy Office, so far
as it seems to affect the political interests entrusted by the
people to our care, and we hereby unanimously resolve:
FIRST — That the allegations of fact which are put forth in
the Circular of the Holy Office are to our knowledge
unfounded, and could not, we venture to affirm, have been
promulgated under the authority of the Holy Office if
statements so prejudicial to the Irish people had been tested by
reference to the Prelates of Ireland and the elected
representatives of the people.
  A. That the assertion that Free Contract prevails as to
the letting of land in Ireland, except in an insignificant
minority of cases, is unfounded and unwarrantable, and is
disproved by the fact that the whole course of agrarian
legislation for Ireland during the last eighteen years, under
successive Administrations, has proceeded upon the non-
existence of Free Contract, and has been directed to
compulsory interference with and curtailment of the
arbitrary powers of eviction and confiscation exercised by
the landlords. Furthermore, even since the inception of the
movement known as the Plan of Campaign, the present Tory
Government have been obliged to enact a statute for the
purpose of breaking over one hundred thousand additional
contracts of tenancy on the ground that they were one-sided
and oppressive, and imposed rents which the conditions of
Irish agriculture render destructive of the legal property of
tenants in their holdings.
  B. That the constitution and adjudication of the rent-
fixing courts afford inadequate grounds for the statement in

the Circular that they so reduce excessive rents as to bring them within the limits of equity, since on the contrary it is well known to all concerned that no provision is made by law or afforded by the courts for such reductions in respect of disaster or failure of crops as are supposed by the Holy Office to be made; that moreover, partisans of the landlords predominate in the constitution of the courts; that rents continue to be fixed upon improvements made by the tenants in defiance as well of the spirit of the law as the dictates of natural justice; that no provision is made for reduction of the arrears of rents now decreed by the courts to be excessive; that the existence of these arrears enables many landlords by the threat of eviction to prevent their tenants from applying to the courts for reduction of current rents; that many tenants are deterred from entering the courts by fear of losing in the costs of appeals — to which the landlords are in every case allowed to have recourse — more than they would gain by reduction of their rents; and that large classes of tenants are still absolutely shut out from courts of law, and are harassed by their landlords for payment of rents which the landlords had fixed and increased at their pleasure, which have never been reduced, and which the tenants can no longer pay in full without yielding up their own subsistence.

C.   With regard to the statement that rent has been extorted from tenants and deposited with unknown persons, we affirm as a matter of common knowledge that in the combinations formed by the tenants the moneys deposited by them were freely lodged with persons whom they knew and trusted, to be held as an insurance fund against eviction, and that these moneys are invariably returned without deduction on the request of the tenants.

D.   That as the unjust and cruel exercise of the legal power of eviction has for generations blighted the lives of the Irish people by depriving them of the homes which their own industry had provided, confiscating the value of their improvements, and banishing them by millions from their country, whereby many were led to moral ruin and loss of religious faith, and multitudes of the innocent and helpless underwent dreadful sufferings, even to death, by pestilence or famine, and as this legal power of eviction, armed with new facilities by an act passed last year in a Legislature controlled by landlords, is directed at the present moment to the destruction of thousands of families, together with the appropriation of their legal interest in the ownership of the soil, we solemnly declare that the merciless exercise of this power has been and is the one great cause of evil passions, conflict, and crime in Ireland, and that the public feeling which in some extreme cases has resulted in the denial of social intercourse to those who ruin families by unjust evictions, or those who encourage harsh landlords to such evictions by taking farms so vacated, is a feeling excited in the minds of the people by their love of natural justice and their desire that Christian charity should mould the law of the land and prevail in the relations of life.

SECOND — That we repudiate the assumption on which the Circular proceeds, that the status of Irish farmers is that of mere tenants-at-will, and assert that not only in equity but in law the dominant interest in the agricultural holdings of Ireland belongs to the tenants by whom the improvements have been executed, and we attribute much of the discontent which now prevails to the disregard of our constant protests against the imposition of rent on those improvements, in defiance of the statute, which tardily recognised dual ownership in the soil.

THIRD — That we cannot refrain from expressing our deep regret, as Catholics and Irishmen, that the Holy Office is silent as to the source and provocation of the evils and disorders which afflict the people of Ireland — namely, the subversion of natural justice by those who have obtained through false promises the powers of legislation and government, and the scorn of Christian charity manifested by those persons, including Catholics amongst them, who use a system of calumny to support coercive laws, and apply coercive laws to maintain extortion.

FOURTH — That this silence of the Holy Office as to the violations of justice and charity by which the Irish people are incessantly agitated, is, in our judgment, the more to be deplored in the interests of religion and of our national cause, because it has enabled the enemies of both to misuse the name of the Holy See by an assumption of its hostility to the political claims of Ireland, and because the direction of the admonition of the Holy Office, not in any degree against the systematic violations of justice and charity committed by way of attack upon the homes and property of our people, but wholly against casual and exceptional incidents in the people's struggle to defend themselves and preserve their natural rights, may be of untoward consequence at the present time, when priests and representatives of the people who have exerted themselves to restore tranquility by preventing unjust evictions are suffering imprisonment by the sentences of arbitrary courts, and when patience has been strained to the point of exasperation by a course of misgovernment which persistently assails the primary right of the individual to live by the fruit of his labour, and which suppresses by means of servile tribunals, and the use of physical force, those public rights which are the indispensable guarantees of justice.

FIFTH — That the demand of the people of Ireland for agrarian reform and political liberty is dictated by necessity, sustained by Natural Justice and conducted by modes of action and methods of organization prescribed or allowed by the constitution under which we live; that to organization and agitation persistently maintained, and to that alone, the Irish people owe whatever they have won of civil or religious freedom; that their just claims are now encountered by unconstitutional coercion and organized calumny; that the force of this National movement, increasing from day to day to day, is a force generated and incessantly renewed by the free opinion and the spontaneous action of the people, that this will continue to be exerted until in despite of coercion and defamation it shall have achieved success.

SIXTH — That while unreservedly acknowledging as Catholics the spiritual jurisdiction of the Holy See, we, as guardians, in common with our brother Irish representatives of other creeds, of those civil liberties which our Catholic forefathers have resolutely defended, feel bound solemnly to reassert that Irish Catholics can recognise no right in the Holy See to interfere with the Irish people in the management of their political affairs.[24]

These resolutions, especially the last, were a very serious embarrassment to the Irish Bishops both at home and at Rome.

The Catholic Members, however, were not content with simply passing their resolutions; they were determined to have them endorsed in the country by the popular will. They began their campaign in Dublin with a monster meeting in the Phoenix Park, on the Sunday, May 20, following their conference. Sexton, Dillon, O'Brien and Redmond were the chief speakers. "By our free consent," Sexton declared, "we are linked in our spiritual affairs with the Holy See."[25] "Against our will," he maintained, "we are linked for the purpose of secular laws to the will of the Parliament of England." "Our religion is independent of England," he affirmed in conclusion, "and our politics are independent of Rome." "Mr. Dillon," the *Irish Catholic* reported, "was singularly eloquent, and outspoken, and his speech exemplified anew his unswerving adherence to

[24] *Freeman's Journal, May 18, 1888.*
[25] *Irish Catholic,* May 26, 1888.

"PANIC AMONGST THE PIGS!"

the pronounced and determined position which he has taken up in reference to the Papal Circular."[26] O'Brien noted in the course of his speech that "it was maddening to think that every rackrenter who cleared a countryside could flourish the Papal Circular in their faces as if it were a sheriff's writ."[27] Redmond, who concluded the relay, observed significantly the importance of the Decree with regard to Home Rule, by remarking, "that by their action the Irish Catholic members had shown to their Protestant fellow-countrymen that Home Rule did not mean Rome Rule, and he maintained that, if the Catholics of Ireland acquiesced in Roman interference in their civil and political affairs, the English people would be absolute fools to concede or restore their Parliament."[28]

On the Saturday, May 26, that the *Irish Catholic,* a weekly, reported the monster meeting in Phoenix Park, it also ran a sub-editorial, "The Priests of Ireland," which was most disturbing, in that it clearly foreshadowed the developing danger to the Clerical-Nationalist alliance. "We sincerely hope," the *Catholic* noted, "that there is no truth in the report, which Mr. John Dillon has received on authority, that disciplinary directions are about to be issued to the priests restricting their liberty in political matters." "It is a grievous trial," the editorial continued, "that, at this hour in our history, when we are almost at the opening of better days, anything should occur to disturb the affectionate relations of the Irish people towards Rome." "But it would be turning that trial," it warned, "which can be temperately borne, into a grave danger both to the Church and to Ireland, if the priests were forbidden to take the creditable part they have been taking as Irish citizens." "For the sake of the Church and for Ireland," the *Irish Catholic* then concluded solemnly, "it is to be hoped that this grave step will not be taken."

The campaign against the Decree, meanwhile, began to gain momentum as the lord mayor and several burgesses of the Dublin Corporation convened a meeting for Thursday, May 24, to endorse the resolutions of the Catholic M.P.'s with regard to the Decree. Walsh, who had just had a final audience with the pope on May 23, telegraphed Sexton that same evening. "It may be useful," he advised the lord mayor, "to

[26] *Ibid.*
[27] *Ibid.*
[28] *Ibid.*

assure the Municipal Council of Dublin in my name that all apprehensions of political interference of the Holy See in Irish affairs are absolutely groundless."[29] "The cause of Ireland," Walsh further assured Sexton, "has nothing to fear from Leo XIII. Accept my most distinct assurance on this point." "Protest by all means," Walsh advised, "in the strongest terms, against the action of those hostile journals which represent the Sovereign Pontiff as a political partisan." "But at the same time," Walsh concluded, "make it clear that, as Irishmen and Catholics, you are not to be misled by any such device of the enemies either of the nationality or of the Catholic Faith of Ireland." When the Nationalists of Limerick followed Dublin's lead, and announced a meeting to discuss the Decree on Sunday, May 28, the bishop of Limerick also responded with a letter of advice to the lord mayor, but its tone and tenor was, as might be expected, quite different from that of the archbishop of Dublin's counsel. Edward Thomas O'Dwyer maintained on May 25, in a letter to the lord mayor of Limerick that the Decree "binds the consciences of those whom it concerns," and that it was also "a grievous sin for any Catholic to disobey it, and a much more grievous sin under any pretext to deny the Pope's authority to issue it."[30] "With this official intimation," O'Dwyer then added, "I have discharged my duty, but I crave your indulgence to make a political remark." "It seems a pity," he shrewdly argued, "for a mere detail of political action which has never been adopted by the National organisation, which the recognised leader of that agitation and Mr. Gladstone have both condemned, to run the risk — nay to incur the certainty — of rending the whole Irish nation to its very base at home and abroad." "Plain speaking," O'Dwyer declared, "is necessary here. Prevention is better than cure." "If we are driven," he warned the lord mayor somewhat romantically in conclusion, "to defend the prerogatives of the Holy See, I trust we shall follow those who, before us, sustained more serious persecution than, thank God, our opponents can yet inflict upon us."

The bishop of Limerick's letter, which was published on Saturday, May 26, provided the text for most of the speeches delivered the following day throughout the country. William O'Brien, who was the principal speaker at a meeting in Limerick, was simply furious as he maintained that he "would

[29] *Ibid.*
[30] *Ibid.*, June 2, 1888.

not be deterred from his duty by threats, the rashest and most disgraceful that ever appeared from the pen of an Irish Ecclesiastic."[31] "They would not forget the respect due to Dr. O'Dwyer's sacred office," O'Brien declared, accusing the bishop of Limerick of the original sin among the Irish (disloyalty), "though he had forgotten it himself when he singled himself out from the trusted Bishops of the Irish Church and rushed into print at a moment when his sacred Brethren were remonstrating at Rome." "He left Limerick the previous day," O'Brien charged O'Dwyer in conclusion, adding cowardice to disloyalty, "taking care to supply his manifesto to every Orange paper in the Three Kingdoms." At a meeting the same day in Kildare, Dillon maintained, "that this was the most important period in the history of the National movement, as it had received a blow from the most unexpected quarter — one from which they had the least right to expect it." "The issue was whether," Dillon argued, picking up Redmond's theme of the previous week, "the Irish people were to take their politics from Rome, and so place themselves in such a position that they could never again ask their Protestant fellow-countrymen to help them in the struggle for Irish liberty." "He denied," Dillon then declared unequivocally, "it was the duty of every Catholic priest and layman to obey the Papal Letter, and he had letters from some of the most reverend and learned of the priesthood in Ireland, and abroad, thoroughly approving of the action of the Irish members."

Michael Davitt finally joined the chorus that same day in a very effective speech at Bray. Davitt argued "that the Bishop of Limerick's letter revealed the worst possible form of clerical dictatorship which has worked such manifest injury to the Catholic Church on the Continent of Europe, and which, if shared by any large number of bishops and priests in Ireland, would shatter to its very foundation the Catholic Church of this country."[32] "As an Irish Catholic," Davitt further maintained, "he denied every contention put forth in Dr. O'Dwyer's epistle, wherein it was claimed either the Inquisition or the Pope had the right to compel him, under pain of grievous sin, to obey his injunction in either 'mere details of political action' or anything remotely bearing upon Irish national or social questions." In reference to a remark by the *Tablet* that he had not ventured to

[31] *Ibid.*
[32] *Ibid.*

tell the Irish people that it was not necessary to obey the rescript, Davitt boldly declared, "that he never intended for one moment to obey the Rescript, and he was pretty certain that the same might be said of ninety-nine out of every hundred lay Nationalist Catholics in Ireland." Davitt then observed eloquently in conclusion "that the Irish people owed it to their own political and intellectual manhood, to their spirit of national independence, and, above all, to their Protestant fellow-countrymen, to withstand every semblance of political dictation, interference, or direction on the part of Rome in their national and secular affairs."

Walsh, meanwhile, who was just about to leave Rome, was both perplexed and alarmed by the mounting lay criticism in Ireland. "I have just written," he explained to Croke on Saturday, May 26, "to the Primate telling him how matters stand"(C). "I must say," Walsh added, "I cannot at all understand the line taken by some of our lay friends. Are they in revolt against Parnell? Judging merely from what we see in the newspapers, I cannot put any other construction on their proceedings. But there is no use in writing mere speculations to Y.G. who is on the spot." "I think," Walsh advised, referring to the next meeting of the episcopal body scheduled for Wednesday, May 30, "a short plain statement from the Bishops pointing out that the decision is a *moral* not *political* judgement would go a great way to keep things quiet." "The reasons," he informed Croke, referring to the Decree, "are thrown overboard bodily. Some people are said to have gotten into trouble about them, but it is hard to put faith in gossip of this sort in Rome." "I am sorry that Dr. O'Callaghan's statement got out," Walsh noted, referring to the bishop of Cork's remarks about the Pope's preference for Salisbury rather than Gladstone, "It is not easy indeed to suppose that he is mistaken as to what the Pope said to him. But on the other hand, it is absolutely impossible to reconcile the view thus ascribed to the Pope with the most distinct statements which H.H. made to me last Wednesday. He protested most indignantly against the idea of his being in favour of one party or the other. '*Salisbury or Gladstone,*' he said, '*it is all the same to me which* of them is in power. Let the Irish go on for the settlement of the land question, and for their "autonomia," as you explained it to me. You know that instead of opposing them in any way, I sympathise with them.' " "I explained to him," Walsh further informed Croke, "that a great deal of the soreness that has arisen comes from the circulation of the view that he is *against* Gladstone and for Salisbury. I then showed him the cartoon in Judy. He has most formally authorised me to do everything I can to remove any such impression." "I hope to leave to-day," he concluded, after his stay of nearly five months in Rome, "but I intend to take my time going home. I want a rest badly, and I am not likely to get much of it when I return."

As Walsh had explained to Croke, he had also written that same day, Saturday, May 26, to the primate, Michael Logue. His letter was as carefully written as it was full and comprehensive, and it was obviously meant to be shown or read to their episcopal brethren at their forthcoming meeting on Thursday, May 30, in Dublin. "At first," Walsh pointed out to Logue, and referring to the regular June meeting of the Bishops, "it seemed as if matters might be allowed to stand until the ordinary meeting at the end of the month."[33] "But from the tone taken by some of the speakers through the country," he observed sternly, and *before* the reaction to the bishop of Limerick's letter had taken place, "it is considered that great harm may be done if the field is left in possession of the lay element much longer." "I had a very long audience," Walsh further explained, "on Wednesday last, when I had from the Holy Father most distinct statements to the following effect.

(1) That he wishes the Decree to be communicated at once to the clergy for their guidance; (2) That he regrets that this was not done before now; (3) That the reasons stated in Cardinal Monaco La Valetta's letter are in no way to be taken as limiting the sense of the Decree; the Decree is an official act of the Holy Office, confirmed by the Pope; the statement of reasons is the act merely of the individual Cardinal who wrote the letter to Propaganda; (4) That it is important that the people should be *at once* instructed that the Decree is a decision in *morals* and is not a *political* interference.[34]

"This, I think," Walsh remarked, "exhausts my official commission. But I may add from myself, as a result of all I have had the opportunity of learning here, that *collective* action on the fourth point would seem to be desirable; without this it

---

[33] *Walsh,* pp. 352-53.
[34] *Ibid.*

would be difficult to secure the unity of action which is so important. Also: there seems to be no idea entertained here of any formal *promulgation* by reading the Decree in the churches. Each bishop is to take the course he deems most prudent in this matter." "I shall probably," he further noted, "write a letter to each parish priest, marking it private, suggesting that he should explain the state of the case personally to the local political leaders, if he finds that any cases of the condemned practices exist in his parish. Where no cases exist I think it better to let matters alone." "According to the official reports," he added, somewhat over-optimistically, "Boycotting is fast dying out; Parnell's advice will probably relieve us of all trouble as regards the Plan of Campaign." "I am authorised," he added, "to give the strongest assurances that the Pope is most friendly as regards our whole popular programme, and anxious to help our people in any way that may be in his power." "He trusts that the bishops will leave nothing undone," Walsh reported, referring of course to the bishop of Cork's indiscreet remarks at the last episcopal meeting, "to remove the impression that has been created that he has in any way been influenced by political considerations in the condemnation. As he views the matter, he has removed obstacles out of our way." "I fear all this is very disjointed," he finally apologized in conclusion, "but I have to write hurriedly to catch the post."

"I am out of Rome at last," Walsh reported to Croke from Pisa the next day, Sunday, May 27, "and I think I never experienced such a feeling of relief from worry in all my life"(C). "I write this," he added, explaining his second letter in two days, "fearing lest by any chance my letters of yesterday to Y.G. and the Primate may go astray. Owing to the vexatious regulations about sealing etc. I was unable to register the letter to the Primate, which enclosed Card. Rampolla's letter to me i.e. to the Bishops. As I mentioned to Dr. Logue, it is considered important that the Decree should be communicated by the Bishops to the clergy Quam primum, the mode of communication is of course for the Bishops themselves to select." "Action should," he advised, "as far as possible be *uniform: collective* action would be the best of all. In the absence of all this, comments are sure to be made on the different lines to be taken by individual Bishops; even merely verbal differences in their letters may be magnified into

something very serious; all this will do harm in the country."
"A joint expression of the episcopal body," Walsh suggested
again, "that the Decree is a moral one, not political, would go a
great way to check the mischief that seems to be growing. If the
people were made to feel that the act is one completely within
the competence of the Holy See, they would not, I suppose,
take part in any disrespectful protest." "I have explained,"
Walsh added, even more naively, "that all the mischief has
come from the Tory newspapers, putting a political
construction on the act." "The resolutions of the members," he
further observed, "*begin* with a mere protest against this. But in
the end they seem more or less to adopt the view that the act is
political. Even the most friendly people in Rome comment on
the continued silence of the Bishops." "It is well," Walsh closed
finally, "for Y.G. and the others to know all this."

The following day, when Walsh wrote to Kirby to thank him
for his hospitality and enclose a check for his extended stay at
the Irish College, he was even more disturbed by the latest
reports from Ireland. "Dr. Donnelly," Walsh reported to Kirby
from Modena, on Monday evening, May 28, and referring to
his auxiliary bishop, "had written in advance to Fiesole. He
gives a very gloomy view of the state of feeling in Ireland"(K).
"As he says," Walsh explained, and referring to his own letter
of May 11, to the *Freeman,* "the field was left in the exclusive
occupation of the laymen; with the exception of my letter, not a
word had come from the episcopal body." "It is a pity," he then
lamented, "the Bishops as a body have not spoken out." "We
had to-day at Florence," Walsh noted further, "a London paper
of Saturday, with Dr. O'Dwyer's letter on the Limerick meeting.
It is to be hoped it had a good practical effect. But, of course, it
is a pity that the duty of interfering did not fall on some other
Bishop in whom the people would have more confidence as
regards general sympathy." "I am sure," Walsh observed
piously, "we have all the help of Y.G.'s prayers that the
Bishops' meeting on Wednesday may turn out well. Dr.
Donnelly says that if the movement is allowed to go on
unchecked much longer, it will be too late to interfere."
"Indeed," Walsh observed gloomily, "he seems to think that,
even as it is, there is some fear that the time for useful
interference has passed."

What other news Kirby had also recently received from
Ireland was almost as gloomy as it was scarce. Once again, as

in previous crises with Rome, Kirby's clerical correspondents, when they wrote at all, were very cautious. The new, young, and very discreet bishop of Raphoe, Patrick O'Donnell, for example, wrote asking Kirby to arrange with Propaganda for the assigning of his mensal parishes on the same day that the Catholic Members were meeting in Dublin. "Our poor country," O'Donnell lamented on May 17, from Letterkenny in Donegal, "is going through a terrible trial"(K). "I trust God and his holy Mother," he further observed cautiously, "will enable it to preserve unabated devotion to the Holy See." "We expect," he concluded amiably, "the trusted Archbishop of Dublin back soon." A week later, another of Kirby's cautious, if less discreet, correspondents, wrote him about the situation in Ireland. "I sincerely trust," the bishop of Cork, T. A. O'Callaghan reported on May 25, "the present feeling will soon subside and leave no trace after it"(K). "I have no doubt whatever," he assured Kirby, "that if the Holy See succeeded in its intentions of benefiting our people all will be forgotten in a moment. You are aware that meetings are being held throughout the Country and one is to be in Cork. If I cannot prevent it I shall do my best to influence individuals so that the evil will be as far as possible diminished." "The idea that is doing harm," he explained to Kirby, "is that the Holy See under the influence of the E. Government would be induced to prevent any reform that may be attempted. I have received this answer on several occasions from those with whom I tried to reason." "Indeed," he added naively, "I think it is the motive for holding the meetings."

Several days later, O'Callaghan again wrote Kirby reporting that he had confirmed some 2,400 children while on visitation, and not twenty missed a question in the catechism. "I have explained my thoughts," he added prudently, in the course of this letter, "on the present state of the Country in the enclosed letter to Card. Simeoni which you may read and if you think advisable you may withhold it"(K). "I may perhaps add," O'Callaghan noted, "that I feel intense pain and sadness but I trust in the goodness of God that the danger will pass over without injury." "All the people," he maintained loyally, "feel most grateful to Dr. Walsh and his presence in Rome has a calming effect on the aggitated [sic] state of the country. Though things are bad enough, I can assure your Lordship that they would have been much worse were it not for the influence

THE NEW PAPAL NUNCIO.

Balfour, who has got on a suit which is kept in the Castle for Chief Secretaries to wear on certain occasions, to Erin.—
"Ha! Ha! See what I have got over from Rome. Now, I think you will give me up that paper?"
Erin.—"**NEVER**!!! That document in your hand was obtained by fraud and misrepresentation, and has therefore no moral force."
Balfour.—"Ho!! Ho!! Then you mean to split with Rome?"
Erin.—"**NEVER**!!! I have always been a faithful child of the Church. and will ever remain so, but I mean to manage my own
domestic affairs, as everyone else does."

of Dr. Croke & other Bishops. How providential it is that the people have confidence still in their clergy and look to them for sympathy." "I am confident," he concluded, "that your Lordship is praying for us. Let us hope that the worst is over and when Dr. Walsh returns that all the Bishops by common action may be able to restore peace and confidence to our people."

The reaction of the Leader and the Party to the Decree had certainly shaken the nerve of the Bishops. The Decree had provided Parnell with the opportunity to demonstrate once again why he had emerged among so many talented men as Leader. He had very effectively reasserted in a moment of great crisis the cardinal principle that, as Leader, he alone determined the priorities of policy as arrived at on the basis of a consensus between himself, the Party, and the Bishops. Home Rule, or *de jure* recognition of the *de facto* Irish State by the British Parliament was still the one thing essential, and solutions to the Land, Education, and Roman questions would not be allowed to trench on it. Since Home Rule, moreover, could only be constitutionally achieved in the political context of the day through the Liberal-Nationalist alliance, the Plan of Campaign and the Decree were only material inasmuch as they affected that alliance. In thus keeping the priorities of the National movement in order, Parnell was not forgetting, however, that the Clerical-Nationalist alliance was also essential to the stability of his *de facto* Irish State. He had, therefore, to decide between the Party and the Bishops in the matter of the Decree. That decision was made, in effect, when he, as Leader officially sanctioned the meeting of the Party that would pronounce on the Decree. In doing so, Parnell provided for the legitimization of the resolutions passed at that meeting, and the Bishops were thus placed in a very awkward political position. They had to decide whether they would or would not endorse the action of the Party and the Leader, and the responsibility for maintaining or weakening the Clerical-Nationalist alliance thus rested squarely with them in that they now had to make the next move. When the Party then proceeded to have their resolutions endorsed by the general will in a series of mass meetings throughout the country, the Bishops found themselves not only in an awkward political situation, but in a dangerous one as far as their power and influence were concerned.

By the time the Bishops met on Wednesday, May 30, they

were a much more chastened group than they had been when they convened three weeks before. Between the injunctions of Rome and the initiative of the lay Nationalist leadership, their course of action, whatever way they trimmed, was bound to be a dangerous one. Their resolutions, however, reflected that they preferred to be wrecked on the rocks of Rome than to chance the whirlpool of Irish public opinion.

1. In obedience to the commands of the Holy See, and in willing discharge of the duty thus placed upon us, we desire to put on public record, that the recent Decree of the Holy Office, addressed to the Irish Hierarchy, was intended to affect the domain of morals alone, and in no way to interfere with politics, as such, in this country.

2. Even this day we have had from our Holy Father the Pope direct and unequivocal assurances of his deep and paternal interest in the temporal welfare of our country, and that, so far from intending by this Decree to injure our national movement, it was the hope and purpose of His Holiness to remove those things which he judged might, in the long run, be obstacles to its advancement and ultimate success.

3. With these facts thus clearly before us, apart altogether from his other numerous titles to our filial affection and respect, we must warn our people against the use of any hasty or irreverent language with reference to the Sovereign Pontiff or to any of the Sacred Congregations through which he usually issues his Decrees to the faithful.

4. While expressing our deep and lasting gratitude to the leaders of the National movement for the signal services they have rendered to religion and country, we deem it our duty, at the same time, to remind them and our flocks, as we most emphatically do, that the Roman Pontiff has an inalienable and Divine right to speak with authority on all questions appertaining to faith and morals.[35]

"Yesterday's Meeting," Croke wrote Walsh hurriedly on May 31, from Dublin, "was a big success — I think"(W). "That is to say," he explained his ambivalence, "we did substantially what we were told to do, or could have been reasonably expected to do, and did *no more*. We gave the world, however, clearly to understand that we would have done nothing if left to ourselves, and that what we had done was done with bad grace." "Dr. Murphy," Croke added, referring to Walsh's secretary, "sent

[35] *Irish Catholic,* June 2, 1888.

you the Freeman. It gives 'resolutions' and W^m O'Brien's comments thereon." "Some were for publishing R's letter in full," Croke reported, referring to Cardinal Rampolla, "— textually — of course in an English garb: but that would have been an awkward course, for, in the first place, it appeared to be a private communication to you, meant, however, for the eyes of the Bishops, and secondly it contained such outrageous misstatements and exaggerations of facts that, if published, it would cause even greater commotion than even the decree itself." "Elphin," Croke noted, referring to Laurence Gillooly, "was for publishing a substantial resumé of it — and nothing more." "Limerick was quiet," he added, and referring to the coadjutor to the bishop of Clonfert, John Healy, "Coadjutor of C. absent, but +E.T. was authorised to sign for him." "That's about the whole of the news," Croke concluded, and affectionately adding in a postscript, "Let me know when you are coming home. God bless you."

Not all the Irish bishops, however, were either so candid or so pertinent in their reports of the Bishops' meeting to Kirby in Rome. "I hope your Grace is pleased," Bartholomew Woodlock, the bishop of Ardagh, wrote Kirby on Saturday, June 2, "and our Holy Father also — with the Resolutions unanimously adopted at our meeting in Clonliffe College on Wednesday last, 30th May"(K). "The Holy Father's instructions," Woodlock explained, "communicated to us by good Dr. Walsh, & also by Cardinal Rampolla, were for us *norma loquendi,* and our rule in guiding our good people. But some of our extreme politicians and newspapers have done & I fear, are doing great mischief — It is very hard to keep them within bounds." "We must pray," he concluded piously, "to St. Patrick our Holy Apostle, to guard Catholic Ireland." That same day, the more garrulous bishop of Cork also wrote Kirby about the meeting. "The Bishops' resolutions," O'Callaghan assured Kirby on June 2, "had a calming effect on the country and I believe the meetings and protests are near an end"(K). "There is one to be held in Cork tomorrow," he explained, "I did my best to prevent it but without success. I am however assured that its tone will be most respectful to the Holy Father and that the utterances will be more guarded than on other occasions." "The feeling throughout the Country," O'Callaghan reported, "was most intense. Cursing the Pope was quite common. Women threw his likeness out of their houses and the excitement extended even to the children."

"With regard to the decree," he observed, breaking unconsciously into Italian in his excitement, "you are aware of our great difficulty was the reasons given for its giusification." "Some of the Bishops said," O'Callaghan confided, "they would laugh in our faces if we published it in the Churches and I am sure in many places the congregations would leave because no one in Ireland thought of upholding boycotting or the plan of campaign in the cases alluded to in the decree. There were certainly abuses but these were quickly disappearing." "As to publication," he explained further, "I immediately on receiving it sent to the paper of the city a translation and the original latin [sic] and both were printed under my name. I also had several copies made and one was sent to each parish priest in the diocese. I am sure when quiet is restored a great deal more can be done but at present it would excite great opposition and formal sin." "At the last meeting of the Bishops," O'Callaghan further informed Kirby, "Cardinal Rampolla's letter was read. It was proposed by some to publish it but as portions of it would give offence and reopen the controversy it was thought better not to do so and the resolutions were published in their present form." "Let us continue to trust," he advised Kirby, "in the great goodness of God and the prayers of our Blessed Mother that the danger may be quickly averted and I would pray Your Lordship to use your influence that the Holy Father may take pity on the weakness of our poor people."

Several days later Croke also wrote Kirby about the Decree and the Bishops' recent resolutions. "I very reluctantly," Croke observed in his letter marked *"Private"* on June 6, "refer to the papal decree about the Plan of Campaign and the embittered discussions to which it has given rise here"(K). "Humanly speaking," he noted, "it was quite a sad affair. Irish feeling has been dreadfully wounded, and the stability of Irish faith severely tested. The Pope is cursed in every mood and tense from Donegal to Baltimore; and wherein his picture was found in private houses, it has been either displaced simply or torn to bits." "The Archbp of San Francisco," Croke further informed Kirby, "tells me it is worse still in the United States. God grant us peace and quietness." "The resolutions," he assured Kirby, "passed by the Bishops at the last meeting will have a highly sedative effect." "There are to be no more 'big meetings' "; he explained, and concluded pointedly, "and if no further provocation be given to the people, the past will be forgiven and forgotten."

Indeed, in concluding his letter, Croke had noted the most significant immediate result of the Bishops' resolutions. The Party had called off the mass demonstrations. The Party had done so because there was no need for them now that the Bishops had, in effect, endorsed the position taken by the Party and approved beforehand by the Leader. The Bishops' resolutions were more remarkable, in fact, for what they did not say rather than what they did say. They had assured the Irish people, for example, that the Decree was a matter of morals, not politics, that the pope was full of good intentions towards Ireland, that neither the pope's name nor that of any of his Sacred Congregations should be taken in vain, and that the pope had an inalienable right to speak authoritatively on all questions concerning faith and morals. Nothing, for example, was said by the Bishops about the assumptions and matters of fact in the Decree labelled either erroneous or unfounded in the resolutions of the Party, nor about the Party's complaints regarding the silence of the Holy Office in matters in which the British government had recently and patently outraged natural justice in Ireland. But most important of all, the Bishops carefully skirted the sixth and final resolution of the Party, which declared in part that as Irish Catholics they could recognize "no right in the Holy See to interfere with the Irish people in the management of their political affairs." The Bishops cleverly parried this dangerous assertion by promptly maintaining in their first resolution that objectively the Decree concerned morals rather than politics, and then upheld the rights of the pope in their fourth and final resolution by subjectively maintaining his ultimate authority in all questions of faith and morals. What the Bishops did not choose to do was to point out that the assertion by the Party that the pope had no right to interfere in politics was a serious error according to Catholic teaching, for this was tantamount to asserting that there was such a thing as politics without a moral dimension. In ignoring this, and in suppressing, in effect, Cardinal Rampolla's letter, the Bishops had gone as far as they could in mollifying the Party, and the Clerical-Nationalist alliance was saved from disruption.

The real question, however, was, would well enough be left

alone. Would Rome continue to insist that the Decree be enforced, and even more importantly, perhaps, what line would Walsh take when he finally arrived home? He had certainly taken a harder line from the beginning of the crisis on the attitude of the lay Nationalist leadership than his brethren in Ireland. His own attitude had obviously been conditioned by the circumstances of his Roman environment, and whether indeed his opinions would begin to vary as his distance from Rome increased was yet another question. In any case, he took special care on his leisurely journey home to keep Kirby fully informed. "I hope the telegram I sent to Y. G. from Milan," Walsh explained on June 5 from Einseeldehn in Switzerland, "containing the early news of the Bishops' resolutions was of use. I have since, of course, seen the text of the resolutions"(K). "There are some points in them," Walsh admitted, "that I do not altogether like. But considering the circumstances in which the Decree was published, and especially the way in which all information from the tenants' side was either ignored or treated as unworthy of belief, it is, I suppose, matter for gratification that the Bishops have allowed it to pass without some sort of protest." "The Limerick letter," Walsh noted, referring to O'Dwyer's pronouncements of May 26, "must have raised a very serious difficulty. The Bishops would naturally shrink from saying anything that might be regarded as endorsing that very imprudent action." "It is a pity, however," Walsh observed, referring to the Bishops' first meeting of May 9, "that they did not act collectively in the first instance, so as to give a proper tone to any action of individuals that might follow. In writing the Primate I mentioned the course that I myself intended to adopt regarding the communication of the Decree to the clergy, namely, to address a *private* circular to the parish priests, giving them all necessary instructions for their guidance. This was announced by the Primate to the meeting, and was, I understand, received with approval, as the course to be adopted generally." "It will be necessary," Walsh had advised Kirby earlier in this letter, "for me to stay a day or two in London, to have a conversation with Cardinal Manning, and with some of our public men, English as well as Irish, before crossing to Ireland."

Walsh had, in fact, written the cardinal several days before from Brunnen, Switzerland. "I left Rome this day week," Walsh explained on Saturday, June 2, "and came on quietly here"(M).

"I do not intend to stay more than a day or two," he added, "as I should find it hard to keep clear of newspaper people if I were to stay in any place for a longer time. I expect to be in London in a fortnight when, of course, I shall call at Archbishop's House, to tell your Eminence all the news." "I thought it better," he further informed the cardinal, "that the Bishops should publish something before my return. Our ordinary meeting will be held in about three weeks from this. By that time we can see whether any further step should be taken. I hope the laymen have not been allowed to run on too far. Looking at the course of affairs as a sort of outsider, I am inclined to think they have been. But I dare say the Archbishop of Cashel and others took all the circumstances into account." "There has been, it would seem," he maintained further, "a good deal of imprudence, the consequences of which, I fear, may not be easily got rid of. But the imprudence has not been confined to Ireland." "I am authorised," Walsh then assured the cardinal in conclusion, "to speak for the Holy Father in a way that I trust, will undo some of the harm that has been done. It would be too much to expect that it would undo all." Walsh wrote the cardinal again some ten days later, on Monday, June 11, from Freiburg in Baden, explaining that he expected to be in London by the end of the week. "I understand," he also reported to the cardinal, indicating that the Bishops and the lay Nationalist leaders had reached an accord, "that the meetings in Ireland are at an end"(M). "My position," he confided to the Cardinal, "is a little difficult just now. All will expect me to say something on the whole question. Of course, I shall do my best to put the Decree in the least unfavourable light." "But with my knowledge of many important facts," Walsh confessed in conclusion, "connected with it, I shall find it hard to do much in this way."

What Walsh apparently did and did not know about the origins of the Decree allows for some very interesting speculation as to who was actually responsible for it. A week after the Decree had been made public, Walsh's auxiliary, Nicholas Donnelly, had granted an interview to the representative in Ireland of several Parisian journals, Arthur Dumesnil. After discussing the Plan of Campaign and Boycotting in French, which Donnelly spoke "fluently, but with an almost imperceptible Italian accent," the journalist asked — "What is your lordship's idea of the effects likely to be produced by the Propaganda [sic] rescript?"[36] "So far as private information is concerned," Donnelly replied, dutifully taking up Walsh's line, "I can state on good authority that most Irish Catholics will submit willingly and loyally to the decree, for the decree does not touch the political situation in any sense. It is simply a moral injunction, and as such the Vatican authorities had a perfect right to issue it." "Its effects," he further explained, "may be already observed in the peaceable demeanour of the people after the sentence imposed on Mr. William O'Brien." "I knew that the rescript," Donnelly added, most indiscreetly, "was prepared and ready to be published even so far back as last February (first), when I was in Rome with my nieces on the occasion of his Holiness's Jubilee." "One of the members of the Sacred College," he declared, even more indiscreetly, "informed me at the time that the document had been written out, but its publication was deferred to an opportune and psychological moment. That moment arrived only when Messrs. Dillon and O'Brien were arrested last month, for the ecclesiastics of the Propaganda feared that the arrest, prosecution, and consequent incarceration of the gentlemen might intensify the policy of the Plan and Boycotting to an alarming extent. Hence it was thought necessary to nip such a movement in the bud."

"Could your lordship," Dumesnil then inquired, "tell me if the Duke of Norfolk had anything to do with the recent rescript?" "The Duke of Norfolk," Donnelly maintained boldly, "had nothing at all to do with it. Of that I am assured, for I happen to know that the document was drawn up before the Duke had at all proceeded to Rome." "The rescript," Donnelly volunteered, and most irresponsibly, "to my mind was based on the reports forwarded to the Vatican by Monsignor Persico, the Papal Legate, who travelled throughout all the dioceses in Ireland and took great pains to glean the most trustworthy information from every possible reliable source." Several days later, on May 9, Monsignor Persico, in a long and eloquent letter to Cardinal Manning, protesting that he had had neither hand nor part in either the origin or the issuing of the Decree, noted hurriedly in an anguished postscript — "Just this moment I have read an interview with a French journalist by Dr. Donnelly, Auxiliary Bishop of Dublin."[37] "Apart from the great

---

[36] *Irish Times*, (Dublin).
[37] *The United Irishman*, April 23, 1904.

indiscretion of communicating such things," Persico informed the cardinal, "Dr. Donnelly affirms that the decree of the Holy Office is given exclusively from my report!" "It would be well," Persico advised in conclusion, "if your Eminence read the interview."

The cardinal obviously replied by return of post, for the monsignor responded hurriedly again on May 10, from Teignmouth in Devon. "I am sorry," Persico apologized in broken English, "I have no more with me Dr. Donnelly's interview with the French journalist, else I would send it to Y. E."[38] "However," he reported, "it has been published in several Irish papers, and hence of public notoriety. Dr. Donnelly having assured the journalist that being with his nieces in Rome on the occasion of the Pope's jubilee, he tried to ascertain everything and had interviews with members of the Sacred College; then in a positive and distinct manner states the following fact: 'That the Decree of the H. O. was made and ready since the 1st. of February!' " "Now," Persico maintained logically, "two inferences can be made from this startling announcement: 1st. That the Irish Bishops knew of the existence of said Decree, whereas I (the Pope's representative *ad hoc*) knew nothing whatever about it. 2nd. The Irish Bishops knew of the Decree, and yet they (*to all appearance*) have remained silent and passive during three months!" "That I knew nothing whatever about it," Persico protested, and enlarging upon his first point, "I would not have the slightest objection to make the following declaration before the whole world, viz. — That I had no idea that anything had been done about Irish affairs, much less thought that some questions had been deferred to the H. O.; and the first knowledge I had of the Decree was on the morning of the 28th of April, when I received the bare circular sent me by the Propaganda." "I must add that had I known of such a thing," he assured the cardinal, "I would have felt it my duty to make proper representations to the Holy See." "For the same reason," Persico explained, turning to his second point, "it seems incomprehensible to me, if the Irish Bishops knew, that they did not represent matters and lay their views and reasons before the H. S." "As it is," he complained, "Dr. Donnelly has done me the greatest possible harm before the Irish people, in denouncing me as their

[38] *Ibid.*

[Rome's] informer, or the instrument of the Decree, etc." "For nothing," Persico observed, all too correctly, "will remove from their minds that I am their enemy, after the declaration of one of their Bishops." "So," he concluded sadly, "the whole onus is thrown on me."

In the light of all this, one thing certainly becomes clear: both Persico and Walsh were treated shabbily, not to say used, by the pope and the Roman authorities. There can be little doubt now, for example, after reading Persico's letter to Manning, unless he was an outright liar and hypocrite, that the monsignor had anything directly to do with the making or the issuing of the Decree. Furthermore, as Persico pointed out to Manning, though Walsh must have known that the Decree had been prepared before February 1st and that this accounts for a certain reticence in his correspondence with Manning and, even more so, with Croke, he must have thought he had at least secured a postponement when the pope asked him to prepare a *relatio* on the Land Question at their audience on February 12, and that nothing, consequently, would be done, at least until Rome had heard the other side of the case. Walsh could hardly have protested the existence of the Decree while the pope was politely asking him to submit his evidence and arguments. In refusing to allow Persico to return to Rome and by asking Walsh to prepare a *relatio* which kept him in Rome, the pope had cleverly and successfully prevented Persico and Walsh from comparing notes, and not only avoided precipitating an awkward crisis, but more importantly secured more time for diplomatic maneuver with the British government.

But if Persico was not directly responsible for either the making or the issuing of the Decree, perhaps the duke of Norfolk was. Donnelly denied, however, that the duke was responsible, and argued that the Decree had been drawn up before the duke had arrived in Rome in early February at the head of the English Catholic delegation assisting at the pope's Jubilee. What Donnelly had forgotten, however, was that Norfolk (and Ross) had also visited Rome officially before Christmas, when indeed the subject of the conduct of the Irish clergy was introduced among other things by the pope as a basis for negotiating the delicate question of diplomatic relations. The duke, therefore, not only supplied the information about the Plan and Boycotting, as indeed had Monsignor Persico in his reports, which allowed for a decision by the Holy

Office, but he had also urged, unlike the monsignor, that the pope should authoritatively proceed to a condemnation without reference to the Irish Bishops. While this certainly makes Norfolk and his friends more responsible than Persico, however, it does not mean the duke was ultimately responsible. The ultimate responsibility, of course, as was made clear in the document itself, rested with the pope. In this case, however, the pope was more than just technically responsible for the initiating and the issuing of the Decree, he was in the deepest sense personally responsible. On the available evidence it simply cannot be argued that he was misled, used, or taken advantage of by Persico, Norfolk, or his advisers. He had himself decided shortly after Walsh's arrival in Rome to proceed to an authoritative pronouncement rather than working with and through the Irish Bishops.

The only question that remained, therefore, was when would it be most advantageous to issue the Decree in order to secure the objects in view — that is, the better conduct of the Irish clergy and British good will. Donnelly had argued that the worsening of the agrarian agitation and the arrests of Dillon and O'Brien had most to do with the timing of the Decree. Since the pope wanted to maximize English gratitude and minimize Irish hostility, however, he naturally ordered his priorities differently. He had, therefore, not only to wait a reasonable period after Norfolk left Rome to lessen the effect of the charge of a *quid pro quo,* but he also had to act before Walsh completed his *relatio,* the consideration of which would have resulted in another delay and destroyed the implicit cause and effect relationship of the duke's visit in the English public's mind. Further, it would be certainly more difficult, if not indeed dangerous, to issue the Decree after Walsh had submitted his considered and conscientious opinion in writing, for while he was eminently reasonable there were limits to his flexibility. Moreover, since Walsh was undoubtedly the strong man in the Irish hierarchy and their acknowledged leader, the issuing of the Decree with Walsh in Rome would maximize Roman influence and pressure on both him and the Irish Bishops.

VII. Enforcing the Law
April, 1888 - August, 1888

Rome was now to learn to its cost, as the British government had been learning for centuries, that it was one thing to make a law for Ireland, but quite another thing to enforce that law in Ireland. Even those who had every reason to be pleased with the issuing of the Decree appear to have had their doubts about how effective it would prove in Ireland. Sir George Errington, for example, who was just about to complete his political metamorphosis from Gladstonian Home Ruler to Liberal Unionist, while delighted about the Decree, was somewhat less sanguine about its immediate effect. "This is," he enthusiastically wrote Smith from the Reform Club in London on April 28, "great news from Rome! I am very glad of it, especially as a Catholic for the honour of the Church, but also for the good it will do in Ireland. It will relieve many a good priest from the false position in which he is placed by the conduct of the Bishops & will force many to choose between this world & the next"(S). "It will not," he shrewdly observed, "have an immediate *political* effect, but I am confident that in the long run it will immensely diminish & check the widely spreading revolutionary and dishonest doctrines among the people. There is no doubt it is a knockdown blow to the violent party." "For some time past," Errington confided, "though I have not *declared* myself a Unionist, I have withdrawn from all sympathy & cooperation with the Gladstonians on account of their shameful tolerance and approval of the very things which when in power they strongly condemned. To them too, this declaration of the Pope's is a terrible reprimand." "I am just as strongly as ever," he maintained, protesting a little too much, "in favour of moderate Home Rule, as the necessary and only possible ULTIMATE solution; but it would be madness to apply it in the present disturbed state of Ireland: if we could have firm & honest government as at present for 4 or 5 years, Home Rule might then be safely tried: this I KNOW to be the opinion & intention of the present Govt." "Pray send me a line;" Errington then begged of Smith in conclusion, "I am *most anxious* to hear all you can tell me about the decision of the Pope in Ireland."

About a week later, the duke of Norfolk, in reply to a letter from Ross, who was still in Rome, reported that the situation with regard to the Decree, especially in Ireland, was still far from clear.[1] While admitting that the effect of the Decree on public opinion in England was "most satisfactory," the duke had to confess that it was "more difficult to judge what the effect in Ireland will be. Father Flanagan's letter you have seen. Lord Kenmare whom I saw yesterday immediately on his return from Ireland speaks in exactly the opposite sense and says that very many people, especially among the Clergy, are relieved and only too glad to catch at the opportunity of escaping from a false position." Earlier in this letter Norfolk had also confided to Ross that pressure just now on the part of Rome for a *quid pro quo* by the British government was most inopportune. Whatever might be said about the Education Question, the duke explained, "I am myself glad that relations should not be pushed forward at this moment. It would be impossible to prevent its being supposed all over the world that the Pope had struck a bargain and this belief hurtful on the one hand to the highest interests of the church and specifically dangerous to Irish Catholics would on the other hand raise up a spirit of Protestant opposition among those who thought the Government had made a surrender to the Pope to get his help in their difficulties. The same may be said about Education, but in a very much less degree." "A bill brought in now," Norfolk then added, "and passed through would look very like part of a prearranged bargain." "I should think," the duke maintained, indicating where the pressure for a *quid pro quo* was coming from, "Rampolla would to some extent feel the force of these considerations. Emly is keen to try some arrangement he thinks practicable to allow of you remaining longer in or near Rome. I do not know what your views may be on this point either from a professional or personal point of view, but there can be no doubt that your presence while this crisis lasts is most

---

[1] Ross Papers(R), Public Record Office, Northern Ireland, Belfast, no date, c. May 5, 1888. This letter and those that follow from the Ross papers have now been catalogued and may be found under the reference numbers D 2004/4/34-51.

important." "I hope you are all right again," the duke then finally concluded solicitously, "Don't knock up."

Of all the immediate reactions to the Decree, however, the most interesting was undoubtedly that of Lord Salisbury, not simply because of where he stood in terms of the chain of command, but also because of the insight it provides into that superb political mind, the cynicism of which appeared to be bottomless. The occasion for Salisbury's comments was a letter from Monsignor Ruffo Scilla, the pope's late representative at the celebration of the queen's Jubilee, and presently papal nuncio in Munich, in reference to the Decree. "I received with the greatest pleasure," Salisbury replied politely, to what was yet another diplomatic gambit on the part of Rome, on May 12, "Your Excellency's letter, which at once recalled to me the agreeable minutes which I passed in your company last year, and reminded me of the enlightened views which you expressed at that time upon the matters referred to in your letter"(Sy). "The opinion which you were able to form upon some of the disputed questions of Irish affairs," Salisbury further observed, indicating that he had taken the measure of his man, "has been singularly justified by the elaborate examination into the facts conducted by Monsignor Persico, and the judgement which the highest authority at Rome has since passed upon them: though your Excellency had little to guide you except your own clearsightedness & practice in public affairs." "I feel confident," Salisbury added, "that that opinion must have had the greatest effect upon the views of the Holy Father." "I believe that the judgement which has been pronounced by the Pope," the prime Minister noted cynically, "upon the moral questions raised by the 'Plan of Campaign,' & the question of 'boycotting,' will have an influence of the most salutary & lasting kind upon all persons of good will & honesty, though of course it is not to be expected that the agitators who are condemned should acquiesce in their own condemnation." "Not the least valuable of the benefits," Salisbury finally concluded ironically, emphasizing that the real world was the world of sanctions, "conferred by this decision will be that it will separate the merely political questions which are in dispute, from the higher precepts of morality which had unfortunately been brought into the issue."

During May and early June, two things certainly emerge from the correspondence of those who had been most involved

in promoting the Decree. One was that the Decree had a good
effect on public opinion in England, or at least those portions of
it that were Conservative and Liberal Unionist. The other was
that the Decree was not proving effective in Ireland because the
Bishops were refusing in effect to enforce it. Robert Bickersteth,
for example, secretary of the Liberal Unionist Association,
wrote Abbot Smith soon after the Decree was published in
England. "We had so many conversations about the Irish
question," he explained on May 9, "that I cannot resist sending
you this week's number of 'Moonshine,' one of the numerous
comic newspapers which are now published in imitation of
'Punch' "(S). "I am sure the cartoon will amuse you,"
Bickersteth added, "and you will not miss the point of the
tattered umbrella. I think it was Lord Rosebery who first gave
currency to the phrase in a speech in which he said that 'Mr.
Gladstone's umbrella was large enough to shelter all sound
Liberals.' But it evidently is not substantial enough to screen the
morality of 'boycotting' and the 'plan of campaign.' " "It would
be difficult," Bickersteth concluded gratefully, "to express the
thankfulness with which the Pope's condemnation of practices
which have done so much to demoralise the Irish peasantry has
been received here." Another of Smith's more intermittent
correspondents, Herbert Vaughan, the bishop of Salford, also
took occasion at this time to write him about the reception of
the Decree in Ireland and in England. "There is still," Vaughan
reported from Salford on May 18, the day after the Catholic
M.P.'s met in Dublin, "a good deal of excitement among the
Irish politicians on the Decree & the M.P.'s are behaving very
ill." "The effect of the Decree in England," he assured Smith,
"has been in the highest degree beneficial to the interests of the
Catholic Religion. No one really believes that it is a political
decree, & everyone sees how great & important is the power of
the Holy See." "This power of the Holy See on behalf of
morality & religion," Vaughan argued in conclusion, "has
come home to the English people with the greatest & most
convincing force, from the fact that the Decree is directed
against Spiritual subjects of the Pope & shews that his
guardianship & morality is superior to what is called his natural
partisanship."

Meanwhile, Smith, who had received Errington's enthusiastic
letter welcoming the news of the Decree in early May, was not
able to reply for more than a month. When he did, however, he

obviously not only asked Errington for more news about the reception of the Decree, but also informed him of Cardinal Rampolla's letter to the Irish Bishops addressed to Walsh, for Errington replied post haste. "In the first place," he explained to Smith on June 9, from London, "the effect of the Papal decree in England has been most gratifying and important. It has immensely raised the position of the Holy Father & the Church generally in protestant estimation"(S). "I am very glad what you tell me of the rebuke:" Errington then observed, referring to Rampolla's letter, and turning to the effects of the Decree in Ireland, "it was most needed. The conduct of the Bishops is nothing less than a painful scandal. Who would have thought that the successors of Cardinal Cullen & Card. McCabe would have shown such want of FAITH as to question & *Cavill* at a solemn act of the Holy See: and as the O'Conor Don points out to me, the Bishops have weakened themselves with the people, for if they now try to enforce the decree, the people will reprove them with having first set them the example of questioning the authority of the Pope!!" "I am becoming daily," Errington then further confided to Smith, "more Unionist. I should like very much (having been so much connected with all these matters) to have some opportunity to publicly express my adherence to the address of Rome, and to say that as a Catholic I feel compelled to withdraw from the National & Gladstone Movement *so far* as it is implicated and upon what the Holy See has censured." "Would you," Errington finally asked, "advise this?" "Do you think," he inquired even more prudently, "it would be approved at Rome?"

Rome may be forgiven, however, if at this critical moment in her affairs she appeared less interested in Errington's political star than in her own. Rome was not only insistent at this time that the Irish Bishops do something to make the pope's recent Decree effective in Ireland, but she was also anxious that the British government demonstrate in some tangible way its appreciation of the pope's recent effort to pacify Ireland. Given all the various reports of the excellent impression the Decree had made on English, if not Irish, public opinion, the pope and his advisers were particularly anxious that so favorable an opportunity on the part of the British government should not be lost. On June 15, therefore, Cardinal Rampolla took occasion to write the pope's old friend, the earl of Denbigh, a letter that was obviously intended for Salisbury. "I am exceedingly obliged to you," Rampolla explained, "for the information you have favoured me with in your esteemed letter of May 30, and I gather from it with pleasure that in high quarters the action of the Holy See in the affairs of Ireland is appreciated as it deserves — and I pray that the English Government may not let slip this favourable opportunity of showing its gratitude to the Holy Father for what he has done in aid of social order."[2] "The Government assuredly," the cardinal observed archly, and referring to the Liberal Unionist support that kept the Conservative government in power, "does not want for means to conquer the selfish opposition of the Radical party." "When you are able to communicate further information," Rampolla concluded encouragingly, and indicating that his letter had the pope's *imprimatur,* "it will always be most acceptable to me, nor will it be less welcome to the Holy Father whom I have made aware of the contents of your letter."

In forwarding a translation of this letter to Balfour on June 19, Denbigh asked him if he would "show it to Ld Salisbury?"[3] Denbigh further explained that Rampolla was "evidently anxious that His Holiness's action in restoring Social order should be appreciated. If Lord Salibury will authorise me to express anything to him I will willingly do so." "I quite understand," Denbigh assured Balfour in conclusion, "that officially we should be able to say, at this moment that no *official* communication has taken place with the Holy See." Balfour, it seems, had been encouraging Denbigh and his Jesuit friend, Baynard Klein, professor of Natural Philosophy at the Royal University, by holding out hopes that the government was now prepared perhaps to enter into negotiations with Rome to consider a measure of higher Education for Roman Catholics in Ireland, for Denbigh had added in a postscript to his letter — "Will you give Dr. Klein some letter of introduction to any one you wish him to work with in Ireland on the question you spoke of the other day?" What Rampolla's letter to Denbigh really signified, of course, was that the pope and his advisers had not been much impressed with the duke of Norfolk's argument, tendered through Ross, that anything

---

[2] B, 49841.
[3] *Ibid.*

done immediately on the part of the British government would
have the unfortunate appearance of a "prearranged bargain,"
and that this in turn would prove a very serious embarrassment
to the government in terms of Protestant public opinion, and
especially with regard to their Liberal Unionist allies who
opposed any official relations with Rome. Rampolla had
cleverly countered this latter argument by suggesting that the
government, by juxtaposing "No Popery" and "Dissolution of
the Empire," both Protestant public opinion and the Liberal
Unionists could be tamed. But Salisbury was too shrewed a
politician to ask an English electorate or even a House of
Commons to make such a choice. In any case, the pope,
through Denbigh, was politely informing Salisbury that he, at
least, expected some reciprocal action on the part of the British
government. What Denbigh, moreover, really wanted to tell the
pope on behalf of Salisbury was that the government was now
prepared, to consider a measure to provide for Catholic higher
education in Ireland.

When the duke of Norfolk heard of Balfour's discussions
with Denbigh and Klein about University Education for
Catholics, he was naturally very upset that he was not to be the
medium through which the negotiations were to be conducted.
He obviously asked Balfour for both an interview and an
explanation, for Balfour laid out the whole case for Salisbury at
this time in an undated memorandum.

> The Duke of Norfolk had some conversation with me today, of
> which, as he is well acquainted with the views of many persons
> in Rome you may like to know the tenor. He alluded to the
> rumour current in the Newspapers that there had been a
> bargain between the Pope and the Go^{vt}: — the Pope to condemn
> the P. of Campaign, the Go^n to concede Catholic University
> Education. He said he was certain that the Pope had acted
> spontaneously in the matter, without any thought of a *quid* pro
> *quo,* and solely in the interests of morality. Never the less he —
> the D. of N. — as a Catholic was anxious to know what the
> views of Her Majesty's Go^n were on the subject of University
> Education in Ireland: as he could not think that, on the one
> hand, it would greatly strengthen the Pope's hands in dealing
> with disloyal ecclesiastics in Ireland to have the last Irish
> grievance removed, and on the other that the task of removing
> it would be much lightened for any Go^{vt} which undertook it, by
> the improvement in the attitude of the Irish Clergy which could

not fail to follow from the recent pronouncements of the Holy
See.[4]

After he had thus repeated what Norfolk had said, Balfour then
informed his uncle what his replies were to the various points
raised by the duke.

> I said that I agreed with him in both points: — that I myself had
> always been in favour of giving to Catholics in Ireland a higher
> education not repugnant to their principles, that I thought some
> scheme carrying out this object should be introduced at the
> earliest date which the state of Parliamentary business and the
> exigencies of public policy allowed, and that I believed that my
> colleagues shared my view on both points. I further said that
> any public announcement of these intentions would in my
> opinion be fatal to the object we both had in view, as it would
> inevitably support the idea of a *bargain,* which would be
> represented as *corrupt*: — and in addition to this it would be
> most inexpedient to say anything which would honourably
> commit us to a policy which unforeseen circumstances might
> make it impossible to carry through in the immediate future. I
> had no ground for supposing that such circumstances would
> arise: but he himself (I added) must be well aware of the
> unexpected difficulties which were apt to arise in carrying out,
> under our Parliamentary System, even the best considered and
> most moderate programme of legislation. These difficulties
> made any specific pledge with regard to legislation absolutely
> impossible under any circ[s], or in respect of any subject.[5]

This whole memorandum, of course, gives evidence of being a
"set piece" on the part of Balfour, and was undoubtedly
preconcerted with his uncle before the duke's visit, as well as
probably discussed and approved in the cabinet. In any case,
the duke could hardly have enjoyed either being dismissed in so
peremptory a fashion by Balfour, or displaced in the
government's dealings with Rome by the earl of Denbigh.

The reaction of Salisbury, who had obviously already
decided to disengage as far as Rome was concerned because of
internal political complications with the Liberal Unionists, to
the confessed anxiety of the pope and his advisers as revealed
through Denbigh for some reciprocal action on his part was, to
say the least, diplomatically imaginative. He simply decided to

---

[4] B, 49821, undated memorandum.
[5] *Ibid.*

forestall the pope's demand for reciprocity by demanding even more. The occasion for the demand was the perennial and embarrassing question of securing an acceptable successor to the sickly and now rapidly failing bishop of Malta. Since the question was again critical, Salisbury decided to press once more for the removal of Monsignor Buhagiar, the bishop of Malta's episcopal administrator, and urge the appointment with the right of succession of Monsignor Peter Pace, the bishop of Gozo. On June 7, the governor of Malta, Sir John Lintorn Simmons, had informed the colonial secretary, Lord Knutsford, that Monsignor Buhagiar had returned to Malta from Rome a few days before. "I am informed on undoubted authority," Simmons further reported to Knutsford, who forwarded this dispatch to Salisbury, "that during his stay in Rome, when the news of Monsignor Siclima's serious attack of illness reached Rome, Monsignor Buhagiar, accompanied by Cardinal Lavigerie, at once, went to the Vatican, and used their best endeavours to secure the nomination of Monsignor Buhagiar to the [almost] vacant See."[6] "I regret to hear," Simmons continued, "from the telegram from the English Embassy, that the Pope is not disposed to nominate Monsignor Pace, and still more regret to learn that he is favourably disposed towards Monsignor Buhagiar. The influence of Cardinal Lavigerie, which is great at the Vatican, is enough to account for the Pope's disinclination to appoint Monsignor Pace, and for his leaning towards Monsignor Buhagiar, but it appears to me that the fact that Cardinal Lavigerie is so strong and so avowed a supporter of Monsignor Buhagiar's claims, is an additional reason why Her Majesty's Gov[t] should refuse to confirm the nomination of Monsignor Buhagiar should it be made." "For myself," Simmons then declared in conclusion, "I can only say, that if war were to break out with France and Monsignor Buhagiar were then to be Bishop here, the first step which the Governor ought to take, for the safety of the Island, would be to send Monsignor Buhagiar out of it."

Why the pope was being difficult was not only that he thought that he had already done enough, but that Salisbury was attempting to turn an acknowledged right of veto in Malta into one of nomination. The British might be well within their rights in objecting to Buhagiar, but in insisting on Pace they

---

[6] F. O., 170/394.

were setting, perhaps, what might eventually be a very dangerous precedent. Salisbury, it appears, was also attempting to keep his Maltese and Irish diplomatic lines clear of each other in that he chose not to negotiate through Ross, who was still in Rome, but through the British Embassy there, and through Gerald Strickland, a Maltese count of some influence at the Vatican and an important British official in the Maltese government. In any case, on June 28, the British ambassador in Rome, J. G. Kennedy, informed Salisbury that in deference to the wishes of the British government, the Vatican had decided to appoint Monsignor Pace to succeed the bishop of Malta and remove Monsignor Buhagiar from the island.[7] In acknowledging Kennedy's dispatch with "satisfaction" on July 7, Salisbury coolly concluded, "and I have now to request that you will avail yourself of any favourable opportunity that may occur for conveying to the Vatican the high sense entertained by Her Majesty's Government of the courtesy displayed by them in this matter."[8] When the pope thus received Salisbury's best thanks for all that he yet promised to do for him in Malta, and, especially all that he had already done, not to say risked, for him in Ireland, his holiness must have realized that he had indeed met more than his diplomatic match.

In Ireland, meanwhile, the truce, which had been effected between the Party and the Bishops by the episcopal resolutions of May 30, and the calling off of the mass demonstrations, was suddenly and rudely shaken by the bishop of Limerick. Just as Irish public opinion was settling down over the Decree, O'Dwyer wrote perhaps the most famous of all those letters, but one, that were to be his hallmark in the Irish Church for the next thirty years. This remarkable document, at once ingenious and contemptuous, was read on June 11 at a synod of the regular and secular clergy of the diocese of Limerick, in St. John's Cathedral. In order to appreciate the letter it is necessary to quote from it at some length.

> VERY REV AND REV FATHERS — It is my duty as Bishop of this diocese to bring to your knowledge officially the decree recently issued by the Holy Office, and sanctioned by the Holy Father, in condemnation of the practices known as the Plan of

---

[7] *Ibid.*
[8] *Ibid.*

Campaign and Boycotting. At our Theological conferences held two weeks ago I was unable, in consequence of a difference of opinion that had arisen as to its interpretation, to go further than to inform you in general terms of its binding force, and I abstained intentionally from a detailed exposition of it. At that time a communication had been forwarded to Rome by the Irish Bishops seeking for information as to whether the condemnation was to be understood as conditional, or limited, or qualified in any way by the reasons given for it by Cardinal Monaco. Some held the reasons to govern the condemnation, and that it would be understood as having effect only where the circumstances implied in them were found to exist, while others maintained that the reasons had no further value than the undoubtedly great weight of Cardinal Monaco's own authority, and were no part of a formal decree. That point has now been decided. At the last meeting of the Bishops, held at Clonliffe on the 30th ult. a letter was read from the Archbishop of Dublin informing us, by the direction of the Pope himself, that the latter was the true opinion; and secondly, that Cardinal Monaco's reasons did not in any way enter into or limit the formal condemnation. These practices, then, of boycotting and the Plan of Campaign as they actually exist in Ireland stand condemned as violations of the moral law of charity and justice. This is no longer a matter of opinion. It is now a settled and certain law of the Catholic Church, which all the faithful of this diocese are bound to take from me as their bishop that these practices are sinful. And it is even more sinful, as being against faith, to deny or impugn under any pretext the right of the Pope to condemn them.

It has been sedulously put about that on this question I am not at one with the other Bishops of Ireland, and consequently that, after all, my views may be treated by the people of this diocese as mere matters of opinion. In this way only can I understand the grotesque manner in which my formal and official statement, as Bishop, of the law of God has been answered by persons who ought to know better than to tell their Bishop that they had their opinion and he might have his own. There is no difference of opinion amongst the Irish bishops as to the meaning or binding force of this decree. I am entirely in accord with them, and surely it ought not be necessary to tell any reasonable man that I am not so ignorant of my duty or so reckless of the salvation of my flock as to impose on them as a certain obligation under pain of sin my own private opinion, no matter how convinced I was of its truth, as long as I knew that the contrary opinion was maintained by others. Take, for instance, these very condemned practices. Some three months ago a priest of this diocese, who held very strong views, consulted me as to his line of conduct. With regard to one of them I said to him, "My own private opinion is against it. Others think otherwise, and consequently you are free with a safe conscience to follow whomever you think is right." But now the case is changed. It is no longer a matter of opinion — *Roma locuta est, causa finita est,* and I am nothing more now than the mouthpiece of the Pope to his subjects in this diocese.

With regard to the manner of publishing this decree, I have to say that in my humble opinion a great deal of the trouble might have been avoided if it had been kept out of the *Freeman's Journal* in the first instance. Now that it has been published, and made a matter of popular agitation and the subject of consideration, not only by that curious body, the conciliabulum of laymen, that sat on the Pope in Dublin, but by public boards in the country down to little village branches of the League, I am convinced the sooner the plain truth is put before the people the better. I have noticed the craft with which Catholic feelings have been worked upon by the leaders of the agitation. They have been assured on the pretended authority of anonymous theologians, and it is even hinted of bishops, that they are opposed to this decree, and that the repudiation of it was quite consistent with their duty as good Catholics. They believed all this, and in perfect good faith went to the meetings and cheered language that, beyond yea or nay, was not only disrespectful and disobedient to the Pope, but even schismatical. I know many of those who have been engaged in such things here. They are good Catholics at least, and if they believed they were committing sin, or were acting disloyally to the Vicar of Christ, they would cast the League and every other worldly consideration to the winds rather than be guilty of such conduct. Now, for such men is it not true prudence, before their minds are poisoned by false principles, and before they have committed themselves too far, to put their duty as Catholics to them; and even if a few reckless and bad men, who thought they were Catholics, have lost the Catholic spirit, revolt against their lawful pastors, better in my opinion to run that risk than permit the Pope's teaching authority, which is the very corner stone of our religion, to be tampered with. It is all very well to talk about allowing the truth to percolate slowly into the public mind, and to avoid scandal. To my mind there never has been in Ireland since St. Patrick planted the Faith here a greater scandal or more injury done to religion than this most deplorable agitation. Whatever may have been the intention of the leaders, and God alone can judge that, the general tendency of these speeches, I am sorry to say, the result has been to impair the loving, and childlike, and undoubting faith and confidence with which the hearts of our countrymen have ever turned to the Chair of Peter. . . .

This is not the place to talk politics, and I don't mean to do so further than I think necessary to prevent a misunderstanding of my position at the present crisis. I am a Nationalist, I believe, as true and as sound as the best of you. I have never wavered in my belief in Home Rule for Ireland. I am a land reformer. I detest as earnestly as any man the oppression of heartless landlords, and would go any length sanctioned by religion to restrain them. I believe there never will be peace in Ireland or prosperity until every farmer is the owner of his own farm, and am prepared to give every legitimate aid, according to my position, to any political agitation for these ends. But from that agitation must be eliminated whatever is against God's law — I don't care what advantage it brings to the farmers or others — if it put a gold mine in the heart of every farm and abolished all rent for ever, if it is condemned by the Church I will not have it, but accept the decision of our own father, Christ's vicar, who is placed by his exalted office above the passions and self-interest that often blind us, and has no motive in all he does but God's honour and our salvation. Cut off what he condemns and there is no bishop in Ireland will throw himself with more heart or determination into this movement than I. I don't think that a state of equilibrium, social or political, will ever be reached as long as the centre of government is outside Ireland; but even for the recovery of all the blessings which Home Rule would bring I will not sanction the violation of God's law, much less the repudiation of the authority of the vicar of Christ, and if disobedience to him is made a test of nationality then I will openly and to the best of my power refuse that test.

There is just one remark of a personal character to which I desire to refer, not so much to affect the opinions of my own people who know me as to let the truth be known to strangers who have been reading every injurious statement against me. It has been said repeatedly that I have habitually associated with the aristocracy, and for years, as a priest, took sides with the rich against the poor, and with the landlords against their tenants. To many men to whom it must have been pain to think that any Irish bishop could be so far forgetful of his duty and the traditions of his order, it will give them, I have no doubt, a great deal of relief to learn that there is not one particle of truth in these statements, nor a shadow of foundation for them. They are simply malicious inventions. They are lies concocted by the leaders of this agitation for the purpose of prejudicing the poor people against me, and thus weakening my authority in teaching them all their duty. Such methods may succeed for a time, but they are not the methods of honourable men, and unless those who have recourse to them against me are prepared to substantiate these charges by some definite facts I should think that they must feel that they have put themselves in an awkward position. It cannot be pleasant for any man to be a convicted slanderer, even if the object of his slander is merely a bishop of his Church who has attempted to teach God's law. To you, the priests of this city and county, amongst whom I have gone in and out for twenty-one years, I appeal, and ask you is there in your whole body, secular and regular, a priest less open to such a charge? But the making of that reckless charge has done a great deal of good. Hundreds of men who were disposed to believe the statements of those agitators stopped when they got so far, and they could not help saying to themselves, "that, at any rate is a lie, probably the rest is no better." But except in so far as it is due to my office to make this statement I assure you I would not give myself the trouble to notice these things. I confess that I feel rather flattered by them, because it is a satisfactory thing that a number of desperate men who were under the necessity of traducing me were driven for their purpose to the invention of falsehood. But I would not wish you from that to think that I retain one atom of rancour in my mind against them. I can make allowance as well as any man for excitement or political passion. These men had got into a most trying position, and although much of their language was wrong, it is easy to understand how they were betrayed into it. Let the whole thing drop now. Let it pass away as a painful incident, and if again the priests and people stand together upon the same platform, I can promise you that no remembrance of the personal ill-treatment which I have received will interfere to disturb the harmony of their reunion.[9]

"I have just returned home (2 o c — P.M.)," Croke wrote William H. Murphy, Walsh's secretary, on June 13, "after finishing my visitations, and found Limerick's Manifesto before me"(W). "It is dreadful," Croke maintained, explaining, "We agreed unanimously not to write anything publickly about the rescript. It was suggested that when promulgating it to the priests, it would be well to do so in writing: but that was overruled unanimously, on the grounds that any letter thus written would surely creep into the public papers, and that consequently the more prudent way would be to have each

---

[9] *Freeman's Journal*, June 12, 1888.

Bishop give such *oral* directions as the [*sic*] thought fit to his priests." "This was agreed to," Croke emphasized, "by Dr. O'Dwyer. Still here he is out in a violent pronunciamento in which he assails everyone, directly or indirectly, right, left, and centre. Tis hard to bear it." "I have found before me, too," Croke also reported to Murphy, "a letter from his Grace of Dublin written at Baden, and dated the 11th int. He says he will be home about today or yesterday week." "I write to him to London tomorrow," he concluded, "or surely the day after to the Grand Hotel London. P.S. Keep me au courant."

"I'm dying to see you," Croke confessed to Walsh the next day, June 14, "and have you safely landed at home"(W). "Of course," he assured Walsh, "I'll be *up* to meet you. But you must let me know *precisely* when you land, and where, and what moves you mean to make afterwards. I reserve all I have to say till we meet. You will have to let 'the cat completely out of the bag' for the benefit of the Bishops. Some of them need it badly." "I had a letter," he explained, by way of example, "a few days ago, from Elphin saying that some stronger and longer pronouncement than our last was needed to protect the privileges of the Pope, and to check the disrespectful utterances of certain Catholic orators. I assured him that the storm had spent its strength, and that any such words of ours as he seemed to wish for would only raise a fresh one more violent and more damaging than the first." "I have not," Croke remarked, "heard from him since."

"The Limerick Manifesto," Croke further pointed out, turning to the immediate crisis, "came on the country with surprise. His Lordship was very quiet and conciliatory at our last Meeting. He took part in drafting the resolutions." "Raphoe," Croke added, referring to Patrick O'Donnell, "he, and I drew them up. It was, at same time unanimously agreed on, that even to the priests, no written communication would be made, lest such a written document may get into the public papers. Directions were to be orally given by each Bishop to his priests, at Conference, or elsewhere: but there was to be *no writing*." "And yet see," he exclaimed angrily, "what the little cur has done!" "It is unaccountable," Croke confessed, "The general impression is that he has lost his head. How else account for his eccentricity and audacious egotism?" "'Tis hard to hold one's tongue under the circumstances," Croke confided, "especially as he has publickly declared that he is *at one* with the other Irish Bishops. His reference to your communication to the assembled Bishops, and to the conclusions come to by the Coetus Episcoporum, is provoking and outrageous in a high degree." "However," Croke observed temperately in conclusion, "tis better to be silent than to further offend the public conscience by shivering a lance over his head."

The *Irish Catholic,* however, was not of the same moderate mind as the archbishop of Cashel. "The Bishop of Limerick's address," the *Catholic* maintained in its lead editorial on Saturday, June 16, "will be painful reading to many *Irish Catholics* as loyal to the Pope as the Most Rev. Dr. O'Dwyer himself." "Until the present moment," the editorial observed, "we have not said a word on the present unfortunate controversy so far as its personal relation to the Bishop of Limerick is concerned." "We fear," the *Catholic* then pointed out, and referring to Limerick's manifesto, "that it will speed forth once more the fiery cross of agitation which had been dropped — openly and deliberately dropped — by the leaders of the Irish people." "If the agitation is revived," the *Catholic* warned in conclusion, "if the excellent effect produced by the general body of the bishops, to which Dr. O'Dwyer has appended so unharmonious a supplement, is destroyed; if there be more heart-burning discussions and dissensions, this address of his Lordship will be the proximate cause."

The agitation was not renewed, however, and it was a tribute both to the good sense and moderation of the lay Nationalist leadership that they allowed the provocation given by the bishop of Limerick to pass. The mood of the country was one of quiet expectation, and it was perhaps best summed up by Kirby's newly appointed vice rector, James Hasson, who was winding up his affairs as president of St. Columb's College in Derry. Hasson, who was certainly no advanced Nationalist, especially where Rome was concerned, explained to Kirby on June 14 that there "is little commotion now about the Rescript, and the Bishop of Limerick is the only one among the Bishops who has come out strong on the point. But I am afraid his solitary action will do more harm than good"(K). "The Archbishop of Dublin," he reported further, "has not arrived yet, and there is great speculation about what he will do." "Let us hope," Hasson concluded, "he will set matters right."

Some three weeks after he had left Rome, Walsh finally

arrived in London on Sunday, June 17, when he had the first of three long conversations with Cardinal Manning.[10] The line of action decided on was made manifest four days later in two long and interesting "interviews," which Walsh granted to the press. The first of these was granted on Wednesday evening, June 20, to the London correspondent of the *Freeman's Journal* and opportunely published on June 21, the day before Walsh arrived in Dublin. It was obviously designed to prepare public opinion in Ireland with regard to the meaning and application of the Decree to Irish politics. "Every question," Walsh explained patiently, "as to whether a particular action, or line of action, is morally right or morally wrong, is a question of morals, and as such it comes within the sphere of authority of the Church."[11] "The action, or line of action in question," he continued, "if considered from a worldly point of view, may be political or social, or medical, or legal. But the question whether that line of action, is or is not in accordance with the principles of morality, that is to say, with the natural law, is not a question of political, or of social, or of medical, or of legal science. It is essentially and exclusively a question of morals."

"Then, as a question of morals," the journalist interposed, "it is to be dealt with by the tribunal —" "It is to be dealt with," Walsh interrupted, "by that tribunal which is competent to deal with it on moral grounds." "Persons who are not Catholics," he pointed out, "have to examine such questions conscientiously for themselves, each man according to the lights of his own private judgement as to what is right or wrong. In matters not decided by the authority of the Church Catholics are left to do the same. But when such a question is decided by that authority, mere private judgement is called upon to give way." "Then, your Grace," the journalist asked, after a further discussion of the limits of the Church's authority, "as to [i.e. what about] the manner in which the decree will be put in force in the different dioceses?" "You must not," Walsh replied, "expect me to go into that question. I have had great pleasure in explaining to you the nature of the authority on which the binding force of the decree rests. But you will see, I think, that at this point we have reached the limits of what I could, for the present at all events, either with prudence or propriety communicate to you for publication in a newspaper." "In the

[10] *Star* (London), June 21, 1888.
[11] *Freeman's Journal*, June 21, 1888.

first place," Walsh explained, "I need hardly say to you, I have nothing to do with any diocese but my own. I am only one out of twenty-eight Irish bishops. I have not as yet had an opportunity of consulting upon this point with any of my episcopal brethren. After consultation with them, I shall be in a position to communicate with the clergy of my diocese, who will of course be guided in their action by whatever instructions it may then be my duty to give them."

"Your Grace, then," the interviewer asked, "will not make those instructions public through the Press?"

A. — I shall be guided by circumstances. You must not take it ill of me if I say that in my opinion a great deal of harm has been done by the extreme anxiety of the press — I should say rather of certain newspapers — to drag this decree, and everything connected with it, into a publicity that I, for one, must regard as singularly inopportune. Very great soreness of feeling, I understand, has been excited in Ireland by the way in which the existence of the decree was first made public.

R. — The news, as your Grace, no doubt, is aware, first appeared in a London Protestant newspaper, a paper most hostile to the Irish national movement. There is in Ireland, and also indeed, as a matter of course, among the Irish population in England, in Scotland, and in America, a strong and even angry feeling on this point. People are saying that whatever the decree may be in itself, the fact that it was communicated for publication in the first instance through such a channel, in a newspaper notoriously hostile both to the land movement and to the Home Rule movement, gives it a decidedly political aspect.

A. — To be candid with you, I do not at all wonder that such a feeling exists. If I did not know the facts of the case, I should feel very strongly on the subject myself. But the hasty judgments that have been formed on this point do a grievous wrong to the Holy Father. Take the case even on broad general grounds. The notion that the Pope was in any way influenced by political considerations, such as you refer to, rests altogether upon the assumption that his Holiness is in some way opposed to the Irish Nationalist movements — to the movement for Home Rule, or to the movement for obtaining a full measure of justice and of protection against oppression for the tenant farmers of Ireland. Now, no assumption could be more absolutely contrary to fact.[12]

---

[12] *Ibid.*

"It is, I may say," the journalist pointed out, and coming to the most delicate question of all, "universally believed, your Grace, that many strong influences of various kinds were brought to bear upon his Holiness within the last year or so, to lead him to take an adverse view of the Irish cause?" "People may believe what they like," Walsh countered, "but I know what I am talking about. It is essential that this point should be fully understood by the Irish people at home and abroad. No matter what influences have been brought to bear upon the Holy Father, no matter how powerful they may have been, their working has resulted in absolute failure." "His Holiness," he assured his interviewer, adroitly side-stepping the main issue, "understands the Irish question fully. He knows what is meant by the demand for Home Rule. And he knows what is meant by the demand for a full and effective measure for protection against oppression and of justice for the Irish tenants." "That is to say," Walsh cleverly explained, blurring the important distinction between understanding and approval, "he knows in the fullest detail what is meant by these demands as I understand them —"

Walsh's second "interview," which was given and published on Thursday, June 21, in the London *Star,* a Liberal and afternoon newspaper, dealt mainly with the Decree as it affected the agrarian agitation, and was obviously designed by Walsh more for English than Irish consumption. "It is hard to know," the interviewer pointed out to Walsh in the course of his remarks, "what this is, if it is not a sweeping condemnation of the Irish Land movement in every shape and form."[13] "But," Walsh maintained, "you may take it on my authority that there is no such condemnation. I cannot deny that statements such as you have quoted are to be found in the letter that accompanies the decree. But the decree itself, approved as it is by the Pope, is one thing; that letter is another." "That is," the interviewer interposed, "the letter of Cardinal Monaco?" "Yes," Walsh replied, "there has been a great deal of foolish writing upon this subject in some of the newspapers. It is all very irritating to our people, and I have no doubt that a great deal of it was meant to be so." "The decree itself," Walsh insisted, "as a decision in morals, is binding upon the consciences of Catholics." "As to Cardinal Monaco's letter," Walsh declared, "it is to be treated,

---

[13] *Star,* June 21, 1888.

of course, with respect; but it has no binding force whatever. It was not intended, and, indeed, it could not have been intended, to have any."

"Then as regards the statements of fact," the interviewer asked, referring to Cardinal Monaco's letter, "contained in it?" "Which of them?" Walsh countered, "It contains a great many." "I mean, your Grace," he replied, "those statements that amount to a condemnation of the whole land movement — the statements that the present rents were fixed by free contracts, and that it is dishonest for the tenant not to pay them, especially as there are tribunals already established to do justice by reducing the rents if they are too high." "As a rule," Walsh then explained, returning to an old theme, " 'freedom of contract' is unknown in Ireland between landlord and tenant. Everyone who knows anything of the country knows how rents have in most cases been fixed there." "In most cases, no doubt," he admitted, "there was a free contract at the beginning of the tenancy. But as the land was improved, or as the landlord happened to want money, the rent was raised; that is to say, the landlord, or rather the agent, went on raising the annual charge which the law empowered him to levy upon the tenant. The tenant from the peculiar circumstances of the country, had no choice but to submit to the extortion. There was really nothing of the nature of a contract in the case. It was rather the levying of a tax."

"Your Grace," the interviewer then noticed, "in a recent letter from Rome implied that you thought some measure of temporary relief could be devised without much difficulty?" "Undoubtedly it could be," Walsh replied, "I have myself sketched out the general outlines of a proposal that I think would go far to meet the present urgent difficulty." "The great problem," he argued, "is how *to provide for the people during the coming winter an effective legal protection against eviction for the nonpayment of excessive rents.* The politicians and statesmen who neglect the consideration of that problem are incurring a fearful responsibility." "Your Grace," the interviewer then noted, "does not refer to a purchase scheme?" "Of course not," Walsh answered, "that must be a matter of time." "What I look to," he insisted again, *"is the stopping of unjust evictions, especially during the coming winter."* "It is," he warned, "a matter of absolute urgency to be dealt with promptly, if it is to be dealt with at all."

"Your Grace at all events," the interviewer finally concluded politely, "cannot reproach yourself that you have neglected to do your part." "I trust not," Walsh admitted, "I have now only to thank you for the opportunity you have given me of stating my views so fully for your London readers. It is important for them to know exactly what the attitude of the Catholic Church is in a matter such as this." "If the Church feels called upon," Walsh recapitulated, "to pass an unfavourable judgment on the morality of some of the means employed for the protection of the tenants, she has no thought of abandoning those tenants to their fate. The issuing of the recent decree has put upon us, in fact, a new obligation. Property has not only its duties, but its rights; and neither the bishops nor the priests of the Irish Church are likely to neglect the maintenance of the poor man's rights, no matter how strenuously they may strive to keep him within the lines of duty. It would be an evil day for the Irish race if we gave cause to our people to think that we could do so. They know themselves that there is little fear of this." "The more clearly," Walsh concluded firmly, "it is made known to others the better."

In his successive interviews Walsh was essentially attempting to protect the Clerical-Nationalist and Liberal-Nationalist alliances. In his first interview, Walsh had really made three main points. First, that the pope had an undoubted right to pronounce in any area, including politics, if a moral issue was involved. Second, that what he, as archbishop of Dublin, would do as far as enforcing the Decree was concerned, could not be determined or communicated until he had consulted with his episcopal brethren in Ireland. Third, that the pope had not been motivated in the issuing of the Decree by political considerations. In making his first point, Walsh had gone somewhat farther than the Irish Bishops had gone on May 30, in their joint resolutions. In stating what was so, however, Walsh did not go so far as to declare explicitly that the Catholic M.P.'s were in error on May 17, when they asserted that they could recognize no right on the part of the Holy See to interfere in the management of their political affairs. By taking this line, Walsh wisely and conscientiously attempted to do what was necessary to maintain the pope's prerogatives without antagonizing any further the lay Nationalist leadership. He then proceeded, in his second point, to assure the leadership that he had not returned to enforce a Roman hard line, but that, in fact, the line would be taken only *after* he consulted with his brethren. Finally, in maintaining the pope was not politically motivated, Walsh emphasized that the main objectives of the Clerical-Nationalist alliance — Home Rule and a peasant proprietary — were not really touched by the Decree.

In his second "interview," Walsh was attempting to achieve two things. First of all he wanted to mitigate the effects of the Decree on English public opinion, and second he wanted to assure all concerned, both in England and in Ireland, that the cause of the tenants would not be abandoned by the Irish clergy. The cry raised in England that the agrarian agitation in Ireland made a legal and moral mockery of the rights of property and the sanctity of contracts had proven very effective. When the pope, therefore, declared the means employed by the Irish agitation to be wrong, the enemies of the Irish movement could not only claim that they had long said so, but that the condemnation came from a quarter that could hardly be considered partial to them. In distinguishing, therefore, between the Decree as such, and Cardinal Monaco's letter, Walsh was attempting to point out to English public opinion that the means condemned by the pope and described by Cardinal Monaco were not necessarily the one and the same thing in Ireland. In announcing, moreover, that the Irish clergy would not abandon the tenants in their efforts to save themselves from eviction, Walsh was, in effect, saying that the conditions described by Cardinal Monaco did not exist, for if they did, how could he allow his clergy to participate in what was patently wrong and rightly condemned? In the last analysis, then, Walsh had taken up Cardinal Manning's position that English law in Ireland was really no law when it was not based on natural justice, and this was the position that had been taken up by the Party on May 17, in Dublin, when they met to consider the Decree. Walsh had, therefore, with considerable skill, done his best in his "interviews" to preserve the Clerical-Nationalist and Liberal-Nationalist alliances by mitigating the worst effects of the Decree in both England and Ireland. Since he must now return to Ireland, however, the time for talking about the Decree was nearly over, and the great question was what would Walsh do about enforcing it after consulting with his episcopal brethren.

When Walsh arrived unannounced at Kingstown on Friday,

June 22, he was met by Croke, and the two archbishops immediately retired to 4 Rutland Square, Walsh's residence in Dublin. The following day they proceeded to Maynooth, where they presumably spent the next four days discussing at length the line of action they would take at the forthcoming ordinary meeting of the Irish Bishops on Wednesday, June 27, at Maynooth. The Bishops met for two days, and at the end of their deliberations they issued a series of resolutions on the Irish Land Question, and, surprisingly enough, left the subject of the recent Decree "severely alone." What actually happened at the episcopal meeting can only be pieced together from the very circumspect letters of those few Bishops who mentioned the meeting at all in their letters to Kirby about this time, and the not so circumspect letters of Walsh to Kirby, who on his return, obviously took the measure, if not the temperature, of his episcopal brethren and decided that, perhaps, Croke had been right in the main after all.

"Our meeting this week," Kirby's old friend, James Lynch, bishop of Kildare and Leighlin, noted on June 29, for example, "went off quietly."[14] "All were edified," he explained to Kirby, preferring obviously to discuss form rather than substance, "with the good grace with which the Archbishop of Dublin yielded the precedence to the Primate of all Ireland." "There is a feeling of depression," Lynch confessed, turning to more general matters, "very general amongst Bishops. Priests and people in consequence of late events. I endeavour to explain the action of our Most Holy Father which you explained to me and which I look upon as a heavenly inspired diplomacy. I tell those, and they are very many, who complain of the manner in which our Country is treated in contrast with that in which other less faithful countries appear to be favoured, that our Common Father treats us like the Father of the Prodigal when his elder son complained of the different treatment he received from that of his brother." "His Father answered," Lynch reminded Kirby in conclusion, " 'Fili tu semper meus es, et omnia mea tuo sunt.' "

About a week later the primate and titular head of the Irish Church, Michael Logue, also wrote Kirby about the Bishops' meeting. "I am glad to be able to inform Your Grace," Logue

---

14   K. This letter is dated June 25, but it is an obvious error and I take June 29 as being the correct date.

reported on July 8, "that our last meeting at Maynooth was everything that could be desired in the matter of unanimity"(K). "Indeed I must say," he complained, "that it was hard for the Bishops to be of one mind for some time past. They were left pretty much in the dark by the authorities at Rome as to what was going forward; and there seemed to be no disposition to trust them or ascertain their views. In these circumstances all is doubt and uncertainty and individuals are left to follow their own lights." "I found the Pallium," Logue then informed Kirby, turning to a subject that was closer to his heart, and referring to the official insignia of his archiepiscopal office, "in the Archbishop's house the last time I was in Dublin; but I don't know well what to do with it. There was no direction as to who was commissioned to confer it on me. I do not even know who brought it. So I brought it home in my pocket, and there it lies since." "If the Archbishop of Dublin," Logue, suggested, "were deputed to confer it on me His Grace would come down here some Sunday for the purpose and the ceremony would edify the people." "I had," he then reported in conclusion, "a collection of the Peter's Pence last Sunday. There was some grumbling, but I trust the result will be the same as usual."

When Walsh, on the other hand, wrote Kirby, less than a week after the Bishops' meeting, he neither mentioned the meeting, nor, more significantly, a letter he had just received from the pope for distribution to the other Irish Bishops. His letter to Kirby, moreover, which was more like the voice of Croke than the hand of Walsh, was ample testimony as to why the Irish Bishops at their recent meeting were quiet, and in what way, as a body, they were unanimous. "I have to thank Y. G. for sending the paper from the Holy Office," Walsh remarked politely on July 3, "allowing the use of meat last Friday"(K). "Fortunately," he added ironically, "it arrived too late to have it published throughout the diocese. It was made known in an informal way, and thus those who cared to make use of the permission did so." "But I need hardly say," he observed dryly, underlining another example of the Holy Office's ignorance with regard to Ireland, "that it was a permission *which very many preferred not to use.*" "The strong feeling of indignation," Walsh continued, "which *the circumstances* of the publication of the former Decree so naturally gave rise to, is very far indeed from having as yet subsided. We had no idea in Rome of the feeling that existed here. It was only since my return that I was able to realise it in some degree. The great prudence of the newspapers in practically suppressing all indications of it is blamed by many. Undoubtedly, so far as I am concerned, I regard it as open to question whether it would not have been better to let the truth be known."

"The testimony from all parts of the country is unanimous," he maintained boldly, "During the present Pontificate, at all events, the old feeling of confidence can never be restored." "The people of course," Walsh explained further, "submit with respect to the explanation given by the Bishops as to the authority of the Holy See in moral questions. But they are now shrewd enough to know that the *exercise* of *that* authority is a matter of discretion: they cannot see why it should have been exercised against them, and in no way against the landlords whose treatment of them is at least equally characterised by injustice and want of charity." "The prolonged visits of the Duke of Norfolk;" Walsh summed up the case for Kirby, "The communication of private information to papers like the Daily Chronicle: The well known fact that the Decree was issued upon onesided information although a sort of sham was gone through of seeking information from me and others, all this has made it simply impossible to remove the impression that the *exercise* of authority was largely influenced by political and diplomatic considerations." "The Bishops," he further insisted, "could not remove *this* impression even if they tried. But the fact is that they have no thought of trying to do anything of the kind. If any sort of respect for ecclesiastical authority is to be saved out of the general wreck, we must abstain from asking the people to believe what they know very well we do not believe ourselves." "As I often remarked to Y.G.," Walsh reminded Kirby, and echoing Croke, "the people of Ireland, Catholic as they are, might easily enough be brought into the same state of mind that now so manifestly prevails throughout the peoples of Italy, France, and other so called 'Catholic' countries." "The same influence is at work," Walsh warned ominously in conclusion, "which has wrought such mischief there. We must be careful how we incur any share of the responsibility."

There can be little doubt that this unusual outburst was in part precipitated both by Walsh's own recent and dismal experience in Rome, and the realization on his return of the alarming effect of the Decree on public opinion in Ireland.

What really triggered the outburst, however, was that he did not know how to deal with the letter he had only just received from the pope without further offending that already much abused public opinion. The pope's letter, which Walsh received on June 30, was dated June 24:

TO OUR VENERABLE BRETHREN, THE BISHOPS OF
IRELAND,
LEO XIII, POPE.
VENERABLE BRETHREN,
HEALTH AND APOSTOLIC BENEDICTION.

From this supreme dignity of the Apostolic office, We have frequently directed Our solicitude and Our thoughts to your Catholic people; and Our feelings have been more than once recorded in published documents, from which all may clearly learn what are Our dispositions towards Ireland. They are sufficiently attested by the provisions which, under Our direction, the Sacred Congregation of Propaganda made in former years respecting Ireland, and also by the letters which on more than one occasion We addressed to Our Venerable Brother, Cardinal M'Cabe, Archbishop of Dublin. Once again, they have been attested by the address which We recently delivered to a not inconsiderable number of Catholics belonging to your nation, from whom we received, not only congratulations and heartfelt wishes for Our preservation, but also expressions of gratitude on account of Our benevolent dispositions, clearly discerned by them, towards the Irish people. Furthermore, within these past few months, when it was resolved to build a church in this City in honour of St. Patrick, the great Apostle of the Irish, We most warmly encouraged the undertaking, and We shall substantially aid it within the limits of Our resources.

Now, this Our paternal affection remaining, as it does, unaltered, We cannot disguise that tidings which have recently come to Us from Ireland have deeply pained and grieved Us. We have learned that an untoward excitement has suddenly arisen because the Sacred Congregation, whose office it is to vindicate the authority of the Church against those who resist it, has decreed that those methods of warfare known as Boycotting and the Plan of Campaign, which had begun to be employed by many, may not lawfully be used. And what is more to be deplored, there are not a few who have come forward and summoned the people to excited·meetings, where inconsiderate and dangerous opinions are set in circulation, the authority of the Decree not being spared. For not only is the real scope of this Decree grievously perverted by means of forced interpretations, but, furthermore, it is even denied that obedience is due to the Decree, as if it were not the true and proper office of the Church to decide what is right and what is wrong in human actions.

Such manner of acting is but little in harmony with the profession of the Christian religion, which assuredly brings in its train the virtues of moderation, respect and obedience to legitimate authority. Besides, in a good cause, it is not fitting to seem in some sense to imitate those who in the pursuit of an unlawful end seek to attain it by disorderly effort.

Such line of action, too, is the more painful to Us inasmuch as We had carefully inquired into the case, so that We might obtain full and reliable knowledge of the state of your affairs, and of the causes of popular discontent. Our sources of information are trustworthy; We investigated the matter in personal interview with yourselves; further, last year We sent to you as legate a man of tried prudence and discretion, with the commission to use the greatest diligence in ascertaining the truth, and to make a faithful report to Us. For this very act of watchful care the thanks of the Irish People have been publicly given to Us. Can it therefore be asserted without rashness that We have given judgment in a case with which We were not sufficiently acquainted — the more so as We have condemned things which fairminded men, not mixed up in your struggle, and thus bringing a calmer judgment to the consideration of the case, unite in condemning!

There is also a suspicion not less unjust to Us — namely, that the cause of Ireland appeals but feebly to Us, and that the present condition of her people gives Us little care. Now, on the contrary, We yield to no one in the intensity of Our feeling for the condition of the Irish people, and We have no more earnest desire than to see them at length in the enjoyment of that peace and prosperity which they have so well deserved. We have never opposed their struggling for a better state of things, but can it be regarded as admissible that in the carrying on of that struggle a way should be thrown open which might lead to evil deeds? Rather, indeed, for the very reason that, under the influence of passion and political partisanship, things lawful and unlawful are to be found mingled in the same cause, it has been Our constant effort to mark off what was right from what was wrong, and to withhold Catholics from everything not sanctioned by the Christian rules of morals.

On this account We gave to the Irish people timely counsels, to be mindful of their obligations as Catholics, and to take part in nothing at variance with natural right or forbidden by the divine law. Hence the recent Decree ought not to have come upon them unexpectedly; all the more as you yourselves, Venerable Brethren, assembled in Dublin in the year 1881 bade the clergy and people to beware of everything contrary to public order or to charity — such as refusing to discharge just obligations; preventing others from discharging theirs; inflicting injury on any one either in person or property; violently resisting the law or those engaged in the discharge of public duties; joining in secret societies; and the like. These injunctions, most just in themselves and given most seasonably, were praised and approved by Us.

Nevertheless, as the people were being carried away by ever-increasing vehemence in the pursuit of the object of their desires, and as there were not wanting those who daily fanned the flame, We perceived that something more definite was needed than the general precepts of justice and charity which we had previously given. Our duty forbade us to suffer that so many Catholics, whose salvation must be Our first care, should pursue a hazardous and unsafe course leading rather to disorder than to the relief of distress.

Let matters, then, be viewed in their true light, and let Ireland read in this decree Our love for herself and Our desire to promote the prosperity she hopes for; since nothing is so harmful to a cause, however just, as recourse to violence and injustice in its defence.

These instructions which We address to you, Venerable Brethren, you will convey to the Irish people. We feel confident that, united in due conformity of views and of purpose, and sustained not only by your own, but also by Our authority, you will accomplish much — and chiefly this, that the true estimate of things shall not continue to be obscured by passion, and most especially that those who have urged on the people to excitement may come to regret the rashness with which they have acted. Since there are many who seem to seek out means of escaping from even the plainest obligations, take all necessary steps that no room be left for doubt as to the force of this decree. Let it be understood by all that the entire method of action, whose employment We have forbidden, is forbidden as altogether unlawful.

Let your people seek to advance their lawful interests by lawful means, and most especially, as is becoming in Christians, without prejudice to justice or to obedience to the Apostolic See, virtues in which Ireland has in all times found comfort and strength.

In the meantime, Venerable Brethren, as a pledge of heavenly favours, and in testimony of our affection, We most lovingly in the Lord bestow on you, and on the clergy and people of Ireland, the Apostolic Benediction.
Given at St. Peter's, Rome, the 24th day of
June, in the year 1888, the eleventh year
of Our Pontificate.[15]

Walsh's efforts to mollify Irish public opinion had been, and still were, so intense since his return from Rome, that the pope's letter must have been a real shock. When he wrote Manning, for example, the day after he received the pope's letter, he was still more preoccupied with his efforts to contain Irish public opinion than with the very serious implications raised by the pope's letter. "I gave directions," he reported industriously to the cardinal on July 1, "for two numbers of the *Freeman's Journal* to be sent to your Eminence, each containing an 'interview.' Tomorrow's paper will contain a statement on the Land Question which I was able without any difficulty to get adopted by the Bishops and signed individually by them"(M). "Curiously," Walsh observed further, indicating that not everyone had been doing their homework in his absence, "there were not a few of them to whom the statement about the Scotch (Crofters) Arrears Act came as a surprise." "I received yesterday," he then informed the cardinal, "a letter 'Ad Episcopus Hiberniae.' " "I hope," he added, either discreetly or numbly, "it will not do harm. Poor Mgr. Persico!" "Your Eminence," Walsh promised the cardinal in conclusion, "will see it in a day or two."

Walsh, however, did not forward the pope's letter to Manning as promised in the next few days, for he quickly realized how difficult it would be to publish the letter without again offending the Irish nation at home and abroad. His embarrassing predicament certainly accounted for his angry letter to Kirby on July 3, but by the following day, at least, he had finally decided on how to proceed. On July 4, at a dinner given in his honor by his cathedral chapter, Walsh took advantage of the occasion to break the news gently to the public that he had received a letter from the pope.[16] In his reply to the chapter's address of welcome, Walsh skillfully dwelled at

---

[15] *Freeman's Journal*, July 16, 1888.
[16] *Walsh*, p. 362.

great length on the pope's concern and sympathy for the Irish
people and their aspirations before finally coming to his real
purpose. "Some incidents of our recent history," Walsh
explained to his canons, "have brought pain to the heart of the
Holy Father. He was much grieved at the thought of the
injustice which seemed to be done to him by some whose words
appeared to indicate a want of confidence in the sincerity and
earnestness of his desire for the welfare of our people. Of all
this, I had, before leaving Rome, an assurance from his own
lips." "I have in my hands to-day," Walsh concluded cleverly
and ambiguously, "an assurance of it, in more enduring form,
in a letter to the Irish bishops."

Walsh also wrote Kirby that same day about the pope's
letter, but the substance and tone of his letter was quite different
from what he wrote to the cardinal. "We are still struggling,"
Walsh explained, on July 9, "to keep our people from being
driven on to anything disrespectful to the Holy See. But the
recent letter raises serious difficulties, especially as it contains a
manifestly inaccurate reference to the opposition meetings as
still going on!"(K). "However," he added stoically, "we can only
obey orders and leave the responsibility for the consequences
where it really lies." "So far as I can judge," Walsh complained
again, "we are being driven along the high road to the same
state of things that exists in Italy and France, and that has to
so large an extent, been brought about in those countries by the
operation of the same causes that are now being set in
operation here."

When Croke received his copy of the pope's letter, his
reaction was easily predictable. "I have forwarded the Pope's
letter," he reported to Walsh on July 10, "to the Munster
Bishops. It contains some strong expressions. I fear very much
that Rome will never stop its letters till it has driven the Irish
people into open revolt against, or silent contempt for, the
pronouncements of the Holy See"(W). "Country as quiet as
possible," he then noted telegraphically, "Past contentions
forgotten, provocation forgiven." "New sores," Croke
concluded, "will be opened, I fear, soon." Walsh, meanwhile,
was doing his best to keep the sores closed. In distributing the
pope's letter to his parish priests, Walsh wrote an equally long
covering letter, dated July 13, explaining among many other
things the pope's good intentions. He then further instructed his
pastors to read his explanatory letter *before* they read the

pope's letter on Sunday, July 15, to their assembled congregations. "The reading of this document," Croke congratulated Walsh, the day before it was read in Dublin, "in churches is a bold stroke"(W). "I thought," he added, "we were done with such perplexities. I shall take publication in 'Freeman' as sufficient for all my purposes." Walsh's letter was truly a masterpiece of its kind and, in order to appreciate fully its shifting subtleties and nuances, it is necessary to read it in its entirety.

4 Rutland-square, E.,
Dublin, 13th July, 1888.

VERY REV AND DEAR FATHER — You will receive with this a translation of an important letter of our Holy Father the Pope, sent by his Holiness as an Encyclical Letter to the Bishops of Ireland.

His Holiness, as you will observe, has addressed this letter to us with the view, in the first place, of removing a painful misconception which seems to have arisen in the minds of some, in connection with the recent Decree of the Holy Office. To those who have not personal knowledge of the warmth and depth of the paternal affection of our Holy Father for the Irish Church and for its faithful children, it may, indeed, seem strange that the Sovereign Pontiff, the successor of the Prince of the Apostles, the Vicar upon earth of our Lord Himself, should condescend to address us as his Holiness has done in this most memorable letter. For in it he seeks, as it were, to justify himself in our eyes, explaining to us with patient care the true bearing of the recent Decree, and protesting with most earnest emphasis against that reproach which has so deeply wounded his paternal heart, that he is wanting in sympathy with the people of Ireland in their present trials.

In words of no ordinary impressiveness the Holy Father now assures us of the depth and fulness of that sympathy: — "There is a suspicion," says his Holiness, "which is unjust to Us — namely, that the cause of Ireland appeals but feebly to Us, and that the present condition of her people gives Us little care. Now, on the contrary, We yield to no one in the intensity of our feeling for the condition of the Irish people, and We have no more earnest desire than to see them at length in the enjoyment of that peace and prosperity which they have so well deserved."

Is there any Irish Catholic to whom those solemn words will fail to bring the fullest assurance? Assuredly there is not one whom they will not most fully satisfy that, no matter what pain may have been brought to the heart of our Holy Father by

those occurrences to some of which he alludes in his letter, they
have in no way lessened the sincerity of his love for Ireland, the
earnestness of his desire to see her sufferings at an end, or the
fulness of his sympathy with every effort, provided only that it
be made within the limits marked by the law of God itself, for
the improvement of the temporal condition of her people, and
for their advancement in the paths of prosperity and peace.

From some expressions in the letter of his Holiness you will
also observe that it was written before he could have known, as
he now knows, that the excited discussions to which he refers in
it have come to an end. In the circumstances it can scarcely be
necessary that I should make further reference to them. The
agitation of which they were the leading incidents took place
during my absence in Rome. It had fully come to an end before
my return to Ireland. Its close was brought about by the
prudent action of our Irish Bishops at their meeting held in
Dublin some six weeks ago. The statement of Catholic truth
embodied in the resolutions adopted by the bishops on that
occasion was at once received with unhesitating loyalty by our
Catholic people. The confusion of thought, then, that for a time
had seemed to stand in the way of the prompt and practical
recognition of the authority of the Holy See in matters of
morals as well as in matters of faith, was at once cleared away.

Those days of painful doubt and misgiving, as they seemed
even to us who were away from Ireland — days of torturing
anxiety as they must have been to those who lived through them
at home — have now passed away. Let us thank God for it, and
let us pray that they have passed for ever. The hasty words that
in the confusion and excitement of the moment may have been
uttered even by men who would willingly lay down their lives in
defence of the Catholic Faith and of the Holy See, are now
forgotten. Or rather, they are now looked back upon with
feelings of deep and lasting regret that even in a time of
agonizing excitement any word should have been spoken in
Catholic Ireland which could be regarded, or represented even
by the bitterest of our enemies, as open to the construction that
it called in question one particle of the divinely-established
authority of the Successor of St. Peter to teach the Church of
Christ.

Looking away, then, from the troubled past, let us take the
words which his Holiness now addresses to us as words of hope
and promise for the future. Differences of view in reference to
our public affairs there may, and must be, amongst the
Catholics of a diocese such as this. But amongst us there is
surely no one who will hesitate to join in the wishes so earnestly
expressed in the letter of our Holy Father, that the present

pitiful condition of our country may speedily come to an end;
that peace may be once more established amongst us; and that
the dawn may not be long delayed of that era of prosperity to
which Ireland may justly look forward as the reward, well and
nobly earned, of her centuries of suffering and of fidelity to the
faith.

But these blessings it would manifestly be idle to hope for,
except as the fruits of wise and beneficent legislation, based
upon the principle of even-handed justice to all classes and
sections of our people, and putting an end to the disastrous
collision of conflicting interests, of which the present state of
unrest in Ireland is the deplorable result.

Within the last few days some ground for hope would seem
to have arisen, that although the present session of Parliament
is now all but ended, it may yet be possible for the Legislature
before the close of the present year to put its hand to the work,
and to make at all events some substantial provision for the
more urgent needs of the hour. That this hope may be fulfilled,
and that our people may thus be enabled to await in patience
and in security the more comprehensive and permanent
measures of the coming year, should be the object of the fervent
prayers of every lover of justice, of charity, and of peace.

Let us unite in earnest application to the Giver of all good
gifts that these blessings may be granted to us, and that,
through them, peace and prosperity may be restored to our
beloved country. And that our prayers may be rendered
efficacious, let us present them through the hands of Her whom
in every necessity we may confidently invoke as the Help of
Christians, and the Comforter of the afflicted.

You will kindly arrange, then, for the public recital, until
further notice, of the Litany of Loretto, with the Antiphon, *We
fly to thy patronage, O holy Mother of God,* and the usual
Versicle and Prayer, after the last Mass every day in each
church or chapel under your care, and also after the parochial
or other principal Mass on Sundays. — I beg to remain, Very
Rev and dear father, your faithful servant in Christ,

WILLIAM; Archbishop of Dublin
and Primate of Ireland.[17]

Two days after both his and the pope's letters were read in all
the churches of Dublin, Walsh in reply to an address of
welcome from the Dublin Municipal Corporation, finally said in
public, though his language was more restrained, what he had
been saying in private to Kirby since his return to Ireland.

[17] *Freeman's Journal,* July 16, 1888.

"Men's minds," Walsh explained to the assembled local dignitaries at Clonliffe College, on Tuesday, July 17, referring to the Decree, "were strangely troubled."[18] "It seemed," he remarked, "almost to be the opinion of some that all the ancient moorings of our Irish Catholicity had been disturbed, and that our nation was in danger of drifting away upon those shoals where other nations, once as Catholic as ours, thank God, still is, had made shipwreck, if not of the faith, at all events, of that hearty loyalty to the Holy See, the loss of which the faith of no Catholic nation can long survive." "So much, indeed," Walsh observed, "was apparent even to those who were at a distance. But I freely confess, that it was not until I had returned to Ireland, and not indeed for some days after my return, that, from the opportunities which I then had of learning the truth in all its fullness from those who were most competent to tell it to me, I was able to realise even in the most imperfect way, the painful intensity of the crisis through which our people had, thank God, safely passed, and the fearful narrowness of their escape from a disaster in which, but for the unyielding firmness of their Catholic Faith, and of their loyalty to the See of Peter, that faith might have been brought to ruin."

Walsh then boldly turned to the subject of the resolutions passed by the Catholic M.P.'s on May 17, and endorsed a week later by the Dublin Corporation. "As to those resolutions," Walsh observed, "since I have referred to them at all, let me say that they have, at least in my opinion, been grievously misrepresented and misunderstood. I wish, indeed, I could think that the misrepresentation was in all cases the result of misunderstanding and not, as it unquestionably in some cases was, the outcome of downright malice." "One very zealous," Walsh then remarked pointedly, alluding discreetly to the bishop of Limerick, "but as I must take the liberty of saying, somewhat overzealous and altogether self-constituted guardian and defender of that respect which he very properly asserted was due to my office and position in the Irish Church, thought it right to make a rather pointed public allusion to your action in reference to me and to the telegram that I sent you on the occasion of your meeting. Your critic, to whom I refer, took it upon himself to declare that your action upon those resolutions was nothing short of an insult to me." "For myself," he confessed, "I can only say that I fail to see it."

[18] *Ibid.*, July 18, 1888.

"As to the resolutions which you endorsed," Walsh noted again after his aside, "while of course I cannot say that as regards their form and phraseology they were such as I should myself have drawn up, they undoubtedly seemed to me to set forth, so far as their substance was concerned, what I cannot but regard as an honest and accurate statement of the case of the Irish tenants, and not only of that case as it stands in itself, but also the view taken of it at the Holy See." "I do not now," Walsh entered his qualification, "of course, speak of the expressions, many of them hasty and unguarded, which were issued at some of the meetings throughout the country on the subject of their resolutions." "Now, looking at these resolutions," he then asked rhetorically, "what do we find the sum and substance of them to be?" "I take it," he replied, "to be this."

> They are made up mainly of three protests. They protest, in the first place, against the action of those who, endeavouring to twist the Decree of the Holy Office to political purposes — "enemies," as the resolution described them — "unscrupulous enemies of the Holy See, as well as of the Irish people," unscrupulous in their use of that Decree "as a political weapon to prejudice the Irish cause, to create misunderstanding and estrangement between the Irish people and their spiritual guides, and to increase the dangers which threaten the liberties, and even the very existence, of our people." That is the first portion of the Irish members' protest; and so far from finding in it matter of censure, or even of regret, I have no hesitation whatever in saying that I cordially, and most unreservedly, approve and endorse it (applause).
>
> In another portion of their resolutions the members formally assert the right of Irish Catholics, and of the people of Ireland, to manage their own political affairs, and to do so free of all external control. This protest has been represented as if it put forward, on the part of the Irish people, a claim which it would be impossible even to suppose that any Christian nation could for a moment entertain the thought of making — the claim that in politics the end should be held to justify the means, and that the political liberties of the nation, or the material interests of its people, could legitimately be advanced by any means that seemed to serve this purpose, utterly regardless of the consideration whether the means in question were or were not in accordance with the law of God. No such preposterous doctrine, I take it on myself to say, was ever yet laid down by anyone who could establish the faintest shadow of a claim to

speak for the Irish people (applause). The criticisms, then, that have been directed against the members' resolution on this score fall harmlessly wide of their mark. There is, in truth, in this portion of the resolutions of the members but one point on which even the most captious critic could fairly lay hold. The resolution seems to contemplate a possible or probable danger of some political interference of the Holy See in the affairs of Ireland. On this point I have already elsewhere clearly spoken. There is no such danger. If I could say so without hurting the feelings of those whose sense of true devotion to the See of Peter I cannot but regard as equal at least to my own, I would add that even the very suspicion that such a thing was possible should be put without a moment's hesitation from the mind of any Irish Catholic who wishes to avoid harbouring a thought manifestly at variance with the respect which, as Irishmen no less than as Catholics, we owe to the Holy See (applause).

Then there is that other portion of the resolutions, in which the representatives of our people protest, and most rightly protest, against the erroneous view presented of the case of the Irish tenants by certain statements of fact to which they refer. Those statements, however, it must ever be borne in mind, are in no sense a portion of the Decree of the Holy Office; they have in no sense been sanctioned by the Holy See; and, within of course the obvious limits of propriety, they are in no way removed from the sphere of respectful criticism. I can speak indeed from my own personal knowledge of the extent of the erroneous impressions conveyed by the statements in question. In correcting those statements — correcting them as they did most temperately and most respectfully — the Irish members, in view, to use their own words, "of the responsibility inseparable from their public trust as the constitutionally elected representatives of the Irish people," were not only within their rights, but they acted in fulfilment of a public duty (hear, hear).[19]

"There may be a hard struggle," Walsh then warned his audience, "yet before you, and before those who, with you, are engaged in striving to obtain for that tenantry the legislative protection which, in spite of so many reforms that have been conceded, is, for so many of them, still withheld." "But it is well to bear in mind," he added finally in conclusion, "that in the closing scene of that struggle, you are in no danger of suffering from the disadvantage of divided or of weakened ranks, and

---

[19] *Ibid.*

that, please God, we may look forward to witness in the very near future the happy termination of it, a result which, you may take my word for it, will be hailed with no more heartfelt gratification in any spot in Europe than it will be in the Vatican, and from the throne of Leo XIII."

Walsh's resources in dialectical device were indeed extraordinary. His ability to move from distinctions between form and substance to a consideration of the meaning of the general propositions embodied in and to be derived from a series of resolutions bordered on the casuistical. The *Irish Catholic*, however, was little disturbed by the archbishop's dialectical refinements and proceeded to nail his colors to his mast for him in a lead editorial significantly entitled "Unchanged and Unchangeable."[20] "The courageous and outspoken words of the Archbishop of Dublin," the *Irish Catholic* declared on July 21, "in reply to the address of the Corporation of Dublin, were undoubtedly needed to clear the air." "His Grace," the *Catholic* emphasized *de trop,* "definitely and decisively has given his adhesion to the substance of the resolutions adopted by the Irish members, and not only given his adhesion to their substance, but acknowledged that the Catholic members of the Irish Party were but discharging a sacred and unavoidable public duty when they vindicated their country in the eyes of Europe against the wrong impression created by the statements of fact appended to the letter conveying the recent decision of the Holy Office." "This will silence the critics," the editorial further maintained, "who saw in this discharge of a sacred duty an act of disrespect to the Holy See; and it will shame the slanderers who construed the action into rebellion." "They will be disappointed, too," the *Irish Catholic* concluded, "to find that the Archbishop of Dublin reaffirms his position in Irish politics, and repeats with emphasis the declarations which won for him the trust and affections of the whole Irish race on his entrance into the See of Dublin."

Within a month, therefore, after his return to Ireland, Archbishop Walsh had definitely come down on the side of the Clerical-Nationalist alliance. In taking this crucial decision,

---

20 *Irish Catholic* (Dublin), July 21, 1888. The reference to "Unchanged and Unchangeable," of course, was to the words attributed to Croke when he returned from Rome in 1883, just after the condemnation of the Parnell Testimonial Fund by the Holy See.

Walsh had finally recognized that the various arguments and their refinements as to the legitimate limits of the pope's authority in matters of fact or politics, not to speak of faith or morals, were in large measure irrelevant as far as the Irish people were concerned. What was at stake in the excitement of the Irish people, as indeed Parnell had immediately discerned, was not the niceties of right and wrong raised by either the Decree or the Plan, but simply that the visible head of their Church had entered into an apparent league against them with their hereditary enemy. For that reason the Decree was bound to be a disastrous failure, and all that Walsh and his episcopal brethren could do was to put the best face possible on the inescapable fact that the Decree could not be enforced without wrecking the Clerical-Nationalist alliance, and with it, the Irish Church's power and influence with the Irish people.

VIII.   Rift with Rome
July, 1888 - December, 1888

The vast majority of the Irish Bishops were indeed of Walsh's opinion as regards what should be done about the Decree. Those who wrote Kirby, for example, were certainly of one mind in that they preferred to emphasize the "prudent" rather than the "effective" in enforcing or even in publishing the Decree. The bishop of Cloyne, James McCarthy, in whose diocese the Plan had really taken hold, reported to Kirby several days before the pope's letter was read in Dublin, that things had quieted down and, while admitting that the recent public speeches by the Nationalist leaders were "inexcusable," that he was also sure that in the end good would come of it all. "Those politicians who initiated the Plan of Campaign," he explained to Kirby patiently but firmly on July 11, "did so, I believe, in good faith as [the] only means left them to protect those tenants from extermination who were required by their Landlords to pay rents for their farms which they did not, or could not, produce for the past few years, & which the decisions of those tribunals appointed by the Government pronounced to be unjust, & they had only recourse to the Plan of Campaign after having exhausted every effort to obtain from the Landlords & the Government fair and equitable reductions of what were admitted to be excessive rents, but as happens frequently in the case of politicians struggling against injustice, they looked rather to the *efficacy* of the means they employed than to their *morality*"(K).

"This omission has now been clearly pointed out to them by the recent Decree," McCarthy added, somewhat optimistically, "& I have no doubt that the originators of the Plan of Campaign who are in all the private relations of their lives good practical Catholics will after the annoyance created by the authoritative censure of the plan they recommended, has passed

282

away, be guided in their future conduct by the expressed wishes
of the Holy Father & regulate their action by the principles He
has laid down." "This course," he advised Kirby, "I have
impressed on my Priests at all the Conferences held
immediately after the Decree was promulgated, & it has since
been acted on by them, & will continue to be so in the sense laid
down by the Holy Father 'prudenter sed efficaeciter.' " Several
days later, the recently appointed bishop of Kilmore, Edward
McGennis, also wrote Kirby. "I hope his Holiness," he
informed Kirby on July 14, from Cavan, while forwarding
£334 Peter's Pence, "will not think it necessary to make any
further pronouncements bearing on the Irish question. The
excitement occasioned by the decision of the Holy Office is fast
dying out and it would not be well to revive it"(K). "I have
never," he further explained to Kirby, "taken any public part in
politics and happily my Diocese is and has been very quiet but
in the interests of Religion I hope nothing will be done to imperil
the influence of Rome with the Irish people." "I am sure Your
Grace," McGennis concluded firmly, "and our other friends at
Rome will continue to watch and counteract English intrigue."

"The latest great event," the bishop of Cork, T. A.
O'Callaghan, explained more naively to Kirby on July 20, "was
the Pope's letter which Dr. Walsh and I published last Sunday.
The other Bishops will I presume publish it later on"(K). "It
was received quietly," O'Callaghan reported, referring to the
fact that the Cork papers had ignored it, "and as yet not much
has appeared in the newspapers about it. Let us hope, that with
God's aid the external calm that exists will help to restore
confidence and that we may be released from the terrible
anxiety that presses on us." "We held the synod last week," he
reported, "and during it I published the original decree for the
second time to the priests and gave them special instructions. I
also published the recent letter, it having come while we were
assembled in retreat. As we are more fortunate than other
dioceses there not being a single instance of the Plan of
Campaign or boycotting that I know of — I felt in duty bound
to congratulate the priests on their prudent management for
much is due to their exertions in settling the differences that
constantly arise." "We are not however to think," he warned
Kirby, "that we are out of the wood. A great deal will depend
on the coming harvest which if with God's blessing will be
abundant we may hope for peace for the moment." "But if the

people," O'Callaghan concluded ominously, "will have to face starvation and evictions during the winter, I fear matters will be worse than ever before."

"Everything is quiet in Ireland just now," Patrick McAlister, bishop of Down and Connor, explained to Kirby on July 25 from Belfast, "except that the evictions go on & the government send police & soldiers to protect the evicting parties in expelling the poor people from their homes & knocking down their houses with battering rams & crowbars"(K). "God help the poor people," he concluded, "It is hard to be quiet in such circumstances." The archbishop of Tuam, John MacEvilly, also wrote Kirby several days later complaining about evictions, and obviously in reply to a letter from Kirby which had quoted a "venerable southern ecclesiastic" as to the horrors of priests being involved in the National League. "The feeling of irritation," MacEvilly, who was nursing an attack of rheumatism in Buxton, England, explained to Kirby on July 29, "though suppressed is deep and I fear lasting"(K). "The cruel evictions," he added, "are extending and maddening the people & clergy. For the first time, we had cruel evictions in the diocese of Tuam within the last fortnight, and this in the very parish of Tuam. The evictors, *pious Catholics,* if you please, people who would dictate to the H. Father himself, and who boast that the priests are now silenced and dare not speak. I publicly denounced the cruel use made of the just act of the H. Father, which was never meant, but *the very contrary* to be made use of to harass & persecute the poor people who were rackrented, disposed to pay a fair rent, but were thrown on the roadside, their houses levelled for not paying *impossible rents.* There was no resistance, the clergy prevailed on the people not to resist. But vengence is deep down in their hearts." "The government," he added, for good measure, "is doing nothing to check these evictions, or the contrary, helping them." "I fear there are a few priests here and there," MacEvilly further remarked, echoing Walsh, whom he had undoubtedly visited in Dublin on his way to Buxton, "like the venerable southern ecclesiastic whom you refer to, who have no sympathy for the people and would have the National League suppressed, to gain the favour of the landlords."

If the National League, which, within due bounds, and guided by prudent priests, is a *perfectly legal association,* were suppressed tomorrow, no power on earth could help the vast bulk of our people from forming and joining in *horrible secret societies,* subversive of altar and throne. While the people are permitted to join openly in legal societies in which to give vent to their feelings, all is right, order observed, but prevent that and drive them *underground,* secret societies would *honeycomb* every parish in the kingdom. I fear clergymen of the cast you speak of, who through indolence or indifference to the peoples wants, and through a hypocritical affectation of loyal sentiments, keep aloof from managing legal associations, and allow them to be in the hands of mercenary would-be local patriots, are doing much mischief in estranging our people from religion. Allow them to go away once, there is no bringing them back(K).

"I have written home," MacEvilly then explained, obviously in reply to another of Kirby's enquiries, "to have copies of the Holy Father's late letter to the Irish bishops sent to every parish of the diocese for publication." "There is no use in concealing it," MacEvilly concluded in quiet exasperation, "The ferment is very great & I pray God may calm it."

The next day, the parish priest of SS. Mary and Peter's in Arklow, wrote Kirby a pathetic account of the evictions in his parish. "Landlordism," the venerable James Dunphy informed Kirby on July 30, "is asserting its rights with ardour totally forgetful of its duties"(K). "I have had a trial of it last week," he confessed, "as two of my very respectable parishioners one with a wife and five small children turned out on the road at the *whim* of the Landlord — though owing him *no rent* he was an ardent Nationalist and [had] the courage of his convictions." "He was a Town Commissioner," Father Dunphy explained, "and sat at the Land Board with the Landlord and voted as his conscience and principles dictated to him. The Sheriff with a hundred and fifty police were brought into this quiet town and ejected him by force from his house and premises." "They then went," he added, "to a poor struggling farmer and ejected himself and wife and eight small children leaving them naked on the cold *dung-heap* though the poor father offered one year's rent out of the two he owed. The farm was rackrented forty percent on the valuation." "These are," Father Dunphy noted simply, "very hard to put up with." "I am now striving," he then observed pathetically, "to get shelter for eighteen [*sic*] human beings and to provide support for them. ..." "The weather now," he pointed out to Kirby forebodingly, "is very bad. The hay crop half destroyed by the constant rain."

"Our harvest is in danger," Dean Walter Lee reported to Kirby from Bray on August 19, "and we are praying for fine weather, we had a few fine days but the rain has come again"(K). Four days later the bishop of Cork, while observing that the country was quiet, sounded an even more disturbing note. "There are however constant reports of cruel evictions," O'Callaghan informed Kirby on August 23, "and what is more alarming the potato blight has appeared in many parts of the country"(K). The weather, however, improved in September, and the harvest, though spotty in various parts of the country because of the rain, was for the most part saved. "Everything," Michael Logue reported to Kirby from Armagh on September 28, "is pretty quiet here at present, thank God. The Winter may be a little troublesome as the crops, especially the potato crop have failed in some parts of the Country. However, Parliament will be in session, and that will afford a safety valve"(K). "On the one side," Logue maintained hopefully, "the Tory Government will be kept within the bounds of moderation by the surveillance of Parliament, while on the other the people will have a legitimate means of ventilating their grievances."

From the other end of Ireland, William Hutch, who had left the Irish College some twenty-two years before, wrote his old rector several days later from St. Coleman's College in Fermoy, confirming all that Logue had reported, and substantially summing up the various accounts of Kirby's other clerical correspondents. "Here in Ireland," Hutch informed Kirby on October 3, "we are agitating & fighting away as hard as ever"(K). "Persons living in Rome," he explained politely, "can have no idea of the barbarity and illegality of the present Tory Government, and of all the suffering our poor people have to endure. But we are bearing all with marvelous *patience*, being buoyed up with the certain hope that another year or two will end it all & give us back our old Parliament in College Green." "The priests & people were never," he assured Kirby, "thank God, more thoroughly united, and *practical* religion was never more flourishing in Ireland. The people took up the devotion to the Souls in Purgatory on last Sunday with wonderful enthusiasm. Enormous crowds went to Communion everywhere, and in many places (Fermoy included) the priests had to remain in the confessional up to midnight on Saturday to dispose of all their penitents." "You need not," he further assured Kirby, "have any fears of the Faith in poor Ireland. The most severe shock it could get would be if the people thought that the Pope would side with England against them." "That indeed," he warned, "would try the Faith of Ireland terribly; & may God grant that no such trial is ever in store for our poor people."

As it became more and more apparent that the Irish Bishops were unwilling to enforce the Decree, the reactions of those who had worked so hard to secure the papal condemnation changed from one of pleasure and delight to fury and frustration. "Have you seen," Errington had asked Smith on June 22, the day Walsh had returned to Ireland, "the admirable letters & conduct of the Bishop of Limerick?"[3] "He acts a noble example," Errington maintained, "how different things would be if all were like him!" "Cardinal Manning's intimacy with extreme Nationalists," he further reported to Smith, "& his strong support of all that is most extreme in England as well as Ireland produces a powerful effect." The bishop of Limerick, however, was under no illusion as to what the real state of opinion towards him was in Ireland. "Yr. letter is marked 'private,' " Father J. S. Flanagan, one of the bishop of Limerick's priests explained to Lord Emly on June 29, " — so I can make no use of it without your permission"(R). "Might I mention the fact," he asked Emly, and referring to O'Dwyer, "to the Bishop?" "I'm very glad," Flanagan added, "that the Pope has noticed his action. He is simply hated by the farmers. I rode up last week to the Southern part of the County — I was to Rockhill, Charleville & Effin, & the feeling ags't him in those parts was vehemently strong. He knows from *me* that this is so — but no one else would tell him." "The Bp.," he then noted, "has just returned (yesterday) from the Maynooth meeting. As far as I know, no public manifesto will come from the Episcopoli by [sic] the Decree." "There will be something," Flanagan concluded, "about the land, & their sympathy with the tenants &c." Emly, in forwarding Father Flanagan's letter to Ross, who had only just returned from Rome, noted in the margin against the concluding sentences — "Is this not monstrous?"

Indeed, before Ross had even received Emly's enclosure, he had had an interview with Balfour in London, and assured the chief secretary that Rome had every intention of enforcing its will with regard to the Decree. "Will you," he asked Balfour the following day July 1, "let me trouble you with a few lines relating to what I said yesterday?"[1] "The Decree has got to be obeyed," Ross maintained, "& however patient Rome may be, there is no intention there of allowing it to be either obscured or shelved. Hence: — (1) The Clergy will have to teach & enforce it to the best of their ability & (2) Any organisation obstructing it, will be liable to condemnation. The National League is aware of this danger (I imagine Archbishop Walsh understands this) & will have to act cautiously." "With reference to the action of the Clergy," Ross further reported, and explaining the silence of the Bishops at their recent meeting, "they do not seem at Rome to be so anxious about public declarations on the part of the Bishops, as they are that the condemned practices should cease. The Bishops have to enforce the Decree, but they may do so quietly. The condemnation has now been known for some time, & if the Plan of Campaign & Boycotting still exist in particular dioceses, the Bishop concerned can be called to account."

"When Card. Rampolla told me this," Ross observed, turning to the old theme of a lack of reliable information, "I knew there was not much change in the districts where the Plan & boycotting were rife. But I preferred not to make any vague statements in so serious & important a matter. Thus, if accurate information were possible, noting Dioceses, I think it would be very useful." "The case of Raphoe Diocese," Ross pointed out, "is peculiarly important. An organized effort appears to be made to prevent Evidence being given to Courts who are empowered to deal with Boycotting. Not only is the attempt to suppress evidence before a Court of Law a very demoralising proceeding & likely to spread, but in this particular instance the crime is one of the practices condemned by the Holy Office — which the Bishop is bound to obey. A very short account of one of these enquiries in Donegal, & what the Bishop has done, would therefore I think be very useful." "This particular Bishop," Ross remarked, referring to Patrick O'Donnell, and a protégé of Walsh's, "has disappointed the Roman authorities; they thought they had taken all possible precautions to ascertain his character beforehand, & believed he would be peaceable, but they report the result has been unfortunate."

---

[1] B, 49821.

Errington was also daily growing more upset with the temporizing attitude of the Irish Bishops. "The Bishops I am sorry [to say]," he reported to Smith on July 2, from Castle Forbes in County Longford, where he was staying with Lord Granard, "are showing a very unworthy & disloyal spirit towards Rome; I hope this will not be forgotten. They were devoted sons of the Pope as long as everything went to their liking, but as soon as the Holy See finds it necessary to thwart them all this vaunted obedience & loyalty vanishes"(S). "Pray look at the Tablet this week," he recommended to Smith, referring to Walsh's London interview with the *Freeman* of June 22, "with the account of Dr. Walsh's interview; its casuitical & minimising spirit is painful & pitiful." "I hope Msgr. Persico," Errington then suggested, "will (as is expected) be sent back here; it would be *most important,* for the Pope cannot afford to show weakness now." Ross was also concerned that the pope should not show any "weakness now," but his concern naturally had more to do with emphasizing to Balfour that the pope must be kept up to the mark with reliable information from the proper sources.

"I think I should tell you," Ross explained to Balfour on July 8, a week after his previous letter, "that Ld. Emly has had information to the effect that Dr. Croke had censured Fr. Mat. Ryan privately, and has informed him that he would remove him from the Diocese if he does not keep quiet in future. Ld Emly gave this news to Dr. Dunne (Sec^y of the R^e University). who was lately in Rome, & the latter having had an audience, repeated it to His Holiness."[2] "The Pope mentioned the fact to me," Ross noted, "with evident pleasure & satisfaction when I had my audience about a fortnight ago & so did Card. Rampolla. Ld Emly also says that Fr. White of Miltown Malbay has suppressed the boycotting [of] Mrs. Moroney, which disgraced his Parish for so many years, & the Pope knows of this too." "My fear then," Ross confided, "is that if those cases are brought forward, the answer will be the Bishop is endeavouring to do his duty with regard to Ryan, & White is also trying loyally to carry out the Decree. Dr. Croke's efforts to keep Ryan in check, & Father White's efforts, may be genuine or not. Whatever they are, they are private efforts (perhaps somewhat like Davitt's denunciations of outrage 'don't

[2] *Ibid.*

do it because it is not politic to be violent')." "At all events," he observed, "such efforts will produce little good in the Country."

"The main point seems to me," Ross continued stubbornly, finding his second wind, "to get the Decree promulgated & taught publicly, & the information asked for by Card^l Rampolla (viz. — 'in what Dioceses do the plan of Campaign & Boycotting exist still') would I believe be useful towards this." "Of course I know generally," he admitted, "that the Decree has not yet broken up the Plan or Boycotting and I should be fairly safe in saying that the condemned practices are in force where they existed before the Decree came out. But if it were possible, I should be glad to think, the information I sent was not merely a vague generality, that it was true in every particular and that it could not be contradicted. There is naturally some responsibility attaching to the formulation of a special complaint to the Pope against an individual Bishop that makes me anxious to be very accurate." "At the same time," Ross assured Balfour, "I must say that it never entered my head to quote my authority to Cardinal Rampolla. I should merely like to have it to guard against making an erroneous statement & to save myself from reporting weak cases when strong ones exist in the Country." "By taking up the case of a particular Priest," Ross then summed up doggedly for Balfour, "the result would be that he will be more or less admonished, and perhaps only told not to do anything in future that draws attention upon him; whereas by taking up the case of a Diocese or two, it is to be hoped the whole people could be taught & Nationalist Priests prevented at the same time, from continuing their hitherto outrageous conduct." "I must apologise," Ross finally concluded, and Balfour must have smiled with relief, "for sending you so long a letter."

Errington, who had meanwhile returned to Dublin, found himself profoundly shocked by Walsh's speech on July 17, to the Dublin Corporation. "It is really a scandal;" he declared to Smith, "after all the Pope's orders & strong expressions, Dr. Walsh in this speech minimises the whole matter in the most unworthy way, indirectly defends those who attacked the Papal decree, & says he has not changed in anything; but not one word does he say directly or indirectly in support or in favour of the Pope's action."[3] "He has a fling of course," Errington added, "at Dr. O'Dwyer." "I assure you," he declared again,

[3] S, fragment of letter, no date, c. July 19, 1888.

"the whole thing is a positive scandal; though he has obeyed in regarding the Popes letter, he openly does all he can to explain it away & make light of it. Still, there is no doubt of the excellent effect produced by the action of the Holy See." "One thing is certain," Errington noted, "the priests go much less to meetings than they did." Several days later Smith received a further report from his cousin James Talbot Power about the activities of Archbishop Walsh.

"Mother has requested me," Power dutifully informed Smith from Leopardstown Park, County Dublin, on July 22, "to send you on enclosures" (S). "There *was*," he emphasized, "a printed slip gummed on the archbishop's letter stating that both the Pope's letter & the archbishop's letter were to be read in all the Churches of the Diocese of Dublin on Sunday last; 'The letter of Archbishop to be read First.' I *saw* this slip. But the Priest who gave me enclosures, tore off this slip before handing them to me." "I take much exception," he then added indignantly, "to the strained translation of the Pope's words 'gente vestra' which litterally [sic] means 'Your Race or People' — whilst the Archbishop translates it 'your Nation.' This trifling wording makes all the difference over here — as the Newspaper cry is 'Ireland a Nation.' " "The 2 letters from the Pope," Power then reported, "have had a most happy & reassuring effect. There never was the least 'painful anxiety' or 'troubled crisis' or any 'intensity' of feeling amongst Catholics in Ireland about either of the Pope's letters." "Everybody," he further declared, "(except the Irish Leaders & their Newspapers) accepted both most loyally & respectfully & most people thanked God the Pope had at last written as we have become appaulingly [sic] 'Dishonest.' The Archbishop is merely trying to let himself down as light as he can. He worked real hard all the while he was in Rome, & he suffered an immense defeat & poor man he is terribly vane [sic] & conceited." "We are really far better off than most Countries," he maintained further "& if we would only work & reduce Drink we would be most prosperous & happy but we will always be lively & volatile Politicians. It is the old story, a stupid but Honest Race (England) trying to govern a clever & dishonest one (Ireland)." "I called on the Archbishop," Power confided, "since his return from Rome — but did not see him." "You know," he assured his cousin in conclusion, "I have always paid him the fullest respect as my Archbishop but regret deeply that he pays so much attention to

Politics." "Father Klein," Power added significantly in a postscript, "is now [in] Dublin & has got copies of all enclosures."

Ross also reported the archbishop of Dublin to Rome. "Your registered packet came this morning," J. T. Campbell, rector of the Scots College in Rome informed Ross on July 26, "and I at once sent off the enclosure to the Cardinal Secretary"(R). "Some people," Campbell noted, "are incorrigible. The Pope's last letter, reproaching, reproving, and condemning, is put forth by them as a Papal apology and humble explanation." "They know their countrymen can only read through spectacles," Campbell declared in a burst of British patriotism, "so they provide them, green ones of course." Several days later Ross wrote to Balfour's private secretary, asking for information in order, undoubtedly, to prepare a report on Croke as well as Walsh for Rome. This letter is an interesting example of the kind of information Ross was forwarding to Rome, as well as the extreme caution shown by him in the mode of eliciting it. "Late last night," Ross explained to Browning on July 29, "I got an extract from a Tipperary local paper giving a letter from Dr. Croke which was published therein, by which letter he sends to a certain 'Sheehy T. C.' £5 as his contribution to the 'Condon testimonial Fund' & excuses himself for not having done so before as he did not know of this Fund"(R). "He says," Ross reported Croke, "Mr. Condon has done good work in troublous times &c." "Now what I want to ask," Ross inquired, "is this: Is this Condon, Condon M.P.? & was this Condon M.P. the man who acted as agent to the league in organising & keeping alive & in enforcing the P. of C. in the Mitchelstown Estate? In fact is it true that the *only* way in which this Condon M.P. has distinguished himself is by his action on this occasion?" "I might add this question," Ross continued, "was this Condon M.P. imprisoned for this very action on the Mitchelstown Estate, & if not what was he imprisoned for?" "If in your power to give any answer," Ross noted hurriedly, "I shall be obliged to you." "It w^d be easier for me," he concluded, obviously wanting to keep official correspondence to a minimum, "if so, if you w^d add the answers to the blank page & return my note." "Yes/Yes," Browning obliged, "/In this way, & in organising resistance to the Leahy Compensation Tax. /He was convicted and sentenced to imprisonment on two charges viz. — /1. Inciting to resistance to the Leahy

Compensation Tax. /2. Taking part in an unlawful assembly, viz. — a meeting for the formation of the Plan of Campaign"(R).

Ross, in fact, had every reason to be concerned about the effectiveness of the pope's action in Ireland. "I have just come from Ireland," Lord Emly reported to Ross from the United Services Club in London on August 5, " — the anti-Papal policy there is very successful"(R). "On the one hand," Emly explained, "the Revolutionary papers there are as violent as ever — Priests are backed by their Bishops [and] explain away the decree of the Holy Office. Boycotting unnoticed by the priests goes on up to the very walls of their churches. In some dioceses the Pope's letter has not been read at Mass." "One of the latest made Bishops," Emly complained, indicating that this letter was meant for the authorities at Rome, since Ross was as aware of these details as he was, "Dr. O'Donnell of Raphoe has been conspicuous for his violence — the Archbishop of Cashel has subscribed to a testimonial to Mr. Condon the organiser of the Plan of Campaign at Mitchelstown." "The Freeman's Journal," Emly also noted, "the special organ of the Archbishop of Dublin, makes martyrs of those who are punished for carrying out the Plan of Campaign. Even so good & able a prelate as the Archbishop of Armagh has publicly, in presence of his priests, expressed his sympathy with Mr. Dillon, who is in gaol for an offence condemned not less by the Papal decree than by the law of the land. On the other hand, not one episcopal voice except Dr. O'Dwyer has spoken out for the Pope — the silence of the other Bishops is ["an eloquent" crossed out] a telling condemnation of him, as well as the Pope."

"The Irish people," Emly maintained further, "must naturally as it seems to me conclude that the opinion of their ecclesiastical superior, the Pope has been misinformed & has made a mistake. Every day this state of things is allowed to go on deepens the impression. A long delay may make it indelible — Quidquid delirant reges plectuntur Achivi. Through the fault of their ecclesiastical superiors our poor people in Ireland, without any fault of their own, may become committed to a false morality." "It would be presumptuous of you or me," Emly noted respectfully, "to advise the high Roman authorities — all we want to do is to keep them well informed. But my opinion is, as it was when we were in Rome, that nothing can come right until we have a Papal delegate in Ireland with ample authority not only to inquire but to act." "Should one be sent," Emly argued, "it must, I think be Msgr Persico. To send any one else would at once be represented to Ireland as throwing doubts upon Msgr Persico's informations, & as the commencement of a new enquiry. The Irish people would believe the Pope felt that He had been badly informed & advised, & that there was to be a new departure." "I earnestly hope," Emly concluded firmly, "that whatever is to be done will be done quickly."

During August, Ross made an even more intensive effort to construct a comprehensive picture of the Irish Bishops' and priests' resistance or indifference to Rome's recent injunctions. He either wrote himself or asked Emly to write, to various people in Ireland for information which would prove useful at Rome. What emerges from his effort is that the clergy, high and low, took their lead from Walsh and Croke, and that the bishop of Limerick, and those few clerics who thought like him, were simply frowned down and isolated. "I was glad to receive your letter," the O'Conor Don reported to Ross from Sligo in the West of Ireland, on August 14, "showing that you had safely returned to England"(R). "As to the popes decree," he added, immediately getting down to business, and referring to the diocese of Elphin, "so far as I know neither the decree nor the letter has ever been published in this diocese, & we know nothing of either except from the newspapers." "I regret to say that boycotting," the O'Conor Don noted, "is as rife here as ever. Quite lately, a man who lives within 100 yards of the parish chapel & whose holding of land is separated from the Chapel only by the public road was declared to be boycotted & since then he can get no one to work for him." "He is a rather old man," the O'Conor Don explained, "a pork butcher, & I should say quite unaccustomed to such hard work as mowing meadow, yet during the last three weeks I have seen him day after day mowing his meadow himself & his wife & daughter alone saving the hay. He was boycotted because he ventured to take a few acres of land adjoining his holding which became unoccupied under the following circumstances."

These few acres & a house were held by a most disreputable character whose wife was little better than a common prostitute, & whose children were noted thieves. This man named Morris did not of course pay his rent, & the landlord Mr. Sandford, finding him in every way a most objectionable character gave him money to give up his holding which in the end he did. He then went into the workhouse, whilst his wife went off with a young fellow, a shoemaker in the town of [illegible]. Everyone in the neighborhood was delighted at getting rid of these people, still the league decreed that no one should take the farm & it remained derelict for nearly two years. About six months ago, the butcher to whom I referred above, whose holding adjoined it, took the land from Mr. Sandford, and immediately a meeting of the league was called. This man who belonged to the league was expelled & ever since has been boycotted(R).

"So far as I know," the O'Conor Don maintained, "not one word has been said against this by the priests, although the first person who told me that the man was boycotted was one of the curates. We have, I consider very good priests in this parish. They have never taken an active part in the agitation, & have kept themselves quite clear from the league. Yet they are absolutely silent as to the decree. Our parish priest, or rather administrator, who is a most excellent good man, would not I am sure do anything without the direction of the bishop, and as the bishop has made no move, at least no outward public move, nothing is said in his diocese about the papal decree." "As to the 'Plan of Campaign,'" the O'Conor Don continued interestingly, "I think that is nearly extinct, but not on account of the papal condemnation, but because the people would not join in it a second time on any estate where it had been tried. I think the next time they will combine not to pay any rents but what they choose, but they will not lodge the rents with trustees as under the Plan, but will simply keep the money in their pockets or spend it on themselves." "I don't believe," he summed up for Ross, "that the papal decrees on either point have had the slightest effect here & naturally they have not when the people see that the bishops have ignored them & that when Dr. Walsh published the popes letter he never said one word in support of the letter & on the contrary defended the conduct of the Irish M.P.'s & others who met to denounce the pope's action."

"What is really required in this country," the O'Conor Don recommended, "is some ecclesiastical head, who would enforce the popes decrees & make the bishops obey. At present there is no head." "I greatly fear that Cardinal Moran's visit," he noted significantly, and referring to the fact that the cardinal, archbishop of Sydney, who had been in Rome on Australian business, was about to visit Ireland, "will do no good, but rather the contrary." "As to O'Kelly," the O'Conor Don further remarked, referring to J. J. O'Kelly, Parnell's trusted lieutenant, and M.P. for Roscommon, "he certainly tried to prevent evidence from being given before the R.M.'s under the Crimes Act. The inquiry was in regard to the establishment of the 'Plan' on Mr. Murphy's, L^d De Freyne's, Mr. Mahon's & Mr. Worthington's estates, & into intimidation in connection with this. A great deal came out in the preliminary private inquiry, but when the public investigation followed the witnesses either refused to give evidence or contradicted what they had sworn at the private inquiry." "Some of the priests," he explained, "in the neighboring parishes were messed up in the starting of the Plan, & so far as I know none of the priests have said a word against it in public." "I don't think," the O'Conor Don then added finally in a postscript, "there is any improvement in this part of the country."

The following day, Canon Arthur S. Griffin, of Millstreet, County Cork, in the diocese of Kerry, wrote Ross a long report on the situation in the Southwest. "Lord Emly has sent me a note from you," Griffin explained on August 15, "in which you ask him to write to me for information on the present ecclesiastical Action in Ireland, and you express a fear that I may be shy in answering you if you wrote to me yourself as I may have forgotten you." "I have been so anxious," he then confided to Ross, after further explaining that he had indeed intended to write to him, and especially when he heard that he had accompanied the duke of Norfolk to Rome, "about the religious aspect of affairs in this unfortunate country, I determined to go over to London and see His Grace after his return from Rome."

And it so happened that I started for Dublin the week after the Papal Rescript appeared. I remained in Dublin during some days and during my stay I sent the Dublin papers to His Eminence Car^d Simeoni in which were published the Speeches of the "*trusted leaders* of the Irish people," the speeches of the men who "did so much for Country and Religion" — but in every and [each] of their speeches grossly insulted the Father of the faithful — and held him up to the scorn of the wide world, and imputed to him the basest motives that could be laid at the door of the humblest priest in the Church. I was in Dublin the day the Bishops first met at Clonliffe College to consider the Rescript, but as my Bishop did not attend I could learn nothing. Everyone I met asked me "What will the Bishops do," and I said "I am sure absolutely nothing"(R).

"I proceed to London,". Griffin continued his odyssey, "and called on His Grace to whom I may say I had written on some former occasions and impressed on him the necessity of having diplomatic relations of some kind established with the Vatican, but on the occasion of my visit I told him I feared much the Irish Bishops would treat the Rescript as they treated some former documents issued on the politico-religious state of Ireland and I presumed to suggest that in case they treated this decision of the Holy See, with regard to the Plan of Campaign and Boycotting, with the same indifference — His Holiness should be advised to send to Ireland an Apostolic Delegate such as Monsignor Persico with plenary Apostolic powers & who would insist on having the Mandates of the Holy See accurately carried out and published to the people when he so ordered." "I gave His Grace an outline," Griffin further reported, "of the general state of things in the Country — and I am sorry to say that my anticipations with regard to the conduct of the Bishops is fully verified. They made no publication of the Rescript throughout Ireland, except alone Dr. O'Dwyer of Limerick — and you know the amount of outrageous insults poured forth on him." "In their published document," Griffin noted, referring to the Bishops' resolutions of May 30, "— they praised his slanderers and why he put his name to such a document astonished everyone." "Notwithstanding all this," Griffin assured Ross, "the Rescript has been steadily doing good work, and it has silenced, at least in public, the utterances of violent priests."

"I never thought," Griffin then confessed, "when I was a young priest — in the days of such men as Car^d Cullen, Archb. MacGettigan, Bishops Delany, Moriarty, etc. etc. that I would live to see the Irish Episcopacy So weak, So vacillating, So *unfaithful* (I can use no other word) to the Holy See, as the present prelates have shown themselves to be. Up to the 12th of July, not a word of publication of the Rescript was made to the priests of this diocese Ardfert and Aghadoe (commonly called Kerry) by the Bishop, and as I lived on the borders of Cloyne I know the same was exactly the case." "At our Diocesan Synod," Griffin added, referring to the very conservative bishop of Kerry, "Dr. Higgins had the Rescript published by one of the Archdeacons, and remarked — that His Holiness never intended that the document should be published in the papers, that it was *only* intended as a decision for the Bishops and Priests, as to the illegality and immorality of the plan of Campaign and Boycotting *where land was concerned* and that confessors should deal with it as with all other sins." "The Plan, he observed," Griffin continued, paraphrasing Higgins, "had not been introduced into the diocese and consequently the Rescript did not apply to us so far, but if it should be introduced on any property the P.P. of the place should at once take action in the matter and denounce it." "— As to Boycotting he regretted to say," Griffin added, "that parish priests were marked out for it in many instances, especially in the Management of their Schools and in the appointment of their teachers — but he did not intend that the Rescript would be published to the people."

"After His Lordship concluded his remarks which were very brief," Griffin explained, "finding that no one appeared inclined to make any comments or remarks I stood up and said —

It may have been the intention of His Holiness not to have the Rescript published first in the Newspapers — but that it appeared very strange to me, if he intended that such an emphatic condemnation of the Plan and Boycotting should be only made known to Confessors. Up to the publishing of the Papal documents several Bishops and Priests openly maintained the legality and even wisdom of both, and taught their people to carry them out, and the people therefore looked upon them as perfectly lawful. How therefore, I asked are they to know that they are unlawful if the Rescript is not to be promulgated by our Episcopal pastor, or promulgated by the Clergy from the pulpits of the diocese?; I believed that the violent speeches and attacks made on the Holy Father imperitantly [*sic*] demanded the fullest promulgation of the papal documents, unless the Bishops are satisfied to see the papal documents trampled on, and the authority of the Holy See entirely annihilated in the Country. Boycotting, I said, is wide spread throughout the diocese — it has caused frightful murders and other crimes too numerous to mention and it promises to continue. Am I not to tell my people publicly that it is condemned by the Pope and that it is a Mortal Sin?(R).

"His Lordship said," Griffin then observed, "that if I thought it necessary to denounce Boycotting in my churches I had better consult him and explain the various cases." "I said I had years ago," Griffin noted, "condemned and denounced Boycotting from my pulpits, and that I would continue to do so, but what I wanted was to have the *Papal Condemnation* read." "I got no seconder," he added, "on the contrary the vast Majority disapproved."

"We went on Retreat that Evening," Griffin continued, referring to Thursday, July 12, "and on the following Sunday the Papal Encyclical was read in the Dublin Churches together with Archbishop Walsh's letter and this made everyone believe that the publication and reading of the letter should take place in every Church in Ireland on the following Sunday — as His Holliness [*sic*] expressly commanded the Bishops to make it known to their people, but to our astonishment we received no notification from the Bishop, and after two Sundays passed I wrote to him and asked him was this last utterance of the Holy Father not to be read for the people in the Churches?" "He wrote in reply," Griffin reported, quoting Higgins, "that 'he hoped no Bishop would promulgate it without united action.'" "It has not been promulgated," he further noted, "in any Southern diocese. Nor did I see by the newspapers that it was promulgated anywhere except in Dublin and Armagh. I met Cloyne Priests last week, and they told me they had no communication from their Bishop about it. I asked in Cork if it was promulgated and I was told not one of the Cork papers said it was read at the Cathedral in the city." "I was away all this day," Griffin finally apologized in closing his long letter to Ross, "at one of my Country chapels and I am writing late in the night in order to comply with your wishes and as I have gone as fast as the pen can go pray excuse all shortcomings in these sheets."[4]

On the same Sunday that Canon Griffin was thus writing Ross from West Cork, Edmund Dease, Errington's old friend, and former Liberal M.P. for Queen's County, wrote Ross from the Midlands. "I know you have the means," he explained to Ross on August 15, "of bringing before the authorities at Rome the needs of the Church over here"(R). "I have just heard," Dease reported, "that Mg^r P. is not expected to return here!"

<hr/>

[4] R, Griffin to Ross, August 18, 1888. See for an account of priests being involved in boycotting.

"If this is the case," he warned Ross, "it will *be disastrous in the extreme*. He, or someone trusted at the Vatican, *must be on the spot*, or we shall surely drift back to those dangerous waters on the borders of which we still rest in great uncertainty. I do hope that this is pressed on the attention of the Holy Father!" "Do you happen to know," Dease inquired of Ross, "where Mgr Persico is." "That unfortunate address," Dease added, referring to the address to Persico drawn up by the "loyal" Irish Catholics some ten months before, "is still unpresented. He wrote twice to me — 'that he would *formally* receive it on his *return to Ireland* & that he would let me know the *when & where* he would receive it.'" "In presenting it," Dease then explained, "care must be taken to call attention to the *date* & to the accidental cause in the delay in formal presentation." "We don't yet know," he concluded, and referring to the fact that the bishop of Kildare and Leighlin, James Lynch, had requested a coadjutor *cum jure successionis,* "who our Bishop is to be."

"Many thanks for your letter," Dease replied to Ross again some ten days later on August 26, "I shall be very glad indeed if you can see Mg^r P. when he receives the address"(R). "The address & answer," he then added, "should be published as well as a list of each class signing. D.I. J.P. P.C. &c &c." "Now as regards Kildare & Leighlin," Dease explained, and referring to one of the candidates for coadjutor, "What you hear as to Father Comerford, as to his being *president of his local league* — is *absolutely false*. I am living in the next parish to him and know the facts."

In consequence of his not joining the league, some of its members, though parishioners of his, boycotted him their P.P. On one occasion the league managed to get the Xtian Brothers to leave their local school room for a meeting. The room belonged to the P.P. though it was used by the Brothers. He heard the meeting was *being held,* & ran off to the school & turned out the *whole meeting* his own curates included! When meetings were afterwards held — on the *road* near the church but *outside his jurisdiction* he *refused* to permit *any priest* from outside his parish to enter or attend & some, who were invited, publicly announced that they could not attend owing to the action of the P P of Monasterevan Parish. In his church to this hour — the *prayer for the Queen* is said every Sunday in *his three Churches*. You will see from this that the information reaching you about Father C is not at all reliable — in fact it is

false. He is over 50 years of age. I cannot conceive that he
would take any other line as a bishop than he has done as a P P
— it is of course, possible, but most improbable(R).

"The 4 bishops of the Province," Dease further informed Ross,
and referring to the bishops' report to Propaganda on the *terna*
commended by the clergy, "including Ab. *Walsh* strongly
recommend Father *Murphy of Kildare.*" "I quite agree with
you," Dease admitted, and referring to Walsh's auxiliary, "that
Dr. Donnelly's appointment, as not at all to be desired, he is
personally a very nice man, but weak as water, & I dont believe
there is any diocese in Ireland, that is in greater need of a firm
Bishop than Kildare — in *all matters,* for the late Bishop, for the
last 10 years let them slip into a bad way; owing to his
advanced age, & infirmities." "Father C. knows this,
well,"Dease added, "& dreads the responsibility of undertaking
the Episcopate & prays earnestly, that it may not fall to him. I
know, he was the means of *preventing* several from *voting* for
him, as he dreads the work of reform needed — but if put upon
him; he will not shrink."
    "As to the 'Decree,' " Dease turned finally to Ross's major
concern, "I never heard that *it* was read anywhere — But the
Popes letter was — In *Meath & here* in *Dublin,* in *Tuam.*" "A
curious fact I heard from the diocese of Meath," Dease then
observed, "the letter was read in the Parish of Moyvore, where
some relations of mine live — on returning from church, some
men were overheard *cursing* the *Pope,* now this is a fact & a
very awful one!" "The truth is," he explained, "that Rome was
too slow *too late* in acting. Bishops allowed Priests to advocate
Boycotting & the P. of C. & even by silence at least, *accepted*
these most immoral practices. It was not for two years or more,
that Rome interfered, & by *then* the *harm was done.* I believe
all the Bishops at Conference, & at the *retreats,* told the Priests,
that the Decree was binding under pain of mortal sin, not
publicly. They have been themselves silent & afraid to speak."
"When the *decree* was *first* published," Dease continued,
referring rather to the reports of the various speeches than to
the *Freeman's* editorials, "the Freeman denounced it in
scandalous language." "When the Pope's *letter* came," he
added more accurately, "— a line of transparent humbug was
adopted, in trying to make it appear that the Pope was really
not opposed to the *People &c* & all the Nat'al press followed

this line." "*Unless*," he warned Ross, "the Bishops *are made* to issue a *united Pastoral* to the entire Irish flock, setting forth all contained in the Pope's letter & *commanding obedience,* everything will be allowed to slide. This will never be done unless there is a *Papal legate here* — unconnected with the Church in Ireland — but appointed *with supreme Power.* Card. Cullen held such a position — but no one in Ireland could hold it now, it must be someone *sent direct* from Rome — who from *the first* must *report to Rome.*" "Without a *Legate* here from Rome," he then urged once again in conclusion, "we shall not be really safe — even if with one, we are!"

In his correspondence with Rome in July and August, Ross was apparently attempting to achieve a number of things. First of all, he was intent on keeping the lines of communication, however unofficial, open between the British government and Rome. By doing so he hoped to keep the prospect, however tenuous, of diplomatic relations alive. Secondly, on the basis of the "unofficial" information supplied through him, he was trying to persuade Rome to enforce her recent Decree. Finally, he was endeavoring to convince the Roman authorities that in order to enforce the Decree effectively in Ireland, especially in the light of the failure of the admonitions of Cardinal Rampolla, and even the pope, to the Irish Bishops, what was necessary was a papal legate, and preferably Monsignor Persico. What Ross and his friends did not understand, however, was that Persico, though the logical choice perhaps, was now an impossible one. He was not only distrusted by the Irish Bishops, but literally, however unjustly, hated by the clergy and people as their betrayer at Rome. Persico's usefulness in Ireland was, therefore, at an end, and both he and the Roman authorities well understood this. He was soon allowed to return to the more congenial climate of Rome, where he was eventually appointed secretary for the Affairs of the Oriental Rite at Propaganda. In this prestigious position, Monsignor Persico became, ironically enough, very influential in Irish affairs, and especially in the matter of episcopal appointments. Still Rome could not but have been deeply concerned about how her authority in Ireland had been compromised by the patent reluctance on the part of the Irish Bishops to enforce her Decree. The real question for Rome now, however, was what was to be done to reassert her authority without making matters worse.

Walsh and Croke, meanwhile, continued within their framework of episcopal and clerical support to attempt to preserve to the Irish Church its power and influence in spite of the recent Roman pronouncements. Cardinal Manning wrote Walsh shortly after he read his letter covering the pope's in the press to reassure him that at least he approved. "It is always the greatest encouragement to me," Walsh acknowledged gratefully on July 21, "when I find I have Your Eminence's approval. The recent letter required careful handling. As I was entrusted with the translation and sending out of it to the Bishops, I was able to secure its presentation to the public in at all events the least objectionable possible form"(M). "I have a project now," Walsh added characteristically, "of writing an article of 12 or 14 pages for the Contemporary Review on the statistics of the Land Courts. Your Eminence asked me to let you have some figures showing the general working of the Act of 1881. Such an article as I contemplate, would put all this in a permanent and easily accessible form." "As we are to have an autumn session," Walsh then pointed out, "I would propose in this article, for the outline of my plan for the temporary settlement of the Land Question." "In this way," he noted in conclusion, "the proposal could be well illustrated by statistics." "P.S.," Walsh added, referring to the question of including Irish representation at Westminster after the grant of Home Rule, "Parnell's view is accepted everywhere simply as a matter of course."

When Manning again read an account some two weeks later of Croke's speech in Kerry denouncing outrage, he wrote to congratulate the archbishop of Cashel. "I have just read," the cardinal reported on August 7, "your noble words at Cahirceveen"(C). "They are," he noted, "what I looked for from you. And they will 'stop the mouths of Lions' or at least leave our slanderers without excuse." "All things are working for good," he added reassuringly. "Every day brings us nearer to our hope. The change in the people of England is spreading fast & widely, greatly hastened by the policy of imprisonment: and hindered only by the disastrous acts you so wisely denounced." "I hope," he added, "you are well. Let me now thank you warmly for your welcome telegram on my 80th birthday." "I hope," he concluded optimistically, "I may live to help Ireland by a few words & to see its day of peace."

A week later, the archbishop of Sydney, Cardinal Moran

arrived in Ireland after having just spent some time in Rome in the interest of both his health and Australian ecclesiastical business. Though he remained in Ireland for some six weeks, and had extended conversations with both Croke and Walsh, everyone seems to have maintained a most circumspect silence about his visit. "I had a line from Card. Moran from Paris," Croke reported to Walsh on August 15, "stating that as he had missed me the last time he was in Ireland, he would surely pay me a visit this time, and naming the 16th of Augt as the day on which I may expect him. So, I suppose he will be here tomorrow"(W). "The Cardinal," Croke further reported on Saturday, August 18, "has just left for Callan. He will be with you on Monday." Even more surprising was that when Walsh wrote Kirby on Thursday, August 23, he not only never mentioned the cardinal or his visit, but his resentment towards Rome seemed to have only increased since he had last written Kirby some six weeks before. "As the Freeman's Journal goes regularly to the Irish College," Walsh noted curtly, "I need not say anything of our public affairs"(K). "But it may be well to know," he added bitterly, "that as regards the feelings of our good people, the mischief that has been done through the Roman intrigues is now beyond recall. The last letter of the Pope showed such an angry and bitter feeling that but for the respect for the Bishops here, whom the people still trust as much as ever, there would have been a most painful outburst of feeling all over the country. The evicting landlords are rampant. For a while the people were fairly satisfied by the assurances, given by myself and others, that the Pope had not gone over to their enemies. There was even a sort of anticipation that the unfortunate decree of the Holy Office would be followed up by a protest of some kind against the way in which the Coercion Government are oppressing this unfortunate Catholic people. When the letter came there was no longer any possibility of concealing the truth." "I did my best in a letter," he confessed candidly in conclusion, "that I sent out to be read in the Churches of the dioceses. But while everyone respected my motive in trying to extricate the Holy Father from the awful position into which Lord Salisbury's agents have succeeded in dragging him, everyone too saw as well as I myself did, how the case really stood."

The reports of "Lord Salisbury's agents," and especially Ross's, to Rome in August and early September, however, had obviously been very effective, for Walsh received yet another letter from the pope's secretary of state. "I received a few days ago," Walsh soberly informed his fellow archbishops on September 15, "from H. E. Cardinal Rampolla a letter written by direction of the Holy Father"(C). "His Holiness wishes me to make it known to the Bishops," Walsh reported, "that he is both grieved and surprised at the manner in which his Encyclical Letter to the Irish Bishops regarding the decree of the Holy Office has been received in Ireland. Neither from the people, nor the episcopate, has come to him that 'dutiful manifestation of sincere adhesion,' 'called for by the circumstances which gave rise to his action.' The absence of all this has been all the more specially noticed by his Holiness inasmuch as he is obliged by virtue of his supreme authority not to permit so solemn an act of the Holy See to remain in any way unobserved." "In charging me," Walsh observed, "with the duty of making this communication, the Holy Father expresses his confidence that the Bishops of Ireland will appreciate the importance of the matter to which he directs attention, and will not fail in the duty of fulfilling in every respect the expectations of the Sovereign Pontiff." "I have communicated directly with the Bishops of the Province of Dublin," Walsh noted circumspectly, "but as regards the Bishops of the other Provinces, I wish to execute my commission by placing the matter in the hands of the respective Archbishops." "I should add," Walsh pointed out coolly, "that in my reply to Cardinal Rampolla I stated to his Eminence that, as regards any collective action of the Bishops, no opportunity for it had as yet arisen, but that a meeting is to be held on the 9th October, when I had no doubt steps would be taken to send a suitable reply to the letter of his Holiness." "It might be well," Walsh advised his fellow Archbishops in conclusion, "in the circumstances to take steps to secure as large an attendance of the Bishops as may be possible."

"I am here," Croke replied from London on Tuesday, September 18, "I leave, however, tomorrow for Chester, and will 'cross over' on Thursday — wind and weather permitting"(W). "I have got yours," he then assured Walsh, "addressed to Thurles. We can talk the 'situation' over. But I see nothing to be done till general Meeting in October." Indeed nothing was done until the October meeting, and in the interim Walsh's temper did not improve. In a long complaining letter to

Kirby about the late arrival of notices from Propaganda on October 8, the day before the general meeting, Walsh noted testily, that if this was an example of the new distribution arrangements, the future did not look bright. "The Cardinal," Walsh also noted, referring to Moran, "left us last week after a visit that we all feel will be of useful results for our Church and Country, if the authorities at the Holy See will only listen to such disinterested advice instead of giving way to the advice of prejudicial partisans"(K). Walsh, it appears, did not write Kirby after the general Meeting to explain what indeed had been done by the Bishops. About a week after the Meeting he did, however, write to Cardinal Manning. "Your Eminence will be glad to know," Walsh explained on October 18, "that the recent meeting of the Irish Bishops led to very definite action being taken. We have sent a letter of adhesion and of thanks for the kindly sentiments and expressions of the Holy Father's letter. But we conclude by saying that we feel it to be our duty to put before him a full statement of the present and recent circumstances of the country as regards the reception of the Decree. This has since been written into Latin and sent to all for suggestions"(M). "It occurred to me at the meeting," Walsh observed, "to suggest that we should all, if possible, *sign*, — as in the case of a Royal Commission Report — dissenters, if any, indicating in the document itself the fact, the extent, and the reasons, of their dissent." "Of course," he assured the cardinal firmly in conclusion, "we shall arrange matters so as to have as little dissent as possible."

"The joint letter of the Irish Bishops," John MacEvilly, the archbishop of Tuam, explained to Kirby over a month later on November 22, "to the H. Father has not, I believe, been sent off yet. It is in the form of a reply to the charges made against us"(K). "We have had very recently," MacEvilly reported, referring to yet another communication, "a terrible letter from Card. Rampolla. It is exceedingly strong, and I must say, with all the profoundest respect, *unfounded*." "So far as this Diocese is concerned," he assured Kirby, "I mean to inform his Eminence with great respect and reverence that there is no foundation for it." Croke naturally was also very upset about Rampolla's most recent pronouncement. "There is one thing," he suggested to Walsh also on November 22, "that should certainly, in my humble opinion, be introduced into the document which is being prepared for the Holy Father, and that is a protest against the utterly unprecedented and apparently, unconstitutional interference of Cardinal Rampolla, Sec of State, in the affairs of the Irish Church"(W). "Only imagine," Croke expostulated with Walsh, referring to Pius IX's celebrated secretary of state, "Cardinal Antonelli sending us a dispatch upon faith and morals. Such a thing was never heard of." "If their Lordships of Elphin and Ardagh," he concluded, referring to Gillooly and Woodlock, the secretaries to the episcopal body, "come to you, as you expected, I feel assured that they will be with me in this matter." "Written," Croke added good humoredly in a postscript, "with a *diamond* pen value £3."

A week later, however, Croke decided to write directly to the cardinal prefect of Propaganda to complain about the "unconstitutional" interference of the cardinal secretary of state in Irish affairs. Croke was, indeed, at his eloquent best in this very dignified protest occasioned by Cardinal Rampolla's latest letter sent individually to all the Irish Bishops. "I write you this line," Croke wrote Cardinal Simeoni on November 29, invoking the court of last resort among men, "urged to do so by my conscience"(C). "As your Eminence knows," Croke noted, "I do not often trouble the Propaganda authorities with the expression of my views on Irish affairs. But, at the present moment, I fear I should be wanting in my duty, were I to keep silent." "The affairs of the Irish Church," Croke explained to Simeoni, "hitherto confided to the guidance of the Propaganda, have now, apparently, fallen into the hands of his Holiness's Secretary of State, a diplomatic official, but partially acquainted with, if not wholly ignorant of, the Irish 'situation' in its various bearings, and naturally more conversant with diplomatic maneuvers than with the feelings and requirements of our National Church." "The Bishops generally," Croke assured the cardinal, "complain of this. We feel that we are safe and in friendly keeping when dealt with by the Authorities of the Propaganda, but we are certainly not satisfied to become the bone of diplomatic contention, and be withdrawn from the immediate control of the Sacred congregation of Propaganda that has managed Irish Ecclesiastical affairs for a long series of years, and managed them, on the whole, both wisely and well." "A good deal will have to be said upon this matter," Croke warned Simeoni politely, "I take it for granted, when the Irish Bishops hold their next general meeting — if not sooner; but I desire to bring it, by anticipation, and unofficially before your Eminence now."

"Permit me to add," Croke observed candidly, "that so long as the Authorities in Rome believe, or affect to believe, that they know more about the actual state of what is called the *'Irish Question'* in all its complicated and varying phases than the Irish Bishops and Priests do, there will be a strong current of revolt against Roman views, and Roman interference, in this country." "Our people are, in fact," he frankly pointed out to the cardinal, "fully persuaded, that they understand their needs and rights better than any extern can; and that their clergy, not being either heretics or infidels, or notorious violators and scoffers of God's law, are more competent to pronounce on the *concrete* merits of the National Struggle, with all its complex and ever varying incidents than any person not an Irishman living in Ireland, but a Roman living in Rome, can possibly be." "This applies, of course, only to the political or secular aspect of our case"; Croke added dutifully, if hypothetically, "for however they may doubt about the *opportuneness* of the document there is no Ecclesiastic, I am sure, in Ireland, and there are but few, if any, amongst even the more fiery and enthusiastic of our Irish Agitators, who dispute the soundness of the *general* decision come to by the Holy Office in their now memorable Rescript, or question the Competency of the Sovereign Pontiff to judge decisively on all matters appertaining in any way to faith and morals." "I write in French," Croke concluded, "as that language is familiar to me, as it is, I know, to your Eminence also."

Meanwhile, the statement promised by the Irish Bishops to the pope at their meeting on October 9, had been put into final form and circulated among the Bishops for their signatures. "I return the document," Croke wrote Walsh on December 1, "having my sign manual duly attached"(W). "It is decidedly an improvement on its predecessor," Croke noted, "being clearer, shorter, and, in many ways, more precise." A week later Walsh forwarded the document to Kirby. "I think it better," he explained to Kirby on December 7, "to send the enclosed letter to Y.G., than to trust it to the post addressed either to Cardinal Rampolla or to H.H."(K). "Let us hope," Walsh then observed wryly, "that it will make some impression." "I wrote to Card. Rampolla a few days ago," Walsh further reported, "protesting against the sending of letters, such as his late letter, to all the

Bishops. I simply demand as an act of justice to my priests that any charges made against them be submitted to me for examination, and that until the facts of the case are ascertained no further defamatory letters be written about our Irish Church." "I am satisfied," Walsh then observed significantly, "the Pope does not know to what political use his name and authority are being turned. Cut off as he is from free communication with the Church this is not to be wondered at." "Kindly seal up the enclosed when Y.G. has read it," he charged Kirby in conclusion, "and *give* it to Cardinal Rampolla for H.H."

The substance, at least, if not the form of the Bishops' collective response to the pope's letter may be easily appreciated from a long "Mem^d for Reply to H.F." drawn up by the bishop of Elphin.[5] This Memorandum, which contained some eighteen points, was obviously drawn up previous to the writing and circulating of the first draft for the Bishops' comments. After expressing (1) their deep regret to the pope for his dissatisfaction, the Bishops (2) promised sincerely to observe his instructions and conscientiously fulfill them. They further explained (3) that not all the Bishops could adopt the same time and mode of publishing the Decree, and it had been decided, therefore, to leave it to each Bishop to be dealt with as he thought best. The resulting (4) delay and diversity in action has been misinterpreted, as the Bishops expected it would, as evidence of a want of obedience and devotion to the Holy See, but the Bishops, (5) knowing that the pope could never believe that Ireland could be disloyal, have remained silent. The Bishops then explained (6) to the pope that they acted as they did because:

(a) to safeguard the authority of the Holy See.

(b) to preserve the Confidence of the people in the sympathy and approval of Rome.

(c) to save the clergy of Ireland from the severeness & hostility of the people, and from the fearful consequences (social, political & religious) that sh^d follow not only in Ireland but in America and the Brit. Colonies from their sudden and united condemnation & abandonment of the political machinery of the N. League, which they had previously approved or at least tolerated.

---

[5] Gillooly Papers(G), Archives of the Diocese of Elphin, Sligo, no date.

(d) to preserve the peaceful constitutional character of the Movement, and to save the people from Secret Societies & Dynamiters — it being well known that if the Bishops & Clergy condemned & opposed the leaders of the people, these would give up public life casting all responsibility of failure on the Clergy and leaving the people to the lowest class of agitators & demagogues.

(e) to save the people from wholesale eviction which w[d] certainly follow the public & simultaneous opposition of the Clergy to the Nat Organisation as unity of action. The only effectual check on Evictions would then become impracticable on the part of the people — and the Landlords w[d] increase their legal powers to the utmost(G).

"To foresee & weigh," the Bishops argued (7) prudently, "the dangers & evils of hasty action was, the Bps assumed, a solemn duty imposed by their office. They have discharged it to the best of their judgement and will continue to do so." The Bishops then maintained (8) that they had never tolerated any certain injustice or lack of charity, but they had at times seen the necessity of tolerating abuses and offences in order to prevent greater evils, and in consequence they have been misrepresented both in Rome and in England.

The people, the Bishops pointed out to the pope, (9) are only protecting themselves under an unusual set of circumstances. "Gladstone," the Bishops added (10), and referring to the propertied classes, "who is saving England from a social Revolution by the gradual enfranchisement of the people, they regard as a robber and arch revolutionist." The property class in Ireland, moreover, was both cruel and arrogant, and it was (11) "to their selfish intolerant Class that the present Gov[mt], itself composed of the same Class, is lending all the power of the State for the exaction of impossible rents and for the wholesale eviction of our people." Coercion Laws are (12) passed to sustain this Class, and the policy of the Government is (13) that there will be no remedial legislation until all opposition to their aims is given up. Under the precedents and customs of the English Constitution, the Bishops further informed the pope, (14) not only passive resistance but even active resistance is justifiable in as much as it can be "practised" in opposition "to this brute-force system of Government." These acts (15) have been defended in Parliament by Gladstone and the Liberal Party. "A great

Social Revolution," the Bishops continued (16), "is being carried out in Ireland; its methods are to some extent necessarily new; they are substantially legal & equitable; and, when by exception unlawful, they are less violent & unjust than what w^d be employed under similar conditions in England or any other Country of the world." "Unjust laws and the unjust administration of them," the Bishops further argued, "have to be denounced and occasionally resisted — because fear alone will obtain the needed reforms from the legislative & governing Class — whose wealth & power depend on maintaining their territorial supremacy." "It is now the general," they finally pointed out, saving the most forceful argument for last for the pope (17) "if not the universal belief that the Irish movement, if not obstructed & weakened from within, will be soon crowned with success." "Its failure at such a critical moment," the Bishops observed, "would be a grievous danger to religion & to Social order, by leading to methods essentially evil and not only uncontrolled by but hostile to religion." "Irishmen would never forget or forgive," the Irish Bishops then warned the Pope, "such cruel ingratitude & betrayal — it would drive millions of them out of the Church." The Bishops concluded (18) by begging the pope, in turn, to believe that they were loyal.

"I wrote a letter to Card. Rampolla," MacEvilly also informed Kirby three days later on December 10, "in reply to the one he sent us in the name of the H. Father"(K). "I assured his Eminence," MacEvilly reported, "that the report of a meeting which took place in this Diocese at Ballyhaunis on 22 October and reported in the Freeman, was falsely and injuriously reported. It was said that in the presence of Priests, the delegates who assembled, said 'they would have recourse to the Plan of Campaign.' The Chairman a P.P. and others remaining silent." "There was," MacEvilly emphasized, "*not one word of truth in the Report* & I got the P.P. to contradict it publicly in the same Paper (the Freeman)." "I then," MacEvilly noted, "in the most respectful words insinuated, that before any accusation could be received, it was right the golden maxim, 'audi alteram partem' should be adhered to." "In truth," MacEvilly warned in conclusion, "if this dictate of natural justice be not adhered to, no one's character is safe against malicious maligners." It was Kirby's old friend, however, James Lynch, the bishop of Kildare and Leighlin, who in the course of a letter several days later, announcing that the

briefs for the consecration of his new coadjutor, Michael
Comerford had arrived, summed up the position and dilemma
of the Irish Bishops best. "I am anxious to know," Lynch
confessed to Kirby on December 15, "how our M.H. Father
took out joint letter. All put their signature to it except the
Bishops of Limerick & Coad. of Clonfert"(K). "I cannot tell
your Grace," Lynch confided in conclusion, "how difficult we
feel our position here, between the undisputed loyalty we owe to
& I hope we forever will to our Most Holy Father & the
confidence of our poor oppressed people."

The proverbial straw for the Irish Bishops, of course, had
been Cardinal Rampolla's letter in September, written at the
insistence of the pope. What the pope was telling the Irish
Bishops was that he knew better than they did what the
situation was in Ireland, and that the Irish Bishops were not
only wanting in loyalty, but were not doing their duty. Cardinal
Rampolla's continued interference during October and
November in the internal affairs of the Irish Church only added
insult to injury. In their joint letter to the pope in early
December the Irish Bishops protested that they were not
wanting in loyalty and that they had done their duty according
to their perception of what was really happening in Ireland.
They plainly told the Pope that they knew better than either he
or his advisers about what was happening in Ireland, and that
there was perhaps even something more important at stake than
his authority with regard to the recent Decree. That something
was, in fact, the faith of the Irish people on which not only the
power and influence of the Irish Bishops rested, but on which
papal authority in Ireland in the last analysis rested as well. If
they enforced the Decree, they would have to withdraw from
the Nationalist movement, and thus break up the Clerical-
Nationalist alliance. The consequences of such action for both
the temporal and spiritual welfare of the Irish people were
frightening to contemplate. The constitutional lay leadership
would retire from politics maintaining that they had been
betrayed in the great moment of promise by the Irish Bishops
and clergy at the behest of Rome in the interest of placating the
hereditary enemy for Rome's own sordid interests. The result
would be not only to throw the whole Nationalist movement
into the hands of the secret societies and physical force party,
but "millions" of Irishmen would forsake the Church of their
fathers. The Irish Bishops, some thirty in number, with two

dissentients, therefore, told the pope they could not conscientiously enforce his Decree, and would continue to discharge their duty as they collectively perceived it. The next move was now up to the pope and his advisers, and they wisely decided not to insist any further on the enforcement of the Decree.

EPILOGUE

In the initial stage of the consolidation of the modern Irish State nothing was perhaps more important or central to that consolidation than the Plan of Campaign. Between the launching of the Plan in the autumn of 1886 and the collective refusal of the Irish Bishops at the end of 1888 to enforce the Roman Decree condemning it, the Plan, in effect, was the Irish question. Basic to the strength of the *de facto* Irish State created by Parnell, for example, was the Clerical-Nationalist alliance, and the Plan, more than anything else, put that alliance to the supreme test. If that *de facto* State, moreover, was to be made as legal as it was real, the Liberal-Nationalist alliance was essential, and the Plan certainly provided a critical testing time for that alliance as well. The efforts of the Conservative government to break up those alliances by coercive measures at home and diplomatic pressures at Rome proved ineffective. The further attempts by Arthur Balfour as Her Majesty's chief secretary for Ireland to ensure that law and order were enforced by and administered through him and not Parnell and his Party was also a failure. Both alliances, in fact, not only endured, but even emerged from the crucible stronger than when they went in, and Ireland, moreover, was still as much in the grip of Parnell and his Party at the end of 1888 as it had been when the Plan had been launched two years before.

Indeed, the essential failure of Conservative policy in Ireland between 1886 and 1888 was witness to the reality of the Irish State created by Parnell. When Gladstone had endorsed that creation in his first Home Rule Bill, and then failed to have it ratified by Parliament in 1886, the responsibility for making the Irish State as legal as it was real devolved mainly on Parnell. His success would depend on whether the Clerical and Liberal-Nationalist alliances could be sustained unimpaired until the next general election. Parnell's policy, therefore, was to protect those alliances, while at the same time increasing his grip on the country. From his point of view, then, the basic threat to those alliances and his own grip on the country came from neither Rome nor Conservative strategy or tactics, but rather from the agrarian wing in his own Party. The danger was that a renewal of the land agitation under the Plan, would both frighten the clergy and alienate English public opinion, thereby undermining the Clerical and Liberal-Nationalist alliances. A revival of the agrarian agitation, moreover, would also pose a serious threat to his grip on the country if it escaped, as it had indeed in the Land League agitation some seven years before, its political harness. Parnell did his utmost, therefore, to emphasize, at the expense of the agrarian agitation, that the main task at hand was still the ratification by Parliament of the existence of the Irish State now in the process of being consolidated.

While the potential dangers envisaged by Parnell in the Plan were certainly real, they did not in fact materialize. In the first place, the Bishops and priests were not frightened by the Plan. Indeed, after Archbishop Walsh publicly endorsed it, they generally took it up with enthusiasm, and they did not even forsake it when Rome condemned it. Secondly, English Liberals, whatever may be said about English public opinion, were more outraged, in the last analysis, by Tory coercion than they were by Irish efforts to reduce rents and resist evictions. Indeed, it may not be too much to say that the Liberal Party was as much "radicalized" by the Plan as it had been by Home Rule. Finally, the potential dangers in the Plan with regard to threatening Parnellite control in the country by giving rise to an indiscriminate outbreak of agrarian violence was circumscribed by both the nature and extent of the Plan itself as well as the attitude of the Leader and the Party to it. Parnell's own reticence, for example, with regard to the Plan, and his general reluctance to support it out of Party funds, certainly contributed to the containing of it in the long run. Then too, the operating of the Plan was much more under the control of the members of the Party than the Land League agitation had ever been. Those who actively supervised the Plan, in fact, probably never numbered more than a third of the 85 members of the Party. This control by the Party, moreover, was only made possible by the limited extent of the Plan, which was never put into operation on much more than 100 estates, and was not sustained for any length of time on much more than a quarter of those estates. The nature of the Plan, as well as its limited extent, also allowed for greater Party control, since the Plan made it possible to sort out the question of reducing rents from that of resisting evictions. The Party was thus better able to curtail that local initiative in Boycotting, which was very difficult to discipline or control and often proved embarrassing to both Party, and its machine on the local level, the National League. Of all the reasons, however, why the potential dangers in the Plan did not materialize, the most important was that the Bishops and priests were so deeply committed to it, and in their commitment exercised a conservative and restraining influence.

But while the Bishops and priests certainly supported the Plan in the interests of sustaining the Clerical-Nationalist alliance, this does not mean, of course, that their position within the alliance *vis-à-vis* the Party and the Leader remained unchanged. When the Clerical-Nationalist alliance had been finally made in October, 1884, the Bishops had joined it as equals. At the time, however, their own serious dissensions, and the evident lack of leadership during the primacy of Cardinal McCabe, Walsh's predecessor in the see of Dublin, had placed the Bishops as a body at a disadvantage in the early working of the alliance, and they were in danger of being reduced from equals to auxiliaries. The appointment of Walsh to Dublin in June, 1885, however, soon changed all that. Under his dynamic leadership, the erosion of episcopal power within the alliance was checked, and indeed by the time the first Home Rule Bill was introduced in April, 1886, the Bishops had recovered all the ground they had previously lost. With the launching of the Plan in October, 1886, however, the Bishops once again began to find it more difficult to maintain their position within the alliance. Walsh's own difficulties with several of his episcopal colleagues, his failure to win any concessions from the Conservative government on the Education Question, and his inability to prevent Rome from veering around once more on the question of reestablishing diplomatic relations with the government, all contributed to the impairment of his effectiveness as leader in the Irish Church. With the arrival of the Persico Mission and Walsh's consequent long absence in Rome, the Bishops began to lose the initiative to the agrarian wing in the Party in what had been previously their joint effort to protect the vital interests of the Irish tenant. When Rome then condemned the Plan and Boycotting in April, 1888, the

Party with Dillon and O'Brien in the vanguard called the Bishops to account. In their subsequent submission to the Party, which was fully endorsed by Walsh on his return from Rome, the Bishops were, in effect, forced to play a more modest role in the Clerical-Nationalist alliance.

This ebb and flow in episcopal power within the alliance, of course, reflected the usual struggle for power basic to any political combination. The struggle here, however, also had a deeper significance, for what was actually being evolved was a unique political system. In creating his *de facto* State, Parnell had undermined the dominant English system of politics by dissent in Ireland. He had not only made the concept of Leader real in himself, but he had also established a One Party System, a mass machine organization, a controlled press, and a single plank National program. The passing of the English system of politics by dissent in Ireland, however, did not result in either the triumph of the general will as articulated by the Leader, or even in the tyranny of the majority as represented by the Party. What was evolved instead was a system of politics by consensus, and the constituent elements in that consensus were the Leader, the Party, and the Bishops. What gave the system its constitutional potential was that no one of the elements could impose its will on the other two. But what really made the system work was that any two could exert considerable pressure on the other one. How the system worked, in fact, is perhaps best illustrated by the impact of the Plan on it. When the Plan, for example, was launched by the Party and approved of by the Bishops, the Leader who was full of misgivings about it, submitted to the consensus and accepted it. When the Plan was condemned at Rome, moreover, and the Leader and the Party were agreed as to the course to be pursued, the Bishops also submitted. What could happen, however, when one of the elements would not submit, and would attempt further to impose its will on the other two, would be only too well illustrated in a few years' time in the fall of Parnell.

The real achievement between 1886 and 1888, then, was the transformation of the Clerical-Nationalist alliance architected by Parnell into a constitutional system that would survive even the fall and death of that great man. But as with all such achievements, the real turned out to be something less than the ideal. One of the hallmarks of the Nationalist political tradition in Ireland was religious equality, and successive Nationalist

leaders, in their various generations, whether in the
constitutional or revolutionary mold, continued to exalt
religious equality over mere toleration. This stand for religious
equality in Ireland, however, was not simply a function of a
rational eighteenth-century humanism projected into a more
romantic age, it was also the result of the demand of a Catholic
majority tolerated by a Protestant minority in a more
democratic age. Whether, indeed, that Catholic majority, when
it acquired real power, would respect its own shibboleths, or
whether Home Rule would become Rome Rule, was a
fundamental question not only for a frightened Protestant
minority, but for those Catholic Irishmen who sincerely
believed in religious equality. What finally emerged, however, in
the making and consolidating of the *de facto* Irish State
between 1884 and 1888 was a compromise in which the new
State was neither religiously pluralistic nor purely clerical.
What actually evolved was a Confessional State in which
Catholic values and interests predominated, and Protestants
had an unusually wide degree of toleration.

What took place, then, in the course of the nineteenth
century in Ireland, was the substitution of a Catholic
Confessional State for a Protestant one. The process, of course,
was long, piece-meal, and involved, but the concluding of the
Clerical-Nationalist alliance in October, 1884, was the
fundamental turning point. That alliance, by including the
Bishops in the governing consensus, and thereby paving the
way for their eventual constitutional status, provided for the
establishment in effect of the Irish Church as the State Church.
By 1888, the Church had, in the persons of its Bishops and
priests, acquired a considerable amount of political power and
influence within the governing consensus. The Bishops were not
only responsible for all aspects of the Education Question, but
they had established the right to be consulted on the suitability
of Parliamentary candidates in their respective dioceses. Their
priests, moreover, had formally secured the right as priests to
be represented in Convention in the selection of Parliamentary
candidates, as well as their more informal, but still recognized
preeminence as officers in the local branches of the National
League. While these rights and privileges of the Bishops and
priests in the Irish political system certainly helped to make the
de facto Irish State more confessionally Catholic, they were not

in the last analysis what distinguished that State as a Catholic Confessional State.

That distinction was made once and for all when Archbishop Walsh declared the Plan of Campaign to be morally unobjectionable, and the Party acquiesced in that decision. Since Walsh might have also found the Plan objectionable, the real principle at stake was not to be found either in his endorsement or non-endorsement, but in his assuming that the right to pronounce authoritatively on the moral dimension of any question was reserved to the Church. If such power rested with the Church, speaking authoritatively through its Bishops, then the State that recognized that power was at best Confessional and at worst Clerical, depending on the extent to which that power was exercised. If that power, moreover, was not effectively limited either constitutionally or extra-constitutionally, then the Confessional State must inevitably become a Clerical one. Why the Irish Confessional State did not degenerate into a Clerical State, of course, was that the Church's power was effectively limited, and limited constitutionally, from the very beginning. In becoming part of the governing consensus, the Bishops had formally acquired considerable political power, but that power had to be exercised within the framework of that consensus. If Archbishop Walsh, for example, had found the Plan to be morally objectionable, which was a real possibility in November, 1886, it would have undoubtedly been either quietly dropped or modified to suit his objections. When the Plan, however, had finally been adopted by the Party, approved by the Bishops, and accepted by the Leader, it was, in effect, Irish-made law, and as such had to be obeyed.

While both the Party and the Leader had implicitly admitted the right of the Bishops to pronounce on the moral dimension, by acquiescing in Walsh's endorsement of the Plan, this was not to say that as far as they were concerned there were no limits on that acknowledged right. For, if there were no limits, they were not only at the constitutional mercy of the Bishops and Rome, but their Confessional State was really only a mask for a Clerical one. First of all, both the Party and the Leader were well aware that the Bishops were constrained by the fear of the consequences involved in their taking any action that might result in the breaking up of the National movement and the jeopardizing thereby of Home Rule. Secondly, the Party and the Leader drew their constitutional line with regard to the Church's right to pronounce on the moral dimension with the Bishops and not at Rome. Finally, and perhaps most importantly, that the right and the veto power implicit in it, had to be exercised in terms of a procedural framework that governed even the consensus. What was absolutely crucial in that procedure was that the Bishops' right to pronounce was part and parcel of the legislative process and not independent of it. In other words, the Bishops' right was to be exercised before and not after the proposed legislation was enacted and became law. This critical distinction not only guarded the integrity of the State by ensuring that the law made by that State was not subject to moral review by the Church, but it also enhanced the dignity of the State by providing a consultative mode in which serious, and perhaps unseemly, differences of opinion between the constituent elements of the consensus might be privately subsumed in the interests of National unity.

This was why, therefore, the Roman Decree condemning what was in effect Irish-made law, precipitated a constitutional crisis. If indeed Rome had such a right, the Irish legislative system was placed in double jeopardy because the Bishops had an effective veto in the initiating of legislation, and Rome had another veto when that legislation became law. No self-respecting State, Confessional or not, could survive such a constitutional arrangement. Patently, the primary responsibility for not only dealing with Rome, but containing her as well, as far as the Party and the Leader were concerned, rested with the Bishops. Since the Bishops, and indeed all Irish Catholics, were agreed that Rome had a legitimate appellate jurisdiction in the Irish Church, the correct constitutional procedure for the Irish Bishops with regard to Rome was clear. If the Bishops were in doubt about the moral appropriateness of proposed Irish legislation, they were bound to consult Rome, and then advise the other elements in the consensus what they could or could not accept. The responsibility, however, for the advice given was the Bishops', whether they consulted Rome or not, and the law arrived at in terms of the consensus, of which they were an integral part, was the law of the land and had to be obeyed. Rome could not be allowed, therefore, to interfere after the fact with regard to Irish-made law without making a mockery of the evolving constitutional process. Since Rome had interfered, however, she would have to back down if the constitutional and confessional nature of the State was to be preserved. The responsibility, moreover, for seeing that she did back down rested with the Irish Bishops. If the Bishops, however, could or would not accept their responsibility, they then would have to learn to live with the political consequences.

In the month following the crisis, the Bishops were indeed given a sharp taste of how disagreeable the consequences might prove to be. Parnell, in quickly turning the Bishops over to the tender mercies of the Party, signified that as Leader, he would take the Party's part in the constitutional crisis precipitated by Rome. The ways in which both the Leader and the Party proceeded, in fact, was a further demonstration that they were part of a still operative political system with a special constitutional and confessional character. All the constitutional niceties, for example, were carefully preserved. The meeting of the Party was both requisitioned by the Party and sanctioned by the Leader. Parnell then decided that as Leader he would make his own position clear before either the Party or even the Bishops met to deliberate on the Decree. He both warned the Bishops that the Decree would prove ineffective, and the agrarian wing in the Party that the Plan as an instrument of National policy would have to be reconsidered, before finally giving the Party *carte blanche* in the immediate crisis. He was obviously still very much the Leader, and his lower political profile in these years was less a function of any diminution in his status or power as Leader, and more an indication that a constitutional process of which he was an integral part was being crystallized. The true confessional nature of the State, furthermore, was made perfectly clear in that the meeting of the Party was to include only the Catholic members. In their sixth and final resolution at their meeting, moreover, the Catholic members assured their Protestant fellow countrymen that Rome would not be allowed to encroach on those civil liberties won by all Irishmen and thus turn what was a Confessional State into a Clerical one. The significant point, of course, was that in religious matters affecting Catholics, Protestants were expected not only to defer, but were actually dependent on the good will and sense of honor of their Catholic fellow countrymen. No one perhaps understood this better than Parnell, for he not only sanctioned the calling of the religiously exclusive meeting of the Party, but then as Leader deferred to the Catholic members in discussing the Decree. At this point, given the risks involved in bringing down the wrath of the Irish people on their own heads, the Bishops did not dare challenge the Party and the Leader. They wisely and prudently decided, therefore, to submit, and endorsed the consensus. By refusing to enforce the Roman Decree, they thus preserved their very real power within the consensus as well as their influence with the Irish people. But what was even more important, at least from the point of view of strengthening and consolidating the *de facto* Irish State, was that the Bishops by their decision helped to transform what had been begun as a working political arrangement in the Clerical-Nationalist alliance into a basic constitutional relationship that is today still fundamental to the Irish political system.

Bibliographical Note

The sources for this study were mainly archival, and the printed materials used were few in number. I have not, therefore, listed the books, articles, and newspapers in a formal bibliography because the reader will easily find what is pertinent in the footnotes. Two works which have been liberally used in the writing of this volume, however, deserve especial mention. One is Conor Cruise O'Brien's *Parnell and His Party, 1880-1890* (Oxford, 1957), and Patrick J. Walsh's *William J. Walsh, Archbishop of Dublin* (Dublin, 1928). The first is what may be termed a basic book, which no scholar or student of the period can do without, while the second contains a considerable amount of original material, sometimes unfortunately inaccurately quoted, which has either been lost or is now unavailable to scholars. The archival materials consulted are to be found mainly in Ireland, England, and Rome.

In Ireland the main bodies of material consulted were:

1. The Papers of William J. Walsh. Dublin Diocesan Archives.
2. The Papers of Thomas William Croke. Cashel Diocesan Archives, Thurles, County Tipperary. Microfilmed and on deposit in the National Library of Ireland.
3. The Papers of Laurence Gillooly, C.M. Elphin Diocesan Archives, Sligo, and have been microfilmed.
4. The Papers of Sir John Ross of Bladensburg. Public Record Office, Northern Ireland.

In England the main bodies of material consulted were:

1. Foreign Office Papers for Italy and Rome. Public Record Office, Chancery Lane.
2. The Papers of Arthur Balfour, British Museum.
3. The Papers of the Marquess of Salisbury, Hatfield House, Hatfield, Herts.

4. The Papers of the Earl St. Aldwyn (Hicks Beach), Williamship Park, Coln St. Aldwyn, Gloucester.
5. The Papers of Henry Edward Cardinal Manning. Archives of the Church of St. Mary of the Angels, Bayswater, London.

In Rome the main bodies of material consulted were:

1. The Papers of Tobias Kirby. Archives of the Irish College.
2. The Papers of Bernard Smith, O.S.B. Archives of St. Paul's Basilica outside the Walls.

Index*

*An asterisk following an index entry indicates identification is not certain.

Table Conference 129; trial, 16.
Diplomatic relations, Rome and the United Kingdom, 28n, 48-53, 57-58, 63, 72, 81-83, 87, 91, 97, 101, 109, 130, 137, 151-152, 155-156, 163-164, 175, 180, 199, 201, 242, 245, 250, 316.
Donnelly, James, bishop of Clogher, 65.
Donnelly, Nicholas, bishop of Canea, auxiliary to the archbishop of Dublin, 60, 172, 183, 231, 239-243, 301.
Dublin, Corporation of, 276; Walsh address to, 277-280, 290.
Dublin Jubilee Committee, 97.
Dublin University, 41.
Duffy, Sir Charles Gavan, Australian prime minister, 122.
Dumesnil, Arthur, French journalist, 239-240, 241.
Dunne, Dr. D. B., secretary of the Royal University, 289.
Dunphy, James, P.P., Arklow, Dublin, 285.

Education Question, xiii, 10, 28n, 29-45, 48, 51-54, 56, 83, 114, 115, 149, 155, 156, 190, 218, 233, 245, 316, 318; Irish education system, 150; negotiations between the Irish bishops and the government, 26-31, 33, 36-38, 40-41, 43-45, 47, 54, 55, 71, 94, 108-109, 250.
Eighty Club, 211, 215, 219.
Election, general, of 1886, 3, 51.
Elections, episcopal, see episcopal elections.
Emly, Lord (William Monsell), 26n, 35, 36n, 117-119, 153, 201, 213, 287, 289, 293, 294, 296.
Episcopal appointments, 63, 153, 170, 183-186; Achonry, 183-184; Dromore, 59n, 61; Kilmore, 183, 185; Malta, 65-66, 81-82; Raphoe, 183-184.
Episcopal elections; Armagh, 64n; Dromore, 59-60; Galway, 58-59, 62, 64.
Episcopal standing committee, 33, 34, 49, 183.
Errington, Sir George, 67, 151, 244, 247, 287, 289, 290, 299; Decree, 248; diplomatic relations, 57, 58, 201; Home Rule, 124, 201; landlords, 123; Persico, 107, 118, 119,

124, 131-133, 200; politics, British, 119, 133; Round Table Conference 123-124.
Eyre, Thomas, 65n.

Fahey, Jerome, V.G., P.P., Kilmacduagh and Kiltarten, Galway, Kilmacduagh, and Kilfenora, 62.
"Fair rent", 7, 111, 115, 126.
Fenianism and Fenians, 77, 111, 136, 138, 141.
Fielding* (either first or second son of the Earl of Denbigh), 199-200.
Finegan, Bernard, bishop of Kilmore, 19.
Finn, M., Dean, vicar capitular, Achonry, 184.
Finnegan, A. C., P.P., Lurgan, Dromore, 60n.
Fitzgerald, William, bishop of Ross, 12.
Flanagan, J. S., P.P., Adare, Limerick, 245.
Forster, W. E., 185n.
Freeman's Journal, 12, 18, 21-24, 34n, 67, 75, 76, 84, 100, 109, 115, 120-123, 141, 142, 157-159, 194, 207, 211, 215, 216, 231, 235, 255, 272, 274, 293, 301, 311; death of Gray, 191-193; Decree, 203; Dillon defence fund, 16; Plan of Campaign, 7; significance of, 191; Walsh interview, 260-262, 289.
de Freyne, Lord (Arthur French), 129, 296.

Gaelic Athletic Association, 140, 141.
Galway College, see Queen's Colleges.
Garibaldi, Giuseppe, 118.
Gillooly, Laurence, bishop of Elphin, 35, 38, 169, 170, 173, 177, 184, 185, 235, 258, 307; Education Question, 35, 41; memorandum, bishops reply to the pope, 309-311.
Gladstone, William E., xiii, xiv, 3, 6, 10, 51, 58, 74, 111, 118, 119, 123, 124, 130, 152, 182, 199, 211, 216, 217, 226, 228, 229, 247, 248, 310, 314.
Glenbigh estate, 100, 112, 113.
Glynn, Patrick J., O.S.A., prior of Augustinian convent, Rome, 143.
Goschen, G. J., 55.
Gosselin, Le Marchant, 148, 150.
Government, see British government.

330 THE ROMAN CATHOLIC CHURCH